SARRA COPIA SULAM

A Jewish Salonnière and the Press in Counter-Reformation Venice

Sarra Copia Sulam

A Jewish Salonnière and the Press in Counter-Reformation Venice

LYNN LARA WESTWATER

UNIVERSITY OF TORONTO PRESS
Toronto Buffalo London

© University of Toronto Press 2020
Toronto Buffalo London
utppublishing.com
Printed in Canada

ISBN 978-1-4875-0583-7 (cloth)
ISBN 978-1-4875-3279-6 (EPUB)
ISBN 978-1-4875-3278-9 (PDF)

Toronto Italian Studies

Library and Archives Canada Cataloguing in Publication

Title: Sarra Copia Sulam : a Jewish salonnière and the press in Counter-
Reformation Venice / Lynn Lara Westwater.
Names: Westwater, Lynn Lara. author.
Description: Includes bibliographical references and index.
Identifiers: Canadiana 20190191945 | ISBN 9781487505837 (hardcover)
Subjects: LCSH: Copia Sulam, Sarra, 1592–1641. | LCSH: Jewish women –
Italy – Venice – Biography. | LCSH: Jewish women authors – Italy – Venice –
Biography. | LCSH: Venice (Italy) – Intellectual life – 17th century. | LCSH:
Salons – Italy – Venice – History – 17th century. | LCSH: Venice (Italy) –
Social life and customs – 17th century. | LCSH: Venice (Italy) – Religion –
17th century.
Classification: LCC PQ4634.S83 Z935 2020 | DDC 851/.5—dc23

University of Toronto Press acknowledges the financial assistance to its
publishing program of the Canada Council for the Arts and the Ontario Arts
Council, an agency of the Government of Ontario.

Canada Council   Conseil des Arts
for the Arts   du Canada

ONTARIO ARTS COUNCIL
CONSEIL DES ARTS DE L'ONTARIO
an Ontario government agency
un organisme du gouvernement de l'Ontario

Funded by the   Financé par le
Government   gouvernement
of Canada   du Canada

Canadä

FSC
www.fsc.org

MIX
Paper from
responsible sources
FSC® C016245

For Jay

Contents

ஒண்

Figures

❧⟶

Acknowledgments

It is perhaps ironic that this book – which follows a seventeenth-century salonnière and the unravelling of her literary coterie – strengthened the bonds of my own intellectual society. I did the research for and wrote some of the book in Venice, where colleagues helped me at every turn. Mario Infelise provided invaluable guidance on research in the Venetian archives and graciously shared his expertise on print culture in seventeenth-century Venice. Daria Perocco gave unstinting assistance on paleography and Seicento literary culture. Sabrina Minuzzi generously shared her expertise in paleography, material culture, and print culture in early modern Venice. Numerous colleagues helped me to locate and decipher documents at the Archivio di Stato di Venezia. I am grateful in particular to Alessandra Schiavon, Andrea Pelizza, Daria Perocco, Franco Rossi, Sabrina Minuzzi, Antonio Mazzucco, and Matteo Casini. I worked on the book manuscript at the Marciana Library, where the staff accommodated my every research need. Stefano Trovato, Alessia Giachery, Tiziana Plebani, and Sabrina Minuzzi provided essential help with my research there and, even more important, their company for coffee breaks.

I am indebted to Howard Adelman for the advice and guidance he has so liberally offered over several years, in particular regarding Sarra Copia Sulam and her close colleague Leon Modena and, more generally, regarding Jewish women and Jewish life. I enjoyed a correspondence with Don Harrán, whose work on Copia Sulam was invaluable to my research. His passing impoverishes the world of Italian Jewish studies.

This book was strengthened enormously by the insightful suggestions offered by the anonymous readers at the University of Toronto Press. I am deeply appreciative of their careful attention to my manuscript. Suzanne Rancourt and Robin Studniberg shepherded the text through the editorial process with great acumen and professionalism. Amyrose

McCue Gill of TextFormations line edited the manuscript with remarkable attention to both detail and the big picture, copy-edited the critical apparatus with an eagle's eye, and created the index with speed and
precision.

A small army of colleagues and friends have provided assistance and
advice at every turn. I am grateful in particular to Julie Campbell, Vir-
ginia Cox, Nathalie Hester, Sally Hill, Dana Katz, Vickie Kirkham, Annie
Jones, Suzanne Magnanini, Shannon McHugh, Davide Papotti, Courtney
Quaintance, Benjamin Ravid, Anne Schutte, Deanna Shemek, Michael
Sherberg, Jane Tylus, and Anna Wainwright for feedback over the years.
Diana Robin offered invaluable perspectives on women's intellectual
networks in early modern Italy and read draft after draft of the manuscript, on which she gave incisive and lightning-fast feedback. Meredith
Ray's detailed comments on drafts of the manuscript and her exper-
tise on letter collections and salons were instrumental. Paolo Cherchi,
Armando Maggi, and Rebecca West supported this project in its infancy.
Elissa Weaver, always boundlessly generous with her time and talents,
read numerous drafts of this work, which she inspired and shaped from
its inception.

I am grateful for the interest in and support for my project from my
colleagues at The George Washington University, especially Tyler An-
binder, Heather Bamford, Masha Belenky, Leah Chang, Holly Dugan,
and Sergio Waisman. Support from the administration of the Depart-
ment of Romance, German, and Slavic Languages and Literatures and
of the Colombian College was essential, and I am grateful in particular to
Antonio López, Ben Vinson, Eric Arnesen, and Yongwu Rong.

Research leave and course release from The George Washington
University allowed me to finish this book, while the GW Humanities
Facilitating Fund and the Columbian College Book Publishing Fund
provided financial support. Fulbright and Whiting fellowships supported
my early research.

Many close friends have helped me and my family along the way. In
the US, I am grateful in particular to Michelle Brydges, Leigh Fraiser,
Ann Hudson, Margaret Hock Koehler, Sumru Krody, Susi Lill, Pamela
Marcantonio, Mary McCain, Debbie McCann, Adinah Miller, Manju Nair,
Amy Sharp, Jill Shenk, Brenna Snider, Elizabeth Spatz, Alex Sundman,
and Julia Torrey, and in Venice, to Elena Pradolin and Paolo Bened-
etti, Sara Bossi and Luca Colombo, Trina Tygrett and Giorgio Nason,
and Jill Weinreich and Andrea Luppi. I am also deeply grateful to the
Mazzucchelli family in Varese, the Cremonesi family in Milan, and the
Solimini family in Rome.

Finally, I wish to thank the members of my family for their roles in shaping this book. My parents, Ann Meredyth and Ed Westwater, have shared their love of learning with me from my earliest days up to the present. They taught me young that words matter and women count. My parents-in-law, Allan and Clemmy Brodsky, have shown boundless enthusiasm for my research, which they in turn have inspired through their tireless advocacy for women and religious minorities. My stepmother, Jerri Perna Westwater, immediately grasped the political importance of this project. My siblings, Kristin McDonald and John Westwater, and brother-in-law, Bill McDonald, have pushed me to work hard, play hard, and cultivate curiosity, while my sisters-in-law, Anne Brodsky and Margaret Chriss, have guided me with their wisdom, industry, and principle. My daughters Sofia, Julia, and Anna have cohabitated quite patiently with this other child of mine, to whom they frequently turned a curious eye and whose graduation from our household they can now celebrate. I hope they will one day draw both inspiration and perspective from this story of a Jewish woman's struggle against intolerance. My husband, Jay Brodsky, not only served as my IT consultant and footnote proofreader, but was also my project's biggest champion. Given the number of car-pools he ran and dinners he cooked to allow me the time to finish this work, he could easily clinch the double title of husband and father of the year. Rather than a trophy, I offer him this book, along with my deepest gratitude and love.

Abbreviations

ASV   Archivio di Stato di Venezia
BUG   Biblioteca Universitaria di Genova
DR   Douay-Rheims Bible (referenced at www.drbo.org)
OED   Oxford English Dictionary, 3rd edition

Timeline

1592?
Sarra Copia is born, probably in Venice's Ghetto Nuovo.

1596
Ansaldo Cebà publishes his first work, *Rime* (Poems), in Padua and
  Antwerp.

1599
Giuseppe Passi's antifeminist catalogue *I donneschi diffetti* (The Defects
  of Women) is published in Venice.

1600
In response to Passi's attack on women, Lucrezia Marinella's *Le
  nobiltà et eccellenze delle donne et i diffetti e mancamenti de gli huomini*
  (The Nobility and Excellence of Women and the Defects and Vices
  of Men) and Moderata Fonte's *Il merito delle donne* (The Merit of
  Women) are published in Venice.

1601
Lucrezia Marinella's *Nobiltà* is published in an expanded edition.

1606
Simon Copio, Sarra's "most adoring" father, dies. He directs that Sarra
  and her two sisters be able to choose husbands to their liking and
  that his estate be split equally among his daughters, provided that
  they remain within the Jewish faith.

1609
Sarra Copia marries Giacob Sulam, from Mantua, who will become a
  moneylender and a leader of the community in the ghetto.

1614
Copia Sulam gives birth to a daughter, Rica.

1615
Rica Sulam dies.

Ansaldo Cebà publishes *La reina Esther* (Queen Esther) in Genoa. The epic poem on the Old Testament heroine will attract Copia Sulam's attention.

1616
La reina Esther is published in Milan.

1618
Copia Sulam initiates a correspondence with Cebà. Her salon is born.

A miscarriage leaves Copia Sulam near death.

The Roman writer Numidio Paluzzi arrives in Venice, along with his associate Alessandro Berardelli. Copia Sulam hires Paluzzi as her preceptor and eventually arranges for his dwelling.

Passi's *Difetti* is published for the fourth time.

1619
The priest and dramatist Baldassare Bonifaccio, whose family hailed from Rovigo, begins to frequent Copia Sulam's salon. They communicate in person and by letter.

Copia Sulam and Cebà continue their correspondence.

Copia Sulam's close associate Leon Modena publishes a play on Esther, *L'Ester*, which he dedicates to Copia Sulam.

In late 1619 or early 1620, Bonifaccio writes a letter to Copia Sulam regarding the immortality of the soul.

1620
Copia Sulam writes a private letter to Bonifaccio, which he later published, in which she questions the soul's immortality.

Copia Sulam and Cebà continue their correspondence.

Paluzzi leaves Venice in October to go to Fruili, without notifying Copia Sulam. He strips the dwelling she had furnished for him at a cost of 100 ducats.

1621
Cebà's *La reina Esther* is suspended by the Congregation of the Index in spring 1621 until appropriately revised, over charges that the work contradicted Scripture and was "obscene." Cebà did not revise the work and the suspension was never lifted.

Copia Sulam and Cebà continue their correspondence, but after *La reina Esther*'s suspension, Cebà becomes noticeably more hostile.

In April 1621, Paluzzi returns to Venice from Friuli. He undergoes treatment for probable syphilis until fall 1621.

Copia Sulam falls ill. She will report in summer 1621 that "I just recovered from a serious illness that oppressed me for some time and threatened my life."

In late June 1621, Bonifaccio publishes his *Dell'immortalità dell'anima* (On the Immortality of the Soul), in which he accuses Copia Sulam in print of denying that tenet.

A few weeks after the publication of Bonifaccio's *Immortalità*, Copia Sulam publishes her *Manifesto* in which she refutes Bonifaccio's charge against her, defending her belief in the soul's immortality in Christian terms. The work is reissued twice within several weeks.

In early August, Bonifaccio publishes a *Risposta al* Manifesto (Reply to the *Manifesto*) in which he argues against Copia Sulam's *Manifesto* and publishes the private letter that Copia Sulam had written him in early 1620, in which she questions the immortality of the soul.

Paluzzi spends the winter (1621–1622) under the sponsorship of an unnamed gentleman.

Marinella's *Nobiltà* is republished.

1622

In spring 1622, the Cebà–Copia Sulam correspondence ends after the exchange had become markedly antagonistic.

When Paluzzi's other sponsor leaves Venice in spring 1622, the burden of his care falls to Copia Sulam. His probable syphilis worsens. Paluzzi spends the spring and summer at a curative steam bath, where Copia Sulam provides him a salary and food. He leaves in August to go to a dwelling Copia Sulam secured for him.

Paluzzi enters into a conspiracy with Copia Sulam's household servants and his Roman friend Berardelli to steal from the Sulams.

Cebà dies in October 1622.

1623

Cebà's literary executor publishes many works posthumously, including his *Lettere a Sarra Copia* (Letters to Sarra Copia).

In late 1623 or early 1624, a French nobleman comes to Venice and visits Copia Sulam. Afterwards, Paluzzi, Berardelli, and the other conspirators pretend to use magical means to deliver letters and gifts to the prince in Paris. They use this ruse to further defraud the Sulams.

1624

In July, Copia Sulam's friend and associate Giacomo Rosa discovers the conspiracy against the Sulams and reveals it to Copia Sulam. She fires the servants involved, cuts off support to Paluzzi, and denounces Berardelli – the ringleader and principal thief – to Venetian authorities.

Berardelli (perhaps with Paluzzi) composes, circulates, and reads aloud in the ghetto and throughout the city a defamatory pamphlet called "Le Sareide"(Sara's Feats).

1625

Berardelli is found guilty of wrongdoing probably in late 1624 or early 1625 and sentenced to a prison term and to time rowing in the galleys, probably in spring/summer 1625.

Paluzzi dies in July 1625.

By this year, Copia Sulam's paternal uncle Moisè Copio converts to Christianity.

1626

Berardelli edits a posthumous edition of Paluzzi's *Rime* (Poems) in which he slanders Copia Sulam by charging that Paluzzi wrote all of the works that she claims. He calls her a "perfidious Jewess" and accuses her of stealing writing from a moribund Paluzzi to hide her plagiarism.

Copia Sulam and associates circulate a manuscript entitled "Avisi di Parnaso" (Reports from Parnassus) that responds to Berardelli's slander.

1627

A poem of Copia Sulam's appears in a collection edited by Gabriele Zinano. This is the last attributed work of Copia Sulam's published for the next two centuries. There is no further clear trace of her participation in literary society.

1630

Copia Sulam and Giacob Sulam both survive the plague, in which a third of Venice's residents die.

1641

Copia Sulam dies February 15 in the Ghetto Vecchio.

1645

Copia Sulam's mother, Ricca Grassini Copia, dies.

Dramatis Personae

Giovanni Basadonna: A Venetian senator and writer who frequented Copia Sulam's salon. Copia Sulam's correspondent Ansaldo Cebà suggested that Basadonna's visits compromised Copia Sulam's honour.

Alessandro Berardelli: A Roman writer and painter who was Numidio Paluzzi's close associate and who frequented Copia Sulam's salon with him. From 1622 to 1624 he orchestrated a conspiracy to defraud the Sulams and, after Copia Sulam denounced him, was imprisoned and sentenced to serve in the galleys. He slandered Copia Sulam in a book published in 1626. He remained an active participant in Venetian literary society into the 1640s.

Baldassare Bonifaccio: A priest and writer with roots in Rovigo, Bonifaccio was an early and enthusiastic participant in Copia Sulam's salon. He betrayed her in 1621 by publishing a treatise that accused her of heresy.

Ansaldo Cebà: A Genoese writer who engaged in a correspondence with Copia Sulam towards the end of his life. Through his letters he sought to convert Copia Sulam to Christianity and reacted with hostility when she did not bend to his will. His letters – first in manuscript, then in print (*Lettere a Sarra Copia*) – played a central role in discrediting Copia Sulam.

Michiel Copio: Copia Sulam's paternal uncle who lived in Zante. He was Simon Copio's business partner in all ventures until the latter died in 1606. Ricca Copia and Michiel Copio separated most of their financial interests in 1607.

Moisè Copio: Copia Sulam's paternal uncle whose conversion to Christianity in the mid-1620s and subsequent misbehaviour created a family scandal.

Rachel Copia: One of Copia Sulam's two younger sisters.

Ricca Grassini Copia: Copia Sulam's mother who managed the family's business and financial affairs after the death of her husband, Simon Copio. She was likely involved in Copia Sulam's education.

Simon Copio: Copia Sulam's father, a moneylender and merchant who died in 1606. In his will he tried to ensure autonomy and financial well-being for Copia Sulam and her two sisters. Copia Sulam showed deep affection for her father, whom she immortalized by dedicating to him her one published work, her *Manifesto*.

Ster (Ester) Copia: One of Copia Sulam's two younger sisters. She married her cousin Gabriel, son of Simon Copio's brother Michiel.

Gianfrancesco Corniani: A Venetian poet and cousin of Baldassare Bonifaccio. Corniani participated in Copia Sulam's salon. In a letter to Bonifaccio, Copia Sulam mentions that Corniani and Numidio Paluzzi came to her house to hear the letter Bonifaccio had written on the immortality of the soul.

Isabella della Tolfa: Wife of the Genoese nobleman Marcantonio Doria and a correspondent of Copia Sulam. Cebà enlisted her help to convince Copia Sulam to convert to Christianity. After Cebà's death, Copia Sulam turned to della Tolfa to request that one of Cebà's letters to her be excluded from the posthumous collection of his correspondence that Doria was planning to publish.

Marcantonio Doria: A Genoese nobleman, Cebà's patron and friend, who published the *Lettere a Sarra Copia* after Cebà's death.

Paola Furlana: Copia Sulam's laundress who orchestrated a conspiracy to defraud her. Into this conspiracy Furlana recruited her three sons as well as Paluzzi, Berardelli, and the Sulams' scullery maid.

Lucrezia Marinella: The other Venetian woman writer whose works were published in the city in the early seventeenth century.

Leon Modena: A prolific writer and scholar who was a close associate of Copia Sulam. He dedicated *L'Ester* (1619) to Copia Sulam and was a key ally of hers in subsequent literary controversies.

Numidio Paluzzi: A Roman writer and copy editor who worked in Venice from the mid-1610s through the mid-1620s. Copia Sulam hired him as her preceptor and he became an important participant in her salon. He later betrayed her by taking part in a conspiracy against her.

Pietro Petracci: A writer and editor whose name appears above introductory sonnets in the first edition of Copia Sulam's 1621 *Manifesto*. He may have been one of Copia Sulam's associates.

Giacomo Rosa: Cebà's agent in Venice who befriended Copia Sulam and later revealed to her that Berardelli and Paluzzi had entered into a conspiracy against her.

Giacob Sulam: Copia Sulam's husband, who was a moneylender and an influential figure in the ghetto. Giacob's sanction of Copia Sulam's literary activities was essential to her career.

Rica (Ricca) Sulam: The Sulam's infant daughter who died near the age of one in January 1615.

Sarra Copia Sulam: Venetian writer, poet, and salonnière who rose to prominence in her home city in the late 1610s and early 1620s through a series of well-publicized controversies with her literary associates. Her one printed work, *Manifesto*, was released in three editions in the summer of 1621.

Gabriele Zinano: A widely published author who was a visitor to Copia Sulam's salon and published a poetry exchange with her in his 1627 *Rime diverse* (Various Poems).

Note on the Text

Primary sources not originally in English are given in English translation, with the original text in an endnote. Secondary sources not originally in English are given in English translation. Where no other source is listed, translations are mine. To avoid confusion with modern English translations, all early modern texts are referred to throughout by their Italian titles; a translation of the title is given at first mention. The spelling of Copia Sulam's name varies in both primary and secondary source material: Sarra/Sara; Copio (Coppio)/Copia (Coppia); Sulam/Sullam. The spelling is here standardized to Sarra Copia Sulam, as her name appears on the title page of the work she published. Other names have been similarly standardized. Birth and death dates for all historical figures are provided when available. Where it is not an impediment to understanding, transcriptions are faithful to the original printed texts, with the exception of diacritical marks, capitalization, and punctuation, which have been modernized; transcriptions of archival documents are modernized according to the criteria given in Appendix A. English translations of biblical verses are from the Douay-Rheims Bible. All dates are given assuming 1 January as the first day of the year (some primary sources give dates according to the Venetian calendar, by which the year began 1 March).

SARRA COPIA SULAM

A Jewish Salonnière and the Press in Counter-Reformation Venice

Introduction

For nearly a decade at the height of the Counter-Reformation in Italy, the Jewish poet, polemicist, and salonnière Sarra Copia Sulam (ca. 1592–1641) hosted Christian and Jewish intellectuals for provocative discussions at her home in the Venetian ghetto. Her salon, which met from 1618 to 1626 and included as many as a dozen regular participants, provided one of the most public and enduring forums for Jewish–Christian interaction in early modern Venice. By 1627, however, Copia Sulam's remarkable literary career had sunk under the weight of slanderous charges against her sexual, professional, and religious integrity.

This book, the first biography of Copia Sulam, examines the explosive relationship between gender, religion, and the press in seventeenth-century Venice through the case study of her literary career. The backdrop to this inquiry is Venice's tumultuous religious, cultural, and political climate and the competitive world of its presses, where men and women, Christians and Jews, alternately collaborated and clashed as they sought to gain a foothold in Europe's most prestigious publishing capital, which was perched, however, on the brink of a precipitous decline.[1]

Starting in 1618, Copia Sulam built a literary salon that nurtured close ties to the publishing industry. There is no evidence that this religiously integrated salon attracted unwelcome attention from the Inquisition, despite the fact that in 1621 Copia Sulam herself was accused in print of heresy. By denying the charge, Copia Sulam entered into debates about the misuse of media that remain current today. While she defended print as a medium to be used judiciously by women and men, Christians and Jews, for high-minded discussion, her associates – who debased her as religiously deviant, dishonest, and unchaste – used print as a vehicle for character assassination.

The media landscape in which Copia Sulam and her group worked is essential to understanding relations between Jews and Christians

as well as between male and female writers who participated in the
rough-and-tumble world of the commercial press in Counter-Reformation
Venice. The close ties between Copia Sulam's salon and the presses have
not been explored in studies on the Jewish writer,[2] despite recent scholarship that has underscored the connection between women-led salons
and the publishing industry.[3]

Copia Sulam's rise and fall as a public intellectual in the first quarter
of the seventeenth century cannot be understood without taking into
account the role of Venice's prominent presses and the writers and editors who worked for them, who were her salon associates. In fact, her career can be seen as a study of the presses' power during this period. When
one member of her salon, the priest and dramatist Baldassare Bonifaccio
(1585–1659), accused Copia Sulam in print of doubting the immortality
of the soul, a press rushed to publish his charge. While his work sought
to defame Copia Sulam, it also provided her with the opportunity to win
public recognition for her ideas with her own printed response, *Manifesto
di Sarra Copia Sulam hebrea, nel quale è da lei riprovata e detestata l'opinione
negante l'immortalità dell'anima falsamente attribuitale dal signor Baldassare
Bonifaccio* (Manifesto of Jewess Sarra Copia Sulam, in which She Refutes
and Disavows the Opinion Denying the Soul's Immortality Erroneously
Attributed to Her by Signor Baldassare Bonifaccio), the only original
work published by a Jewish woman in early modern Italy. Copia Sulam's
Manifesto, in which she espoused her belief in the immortality of the
soul while defending her Jewish faith, was a sensation. The *Manifesto* was
printed three times in Venice within a matter of weeks in summer 1621
by publishers of the first rank. Fuelling the controversy over – as well as
the sales of – Copia Sulam's volume, Bonifaccio published his stinging
Risposta al Manifesto (Reply to the *Manifesto*), which he claimed contained
proof of her heresy, mere weeks after the *Manifesto* first appeared. This
controversy was the first of several broadcast in the press: over the next
five years, close associates published two other works that maligned her.
Whereas Bonifaccio's first published diatribe prompted Copia Sulam to
publish a response, she did not answer these later attacks in print. She
made her final reply, which rejected a literary culture based on slander,
in a manuscript circulated in 1626. A lone poem of hers appeared in a
collection printed in 1627, and thereafter any trace of her participation
in literary society vanished.

This book examines the unfolding of this literary drama from its initially hopeful moment – in which Copia Sulam's salon seemed to offer
the possibility for respectful intellectual interactions between Jews and
Christians, women and men – to the eventual dashing of this hope. Since
this story unravels precisely because Copia Sulam was a woman and a

Jew in a literary culture dominated by Christian men, it must be situated in the dual contexts of the situation of Jews and the position of female intellectuals in seventeenth-century Venice.

An Intellectual Woman in the Venetian Ghetto

By the time Sarra Copia Sulam rose to prominence in 1618, the ghetto in which she lived was a thriving centre of Jewish life, but residents were nevertheless subject to constant humiliation and crippling taxation at the hands of Venetian authorities. From its founding a century before, in 1516, the ghetto – situated in a marshy area of Cannaregio and separated from Venice by locked gates – had always represented a profoundly ambivalent space: it allowed Jews a permanent place of legal residence in Venice but also strictly limited their freedom.[4]

The conditions within the ghetto ranged from uncomfortable to unsafe as the Jewish population in Venice increased severalfold between 1581 and 1630.[5] Though the Jewish quarter was enlarged from the *Ghetto Nuovo* (new foundry) to include the *Ghetto Vecchio* (old foundry) in 1541 and the *Ghetto Nuovissimo* (newest ghetto) in 1633,[6] this expansion did not keep pace with the growth of the population. Structures were built perilously upwards, rising far above most of the cityscape of Venice.[7] Living space nevertheless remained inadequate. Several times during the sixteenth century Venetian authorities became concerned about the overcrowding of the ghetto because of the health hazard it represented. Despite the substandard conditions, Jews were charged rents one-third higher than those the earlier Christian residents had paid.[8] By the middle of the seventeenth century, population density in the ghetto was up to four times greater than elsewhere in Venice.[9]

Venetian law restricted Jews' commercial activity and subjected them to onerous taxes and fees. They were allowed to loan money at interest, but as the permitted interest rate decreased across the sixteenth century, the activity became an economic burden rather than a boon. The Jews' involvement in moneylending was convenient to the Republic, since capital on loan was essential to the urban poor, but it was considered sinful for Christians to loan money at interest.[10] The many trading connections of the Jewish community – particularly Jews from the Iberian Peninsula and the Levant – were also useful to *La Serenissima*. Despite the numerous advantages a Jewish presence brought to Venice, the position of Jews was far from secure, and the threat of expulsion always hung over the community.[11] Copia Sulam's close associate Rabbi Leon Modena worried that the misbehaviour of any Jew could imperil the community, writing that "when one Jew is guilty, all are blamed."[12] In a similar vein, when Copia Sulam was charged with heresy, she considered the accusation not only a personal threat but also an attack on all Jews. In her response, therefore, she sought to protect both herself and her community.[13]

The movement of Jews within Venice was tightly controlled. They were free to leave the ghetto during the day but were locked in after sundown behind gates guarded by Christian watchmen whom the Jews were forced to salary. Authorities sought to ensure that windows in ghetto structures could look only into the ghetto itself, since they feared Jews looking out at Christians as well as Christians looking in.[14] Jews leaving the ghetto had to wear attire that distinguished them as Jewish.[15] Most Jews were subject to fines and punishment if they were caught outside of the ghetto after dark,[16] though Jews in special circumstances were allowed to exit at night.[17] The elite class to which Copia Sulam belonged enjoyed the most mobility, both within the city and beyond.[18] She is reported to have gone personally to tend to a legal issue[19] and may have travelled to Mantua for her cousin's wedding in 1623.[20] Just as Jews frequently crossed the ghetto boundary to conduct their affairs in the outside world, so Christians often entered the ghetto.[21] This movement was normal enough that Christians frequenting literary gatherings in Copia Sulam's home in the ghetto over an eight-year period did not attract negative attention from authorities, even though the nature, closeness, and duration of Copia Sulam's interactions with Christians were highly unusual.

As one of the most diverse and populous Jewish communities in Europe, the Venetian ghetto enjoyed an intense cultural life. Copia Sulam participated in a particularly interesting cultural flowering in the mid-seventeenth century, along with such prominent figures as rabbis Leon Modena (1571–1648) and Simone Luzzatto (ca. 1580–1663). These intellectuals tended towards rationalism and favoured cultural ties with the outside world. But Copia Sulam's attempts to establish dialogue across religious lines, which ended in hostility from her Christian contacts, also ran contrary to the beliefs of some Jews. Similarly, her status as a public intellectual, which eventually brought her trouble with her Christian associates, also violated proscriptions in the Jewish world.

Jewish communities in Venice (and elsewhere in Italy) felt a deep ambivalence towards women's learning.[22] On the one hand, women's literacy was considered useful and modest learning was not uncommon. Well-educated daughters were a sign of prestige for elite families, since such education proved that a family was able to invest considerable resources in something not considered a necessity. But fears (common also in the Christian world) that women's learning correlated with promiscuity kept most women from advanced study, and very few women achieved genuine erudition. Copia Sulam, who wrote about philosophy and religion, published a polemical work, and presided over a salon attended by prominent male intellectuals, was the most learned and accomplished Jewish woman in early modern Italy.

Women's Writing in Venice

When Copia Sulam began her public literary career in 1618, she joined a tradition of acclaimed women writers in Venice who found success in the city's dynamic literary environment and published works with the city's famous presses.[23] But the legacy she inherited from them was fraught: while these women earned recognition for their literary skill, male associates often responded to them with slander, sexual interest, or indifference. In the mid-fifteenth century, Veronese humanist and religious scholar Isotta Nogarola (1418–1466) earned praise throughout the Republic for her learning. She cultivated literary relationships with several Venetian noblemen and lived in Venice for a time. While some contemporaries inaccurately portrayed her as a "holy woman" – a sort of living saint of letters and thus an accepted model for female behaviour – an antagonist accused her of promiscuity, adultery, and incest.[24] Venetian humanist Cassandra Fedele (1465–1558) earned broad fame and praise as a young woman for her erudition and writing, yet male writers were often more interested in her appearance than her ideas; when she was no longer considered a prodigy or pretty, her success dried up.[25] By the time she stepped back into the limelight in the mid-sixteenth century,[26] after long years of obscurity, the commercial presses had brought many other women's intellectual achievements into full public view.

Venetian presses printed more than a dozen versions of the enormously popular *Rime* (Poems) of Vittoria Colonna (1490–1547) by 1559[27] and an extensive array of other female Petrarchist poetry.[28] The city was home to several talented women writers of the era, most importantly singer and poet Gaspara Stampa (ca. 1523–1554) as well as poet and courtesan Veronica Franco (1546–1591). These two poets rose to prominence in the city and won powerful defenders, but they also encountered vicious slander. Stampa was the object of obscene satirical attacks that labelled her a whore and a plagiarist.[29] Franco was the target of both poetic and religious defamation: a Venetian nobleman wrote satirical invective against her that termed her, too, a whore,[30] and a man she employed denounced her to the Inquisition for heresy.[31] The city allowed these writers opportunity but at a high price, and their literary

experiences signalled the existence – already in the latter half of the
sixteenth century – of strong hostility in the Republic towards women
writers.[32] Moderata Fonte (Modesta Pozzo de' Zorzi, 1555–1592) and
Lucrezia Marinella (1571–1653) both wrote and published in Venice in
the late sixteenth century (Marinella continued to publish until the middle of the seventeenth century). They published in several genres but are
best known for their 1600–1601 protofeminist entries into the *querelle des
femmes*, the contemporary debates over women's nature and roles discussed below. While these writers – who were both of the elite citizen
class – did not encounter the sort of malicious slander that Stampa and
Franco faced, Fonte published under a pen name to avoid the "public
censure" that might otherwise have resulted,[33] while Marinella encountered charges of plagiarism in the early 1600s that would haunt her for
the next half century.[34]

The negative attitudes towards women's writing that persisted in
mainstream literary society into the seventeenth century can be seen in
Traiano Boccalini's enormously popular *De' ragguagli di Parnaso* (News
from Parnassus), the first century of which (with 100 *ragguagli*) was published in Venice in 1612 and the second (with 100 additional *ragguagli*)
in 1613, just a few years before Copia Sulam started her public literary
career. In a series of fictional reports, the work imagines the reaction
in Parnassus to certain contemporary events. One particularly salacious
report from century I (*Ragguaglio* XXII) recounts that Apollo had questioned the merit and virtue of famous sixteenth-century women poets
who had begun literary associations with men.

> Some months ago, the Academy of the Intronati, contrary to their origi-
> nal institution, admitted into their society the ingenious Victoria Colonna,
> Veronica Gambara, Laura Terracina, and some others of the most cele-
> brated poetesses of Parnassus ... But in a little time Apollo began to smell a
> rat, and commanded the chief of the Intronati to put a stop to that custom.
> He told them he was at last convinced that the fittest poetry for females
> was the needle and the distaff, and in short that the exercise of learning
> between them and the virtuosi is but like the play of dogs, which soon ends
> in their mounting one another.[35]

This seventeenth-century derision of the preceding generation's female
poets, including the greatly esteemed Colonna and Gambara (1485–
1550),[36] shows profound disdain for women's intellectual activity. The
report depicted women's writing as a distraction from their proper (that
is, domestic) work and their literary association with men as little more
than sexual foreplay.

The *Querelle des Femmes* and Venetian Women Writers

Boccalini's demeaning *ragguaglio* is best understood in the context of the *querelle des femmes*, the centuries-long pan-European textual "quarrel about women" that reached a fever pitch in the early modern period.[37] Venice was a key locus of the *querelle*. Writers living in the city actively participated in the debates and scores of texts that intervened in the conversation – either to vilify or to celebrate women[38] – were published there, including Giuseppe Passi's inflammatory antifeminist *I donneschi diffetti* (The Defects of Women), issued in 1599.[39] This catalogue of women's faults, more exceptional in its length than its originality, had the ironic effect of initiating an exceptionally dynamic period in women's writing in the city.[40] Fonte's *Il merito delle donne* (The Worth of Women) and Marinella's *Le nobiltà et eccellenze delle donne et i diffetti e mancamenti de gli huomini* (The Nobility and Excellence of Women, and the Defects and Vices of Men) – both published in 1600 – were presented as responses to Passi.[41] Marinella immediately revised and expanded the *Nobiltà* into a second edition published in 1601. Both the *Merito* and the *Nobiltà* were notable since they were female-authored entries into the *querelle*, which had been fought mostly by men.[42] These incisive texts also gave a preview of the media spectacle that such debates created as publishers jockeyed against one another to extract profit from the cultural controversy.[43] The *Diffetti* volume was in its fourth edition by 1618; the *Nobiltà* went into its third edition in 1621, perhaps in response to the Copia Sulam–Bonifaccio debate, and was reprinted again in 1622. The 1621 media frenzy around Bonifaccio's *Dell'immortalità dell'anima* (On the Immortality of the Soul) and Copia Sulam's *Manifesto* – both of which used tropes of the *querelle* – can only be understood in this context. Copia Sulam may have written another entry into these heated debates: "two books of paradoxes in praise of women and against men," now lost.[44] The *querelle* continued to be hard fought in Venice over the next quarter century. In 1645, Marinella published another work on women's nature and roles – her *Essortazioni alle donne e agli altri* (Exhortations to Women and Others) – that in some ways was a palinode of her *Nobiltà* but still sought to prove women's nobility and excellence.[45] Also in the 1640s the Venetian polemicist and dissident Arcangela Tarabotti (1604–1652) emerged as a leading intellectual figure. Her call for the fair treatment of women – whose rights, she argued, were trampled by biological fathers as well as fathers of Church and state – catapulted her to fame throughout Europe.[46] Tarabotti's blistering responses to those who attacked either her or women in general recall the forceful language that Marinella and Copia Sulam used to counter their opponents in earlier debates.

The Accademia degli Incogniti and the *Querelle*

The ferocity of debates over the "woman question" in Venice intensified around the Accademia degli Incogniti. The academy, "the biggest and most significant one in Baroque Italy,"[47] was a central cultural and political force in Venice during the early to mid-seventeenth century.[48] Although women could not join the academy,[49] the group's powerful role in the city's cultural life forced any writer in Venice to contend with the academy as an institution and with its prominent members. Marinella, Copia Sulam, and Tarabotti – the three women who led careers as public intellectuals in Venice during the years of the academy's dominance – had, naturally enough, important ties to the academy.

Though the founding of the Accademia degli Incogniti has traditionally been dated to 1630, this book supports more recent scholarship that has suggested the academy was founded as early as 1623 and certainly by 1626.[50] The 1647 inclusion in its membership rolls of the long-deceased Genoese writer Ansaldo Cebà (1565–1622), a correspondent of Copia Sulam, shows that the group traced its origins at least to the early 1620s, when Cebà – thanks to Copia Sulam's interest – was in the city's limelight (see chapter one). By 1626, several future academy members had banded together to slander the Jewish writer, turning her vilification into a rallying point for their coalescing group (see chapter five). Copia Sulam's case shows that, regardless of the official date of the academy's founding, by the early to mid-1620s, the intellectual and editorial networks that the academy would formalize were already developing.

Surviving academy discourses show that the vices and dangers of women were among the academy's favourite topics for discussion.[51] Though academy members, intentionally contrarian, relied on paradox and play in these debates and prided themselves on examining issues from multiple viewpoints,[52] the debates communicate a roundly negative view of women, since frequent, zealous attacks overwhelm occasional tepid defences. For instance, the academy's central animator, Giovan Francesco Loredano (1606–1661), the most powerful figure in mid-century Venetian culture, presented a discourse to the Academy, first published in 1638, that justified the rape of women.[53] He presented another discourse, first published in 1646, entitled "In biasimo delle donne" (In Censure of Women), that declared women "an evil so great that it cannot be described."[54] These discourses were repeatedly printed throughout the seventeenth century.[55] In the Incogniti's preferred genre, the novel, academy members also portrayed women – and particularly women's sexuality and expression – as threatening.[56] Other Incogniti wrote and published works that insulted and debased women even more virulently. *L'Alcibiade fanciullo a scola* (Alcibiades the Schoolboy, ca. 1630) – attributed to the influential Incognito friar Antonio Rocco (1586–1653)[57] and called "the most obscene text of seventeenth-century Italian literature"[58] – describes the female body as dirty and corrupting and contends that women use their sexuality to ruin men. The notorious Incognito Ferrante Pallavicino (1615–1644),[59] whose ferocious attacks on the Church and on the Barberini family eventually cost him his head, intertwined an attack against the Jesuits with one against women in *La retorica delle puttane* (Rhetoric of Whores, 1642). This dialogue ridicules religious rhetoric by comparing it to the purportedly deceptive speech of prostitutes;[60] Pallavicino equates all women with prostitutes.[61] In 1647, the Incogniti – led by Loredano – published an Italian translation of a heretical work that contended women had no souls.[62]

In regard to the negative portrayals of women that emerged from Incogniti circles, Ellen Rosand argues that "the rhetorical stance assumed by the academy as a group toward the female sex did not, however, preclude respectful intellectual relationships with women."[63] But the experiences of Copia Sulam – along with those of her female contemporaries – show that many academy members were unable to maintain such relationships. The slanderous accusations of intellectual, religious, and sexual impropriety that Copia Sulam faced were the first sign of the ugly turn these discussions would take, where the general, stereotyped denigration of women went hand in hand with attacks on the character and credibility of individual female associates. The singer Barbara Strozzi, who was also tied to the academy, was attacked as unchaste in an anonymous 1637 manuscript from Incogniti circles.[64] Tarabotti was repeatedly attacked by her male associates and accused of not writing the works she published under her name. Writing at mid-century in a climate controlled by the Incogniti, Marinella reflected bitterly on the enmity that prominent women encountered. She observed in her 1645 *Essortazioni*, a reflection on her half-century of experience in Venetian literary society, that women were often denied credit for their ideas and, when they sought fame, were "like those targets that archers use which are struck and torn by everyone and from every side."[65] Other factors beyond the academy were also at play and surely contributed to the fraught experiences of these elite, erudite women. For example, a male oligarchy ruled Venice and excluded women from public life, in contrast to other parts of Italy where women were key participants in court life. Additionally, several trends that intensified among the Venetian patriciate in the late sixteenth and early to mid-seventeenth century, such as rapid dowry inflation and a tightening marriage market, created anxiety about gender roles and men's proper social position.[66] Such factors in any case cannot be seen as separate from the dynamics in the academy, which was dominated by powerful patrician men, since these factors also influenced the group's ideology.[67]

While the experiences of Marinella and Tarabotti provide essential context, Copia Sulam's case is more complex since her position as a public intellectual provoked religious bigotry as well as misogyny. Her Christian male associates pressured her to convert; when she resisted, they attacked her religion, accused her of heresy, and depicted her as anti-Christian. These charges were part of a systematic campaign to discredit a non-Christian female writer whom associates also persistently accused of intellectual dishonesty. But most damaging to her were accusations of promiscuity. Such charges tapped into age-old Christian anxiety over sexual contact between Christians and Jews and fear of miscegenation.[68] Copia Sulam was more vulnerable to these accusations since, although she was a member of a reviled minority group that was locked into the ghetto at night, by day she enjoyed, in one of the most vibrant Jewish communities in Europe, a freedom of movement and association that would have been unfathomable to either Marinella or Tarabotti. Tarabotti, after all, was a strictly cloistered nun; Marinella was a woman of the *cittadina* class who, like all citizen and patrician woman in Venice, faced tight limits on where she went and with whom she kept company. The close contact Copia Sulam had with her male associates led to charges of sexual misconduct – accusations that then invited new attacks on her religious and intellectual integrity.

Sarra Copia Sulam: A Jewish Salonnière and the Press in Counter-Reformation Venice

This book could not have been written without the scholarship on Copia Sulam that has been produced over the last forty years. Carla Boccato was the first modern critic to study seriously Copia Sulam's life and works. Beginning in 1973, Boccato published a series of articles based on careful research in the Archivio di Stato di Venezia (ASV) and other Venetian institutions that reintroduced Copia Sulam to modern readers and established many of the facts that are now cornerstones of our understanding of the writer. Corinna de Fonseca-Wollheim, in a remarkable dissertation and several important articles published in the late 1990s, sensitively analyzed Copia Sulam's writing and intellectual experiences from a gender studies perspective and encouraged scholars to take her literary production seriously. Umberto Fortis did exactly that in an important 1998 article then expanded into a pithy 2003 monograph entitled *La "bella ebrea": Sara Copio Sullam, poetessa nel ghetto di Venezia del '600* (The "Beautiful Jewish Woman": Sara Copia Sullam, Poet in the Seventeenth-Century Venetian Ghetto). The volume contextualized Copia Sulam's literary career within the cultural life of the ghetto and provided subtle and convincing readings of the salonnière's writing and particularly of her poetry. The text also provided a modern edition in Italian of Copia Sulam's prose and poetry, the latter presented with extensive contextualization and analysis. In a broader context, Howard Adelman's numerous articles over the last quarter-century that discuss Copia Sulam have established her importance and exceptionality in the history of Italian Jewish women and in the context of contemporary Venetian and Jewish culture.

In 2009, Don Harrán published a monumental edition and translation into English of all known writings by and about Copia Sulam. With a lengthy introductory essay, synthetic prefaces to each of the works translated, and exhaustive notes, this critical edition – the first volume to disseminate works by and about Copia Sulam in English – brought these writings into the scholarly mainstream. Harrán's meticulous research on all aspects of Copia Sulam's life and works, along with his nuanced and detailed analysis of her writing, have constituted the definitive scholarly account of Copia Sulam and her associates. His volume is a necessary point of departure for critical studies of Copia Sulam.

The groundbreaking research undertaken by these scholars provides the foundation for this book. At the same time, my approach departs from previous research in the perspectives it adopts and the contexts it illuminates. This book seeks to understand the arc of Copia Sulam's astonishing career as a public intellectual – including her final retreat from the public stage, and, seemingly, from literary activity – in terms of the dynamics of contemporary culture. While studies have thus far ignored the ties between Copia Sulam's salon and the Venetian presses, this study foregrounds these connections, demonstrating that they are essential to understanding her precarious and provocative role as a cultural mediator in the tumultuous intellectual world of seventeenth-century Venice. My long study of Venetian women's writing of this period – in essence, the writing and literary careers of Tarabotti and Marinella, alongside Copia Sulam – has fundamentally shaped my approach to the Jewish writer. Framing her literary career in relation to the experiences of these other female intellectuals in the battles waged in the Venetian presses, this book – in contrast to others – suggests that Copia Sulam's experiences are part of a common pattern that conditioned interactions between intellectual women and the male literary establishment.

Copia Sulam, whose *Manifesto* states that writers should use the press
sparingly and judiciously,[69] brought only one work to press. Her other extant poetry and prose come down to us through scattered sources. This
limited oeuvre, a sign of her adherence to her own dictates, compels
the critic to engage seriously with the words that remain – as well as with
those that were written to and about her by contemporaries. Employing
this approach, the present study provides wholly new readings of Copia
Sulam's writing, which – despite the numerous studies dedicated to her –
still provides fertile ground for original literary criticism. My study, for
instance, rereads a letter she wrote to an associate that was later used as
"proof" of her heresy. While I contend that the letter shows more clearly
than critics have said that Copia Sulam flirted with dangerous ideas,
I also argue that it demonstrates her commitment to the rigorous and
unfettered examination of religious and philosophical ideas, more than
to any specific belief. She would later defend such freedom of inquiry –
for women and Jews as well as Christian men – in her *Manifesto*. My study
also reads anew this important work, underscoring that the *Manifesto*,
much more than Copia Sulam's defence of her own beliefs, is a religious apology designed to protect her whole community. The *Manifesto*
deflects the religious danger her associate's charge of heresy created for
her and her co-religionists in several ways: by downplaying differences
between Judaism and Christianity; by focusing on her antagonist's abuse
of the press; and by shifting her debate with her male associate onto the
terrain of the contemporary *querelle des femmes*.

As regards Copia Sulam's other writing, my study suggests that partial authorship of a 1626 manuscript defence of Copia Sulam may be
attributed to the writer herself. I show how this collaboratively authored
manuscript offers insight into the endurance of her literary network and
her final decision to withdraw from a public literary life. In addition to
rereading works *by* Copia Sulam, this volume provides new understanding of works written *about* her, emphasizing the escalating damage that
Copia Sulam's associates did to her as they maligned her in print. This
vituperation includes insidious attacks on her sexual "honesty." These
attacks, when paired with the accusations of heresy and intellectual dishonesty that were unleashed against her, destroyed Copia Sulam's will to
pursue a career as a public intellectual.

This study of Copia Sulam's intellectual life in the context of contemporary Venetian literary society unfolds in the six chapters described
below. The book concludes with a biographical note on Copia Sulam
and her family based on documents I discovered in the Archivio di Stato
di Venezia, including her father's will and household inventory, which
are published in the appendices.

Chapter One: The Birth of a Salon (1618–1621)

The opening chapter traces the rise of Copia Sulam's literary salon, which fostered Christian–Jewish intellectual interaction of an intensity and duration unique in early modern Venice. The group consolidated around Copia Sulam's correspondence with the Genoese writer Cebà, who attempted to convert her though she strongly resisted. By 1621, at least ten Christian men, in addition to at least two Jewish men, frequented the salon. The group's close ties to the Venetian publishing industry made it especially attuned to the religious and cultural climate of the city. Associates exchanged poetry and letters and debated philosophy and theology in an atmosphere pervaded by heterodoxy.

As Copia Sulam's salon grew in size and importance, Cebà's letters became hostile. He not only criticized Copia Sulam with increasing frequency for her intellectual "speculations," but he also accused her of making herself sexually available to the men who surrounded her. Such charges were especially provocative because of the numerous taboos and legal proscriptions against sexual contact between Christians and Jews. When Copia Sulam faced a serious challenge to her orthodoxy after Baldassare Bonifaccio accused her in print of heresy, Cebà did not back her. He was facing his own trouble at the time: the Congregation of the Index, an arm of the Roman Congregation of the Holy Office (the Roman Inquisition),[70] had suspended his epic poem on the Jewish heroine Esther until it was revised. With his orthodoxy under question, Cebà distanced himself from the free-thinking salonnière.

Chapter Two: A Rupture in the Salon (1619–1621)

Copia Sulam claimed she was stunned when, in June 1621, her associate Bonifaccio used one of the most prominent presses in Venice to publish a treatise that attacked her on religious grounds. His *Immortalità dell'anima* charged her with denying that doctrine, which was considered orthodox for Jews as well as Christians in the seventeenth century. The *Immortalità* mocked Copia Sulam as a female intellectual and depicted her as a danger to men's salvation. She quickly composed a treatise in response.

Chapter two situates the Copia Sulam–Bonifaccio conflict in the history of debates on the soul's immortality and discusses the currency of these ideas in contemporary Venice in both Christian and Jewish intellectual society. Bonifaccio's charge derived from positions Copia Sulam took at salon debates and from a letter that she wrote – which he later published – in which she expressed unequivocally an anti-Aristotelian and materialist concept of the soul. Bonifaccio responded to Copia

Sulam's letter – which constitutes the most developed extant example of her philosophical reasoning – with his published treatise. By broadcasting their discussion publicly, he violated the salon's implicit bonds of trust.

Chapter Three: The Salon and the Venetian Presses (1621)

Copia Sulam answered Bonifaccio's treatise with her *Manifesto*. Since Bonifaccio had challenged her in print, she embraced the opportunity to expand her fame and to immortalize the Copio name by using the same medium. Nevertheless, she criticized Bonifaccio's misuse of the press, charging that he rushed to print an ill-conceived and poorly executed work.

Chapter three shows how, as Copia Sulam focused on the publishing questions that Bonifaccio's attack raised, she minimized the religious ones. Realizing the seriousness of his accusation for her and her co-religionists, she sought to defend herself and her religion with a tactic used in other religious apologies issued by Venetian Jews in the same period: Modena's *Historia de' riti hebraici* (History of Jewish Rites, composed ca. 1616 and printed in 1637 and again in 1638) and Luzzatto's *Discorso circa il stato de gl'hebrei et in particolar dimoranti nell'inclita città di Venetia* (Discourse Regarding the State of the Jews, and in Particular Those Living in the Illustrious City of Venice, 1638). Like Modena's *Riti* and Luzzatto's *Discorso*, Copia Sulam's *Manifesto* presented a vision of Judaism palatable to a Christian audience. With this approach, Copia Sulam sought to protect herself and her community in a cultural climate that was always precarious for Jews.

The provocative religious debate was not the only reason that the *Manifesto* was a print phenomenon in the summer of 1621, coming out in three editions in a matter of weeks. The quick sales of the volume were also due to Copia Sulam's withering attack on Bonifaccio, a Catholic priest several years her senior. Her scathing response used the language of the feminist and antifeminist controversies that roiled in Venice during these years.[71] She tried in other ways to transform the debate into a gendered one – for instance, depicting Bonifaccio's attack on *her* as a general attack on *women*. By recasting the dispute in this way, Copia Sulam again sought to deflect attention from the theological aspects of Bonifaccio's charges. The gendered element, in other words, was another aspect of her religious apology. It was also part of her appeal to a reading public eager to follow the contemporary gender wars that were being fought in the city's presses. Bonifaccio's vicious reply to the *Manifesto* and the slanderous attacks other writers launched against her in the wake of this controversy showed that those around Copia Sulam were also anxious to capitalize on the public interest, at her expense.

Chapter Four: Copia Sulam Compromised (1622–1623)

This chapter outlines how Copia Sulam's correspondence with Cebà cooled immediately after Copia Sulam wrote and published her provocative *Manifesto* in the summer of 1621. In this period, Cebà was fighting his own battle against charges of religious irregularity as he sought to defend *La reina Esther* (Queen Esther), which the Congregation of the Index had censured on the charges that it contaminated the sacred Old Testament story and was lascivious.

As Cebà mounted a defence against the Congregation's charges, Copia Sulam organized her own defence against Bonifaccio's attack by – among other things – seeking Cebà's support. Cebà was unwilling to provide it: after receiving the *Manifesto* she sent to him, he ended the correspondence definitively with two angry letters in spring 1622. In addition to making a renewed attack on her sexual conduct, these last letters insulted her as a woman, dismissed her as an intellectual, and disparaged her as a Jew.

After Cebà's October 1622 death, a volume of his letters to Copia Sulam entitled *Lettere d'Ansaldo Cebà scritte a Sarra Copia* (Ansaldo Cebà's Letters Written to Sarra Copia) was published in 1623.[72] The work was compromising to Copia Sulam, since it voiced concerns about her excessive sexual availability to her salon associates and attributed several anti-Christian statements to her. She succeeded in suppressing one particularly dangerous letter from the collection, which is a measure of her awareness of and concern over the volume's publication. Her concern was merited: the *Lettere a Sarra Copia* collection, like Bonifaccio's *Immortalità*, was issued by a former friend who used the presses to sully her reputation and to advertise his own orthodoxy by attacking hers.

Chapter Five: Friends and Enemies (1621–1626)

Chapter five explores how Bonifaccio's disappearance from Copia Sulam's salon created an opening for two desperate men who were eking out a living at the edges of the Venetian print economy. Their power within the salon grew when Copia Sulam's correspondence with Cebà ended in 1622. The men, Roman writers Numidio Paluzzi and Alessandro Berardelli, used the salon's atmosphere of trust to bilk the salonnière. When she discovered and punished their dishonesty in summer 1624, they sought to ruin her reputation.

First, the men circulated a reportedly provocative and offensive text, "Le Sareide" (Sara's Feats), now lost. Then, immediately after Paluzzi's 1625 death, Berardelli published Paluzzi's *Rime* (Poems [Venice: Ciotti, 1626]), in which he sought to discredit Copia Sulam, a "perfidious Jewish woman" who, he claimed, had stolen writings from the moribund Paluzzi and presented them as her own. That the prominent printer Giovanni Battista Ciotti (ca. 1564–ca. 1635)[73] published the *Rime* lent credibility to Berardelli's accusations. Copia Sulam's defenders would later claim that this vitriolic work debased the print medium as well as Ciotti's own presses.

Rather than to defame Copia Sulam, however, the *Rime*'s explicit aim was to memorialize Paluzzi. Berardelli, who used the volume to burnish his own literary credentials, shamelessly touted his loyalty to his friend Paluzzi. His insistence on male friendship ties grounded in sacrifice recalled the "heroic friendship" between the Venetian noblemen Nicolò Barbarigo and Marco Trevisan, which became a cultural and editorial cause célèbre in these years. This well-known friendship, like Paluzzi and Berardelli's, celebrated a homosocial male bond that pushed women to the margins. It was a meme that, like the revilement of Copia Sulam, provided a rallying point and an editorial opportunity for the writers who were coalescing into the Accademia degli Incogniti.

A group of writers responded to Paluzzi's *Rime* with a satirical manuscript composed and circulated in 1626. The work, titled "Avisi di Parnaso" (Reports from Parnassus), attacked Paluzzi and Berardelli and defended Copia Sulam's honour. Critics have generally accepted at face value the attribution of the manuscript to the many writers who signed their names to its poetry and prose. I propose instead that these names were pseudonyms for members of Copia Sulam's inner circle and for Copia Sulam herself. The manuscript shows that the salonnière maintained an effective literary network through 1626, despite the many associates who had betrayed her in print attacks. The text of the "Avisi," importantly, also includes five signed poems by Copia Sulam that constitute her last literary testament, which champions the nobility of intellectual pursuits but rejects an intellectual life ruled by confrontation and slander. Though the work itself was not printed, it is her final plea for a responsible use of the press.

Chapter Six: The Afterlife of the Salon (Post-1626)

Copia Sulam pledged silence after her last public row with Berardelli, which dragged on through 1626. But she didn't immediately disappear

from the literary stage. The next year, the widely published writer
Gabriele Zinano (1557–ca. 1635) advertised his former connection to
her and to her salon in his 1627 *Rime diverse* (Various Poems), in which
he published a sonnet of hers – the last of her writing to be published
under her name in the seventeenth century.

As chapter six shows, Copia Sulam's withdrawal from Venetian literary
circles created an opening for her most venomous enemy, Berardelli,
who succeeded in carving out a place for himself in mid-century literary society. He gained friends and opportunity through his membership
in the Accademia degli Incogniti and his name continued to appear in
print until the mid-1640s. In contrast, Copia Sulam left no trace of her
activity in the final fifteen years of her life. It is all but certain that the
literary society she had built disintegrated after she refused to continue
the sort of literary battles that had, by dint of circumstance, become her
salon's lifeblood. She died in the ghetto in 1641.

Copia Sulam remained largely forgotten for the rest of the seventeenth
century, until she was again defamed in print in 1692 by a report written
decades earlier by the writer, literary chronicler, and Incogniti member
Angelico Aprosio (1607–1681), who accused the salonnière of plagiarism and promiscuity. Aprosio's account was not the only one available
to readers in the latter part of the seventeenth century, however. The
Florentine writer Giovanni Cinelli Calvoli (1625–1706) was also preparing his wide-ranging bibliographic repertory titled *Biblioteca volante* (The
Flying Library) during this period. Cinelli Calvoli defended Copia Sulam
against Aprosio's charges: he was the first to question both the motives
and the reliability of those who reviled her, and he seems to have seen
the character assassination against her for what it was. His report was
first published in 1682 but had limited initial circulation; it only became
widely available in 1746, more than a century after Copia Sulam's death.

Literary historians from the seventeenth and eighteenth centuries
ascribed importance to Copia Sulam by mentioning her in general histories of Italian literature, but they dismissed her writing, and doubts about
her authorship have persisted into this century. Nevertheless, starting
in the eighteenth century she attracted positive attention in studies of
female writers and Jewish writers. As the fields of women's studies and
Jewish studies have burgeoned over the last forty years, Copia Sulam has
become the focus of critical attention that has prepared the ground for
this first biography of her life.

Biographical Note: Sarra Copia Sulam in the Venetian Ghetto

The biographical note at the end of this book presents significant new archival information on Copia Sulam's family, who were affluent and influential moneylenders and merchants. The documents showcased illuminate the Copio family's position within the ghetto and allow an accurate dating of Copia Sulam's birth and marriage,[74] while also helping to explain how she was able – despite barriers inside and outside the Jewish community – to conduct a public literary career. Her father's 1606 will was decisive: he sought to ensure the autonomy and financial independence of Copia Sulam and her two sisters. The role of Copia Sulam's mother, Ricca, was also fundamental. Clearly literate, Ricca was a successful business woman who, after her husband's death, continued to advocate for and to educate her daughters.

Archival documents also chart the case of Copia Sulam's paternal uncle Moisè Copio, a leader in the Jewish community who converted to Christianity between 1621 and 1625 – the very years in which Copia Sulam's associates reviled her savagely and publicly. Moisè Copio's conversion – surely a great source of shame for the Copio family – only became more humiliating for his relatives since his scandalous post-conversion conduct repeatedly required judicial intervention. His disgrace may have weakened the Copios' status in the ghetto, where the family's power – not to mention wealth – had enabled Copia Sulam to flout the many Jewish proscriptions on female intellectual activity and Christian–Jewish interaction, particularly interactions that crossed gendered lines.

The Birth of a Salon (1618–1621)

Overview

Between 1618 and 1626, Sarra Copia Sulam hosted a salon at her house in the ghetto. By 1621, at least ten Christian and several Jewish men frequented the salon, which attracted curious visitors from the Veneto and beyond. It provided an exceptional forum in which, for nearly a decade, free-thinking Christians and Jews discussed literary, philosophical, and religious matters and exchanged writing in an atmosphere pervaded by heterodoxy.

Copia Sulam built up this thriving literary community around a correspondence she initiated in spring 1618 with the aging Genoese writer and monk Ansaldo Cebà (1565–1622). She was inspired to write to him after reading his 1615 epic poem *La reina Esther,* whose celebration of the Old Testament heroine seemed to Copia Sulam an invitation for cross-faith dialogue. The letter she sent became the first in a four-year-long correspondence. Their exchange had a pretext of spiritual love but hinged on his relentless efforts to convert her to Christianity and on her resistance to these attempts. In addition to letters, the correspondents exchanged poetry, elaborate gifts, their portraits, and – most valuably – their literary contacts.

When Copia Sulam first wrote Cebà, she was all but unknown within Venice, let alone in other parts of northern Italy. She had ties with other Jewish writers in Venice, but we have no evidence that she previously had any Christian literary associates. Her correspondence with Cebà, a much older and widely published author, thus brought her into contact with the Christian literary world. The exchange helped her establish her name and a network of contacts in Genoa and propelled her to prominence in her home city.

From the beginning, Copia Sulam involved other writers in her relationship with Cebà. She commissioned a Jewish writer to compose a poem for him that she included in her initial letter. By 1620, she was commissioning poetry for Cebà from the growing list of salon associates, all of whom were eager for the opportunities that a link to the Genoese writer could bring. Copia Sulam shared Cebà's letters with her associates, whom he greeted in his letters and whose reactions she reported in hers. Participants in the salon, where the debate of religious ideas was a cornerstone, eagerly followed the religiously charged correspondence. Cebà, for his part, sought to enlist her associates in his efforts to convert her. As the correspondence became one of the focal points of the salon, it created a nexus of relations among Venetian writers and between Venetian and Genoese writers that would outlive the correspondence itself. The letter exchange began to take a negative turn when Cebà became jealous over Copia Sulam's contact with other men.

Early Contacts

Jewish Literary Contacts

Copia Sulam accompanied the first letter that she sent to Cebà with two sonnets in praise of *La reina Esther*: one in Italian that she wrote herself and one in Spanish that Cebà reported was written "by an unknown Jewish author at the behest of signora Sarra Coppia."[1] Cebà responded to both poems *per le rime* – that is, using the same rhymes. In orchestrating this three-way poetic exchange between writers of different faiths, states, and genders, Copia Sulam offered an early idea of the sort of open intellectual exchange she sought and would later seek actively to cultivate at her salon. She also showed herself to be a skilled cultural intermediary who helped other writers widen their literary networks as she broadened her own.

At the same time, this opening exchange shows that Copia Sulam's literary network was limited: she commissioned only one other poem, from another Jewish writer whose limited fame may have led either her or Cebà to suppress the poet's name: Jacob Uziel (d. 1630 in Zante), a Jewish doctor and writer with Spanish origins who lived and worked in the ghetto.[2] If, at the opening of the Copia Sulam–Cebà exchange, Uziel had not yet firmly established himself as a writer, by the mid-1620s he had gained a strong foothold – in part through his association with the salonnière. In 1624, he published his own epic poem (in Spanish) on an Old Testament hero – *David, poema heroico* (David, an Epic Poem) – doubtless inspired by Cebà's example. Three years later, Gabriele Zinano – a well-known author and participant in the salon – would publish sonnets he had exchanged with Uziel.[3]

By the time Copia Sulam contacted Cebà, she had also developed a close intellectual relationship with another Jewish scholar, the famed polymath rabbi and writer Leon Modena (1571–1648; see figure 1.1),

1.1 The title page of Leon Modena's *Historia de' riti hebraici* (Venice: appresso Gio. Calleoni, 1638) with a portrait of the author. Courtesy of the Library at the Herbert D. Katz Center for Advanced Judaic Studies, Kislak Center for Special Collections, Rare Books and Manuscripts, University of Pennsylvania.

an extremely prolific author and an influential religious authority.[4] Modena had known her for many years: he was related to the Copio family through his wife and in 1608 lived with Moisè Copio, Copia Sulam's uncle and her mother's and husband's close business associate.[5] The salonnière's early contact with Modena, who was some twenty years her senior and already an important intellectual figure in the ghetto and far beyond, was of utmost importance to her as she began to establish herself as a writer. In 1619, the year after she started her correspondence with Cebà, Modena published his own work on Esther and dedicated it to Copia Sulam.[6] The dedication refers to his long-standing relationship with her and to their exchange of views on scholarly and literary matters. Modena recalls that they were drawn together by Cebà's text, which "on several occasions we fell into discussing."[7] Copia Sulam sent Modena's *L'Ester* (Esther) to Cebà.[8] Modena, who would remain one of her most important contacts throughout her public literary career, had broad cultural interests and the same commitment to dialogue with the Christian world that drove her intellectual life. A case in point was the work he wrote around 1616 entitled *Historia de' riti hebraici*, composed at the behest of an English lord (probably the English ambassador to Venice, Sir Henry Wotton) who intended to present it to James I of England.[9] This book on Jewish rituals was, as Mark Cohen describes, "one of the first Jewish books composed in European languages for non-Jewish consumption" and part of "incipient Jewish attempts to re-orient Christian attitudes toward the Jews."[10] Copia Sulam would make similar attempts throughout her literary career.

If Copia Sulam perceived Cebà's *La reina Esther*, a text written by a Christian man in praise of a Jewish woman, as a bridge for Christian–Jewish dialogue, it first fuelled her interactions with her fellow Jewish writers, Uziel and Modena. These interactions provided the first glimmers of a salon, as Copia Sulam and her associates discussed Cebà's *La reina Esther* and planned responses to it. These relationships provided her a springboard for entry into a Christian literary world where she made advances for her Jewish associates as well. Her overture to Cebà was both a result of and a catalyst for a cultural flowering in the Venetian ghetto in the mid-seventeenth century driven by Jewish intellectuals who sought cultural ties outside the ghetto.

The Beginning of the Cebà Correspondence

The correspondence between Copia Sulam and Cebà (figure 1.2) comprised around one hundred letters exchanged over four years: May 1618 to April 1622. The manuscript letters have been lost, so the exchange

1.2 A portrait of Ansaldo Cebà from *Lettere a Sarra Copia* (Genoa: per Giuseppe Pavoni, 1623). Courtesy of Beinecke Rare Book and Manuscript Library, Yale University.

must be studied through the 1623 edition of Cebà's letters, *Lettere a Sarra Copia*, which was published immediately after his death and includes only his letters. Though the correspondence began around the pretext of spiritual love – a leitmotif in the Italian literary tradition – over the course of the letter exchange Cebà expressed increasing desire for a physical union with Copia Sulam. This rhetorical shift – from love conceived in Neoplatonist terms to desire based on erotic fantasies – became a source of increasing alarm for Copia Sulam.[11]

Copia Sulam's letters are referenced in all of Cebà's responses, and specific statements she made are paraphrased in forty notes that appear at the beginning of his volume. The work includes fifty letters from Cebà to Copia Sulam, plus one letter to her husband, Giacob Sulam (d. post-1641), and two to one of Cebà's agents in Venice, Giacomo Rosa (d. 1630). The volume also traces the correspondents' exchange of poetry and includes four compositions by Copia Sulam, all answered by Cebà. Since the actual letters that the writers exchanged have not survived, we cannot know if the published letters correspond precisely to those Cebà actually sent, though his death and a scandal near the end of his life may have limited his ability to rewrite the correspondence. Chapter four provides an in-depth discussion of this matter.

The letters Copia Sulam and Cebà exchanged became a cultural phenomenon. The correspondence created a network of relations not just among writers, but also among musicians, artists, and patrons from Venice and Genoa. As we have seen, Copia Sulam commissioned associates to write poetry for Cebà, and her salon became an important venue for the discussion and dissemination of his works. Cebà, for his part, sent several agents to Venice to meet face-to-face with Copia Sulam, including Rosa, a musician who became one of her most loyal supporters. Cebà also introduced Copia Sulam, by letter, to his patron Marcantonio Doria's wife, Isabella della Tolfa (d. 1650), an enormously wealthy and powerful noblewoman.[12] She would prove to be an invaluable contact. He also connected Copia Sulam to the famed Genoese artist Bernardo Castello (1557–1629),[13] with whom Copia Sulam also corresponded and who would paint a portrait of Copia Sulam.[14] On at least one occasion, she also wrote directly to Doria (1572–1651), son of a doge of Genoa.[15] The correspondents exchanged their precious contacts for personal gain, but each came to use the connections for their own ends, often at cross-purposes with the other. Cebà used his new contacts to increase pressure on her to convert, while she used the new connections to influence the posthumous publication of his letters.

Cebà was nearing the end of his life when he began to correspond with Copia Sulam. An author of lyric and epic poems, treatises, letters, and dramas, he had played an important role in Genoese and Italian letters for several decades. From a noble but impoverished Genoese family that had produced two doges,[16] Cebà studied in Padua but spent most of his life in Genoa. He had initially undertaken a life in politics, but after "some disappointments" he retired from public life, took minor orders, and pursued a life of learning.[17] He and other writers in late-sixteenth- and early-seventeenth-century Genoa, including Angelo Grillo (1557–1629), Gabriele Chiabrera (1552–1638), Livia Spinola (fl. 1588–1599), and Laura Spinola (fl. 1580s), as well as publishers Girolamo Bartoli (fl. 1558–1591) and Giuseppe Pavoni (ca. 1551–1641), worked to establish the city as a literary capital.[18] Pavoni, active in Genoa from 1598 to 1641, published most of Cebà's works,[19] but the writer also published with presses in Padua, Rome, Milan, Venice, and Antwerp.

By the time Cebà released *La reina Esther* in 1615 (figure 1.3), he had already established himself as a writer of note with two significant collections of rhymes and a previous epic poem.[20] He aimed to broaden his fame with this second epic poem, which he hoped would challenge the dominant model of Torquato Tasso's late-sixteenth-century *Gerusalemme liberata* (Jerusalem Delivered), even though *La reina Esther* – also an epic on a religious theme – is derivative of Tasso's canonical work. Cebà's poem, which narrates Esther's story in twenty-one long cantos, digresses continually and evokes a Baroque sense of marvel for its plot complications, innumerable characters, and exotic elements.

The poem was based on the biblical Book of Esther, though Cebà acknowledged significant departures from the sacred text in his note to readers. The Book of Esther tells the story of a Jewish community living in exile in Persia in the fifth century BCE. The community's precarious existence is threatened when a malevolent minister seeks to destroy the Jews, but they are saved by the heroic actions of the beautiful Queen Esther, who risks her life by visiting the king unbidden, revealing to him that she is Jewish and evoking his sympathy for her people, who are then saved. Cebà's retelling of this deliverance of the Jewish people would have caught Copia Sulam's eye for many reasons. The victory commemorated in the story, around which Purim is celebrated, "was a model for Diaspora Jewry, a success story that served as a source of comfort and inspiration for them."[21] The book surely held particular interest for Copia Sulam, whose literary career was centred on cross-faith dialogue, since it showed Esther successfully acting as a bridge between the Jewish people and the majority culture.[22] The beauty and bravery of the heroine would also have spoken to Copia Sulam, who was praised by contemporaries for her appearance and would give ample proof, in the tribulations of her literary career, of her fortitude. Though Cebà's depiction of Esther was

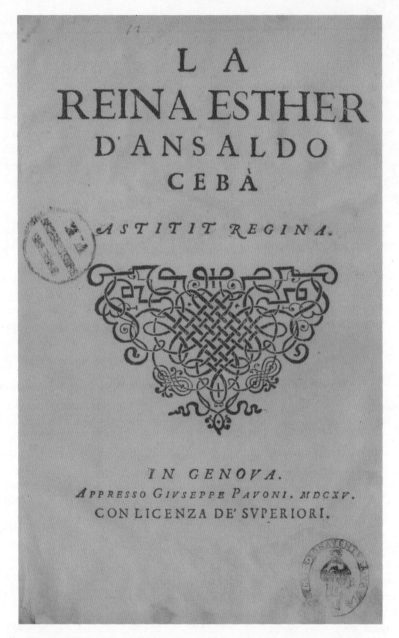

1.3 The title page of Ansaldo Cebà's *La reina Esther* (Genoa: appresso
Giuseppe Pavoni, 1615). Courtesy of the Universitätsbibliothek, Universität
Mannheim.

Christianized, his emphasis on the queen's power – a "strength of soul ... so great / that it surpassed both her age and her sex"[23] – would naturally have appealed to Copia Sulam.

The Book of Esther was enormously popular in seventeenth-century Europe,[24] part of a larger interest in biblical epics and dramas. These stories allowed audiences – Catholic, Jewish, and Protestant – to view the religious upheavals of the period and their own religious struggles through the lens of the Bible.[25] Cebà was by no means the first Christian Italian who had versified the Esther story: Florentine writer Lucrezia Tornabuoni (ca. 1425–1482) had written a version nearly 150 years earlier.[26] Visual representations of the episode by Christian Italian artists also abound.[27] Taking up the popular theme of Esther, and seeking to develop the epic genre in new directions, Cebà expected that *La reina Esther* would establish him as a major Italian writer. Driven by these high hopes, he sent the work – lavishly printed in quarto – to "all the most illustrious figures of Italy."[28] Though the work was printed again the next year, in Milan,[29] it received lukewarm responses and some outright criticisms, which deeply embittered the author.[30] It was also a commercial flop.[31]

Therefore the positive reaction that *La reina Esther* elicited from Copia Sulam, which she communicated in her first letter, buoyed Cebà.[32] With the letter she included a sonnet that, as the first poem she sent outside her immediate literary circle, can be considered her public poetic debut.[33] Cebà later published the poem along with his own response *per le rime*. Though Copia Sulam's poem flatters Cebà with mention of his *La reina Esther*'s glory, the true focus of the poem is on Esther herself, whose pre-eminent place in heaven and central role in Cebà's artistic creation and salvation Copia Sulam underscores.

La bella hebrea, che con devoti accenti
Gratia impetrò da' più sublimi chori,
Sì che fra stelle in ciel nei sacri ardori
Felice gode le superne menti,
Al suon che l'alme dai maggior tormenti
Sottragge, ANSALDO, onde te stesso honori,
Spiegar sentendo i suoi più casti amori
I mondi tiene a le tue rime intenti.
Quindi l'immortal Dio, che nacque in Delo,
A la tua gloria, la sua gloria acqueta,
Né la consumerà caldo né gelo.
Colei ancor, che già ti fe' poeta
Reggendo questa, da l'empireo Cielo
Darà per sempre ai carmi tuoi la meta.[34]

(The beautiful Jewess – who with devout words
beseeched the sublime choirs for grace
and therefore now, in sacred ardor among the stars in the heaven
revels blissfully in the divine intellect –
at the sound the saves souls from the greatest torment,
Ansaldo, with which you bring honor to yourself,
draws all the worlds[35] to your verses
as she hears her most chaste passions described.
Therefore, the immortal God who was born in Delos
fulfills his glory in your glory
which neither fire nor ice will destroy.
She, who already made you a poet
by sustaining your glory, will from her place in the empyrean heaven[36]
always provide an aim for your song.)

The figure of Esther in the poem is clearly a double for Copia Sulam:
she claims also for herself the religious privilege and artistic power she
attributes to the Old Testament queen. In his sonnet of response, Cebà
claims he will uplift Copia Sulam as he did Esther, but he insists on
his new correspondent's spiritual inferiority: "Ma non t'avvedi, ohimè,
ch'errante zelo / Miseramente il passo al Ciel ti vieta" (But you do not
see, alas, that errant zeal / cruelly blocks your path to heaven.)

Along with this sonnet, Cebà wrote an enthusiastic letter in which he
praises Copia Sulam for contacting him about his poem, which "compelled [him] to form a different opinion of [her] than one ordinarily
tends to have of [her] sex."[37] Although he says that Copia Sulam's epistolary initiative burnished her image, his eagerness to engage in the
exchange and his almost immediate interest in publishing it suggest
that he also believed the correspondence reflected quite positively on
him. He may have hoped that the letters – which have as their premise
La reina Esther's merit and influence – could redeem his beloved poem.

Though this latter task would prove impossible, the correspondence
did initiate a particularly productive period in Cebà's literary career.
From 1619 to 1622, he published (or prepared for publication) twelve
of the eighteen works that he would author in his lifetime.[38] The letters
and poetry he composed for Copia Sulam gained him welcome attention in Genoa and Venice, and their correspondence became a central
point of discussion with many of his contacts, as seen in his general letter
collection, which was published posthumously in 1623.[39] He exchanged
letters and verse with the other writers who surrounded Copia Sulam,
participating long distance – at least for a time – in her salon. The ties
he established in Venice through his link to her salon brought concrete

advantages. Whereas he had never before published a work in that city,[40] in 1620 he issued in Venice a new edition of his *Cittadino di republica* (Citizen of a Republic), a meditation on civic virtue that Copia Sulam had praised.[41] The fame that their correspondence earned Cebà in Venice was enduring: he was advertised in 1647 as a member of the influential Accademia degli Incogniti,[42] the most important literary academy in seventeenth-century Venice, whose founding postdated his death. Copia Sulam knew many of the men who would join together to form this new academy.

First Christian Literary Contacts in Venice: Numidio Paluzzi and Alessandro Berardelli

As Copia Sulam undertook her correspondence with Cebà, she also began to establish connections with Christian writers in Venice. The first of these was the Roman author Numidio Paluzzi (1587–1625). Paluzzi, some years Copia Sulam's senior, displayed an intellectual confidence and enough erudition to convince many of a literary potential that he never fulfilled. Paluzzi left Rome in the mid-1610s, seeking "more favorable skies" (as the literary chronicler Aprosio later wrote)[43] and wandering through central and northern Italy as he sought a foothold for his literary career. Aprosio reports that Paluzzi stayed in Tuscany and in Emilia.[44] The poetry he addressed to Florentine and Ferrarese nobility, included in his posthumous *Rime*, shows his attempts to find a patron in these places; his lack of success in securing support led him to Venice.

It is likely that Paluzzi was in Venice by 1616, when he was among the writers who contributed to a collection of verse in memory of the poet and dramatist Battista Guarini (1538–1612), issued that year by Giovanni Battista Ciotti.[45] By 1619, Paluzzi had established himself as a proofreader in the city, likely working for Ciotti, who was in regular contact with Paluzzi by that year.[46] His name also appears as a proofreader for an admired 1619 edition of Caesar's *Commentari* (Commentaries), printed by Nicolò Misserini (figures 1.4 and 1.5).[47] The advertisement of Paluzzi's contribution on the volume's last page shows that he had gained respect in the industry for his editorial skill.

In his early years in Venice, Paluzzi forged important ties with other writers. Pier Francesco Paoli (ca. 1585–ca. 1637), who wrote dedications to several editions by the famed author Giambattista Marino (1569–1625), exchanged poetry with Paluzzi in the 1616 collection in memory of Guarini.[48] Marino himself, the most celebrated Italian writer of the generation, vouches for Paluzzi in a 1619 letter to Ciotti: "About

1.4 The title page of Julius Caesar's *Commentari* (Venice: appresso Nicolò Misserini, 1619). By permission of the British Library, General Reference Collection 293.h.11. © The British Library Board.

T A V O L A

I L F I N E.

Numidio Palluzzi Correttore.

IN VENETIA, M DC XIX.

Appreffo Nicolò Mifferini.

1.5 The colophon of the 1619 Misserini edition of Caesar's *Commentari* advertises Paluzzi's editorial contribution. By permission of the British Library, General Reference Collection 293.h.11. © The British Library Board.

the virtues of signor Numidio Paluzzi I am much better informed than
you and have been for many years. I recognize his worth and the scope
of his genius. I aim to have him speak honorably of me and I will be
most proud if he does so, and I assure him that he won't be poorly
rewarded."[49] In addition to reassuring Ciotti about Paluzzi, Marino here
indicates that Paluzzi had gained enough status as a writer that Marino
sought Paluzzi's accolades. Marino renewed his greetings to Paluzzi in a
1620 letter to Ciotti.[50]

As Paluzzi became part of the literary scene in Venice, he came into
contact with Copia Sulam. They began to work together in 1618, the
same year in which she initiated the correspondence with Cebà.[51] As we
have seen, Paluzzi already had useful editorial and literary contacts, and
he immediately impressed Copia Sulam with his erudition.[52] She became
his patron, providing him money, lodging, and food; in exchange, he
gave her lessons and sometimes wrote her encomiastic verse.[53] Although
others among her associates exerted strong pressure on her to convert,
there is no evidence that Paluzzi was one of them. Paluzzi's enemies later
accused him of Epicurean beliefs and lack of faith in God.[54]

When Copia Sulam established contact with Paluzzi, she also encountered the Roman painter Alessandro Berardelli (d. post-1644).[55]
Contemporary reports describe Berardelli as Paluzzi's constant companion: he left Rome and travelled around Italy with Paluzzi and then
lived with him in Venice, perhaps as his valet.[56] He is repeatedly called
Paluzzi's "servant" or "scullery-boy" in a manuscript that attacks the two
friends.[57] Berardelli, who followed Paluzzi into the publishing industry and also worked as a proofreader for Venetian print houses,[58] was
a peripheral participant in Copia Sulam's salon as it developed over
the coming years, connected to it as he was mostly through Paluzzi.
The painter's humble status and apparent lack of literary contacts in
his early years in Venice made him a less appealing participant than his
friend. But over time he established connections and experience within
the publishing industry that would bear fruit for him, if not for Copia
Sulam: in 1626 he published Paluzzi's posthumous *Rime* with Ciotti in
an edition that glorifies Berardelli's own contributions and slanders
Copia Sulam.

The Salon Begins

By 1619, Copia Sulam was hosting regular intellectual gatherings at
her house that took on the contours of a salon. The term "salon" –
used by most scholars for Copia Sulam's circle[59] – indicates a group
drawn together for informal gatherings where men and women could

interact, in contrast to an academy, a more rigidly structured association usually governed by statutes and strict membership rules, where women were often excluded.[60] In addition to structured membership and written constitutions or by-laws, academies – which proliferated in early modern Venice[61] – generally also had official names, Latin mottos, emblems, formal offices, regular meeting times, and sometimes dues; kept minutes and other records; and encouraged members to adopt pseudonyms.[62] Academies could have ambitious, formalized cultural and political agendas that intertwined with those of the state.[63] As far as scholars know, Copia Sulam's group had none of these attributes. But it was precisely the flexibility of the salon – which contemporaries may have called an *accademia*,[64] a term used loosely[65] but which indicates the stature of the group[66] – that provided a promising path for Copia Sulam to enter intellectual society. Copia Sulam's group gathered participants of different status and class (nobles rubbed elbows with down-on-their-luck proofreaders) and from various parts of Italy, showing the social heterogeneity that was a defining feature of private salons in Venice in the sixteenth century as well.[67] As Martha Feldman has noted, "salons encouraged the sort of juggling for position and exposure common to places of barter."[68] Like the women-led salons of mid-sixteenth-century Italy studied by Diana Robin, Copia Sulam's salon was closely tied to the publishing industry.[69] In their close connection to the presses, academies and salons were similar.[70] They mirrored each other in another way: they could prove perilous places for women's reputations.[71]

The growth of Copia Sulam's salon can be traced through Cebà's letters and in several subsequent works about Copia Sulam.[72] In letters throughout 1619, Cebà indicates his increasing awareness of her literary associations with both Christians and Jews in Venice. In March, for instance, he suggests that her associates might add their voices to his in pressuring her to convert.[73] But during the same period he expresses the fear that the salon might also represent a spiritual hazard to her, warning her that – in contrast to his interest in saving her soul – Modena and others might "interact with you only for the delight of your conversation."[74] In August, Cebà insinuates that she was receiving help with her writing from her associates.[75] These scattered mentions of the salon's influence throughout spring and summer 1619 suggest not only that the group may already have added new associates but also that Cebà was keenly aware of its activity. By summer 1619, Copia Sulam had used her correspondence with Cebà to broaden her contacts in Genoa as well as at home. In June, she exchanged letters with della Tolfa and perhaps with Doria himself.[76]

The death of Cebà's brother Lanfranco provided the impetus for a
new poetic exchange between Copia Sulam and Cebà during the spring
and summer of 1619, when she sent him two sonnets memorializing the
event. In the first sonnet, Copia Sulam comforts Cebà by focusing on his
brother's salvation:

> Signor, pianto non merta il gran Lanfranco,
> Ché s'ei, mentre già fu nel human velo,
> Illustrò d'opre il mondo, hor gode in Cielo,
> Giunto al porto di gloria, invitto e franco.[77]

> (Signor, the great Lanfranco does not deserve your tears
> since, if he illuminated the world with his works
> while in his mortal veil, he now rejoices in heaven,
> having reached the harbor of glory, unvanquished and free.)

Copia Sulam's poem not only reassures Cebà about his brother's salvation, however; it also suggests a consonance between Jewish and Catholic
beliefs on the afterlife.[78] At the same time, she explicitly posits the
Ottoman Turks as the religious other against whom Lanfranco, a member of the Knights of Malta, was pitted.[79] She tells Cebà to look to the east
for his brother's shining flame,

> che sol degli empi' il cor pavente.
> Del tuo fido german la luce è quella,
> Che contra il Trace ancor cometa ardente
> In ciel si mostra e minacciante stella.[80]

> (which only the hearts of the impious must fear.
> That is your faithful brother's light,
> which shines in heaven against the Thracian[81]
> as a burning comet and a threatening star.)

While sublimating differences between Christianity and Judaism, Copia
Sulam represents Islam as the true threat.

In a second sonnet on Lanfranco's death, one that meditates on the
connection between the living and the dead and again suggests similarity
in Christian and Jewish beliefs on the afterlife, Copia Sulam adopts the
role of spiritual guide to warn Cebà to restrain his grief:

> Deh, frena il pianto e 'l duol ch' in te s'accoglie;
> Odi ch'ei dice in sì felice stato
> Che 'l pianger tuo del suo gioir lui toglie.[82]

(Alas, stop the tears and the sorrow that are building in you
Hear him say in his blessed state
that your crying disrupts his rejoicing.)

Cebà again answered the composition *per le rime*. Taking Copia Sulam's advice literally, Cebà rejects the idea that the lamentation of mortals can affect those in the afterlife. But if his brother could come back, Cebà says, he would do so not to comfort Ansaldo

> Ma per veder l'hebrea che mi discioglie
> Da l'amorosa lingua un suon sì grato
> E chiude in sen sì pertinaci voglie.[83]

> (But to see the Jewish woman who releases
> such a sweet sound from my loving tongue
> and who hides in her chest such pertinacious desires.)

If Copia Sulam seeks to elide Christian–Jewish differences in her sonnet, Cebà, in his response, while casting her as his muse, insists on her religious difference and her "pertinacious desires" – that is, her steadfast adherence to her religious faith.

By the end of 1619, Copia Sulam had established several important new contacts. The priest and dramatist Baldassare Bonifaccio – who had important scholarly credentials and ties to academies and other writers, and had published several works in Venice in 1618 and 1619 – was the most prominent Christian writer to join the group up to that point. He may have met associates of the salon through shared connections within the publishing industry.[84] His cousin and collaborator Gianfrancesco Corniani (1582–1646), an established Venetian writer and jurist, was closely involved in the same literary circles as Bonifaccio,[85] including the group around Copia Sulam.[86] Trained as a lawyer, Corniani became a powerful figure in the Venetian bureaucracy, rising to the post of *primario* (senior notary) of the Magistracy of the Avogaria di Comun, which was responsible for enforcing the laws of the Maggior Consilio and Senate.[87] In addition to Corniani, Bonifaccio probably introduced other writers to the group, including two he worked with closely: his brother Gaspare Bonifaccio (b. 1585)[88] and his close friend Giovanni Maria Vanti (1584–1641).[89] Vanti later provided a detailed account of Copia Sulam's salon to Aprosio, which the latter used as ammunition to slander her.[90]

A Salon Debate

As participation in the salon grew, so too did the intensity of discussions

on controversial philosophical and religious issues. Copia Sulam's later
debate with Baldassare Bonifaccio over the immortality of the soul grew
out of such charged conversations. In that published exchange, Copia
Sulam recalls salon discussions, probably from fall 1619, in which she and
Bonifaccio debated controversial ideas.[91] She tells Bonifaccio: "If in one of
our conversations I posed any difficult philosophical or theological questions, that was ... only on account of the curiosity I had to hear from you,
with the resolution of my arguments, some curious and rare knowledge,
since I thought that was the right of every person who professes learning,
and moreover of a woman, and a Jewish woman, who always is pushed into
these discussions by people who toil to convert her, as you know, to the
Christian faith."[92] Thorny intellectual and religious matters, approached
from Jewish and Christian perspectives, clearly attracted the interest of the
group, and some associates repeatedly contested Copia Sulam's continuing
adherence to the Jewish faith. Copia Sulam claims that such conversion-
ary pressure against her as a Jew and particularly as a Jewish woman gave
her a special privilege to engage in an intellectual inquiry that pushed
the bounds of orthodoxy. Her emphasis on her gender alongside her religious identity may indicate that she faced more intense pressure to convert than did Jewish male participants in the salon – for example, Modena
and Uziel. Copia Sulam also defended a more general right to intellectual
inquiry based upon curiosity and a thirst for knowledge.

Bonifaccio and Copia Sulam's salon discussion was compelling
enough that they continued it in a written epistolary exchange.[93] This
intense debate – undertaken in person and by letter – played out over
several weeks, possibly months, and riveted fellow salon participants:
when Copia Sulam received Bonifaccio's letter on the topic, Corniani
and Paluzzi rushed to her house to hear it read.[94]

Portraits and Poetry

Amid this debate, another important event drew salon associates' interest in late 1619 and early 1620: a portrait that Cebà commissioned of
himself for Copia Sulam had arrived in Venice. Copia Sulam reacted
ecstatically to this gift, which was displayed at the salon.[95] She composed
several poems of her own in praise of the portrait and urged her associates to do the same.[96] Paluzzi wrote at least one sonnet on the image;[97]
Bonifaccio wrote three, which he eagerly recited to Copia Sulam;[98] and
other salon associates also contributed verse.[99] Praising Cebà was an
important activity in the salon that took place alongside the philosophical and religious debates: Bonifaccio and Copia Sulam, as they engaged
by letter in the intense philosophic and religious debate over the soul

that played out in these months, also exchanged news on the sonnets Bonifaccio wrote to commemorate Cebà's portrait.[100]

The salon's dedicated attention to his portrait bonded Cebà to the group. In a February 1620 letter he suggested that he participated in the group through his portrait's presence and talked of the men at Copia Sulam's salon as his "worthy companions";[101] he declared himself in the same letter to be a Venetian.[102] As he embraced the group wholeheartedly, the salon became one that operated *between* Genoa and Venice: artistic and literary gifts sent from one city to the other spurred further creativity and connections. The same letter mentions Copia Sulam's ongoing correspondence with some of her new Genoese contacts, della Tolfa and the painter Castello.[103]

By April 1620, Copia Sulam had reciprocated Cebà's gift by sending him a portrait of herself,[104] though he had asked her not to do so.[105] The portrait would serve as a model for Castello to create his own portrait of the salonnière, now lost, though some critics have hypothesized that a copy may be extant (see figure 1.6).[106] Copia Sulam accompanied the portrait with an ekphrastic sonnet in which she expresses, in spiritual terms, her love for Cebà:

> L'imago è questa di colei ch'al core
> Porta l'imago tua sola scolpita,
> Che con la mano al seno al mondo additta
> "qui porto l'Idol mio, ciascun l'adore."
> Sostien con la sinistra arme d'amore
> Che fur tuoi carmi, il loco ov'è ferita
> La destra accenna, e pallida e smarrita
> Dice: "ANSALDO, il mio cor per te si more."
> Pregionera se n' viene a te davante
> Chiedendo aita, et a te porge quella
> Catena ond'è 'l mio amor fido e costante.
> Deh, l'ombra accogli di tua fida ancella
> E goda almeno il finto mio sembiante
> Quel che nega a quest'occhi iniqua stella.[107]

> (This is the image of that woman who in her heart
> carries only your image engraved,
> who with her hand to her chest points out to the world
> "here I carry my idol, may all adore him."
> She holds with her left hand the weapons of love
> that were your songs; the place where she was wounded
> the right hand indicates; and she, pale and disoriented,

1.6 A portrait by Antonio Logorio (fl. 1652–1690) that some critics have
suggested may represent Copia Sulam (the portrait would be a copy of a
painting by Castello from the early 1620s). The sitter's hands are reversed, with
regard to Copia Sulam's description of her portrait. Harrán suggests that such
a reversal could have occurred when it was copied ("Introduction," in Copia
Sulam, *Jewish Poet and Intellectual,* 25).

says "ANSALDO, my heart dies for you."
She comes as a prisoner before you,
asking for help, and she presents you that
chain, whence my love is faithful and constant.
Oh, receive the shadow of your faithful servant,
and at least may my feigned visage enjoy
what an unlucky star denies these eyes.)

Copia Sulam is the subject of this poem in several ways: as the writing subject, of course, and as the subject of the image she describes, but also as an actively loving subject. She describes, in Petrarchan terms,[108] her lovesickness, here occasioned not by the glimpse of her lover's eyes – a view her adverse fortune prevents – but by his poems. Though she casts herself as prisoner to his love – a suggestive metaphor for one who lived enclosed in the ghetto – she demonstrates a high degree of mobility between the artistic and literary landscapes of Venice and Genoa. The exchange also underscores her artistic agency: she not only commissioned the portrait but determined its imagery and then directed its reading through her verse. This poem, which Cebà again answered *per le rime*, is the final poem of Copia Sulam's included in Cebà's letters.

The correspondents' exchange of portraits and related poetry brought their relationship to its apex. The writers asserted a physical presence in each other's city by means of their likenesses, a presence solidified, in Cebà's case, by the literary tributes to the portrait that Copia Sulam arranged within her salon. Soon, however, Cebà began to chafe at the quantity of writing that she and her associates produced for him. In June 1620, he wrote: "You will have a hard time lifting me up from the dust, signora Sarra, even if you write of me with such solicitude and have others do the same. Please stop, I pray you, your pen and others'. And make sure that whoever until now has taken up the topic of my name exert himself henceforth in discussing yours, since the greatest favor that can be done for me is to see that you are praised and revered by everyone."[109] In this letter, Cebà suddenly expresses unease at the literary capital that Copia Sulam was marshalling on his behalf at a moment when her salon was thriving. He also sends back a certain sonnet and letter, probably written by Bonifaccio.[110] If earlier in the year he had welcomed the associates' praise and had considered himself a participant in the circle, he now began to reverse course. Copia Sulam and her associates nevertheless persisted in including Cebà in the salon's literary activities, and participants continued to seek his favour: in September, Cebà indicates that he had received compositions that she had sent him from another writer, referred to only as a "Dottor Vicentino"

(Vicentine doctor),[111] but who was likely the Italian jurist and librettist Pietro Paolo Bissari (1595–1663).[112]

New Associates

Copia Sulam's salon, meanwhile, continued to grow. By fall 1620, it had attracted its most highly placed and powerful participant, the Venetian nobleman Giovanni Basadonna (1562–1647), who was several decades Copia Sulam's senior.[113] His family had ties to Rovigo,[114] where Bonifaccio's family had its roots, and this shared link may have brought him into contact with the salon. Basadonna, a lieutenant in Udine in 1617–1618,[115] was by the 1620s an eloquent and influential Venetian senator and *savio grande*,[116] who attracted accolades for his service to the Republic. In a moment of crisis in 1624, he gave a long speech in the Senate that swayed his fellow senators.[117] Agostino Superbi counted Basadonna among the most prominent figures in the Republic by including him in his *Trionfo glorioso d'heroi illustri et eminenti dell'inclita, & maravigliosa città di Venetia, li quali nelle lettere fiorirono* (The Glorious Triumph of the Illustrious and Eminent Heroes of the Noble and Marvelous City of Venice Who Excelled in Literature) issued at the end of the decade.[118] Superbi lavishes praise on Basadonna:

> in his seriousness and prudence, and in his heroic actions, he is beloved, exceptional, and most wise. He is tireless in his public service, and admirable in his private. He excels in Latin letters, and in vernacular literature is quite skillful. He is richly endowed with intelligence and good fortune in equal measure. Everyone in his glorious *patria* admires his spotless reputation, respectability, and splendor.[119]

Basadonna continued to earn accolades into the 1630s. For instance, the famed classical scholar Ottavio Ferrari (1607–1682), professor of Latin and then Greek at the University of Padua, wrote Basadonna a letter in 1637 that praised him for his eloquence and service to the state.[120]

The association between the powerful and respected Basadonna and Copia Sulam – a warm and respectful contact that would continue for many years – reveals that, by 1620, her salon was a thriving centre of intellectual activity that was drawing interest from the upper echelons of Venetian political and cultural life. Their connection – a remarkable example of Jewish–Christian interaction in early modern Venice – would prove vital to Copia Sulam. Not only did Basadonna provide important cachet for her salon, he also defended her when associates later attacked her.

Copia Sulam eagerly involved Basadonna in her correspondence with Cebà, and the two composed and sent poetry to the Genoese writer. The poetic offerings she arranged introduced the two men while demonstrating to each the strength of her network of contacts, not to mention her literary skill. But Cebà was less than eager to receive this gift, responding on 3 October 1620:

> I like your poems, since I like your person. But those of Basadonna frighten me, since his last name frightens me. And therefore, when he comes to visit you, if he could leave it [his last name] outside, I think I could speak of him with a sweeter tongue.[121]

With this letter, Cebà ratcheted up his complaints about the writing he received from Copia Sulam's salon. Whereas previously he discouraged as misguided the verse she and her associates produced in his praise, he now worried that the salon's literary exchanges – and specifically the poems Basadonna and she had arranged together to honour him – might endanger her reputation: feigning concern over Basadonna's last name – basa (bassa) = low, donna = woman[122] – Cebà warns her to be wary of the (sexual) threat Basadonna might pose to her, though claims he does so "jokingly" (scherzando). Only at the end of the letter does he thank "that eminent gentleman" (quel clarissimo) for his verse. Cebà reacted with hostility to the powerful literary alliances that Copia Sulam was building even as she sought to share the advantages such contacts might bring by introducing him to her new and influential associate. Cebà reports in his next letter (10 October) that when Copia Sulam showed Cebà's letter to Basadonna, who no doubt expected only gracious appreciation for his poetry, Basadonna was "scandalized" (scandalezzato) by Cebà's jealous response.[123] Far from backing down from his insinuation that her salon contacts could harm her reputation, however, Cebà claims "many people ..., without your fault, would perhaps like to become intimate with you," though he protests that Copia Sulam was "as firm in countering lascivious love" as she was "gracious in exercising continent ones."[124]

As Cebà began what would become a sustained campaign to throw into question Copia Sulam's chastity, it is important to note that his attacks were not only against her honour but also her husband Giacob's. There is little discussion of Giacob in the correspondence, but the few exceptions are compromising to both husband and wife.[125] Even early mentions show glimmers of Cebà's later attacks. For example, in a composition from January 1619, Cebà criticizes Copia Sulam for her lack of faith but specifies that he means religious faith, not fidelity to her husband: "Né dich'io, che disleale / Tu sia verso il tuo marito" (Nor am I saying you are / disloyal to *your husband).*[126] In fact, Cebà, by using paralipsis[127] – later his weapon of choice in his attacks on Copia Sulam's virtue – suggests that the faith she lacks may not only be Christian.[128] In the same composition Cebà conveniently "forgets" Giacob with a pun on Copia Sulam's name: "If our faith is double, we'll never make a nice COUPLE."[129] (He doesn't acknowledge, in other words, that Copia Sulam's marriage, in addition to her faith, was a barrier to their union.[130]) Copia Sulam immediately rebuffed Cebà's overture, going so far as to change the spelling of her name from "Coppia" ("Couple") to "Copia."[131] Cebà responded in October 1619: "I took your last name as a good sign at the beginning, hoping we would make a couple as Christian man and Christian woman; but you, subtracting a consonant quite quickly from it ... showed me that you refused to match me in matters of faith."[132] He again neglects to mention her husband.

Because of the obedience expected from a Jewish wife towards her husband,[133] we must assume that Giacob condoned Copia Sulam's correspondence with Cebà and, more broadly, her literary pursuits. Yet his acceptance of the correspondence and her literary career is perplexing. The biographical note later in this book gives some context regarding this issue.[134] Though it is not clear that Giacob would have known the contents of the letters at the time Cebà and Copia Sulam were exchanging them (Did he read Cebà's letters for the first time when they were published in 1623 as *Lettere a Sarra Copia*?), he did allow his wife to engage in a frequent correspondence with a Christian man and to have close contact, in her home, with other Christian men. Cebà would not be the only writer to suggest that, through this contact, Copia Sulam compromised her own (and by implication, Giacob's) sexual honour.[135] But Cebà was the first writer to make these suggestions, and as they became more overt in fall 1620, he explicitly acknowledged their effect on Giacob.

In fact, in the 10 October letter discussed above that suggests Copia Sulam's associates would like to "become intimate" with her, Cebà acknowledges that Giacob "might not be too happy with the traffic of our letters, not because he is worried about attacks from an old lover, but because he fears the siege a Christian man will lay."[136] But the danger Cebà increasingly emphasized is not the sexual threat that *he* poses, but the threat posed by others. Cebà wrote his next letter to Giacob himself. The timing of the letter – the only one in the collection to Copia Sulam's husband – is striking, since it immediately follows Cebà's insinuations about her excessive sexual availability to her male associates. Perhaps the letter to Giacob, whom Cebà terms "honourable everywhere" because of his consort's virtue,[137] was Cebà's attempt to dial back his attack on Copia Sulam's virtue, which he recognized was also an attack on Giacob's honour. Or perhaps the letter could be read as sarcastic, as Cebà taunting Giacob because his position was anything but honourable.[138] It is not clear how Giacob received the letter, if it was in fact sent, or whether it was part of his decision to allow Copia Sulam's continued correspondence with Cebà or her other literary activities, even as these pursuits of hers risked compromising him.[139]

In late fall 1620, Cebà engaged the agent Rosa to represent him in Venice, hoping he would further Cebà's efforts to convert Copia Sulam. A musician and perhaps merchant, probably Genoese, Rosa lived in Venice permanently at least from the time of his association with Copia Sulam until his death.[140] He was a person of some prominence in Venice and became, alongside Basadonna, one of Copia Sulam's most loyal associates: he frequented her house for at least the next four and probably six years and also developed a strong tie to her associate Paluzzi.[141] In addition to his association with the free-thinking salon, Rosa was well acquainted with Archdeacon Giovanni Pagnoni, a known purveyor of prohibited books.[142]

There is evidence that at least one other writer may also have participated in the flourishing of the salon. The "ecclesiastical figure"[143] Pietro Petracci (fl. early 1600s) was a well-known but by no means illustrious literary professional who collected and edited other writers' poetry and letters.[144] He also published his own works, which were often written in praise of powerful men,[145] and his verse appeared in many other writers' works. He had several ties to Copia Sulam's salon: he engaged in a poetry exchange with Paluzzi[146] and (like Paluzzi) had connections to Marino and Ciotti.[147] Petracci also collaborated with and worked as a copy editor for Giovanni Alberti, who printed two editions of Copia Sulam's *Manifesto* in summer 1621.[148] Additionally, Petracci published works in 1618 and 1619 with Antonio Pinelli (ca. 1571–1631), Bonifaccio's publisher, who would print both sides of the Copia Sulam–Bonifaccio polemic. This group of writers – Copia Sulam, Bonifaccio, Paluzzi, and Petracci – and publishers – Ciotti, Alberti, and Pinelli – were bound in a very tightly woven web. Even beyond their shared connections, Petracci is linked to Copia Sulam by a printing error in the first edition of the *Manifesto*, which may indicate that he had been slated to contribute verse to it: the words "Del Signor Pietro Petracci" appear at the top of the page that features two introductory sonnets.[149] His name was removed in the two subsequent printings of the volume.

A Cultural Hub

Copia Sulam sought interaction and collaboration in her intellectual life rather than solitary study. Her literary life was in fact deeply social: she worked in concert with her associates and carried out epistolary conversations – with Cebà, Bonifaccio, della Tolfa, Castello, and others – that fed (and were fed by) intense in-person intellectual dialogues at the salon. By the end of 1620, Copia Sulam's salon was an important meeting place for a variety of figures in Venice's cultural and political life – some powerful and most with useful experience and connections. As described in detail above, we know with certainty that two Jewish and seven Christian men were her associates: Modena, Uziel, Paluzzi, Berardelli, Baldassare Bonifaccio, Corniani, the "Vicentine doctor" (Bissari), Basadonna, and Rosa. Three others – Gaspare Bonifaccio, Vanti, and Petracci – were likely also associates. Cebà participated for a while as a sort of corresponding associate of the salon, exchanging verse, letters, and greetings with all but Berardelli and Corniani among the regular participants, in addition of course to his primary literary exchange with Copia Sulam. The group drew strength from the literary accomplishments of its participants while also spreading their renown and providing them important connections that would propel their careers forward.

As the salon became a hotbed for literary activity as well as for philosophical and religious conversation, it drew many (male) visitors. (There is no record of any female visitors to Copia Sulam's salon besides the female household staff who may have been present for portions of the gatherings.) Reports from various sources about regular visitors to the salon indicate that the group was relatively open to newcomers. Visitors could gain entrée through a trusted associate or perhaps on the strength of their reputation. The literary chronicler Aprosio later reported that "lettered men not only from nearby but also from Treviso, Padua, Vicenza, and even more distant places competed for the chance to hear [Copia Sulam] speak."[150] Curious Genoese visitors also sought out the group. In spring 1621, Cebà sent his friend Giovan Benedetto Spinola to visit Copia Sulam and to bring her some of his books.[151] Cebà also reports that other members of the Spinola family, Giovanni Francesco and Agostino Spinola, went to see her.[152] Genoese patrician, poet, and travel writer Gian Vincenzo Imperiale (1582–1648), a friend of Cebà's, visited Copia Sulam in early May 1622, as her correspondence with Cebà was ending. In his travel diaries, Imperiale called her "a female Jewish poet of great fame."[153]

During a stay in Venice in late 1623, Zinano was a frequent salon attendee.[154] In his 1627 *Rime diverse*, Zinano included four poems from around the same time that regard Copia Sulam,[155] documenting his participation in her salon through his presence at gatherings[156] and the poetry he exchanged with her, of which he published both sides.[157] The collection also showcases his relationships with Paluzzi, Berardelli, and Uziel, to the latter two of whom he addressed poems.[158] Zinano's poems give a rare glimpse of the active salon presided over by Copia Sulam. In a 1623 poem, addressed to the Venetian nobleman Gironimo Bembo – who also attended a gathering – Zinano indicates that Copia Sulam held attendees rapt while resisting their attempts to convert her.[159] The poetic exchange with her that he published, likely dating to 1624, was probably an outgrowth of a salon discussion about poetic and spiritual immortality after Cebà's death. These poems document the salon's productivity into the mid-1620s, when salon discussions continued to fuel written exchange and religious difference spurred creativity.

Salon participants likely gathered during the daytime because of the restrictions on movement into or out of the ghetto after nightfall.[160] We do not have precise information on the frequency of gatherings, although from the numerous descriptions of the group's habitual activities in multiple sources,[161] we can deduce that the group met regularly, perhaps as often as weekly, at least in the years 1618–1622. Each gathering, under the aegis of Copia Sulam and at her home, could draw more than a dozen men.[162] Participants recited poetry, discussed newly published books, presented their own in-progress works, and entered into heated debates about philosophy and religion.[163] Reports indicate that Copia Sulam was the principal animator at events, occupying a central role in discussions and debates – far from the hushed women with a merely ornamental function in conversation seen in Renaissance literature,[164] a model "formulated by male fantasy and desire,"[165] and instead similar to the precedents established at women-led salons in the mid-sixteenth century.[166] Copia Sulam, who would show her acumen at debating in her *Manifesto*, likely parried her male interlocutors. Music was also a focus at the salon: Copia Sulam entertained visitors with song[167] and Rosa, a musician, may also have entertained the group. In addition to the more structured and larger gatherings that featured debates, songs, and recitations, associates in the group also met informally, and sometimes spontaneously, in small numbers.[168] Reports from all available sources indicate that Modena, Paluzzi, Berardelli, Basadonna, and Rosa came to Copia Sulam's house most frequently.

A spirit of intellectual inquiry drove discussions at the salon gatherings well beyond Catholic orthodoxy, as Copia Sulam admitted in print in her later exchange with Bonifaccio. Several of her close associates – including Modena, Paluzzi, and Rosa, not to mention Copia Sulam herself – nurtured intellectual inclinations that could have created problems with religious or secular authorities. Cebà, too, would have his own difficulties with the Inquisition. Copia Sulam's continuing adherence to Judaism was a frequent topic of conversation; as associates sought to convert her, they may also have sought to provide a veneer of religious orthodoxy to the free-thinking salon or to their own participation in it. The involvement of at least two powerful noblemen – Corniani and, most important, Basadonna – may have helped to ensure the group's freedom of inquiry. There is no evidence that the salon – where Christian and Jewish regulars discussed dangerous religious ideas at highly visible gatherings in the ghetto, attended by a variety of curious onlookers – ever encountered problems with authorities.

Debate rather than discussion seems to have dominated interactions at the salon, but at least for in-person meetings, civility and cordiality ruled. In the later controversy over the immortality of the soul, Bonifaccio would revile Copia Sulam only through the medium of the press, and she expressed shock when he did so. His disparagement of her (and Modena, whom he also insulted in print) indicate, however, that latent tensions existed within the group. Paluzzi was reported to have responded viciously against Bonifaccio in the immortality debate, offending Copia Sulam with his aggressiveness;[169] he, along with Berardelli, would later unleash a similar animus directly against her. These male associates (along with Cebà) resented the position of power that Copia Sulam occupied at the salon and sought to demean her.[170] However, other participants in the salon acted with great loyalty to Copia Sulam and authored several manuscript works to defend her.[171] Whereas Bonifaccio would violate the salon's integrity by thrusting a private group debate into the public medium of print, these writers reaffirmed their allegiance with manuscript works that were circulated according to bonds of trust.[172]

A Crisis in the Salon

Cebà Attacks Copia Sulam's Reputation

Already in fall 1620, the Copia Sulam–Cebà correspondence showed signs of tension as Cebà began to react negatively to her literary associations – at the very moment in which her salon was reaching its apex. In spring 1621, Cebà transformed what had been "joking" innuendo into ever more open accusations that Copia Sulam's sexual honour was being compromised by her salon. Cebà intensified these attacks as his own religious orthodoxy came under assault: during this same period, the Congregation of the Index moved against La reina Esther, charging – among other things – that its representation of the Old Testament story was lascivious.[173] The accusations also came during a time when both Copia Sulam and Cebà reported gravely compromised health.[174]

Cebà first expressed unease at his agent Rosa's growing admiration for Copia Sulam. In a letter from March 1621, Cebà tells Copia Sulam

that Rosa had described her person "with overly poetic strokes."[175] Given
Rosa's veneration, Cebà informs her that Rosa had his "permission to
make love to [her], too."[176] Complimenting himself on his generosity,
he contends: "I am such a fine gentleman, really, that I pass my mis-
tress around so easily to everyone. But don't take offense, signora Sarra,
because your treasure is not made to enrich the poverty of just one person. A good is more good the more it is passed around. Therefore allow
everyone to share in your graces. And since you see that I don't mind,
just throw me in with all the others."[177] He suggests, in other words, that
Copia Sulam – depicted here as an object of exchange – should circulate freely among men. Almost as if to encourage her in such a pursuit,
he highlights the wealth her "circulation" would generate – "a good is
more good" if shared – rather than the inevitable devaluation of her
"currency" were she to circulate freely among men. Earlier in the correspondence Cebà had apparently felt part of the salon through literary
exchange. Now he sarcastically suggests he would be happy to participate
in other, less honourable, exchanges.

In a letter dated 10 April 1621, Cebà again expresses his desire to
participate in the "delight" that Copia Sulam provided at her salon, a
pleasure he now presents most explicitly as sexual. He writes: "My love
is so generous that it has much more regard for your person than for
my own. As for my person, if I were as quick as perhaps some of the
men who court you, I would feel most unfortunate not to be able to
come to see you and to try to take from you that delight that your virtue,
I know, would be loath to concede to me, and my mind is most far from
desiring."[178] Here Cebà, who was in his mid-fifties and beset by illness,
envisages himself as one of the young and vigorous men at her salon,
which he imagines offered the tantalizing possibility of sexual contact.
He longingly envisions (but denies desiring) Copia Sulam both granting
and refusing him this satisfaction.

By 1 May, Cebà had received a letter from Copia Sulam that, in his
report, expressed her alarm at the danger to her reputation created by
his insinuations. In his letter of response, he pretends to allay her concerns but instead redoubles the attack against her by repeating each of
his charges while feigning to deny that he made them.

My jokes were not such that they injured (to use your words) your honor.
Read my letters as much as you want: you will see yourself exalted more
than any other woman ever has been. But you will not find, speaking of
lasciviousness, that I have ever judged you anything but most continent ...
And if I must confess the truth, I am not as curious as you believe to make
inquisitions [far inquisitione] as to whether you have dealings with Venetians

and if you write to Genoese since, beyond the fact that I hold you to be
most chaste, my sickness and my other worries give me no space to become
jealous, nor do they leave me time to waste. It is certainly true that I little
believed that you love me much, but neither did I think that you were infat-
uated with others. Nor did it ever cross my mind that you allowed in your
house other trade than one in speculations and letters.[179]

Cebà dismisses Copia Sulam's concerns over his "jokes" about her sexual
honour. But while it is true – as he asserts in his response – that he always
explicitly underscores her continence, she understood that his very
insistence upon her chastity threw it into doubt. Alongside such insinuations he includes protestations of his continuing love. Cebà declares that
he exalts Copia Sulam more than any woman was ever exalted, a claim
so absolute as to echo Dante's youthful desire to celebrate Beatrice as
no other woman had ever been before.[180] But rather than exalt her, he
puts forth suggestion after suggestion that she had inappropriate contact with men. He expresses jealousy (portrayed as disinterest) at the fact
that she wrote to Genoese associates and had "dealings" with Venetians.
He writes that he is not interested in making "inquisitions" about these
links, a turn of phrase suggesting a motivated search for guilt that could
hardly be read as innocent in these years of the Roman Inquisition.[181]
More damning still, he hints – again through denial – that there were
other sorts of "trade" in her house beyond the already suspect literary
exchanges and "speculations," a code-word for heterodoxy.[182]

Towards the close of the same letter, Cebà redoubles his attack on
her sexual honour by feigning to accept her defence of it: "In regard to
what you report, that you were out for the blood of anyone who had less
than honorable intentions with you, you certainly have not only given
me a sign of your virility, but also warned me to curb my desire, if it ever
arose in me (though I don't believe it would), to become more intimate
with you."[183] Here, Cebà represents Copia Sulam as a woman already
compromised, since she had exposed herself to men with ignoble intentions who had already tried to violate her. He threatens to count himself
among them as he imagines her fighting off his advances.

This same string of letters dating from mid-March to early May
1621 – in which Cebà suggests that Copia Sulam is compromising her
reputation and where he casts doubt upon the nature of the salon's
activities – still shows Cebà's participation (at distance) in the salon. He
thanks one associate for the poetry he had sent and passes information
along to others. Cebà explicitly underscores his importance to Copia
Sulam's literary enterprise. In the middle of his attack on her reputation
in his April letter, for instance, he observes: "I see that you entrust your

whole reputation to me."[184] Threatened by her growing list of literary associates,. Cebà had every reason to exaggerate his importance to her. His statement nevertheless reflects an important truth: Copia Sulam's correspondence with Cebà remained the linchpin of her reputation in the salon that had grown up around the exchange.

An Attack on Cebà's Orthodoxy

In March 1621, the Congregation of the Index took action against Cebà's *La reina Esther*, suspending it *donec corrigatur*, or until appropriately revised.[185] As later correspondence on the matter revealed, the Congregation objected to some fifty different aspects of the epic.[186] The most important objections regarded its contamination of the biblical story of Esther with many extraneous episodes and with obscenity.[187] Cebà received official news of this action in a letter from the secretary of the Congregation sometime between March and June.[188] Such reports would have confirmed worries about ecclesiastical censure that had plagued him for some time because of criticisms made against the work.[189] In the face of the censure, Cebà found himself "so mortified ... that he would rather suffer death than this disgrace."[190]

When official news of the suspension arrived, Cebà and his associates mounted a challenge to it by invoking the help of the powerful cardinal Alessandro d'Este (1568–1624), Cebà's friend from his time as a student in Padua.[191] Cebà's patron Marcantonio Doria wrote Este a letter dated 16 July.[192] Another friend, the writer Agostino Mascardi, wrote to Este on 11 July, advocating for Cebà on the same matter.[193]

During these very same days, Copia Sulam faced a serious challenge in Venice against her own orthodoxy. In late June 1621, Baldassare Bonifaccio published his *Immortalità*, which had as its centrepiece the accusation that Copia Sulam denied the soul's immortality. This dangerous public attack had long been in the works.[194] On 9 July, Cebà reported, Copia Sulam sent him a letter in which she informed him of Bonifaccio's attack and of her intention to respond. On 17 July, just a day after Doria wrote to Este on Cebà's behalf, Cebà responded to her letter. He expresses sympathy for her, voicing regret that "without any guilt, you have been blamed,"[195] but he provides little support, counselling her to pay no heed to the criticism and to keep silent: "Since you have a clear conscience, my signora, laugh off whoever tries to stain your reputation, and don't deign to respond to somebody when there is no reason you should even open your ears to listen to him."[196] He advises her instead to focus on her spiritual health: "Save the defences you are planning against the one who called you an infidel in Judaism and convert them

into sermons when you will fight for Christianity."[197] He further urges
her to meditate upon a spiritual work he had sent her, assuring her that
"it will be more useful to you for finding peace with God than it will
be honorable for you to write defences in an attempt to make war with
men."[198] While counselling silence, Cebà makes it clear that, as long as
Copia Sulam – whom he professes in this same letter to love with "such
tenderness"[199] – adhered to her Jewish faith, he could not take her side
in the debate.

Though their correspondence lasted for many more months, there
is no evidence that Cebà revealed the charges regarding *La reina Esther*
to Copia Sulam. But, at the end of his 17 July letter, he refers to tribulations that would make it difficult for him to write. He also makes
an oblique comment that suggests he understood the similarity between
Copia Sulam's situation and his own, as they both faced attacks on their
religious orthodoxy. After counselling her to keep silent, he admits:
"I wish I knew how to follow my own advice when I have the chance to do
so, but I recognize in fact that I am a better philosopher in words than in
actions."[200] While recognizing their common plight, the vulnerable Cebà
could not afford to express outright sympathy for a Jewish woman who
was preparing to enter into a public showdown with a Catholic priest
over charges of heresy.

2
A Rupture in the Salon (1619–1621)

Overview

Copia Sulam's salon was gaining in prominence when the salonnière began a discussion about the immortality of the soul with the priest and dramatist Baldassare Bonifaccio in fall 1619. Their discussion – which would eventually be broadcast in the Venetian presses – started in person when Copia Sulam challenged Bonifaccio with "difficult philosophical [and] theological questions" about the soul's immortality.[1] He continued the conversation with a letter of new year's greeting in late 1619 or early 1620. She responded with a letter in which she poses several challenges to the doctrine of the immortality of the soul. Later reprinted by a vengeful Bonifaccio, this letter, the most developed extant example of Copia Sulam's philosophical and theological argumentation, ventures far afield of both Christian and Jewish orthodoxy. When he responded to her letter not with a manuscript letter but with a printed work, *Dell'immortalità dell'anima*, in which he accuses her of denying the validity of the doctrine, Bonifaccio thrust Copia Sulam into the public light as never before.

This chapter will examine the initial volleys in Copia Sulam and Bonifaccio's debate over the immortality of the soul. By the seventeenth century, this tenet had attracted intense attention in Venice among both Christian and Jewish intellectuals. We thus begin with a history of earlier debates that prepared the terrain for Copia Sulam and Bonifaccio's battle.

The History of the Debate over the Immortality of the Soul

Ancient Philosophers and Commentators on the Immortality of the Soul

The immortality of the soul was a doctrine fundamental to both Christianity and Judaism. Belief in the concept dated back to ancient Greece. Plato (ca. 429–347 BCE) proposes in the *Phaedo* (Φαίδων, also

known in antiquity as *On the Soul*) that the soul could survive after the
death of the body.[2] Aristotle (384–322 BCE), in his *On the Soul* (Περὶ
Ψυχῆς; in Latin, *De anima*, ca. 350 BCE), is more ambiguous, and his
views were variously interpreted by later thinkers as supporting or denying the soul's immortality. On the one hand, Aristotle rejected a Platonic
dualism that separated body and soul; on the other hand, he allowed for
the possibility that a certain part of the soul, or type of soul, could be separated from the body.[3] Aristotle's view on the soul relates to his concept
of hylomorphism: substance or being (οὐσία) is a composite between
matter (potentiality) and form (actualization).[4] In *On the Soul* he proposes that body is to soul as matter is to form[5] and that body and soul are
fundamentally linked, arguing that "just as an eye is pupil and sight, so
in this case too an animal is the soul and the body. Therefore, that the
soul is not separable from the body, or some parts of it if it naturally has
parts, is not unclear. For the actuality of some parts belongs to the parts
themselves."[6] Yet he goes on to qualify this statement: "Even so, nothing
hinders some parts from being separable, because of their not being the
actualities of a body."[7] He specifies that reason and the power to con-
template "seems to be a different genus of soul, and this alone admits of
being separated, in the way the everlasting is from the perishable."[8]

As with many aspects of Aristotle's thought, which often lent itself to
competing – and often ideologically inflected – interpretations,[9] there
was intense debate over time regarding his stance on the soul's immortality.[10] The Aristotelian commentator Averroes (1126–1198) interpreted
the philosopher as having meant that only the human being's active
intellect (which he did not term "soul") was eternal – and then only collectively, not individually. Thomas Aquinas (ca. 1225–1274), who sought
to harmonize Aristotle's philosophy with Christian theology,[11] instead
read him as upholding the soul's individual immortality. With Aquinas's
influence, the doctrine of the soul's immortality became canonical.[12]

The Doctrine of the Immortality of the Soul in Early Modern Christian Italy

The tenet attracted intense scrutiny as the early modern period dawned.
From the second half of the thirteenth century, a strong tradition of
secular Aristotelianism – sometimes but not always connected with
Averroism – emerged at northern Italian universities, especially at Padua
and Bologna, where the study of philosophy was guided by rational principles and was not, as elsewhere, connected to theology.[13] But towards
the close of the fifteenth century, a new climate was developing in which
philosophical doctrines were supposed to confirm religious ones.[14] The
Aristotelian Nicoletto Vernia (1420–1499), who had been the leading

Averroist of the day, was forced near the end of his life – under pressure from the Church – to renounce his Averroist views and to proclaim that philosophy could prove the Christian belief in the immortality of the individual soul.[15] The great Neoplatonist Marsilio Ficino (1433–1499), who rejected the separation of reason and faith, attempted to harmonize Platonic reason and Christian faith on the issue and defended the dogma of the soul's immortality against Averroist tendencies in his *Platonica theologia de immortalitate animorum* (Platonic Theology on the Immortality of Souls, 1482).[16] He argued that the survival of the soul was a foundation of religion and he connected belief in the immortality of the soul with belief in God.

The greatest challenge to the independence of philosophy, however, was still to come. The bull "Apostolici regiminis" (On Apostolic Rule) of Pope Leo X (Giovanni di Lorenzo de' Medici, 1475–1521; pope 1513–1521) was promulgated on 19 December 1513 at the eighth session of the Fifth Lateran Council (1512–1517). The bull condemned the Averroist notion of the collectivity of the active intellect and established the individual immortality of the human soul as an article of faith. It declared as heretics philosophers who defended, even on purely philosophical grounds, views on the soul that denied personal immortality.[17]

The heterodox Aristotelian philosopher Pietro Pomponazzi (1462–1525), a professor at Bologna who had spent many years at Padua and studied under Vernia, directly challenged this decree with the 1516 publication of his *Tractatus de immortalitate animae* (Treatise on the Immortality of the Soul).[18] In his treatise, Pomponazzi – while rejecting the Averroist notion of the collective soul – shows that neither reason nor Aristotelian principles can demonstrate the immortality of the soul and that rational examination in fact leads to the conclusion that the soul is mortal. But in the work's final chapter, Pomponazzi abandons the philosophical approach to examining the soul's mortality, saying it only leads to *probable* results, while Christian doctrine, sanctioned by the God-given authority of the Church, provides *certainty* that the soul is immortal. The conclusion of the treatise underscores that the immortality of the soul can only be proven by means of faith, not by reason or philosophy.[19] Pomponazzi in essence denied that Aristotelian philosophy could prove the dogma of immortality – a conclusion that provoked widespread outrage. The treatise was burned publicly in Venice and many works were published to counter its author's conclusions. Pomponazzi responded to these attacks in his *Apologia* (Apology, 1518), where he includes pointed criticism of the Church, and in his *Defensorium* (Of the Defendant, 1519).[20] Though he expressed views that flew in the face of the Fifth Lateran Council's declarations, Pomponazzi never encountered any repercussions from the Church for the views he

expressed, even after he failed to comply with the 1518 order of Leo X to
retract the most problematic of his statements.[21] His immunity was guaranteed by the support of the famed writer and cardinal Pietro Bembo
(1470–1547), a former student of Pomponazzi and Leo X's secretary, who
assured the pope that the work was not heretical.[22] The pope's attention
may also have been diverted by a much greater threat: Luther's posting
of his *Ninety-Five Theses* at Wittenberg in 1517.[23] Pomponazzi's *Tractatus* –
which was never placed on the Index of Forbidden Books – was enormously influential and essentially succeeded in freeing natural philosophy from the bonds of theology: defenders of the immortality of the soul
thereafter were more likely to resort to metaphysics for their proofs rather
than to natural philosophy.[24] The issues that the *Tractatus* raised remained
at the centre of philosophical debate for the rest of the century, years
in which interpretation of Aristotelian thought became increasingly contested terrain. Jesuits and other religiously inclined writers interpreted
Aristotle in support of Church doctrine, while lay professors tended to
interpret him in opposition to it.[25]

The philosopher Cesare Cremonini (1550–1631), a heterodox
Aristotelian professor at Padua, added new vigour to debates over the
soul's immortality in the late sixteenth and seventeenth centuries. He
was considered one of the greatest philosophers of his time and received
twice the salary from the University of Padua that Galileo did – even after
the scientist's discoveries with the telescope.[26] In 1591, Cremonini led the
Republic's successful campaign to suppress a Jesuit school whose establishment in Padua was seen as an encroachment on civic power. After that
early scuffle with the Church, the philosopher attracted the special attention of the Roman Inquisition and from 1598 on was repeatedly accused of
spreading views contrary to the doctrine of the soul's immortality, among
other heretical ideas.[27] The denial of the immortality of the soul was often
assumed to have atheism as its natural consequence.[28] In 1613 in Venice,
Cremonini published his *Disputatio de coelo* (Disputation on the Heavens),
the work that provided the lightning rod for the Sant'Uffizio. In the
Disputatio, Cremonini interpreted Aristotle without a Christian lens; said
that, according to Aristotle, God was not provident; and expressed doubt
about Aquinas's reading of the philosopher. As noted above, Aquinas had
interpreted Aristotle as saying that the soul was individually immortal.
Cremonini wrote instead that, according to Aristotle, the soul was not
immortal by its essence or nature but, rather, because it informed the
body, was tied to the body and therefore mortal.[29] The Roman Inquisition
made a number of objections to the *Disputatio*[30] and eventually ordered
Cremonini to emend the work. He promised to do so in a new work titled
Apologia dictorum Aristotelis de quinta caeli substantia (Apology for Aristotle's

Words on the Quintessence of the Heavens, 1616),[31] but in that work he instead defended his approach to Aristotle and asserted the independence of natural philosophy from theology.

In 1619 – the very year in which Copia Sulam and Bonifaccio began to exchange letters on the topic of the immortality of the soul – the Roman Congregation of the Holy Office intensified its pressure against Cremonini, communicating with him through the Inquisition of Padua. By means of a letter dated 3 July 1619, the Paduan Inquisitor pointed out (on Paul V's orders) that Cremonini had not, as instructed, emended his *Disputatio* to explain Aristotle according to the decrees of the Fifth Lateran Council and to defend the Catholic faith,[32] and that Rome had threatened to ban his books if he did not emend them appropriately.[33] The Inquisitor appended two documents that underscored the *Disputatio*'s divergence from Catholic dogma, contested Cremonini's reading of Aristotle and Aquinas, and objected to Cremonini's view of the immortality of the soul. The letter added that the Aristotelian had not fulfilled his pledge to correct his *Disputatio* with his *Apologia* and demanded that he issue a retraction of his views that was "clear and manifest, without any convolution or ambiguity."[34]

Cremonini wrote an irritated letter of response to the Inquisitor of Padua in which he claimed he could not alter the *Disputatio* since he had already, at the doge's orders, issued his *Apologia*, and the Venetian Senate would prohibit further intervention. While he made some concessions,[35] he said that he could not change his interpretation of Aristotle: "I cannot retract my explanations of Aristotle, because I understand him thus, and I am paid to explain him as I understand him, and if I did not do so I would be obliged to give back my salary. Similarly, I cannot retract my views on the various commentators nor the refutations you made to their explications: this is a matter of my honor and concerns the integrity of my teaching appointment and therefore of the doge."[36] Cremonini defended his fundamental right – and indeed duty as a professor at Padua, under the jurisdiction of Venice – to interpret Aristotle as he believed. He also composed a longer response to the Inquisition's complaints, addressed to the Paduan Inquisitor, in which he defended his reasoning, pleaded his right to free expression, and refused to alter his work.[37] In the face of his intransigence, the Congregation of the Index placed the *Disputatio* on the *Index*.[38] Cremonini himself, however, never suffered negative repercussions, though he remained a person of interest to the Roman Inquisition.[39]

Cremonini taught a generation of Venetian patricians and was protected by them;[40] his views thus informed early seventeenth-century Venetian intellectual life.[41] He also had close ties to the Accademia degli

Incogniti, which was coalescing in the 1620s and to which both Bonifaccio and Copia Sulam had links.[42] Despite the currency of the debates over the immortality of the soul in contemporary Venetian intellectual life, Copia Sulam feigns ignorance of them in her response to Bonifaccio's accusatory treatise. Claiming surprise that her antagonist would write a treatise to prove such an obvious point as the soul's immortality, she asks: "What need is there now, and above all in Venice, for such a treatise, and to what end are such topics printed among Christians?"[43] In the printed forum of the *Manifesto*, Copia Sulam likely sought to deny any knowledge of the sort of heterodoxy that Cremonini's thought represented, even though the letter she wrote in 1619 (discussed in detail below) suggests that she was well acquainted with the philosopher's views on materialism and the soul's mortality.[44]

The Doctrine of the Immortality of the Soul in Early Modern Judaism

During this same period, debates over the immortality of the soul riveted members of Jewish intellectual circles. Whereas the immortality of the soul is a central doctrine of Christianity, consonant with its focus on resurrection and salvation, there is no such dogma in Judaism.[45] Nevertheless, the personal immortality of the soul had become dominant in rabbinic teachings and was considered traditional across Europe.[46]

In the early seventeenth century, interest in the immortality of the soul was particularly intense among former conversos, Jews from the Iberian peninsula who had converted to Catholicism under duress but found their way back to Judaism after emigrating. Belief in the rewards of martyrdom, absorbed from the dominant Catholic culture, attracted former conversos because it assuaged what Talya Fishman has called "survivors' guilt" over the deaths of fellow Jews who had not converted.[47] Belief in the immortality of the soul allowed survivors to imagine those who had been killed as martyrs rewarded with eternal life.[48]

Uriel da Costa (ca. 1585–1640) was a Portuguese converso who fled Portugal in 1615 for Amsterdam and there returned to Judaism. But da Costa soon publicized heretical beliefs: the next year, he sent a polemic broadside to Venice that catalogued what he claimed were the discrepancies between the Torah and Oral Law.[49] Modena, the famed Venetian rabbi and polymath – who in this same period became Copia Sulam's close associate – responded anonymously to da Costa, calling him "a total heretic in the effrontery which he shows toward the words of our sages of blessed memory."[50] In this response, titled *Magen Vi-Tzinah* (Shield and Buckler),[51] Modena – positing the immortality of the soul as an uncontestable truth – points to the absence of discussion of the immortality of the soul in the Torah as one of the "proofs for the necessity of the Tradition and the Oral Law." He writes: "And as to beliefs, where [in the Law of Moses] do we find clearly set out the survival of the soul, posthumous reward and punishment, paradise and Gehenna, resurrection, etc.?"[52] Modena presided over the symbolic excommunication of da Costa from Venice in 1618.[53] Da Costa then wrote and circulated a longer manuscript work, sometime before 1623, that had as its centrepiece a denial that the human soul was immortal.[54] The text shows many signs that da Costa had read Modena's objections in *Magen Vi-Tzinah*, to which he responded in order to strengthen his own argument.[55] Whereas Modena had reasoned that the absence of mention of the soul's immortality in the Torah proves the necessity of the Tradition and Oral Law, da Costa argued instead that the Law's silence undermines the validity of the belief: "The Law nowhere indicates the human soul is immortal or that another life, whether of punishment or glory, awaits it; how inconceivable for the Law not to have mentioned such things! for God is not in the habit of concealing chastisement from man, but rather does He set it before him again and again, that its threat might dissuade him from evil, as may be seen in the Law."[56] Another former converso, Semuel da Silva (ca. 1570–1631), obtained a manuscript copy of da Costa's work that da Silva published (in part) and refuted in his *Tratado da immortalidade da alma* (Treatise on the Immortality of the Soul), published in Amsterdam in 1623. Da Silva, who did not name his opponent, wrote that he had seen his "scandalous and insolent" writings, including the claim "that man's soul is mortal and perishable and ends together with the body, just like the souls of horses and mules in whom there is no understanding ... Incredible as it might seem that such contagion might infect any good Jew, there is no denying that we are here confronted with just such an instance."[57] Da Costa issued a counter-reply to da Silva in Amsterdam in 1624, *Exame das tradições phariseas* (Examination of Pharisaic Traditions),[58] in which he held that there is no evidence to support the belief in the immortality of the soul: "Those who proclaim the immortality of the soul and resurrection are like people who want to climb a smooth wall without a ladder. Since there is nothing to grasp, every time they stick out a hand or think they have a foothold, they slip and fall."[59] Following publication of the *Exame*, da Costa was imprisoned for a short period and the book was condemned to a public burning.[60] It was placed on the Spanish Index in 1632.[61]

Some critics see a link between da Costa's notions and the arguments given voice in a text entitled *Kol Sakhal* (Voice of a Fool).[62] *Kol Sakhal* is a critique of rabbinic culture that masquerades as a turn-of-the-sixteenth-century text from Spain.[63] Some recent scholarship maintains that Leon

Modena wrote it in seventeenth-century Venice,[64] though other studies
contest his authorship.[65] The composition of the text is dated to 1623.[66]
Though *Kol Sakhal* was prepared two years after Copia Sulam's debate
with Bonifaccio, the issues it addresses had been raised seven years
before in da Costa's broadside and in Modena's response. *Kol Sakhal*
does not deny the immortality of the soul, as da Costa had, but it takes
an ambiguous stance towards the soul's condition[67] and maintains that
there are "no decisive and compelling demonstrations that the soul of
man remains after the death of the body."[68] The work also points out the
absence of reference to the immortality of the soul in the Torah: "The
thing that is most terrifying and frightening to any son of Israel is that
when we review the entire Torah, from 'In the beginning' to 'before the
eyes of all Israel,' we do not find in all the words of Moses ... even a single
statement testifying to the survival of the soul after the death of the body
and [to] another world after this one."[69]

It is not clear whether Modena, if he was in fact the author of *Kol
Sakhal*, expressed his true beliefs or merely created a foil against which
to debate. Modena's incomplete *Sha'agat Aryei* (The Lion's Roar) says
that the author of *Kol Sakhal* was a heretic.[70] The rabbi's knowledge of
and participation in these debates is highly relevant to the debate that
would take place in Copia Sulam's salon, where Modena was a prominent
participant. To dismiss the importance of her contribution, Bonifaccio
would later claim that it was Modena and not Copia Sulam who wrote
the *Manifesto* she published under her name. In contrast, we can argue
that Copia Sulam's *Manifesto* debate fuelled Modena's continued interest
in this topic.

Bonifaccio and Copia Sulam's Letter Exchange
on the Soul's Immortality

The question of the soul's immortality permeated the atmosphere in
which Copia Sulam and Bonifaccio interacted, positioned as it was
between Christian and Jewish worlds and receiving influences from both.
The issue was debated in her salon, where it seems she questioned the
doctrine at a gathering in fall 1619 that included the priest. Bonifaccio
(figure 2.1), born in Crema to a family hailing from Rovigo, studied in
cities around the Veneto, received his degree in law from the University
of Padua, and became a priest in 1611.[71] His first work was published in
Venice in 1618; he would publish four others by 1620. He continued
to publish frequently after the 1621 controversy with Copia Sulam, and
he issued his celebrated tragedy, *Amata*, the next year.[72] He maintained
ecclesiastical ambitions alongside his literary ones: in the early 1620s, he
turned down a bishopric in Candia but accepted a position as archdeacon and vicar of Treviso; towards the end of his life, in 1653, he accepted

2.1 A portrait of Baldassare Bonifaccio, from *Le glorie de gli Incogniti* (Venice: appresso Francesco Valvasense, 1647). By permission of the British Library, General Reference Collection 132.b.3. © The British Library Board.

the bishopric of Cápodistria.[73] He was also advisor to the Inquisition for the Church of Treviso.[74] His interaction with Copia Sulam allowed him an early opportunity to marry his religious and his literary pursuits.

As mentioned above, in late 1619 or early 1620 Bonifaccio wrote a letter of new year's greeting to Copia Sulam (figure 2.2).[75] He begins in media res, seemingly taking up a conversation that he and Copia Sulam had been having in person.[76] Commenting melancholically on the year's end and the passage of time, he lays out a defence of the soul's immortality.[77] Perhaps returning to a recently discussed question, Bonifaccio voices a sceptical query: "If there can be no transformation between things of different species, and if the corruptible differs in its species from the incorruptible, how can it be that at one time man was immortal if now all men are mortal?"[78] He then provides his own answer: only in its sinless state could man's body and soul be immortal, since the soul, by divine grace, could preserve the body. Original sin, he continues, subjected the body to degradation, yet the soul – though sinful – could still be preserved by repentance. Meditating on the scriptural description of death as a spilling of water,[79] he suggests that man is like water, which can both sink into the earth and rise: the material part of man is corrupted in the grave but the spiritual part can rise to heaven. Bonifaccio proceeds to reflect on the brevity of human life and the fragility of the human body, which he says is a temple for the soul that only Christ can renew. He closes the letter urging Copia Sulam to renew this temple – that is, to convert to Christianity – as the year is reborn, which he hopes will provide such sunny days that her "mind will be cleared of clouds."[80]

Bonifaccio's letter occasioned new discussion among members of their shared literary circle. In a letter of response, Copia Sulam reported that at least two of their associates – Paluzzi and Corniani – came specifically to her house to hear the priest's letter. She wrote that Paluzzi praised its "great learnedness" and that they discussed it "more than once."[81]

Copia Sulam countered Bonifaccio's points in detail in a letter dated 10 January 1620,[82] which he later published.[83] Her letter is the most developed extant example of her philosophical inquiry. It shows her familiarity with Aristotelian philosophy and its detractors – among whom, the letter shows, we can count the salonnière herself, even though she uses the Aristotelian categories of matter and form, species and essence, to argue against the ancient philosopher. Her use of, and arguments against, Aristotle suggest that she had engaged extensively with his thought, though it is not clear – since she seems to argue with a Christianized Aristotle – if she knew his works directly. As she develops her own anti-Aristotelian – and clearly heterodox – argument against the soul's immortality, she also critiques the anti-Aristotelian

2.2 The final part of an autograph letter from Bonifaccio to Copia Sulam (B. Bonifaccio, *Delle amene lettere*, 1619/1620), 226/21, 12r. With permission of the Accademia dei Concordi.

Berardino Telesio (1509–1588), several of whose works appeared on the 1596 Clementine Index.[84] Though she takes issue with the ancient philosopher, her conclusions overlap closely with the sort of heterodox Aristotelianism promulgated by Cremonini.

Copia Sulam's letter undoubtedly provided Bonifaccio the grounds to accuse her of heterodoxy, but it is not clear that it was only her materialist notions that rankled him, since such controversial ideas had previously been discussed in the salon in which he had so enthusiastically participated.[85] The letter exchange drove Copia Sulam to commit her argumentation to paper, stepping more firmly onto the "male" terrain of philosophy, where she dared to challenge Bonifaccio's ideas.[86] Her response seems to have infuriated Bonifaccio, prompting him to begin work on the long treatise he would publish a year and a half later to rebuke her for her beliefs. Her letter also provided him material proof of her unorthodoxy, should she dare to deny it.

Her letter gives no sign, however, of the negative turn their relationship would take. She instead expresses a warm bond with Bonifaccio that was nurtured by their common interests and common friends within a shared literary community. In fact, in addition to reporting Paluzzi's accolades for Bonifaccio's letter, Copia Sulam lavishes praise upon three sonnets Bonifaccio had sent in celebration of Ansaldo Cebà's portrait, whose arrival at the salon had exhilarated the group. These sonnets show that Bonifaccio was still an active, even eager, member of the group.[87]

After these initial compliments, Copia Sulam turns to address the substance of Bonifaccio's letter. Her carefully structured argument begins and ends by commenting upon Bonifaccio's lament in his greeting about the passing of time and the inevitability of aging, which she transforms into an extended consideration of the condition of body and soul. She jocularly criticizes the brief opening reflection he had made on the new year, where he expressed envy that the year grew young again while they continued to age.[88] She points out that a year, known by its number,[89] only exists for one rotation of the solar sphere and then becomes another, as its altered number demonstrates (that is, 1620 is not 1619).[90] Mankind, on the other hand, is not so constrained by time. She argues that if Bonifaccio were to reply that the new year was still of the same species – that is, essentially the same[91] – despite its altered number, then he should agree that the same is true of man as he ages.

Copia Sulam then passes to a more general consideration of essence and species, arguing against the Aristotelian notion that essence corresponds to a species whereas individual characteristics are accidental.[92] She instead defines essence as related to an individual.[93] She then takes issue with the Aristotelian view that matter is the corruptible part of the compound of matter and form. In Aristotle, matter is equated with the body, while form is equated with the soul. Copia Sulam argues instead that matter is incorruptible, since a compound can undergo dissolution and corruption but matter in its basic elements always persists. So she asks, provocatively: "If of the two components that we see in natural things – by this I mean matter and form – one lasts eternally and the other disappears, to which one must we logically attribute corruptibility?"[94] Put simply, Copia Sulam responds "with due respect of course to Aristotle"[95] that it is form that is corruptible, since matter – which she has already said is incorruptible – desires always to be "informed" (*informata*, given a form), but these forms show "scant durability" (*poca durabilità*) and must be replaced infinitely. The argument that form (soul) is corruptible is, in short, an argument for the soul's mortality.

Copia Sulam continues to explore this materialist line of thought – arguing for the body's preservation and against the soul's immortality – as she moves to question Bonifaccio's assertion that the human body was immortal by divine grace before original sin rendered it corruptible. She challenges this view as nonsensical: "Why did the Creator not make man immortal by nature, if he intended such to be his state? Or, if he had not ordered that it be so, why miraculously create him in a state that was not going to last?"[96] By arguing that Bonifaccio's account of original immortality by divine grace was flawed since it showed God acting inconsistently, Copia Sulam implies that mankind was mortal from the beginning. She further challenges his view by asking him to explain how, if mankind had retained its original state of immortality, this would have affected generation. If immortal man had continued to generate, how could there be infinite generation in a finite world? But if mankind had not continued to generate, the communicability of his being – which is the highest good[97] – would have ceased. Copia Sulam seeks, in other words, to show that it is logically impossible that man had been created immortal, since it "seems intolerable for men and moreover for God to constitute something in a state in which it cannot last."[98]

Copia Sulam wraps up her argument by underlining the inevitability of the conclusion that mankind is mortal. She urges Bonifaccio to concede – as was implicit, she said, in his own argumentation –

that man always was of mortal nature, and therefore did not pass from one species to another in his fall from his state of grace and ... [therefore] that *like waters ... we fall down*[99] – truly a most striking passage in Holy Scripture, because just like a flowing river shows us, right before our eyes, waters that flow and pass by in an instant, and yet the river is always the same even if the waters are not, similarly the human species features at any moment transitory individuals who are not always the same although the species is always the same.[100]

She says that given the transitory nature of human existence "we can hope for nothing more from the existence of these individual bodies of ours than endurance."[101] In other words, she proposed that the life of the individual was the life lived on earth, without hope for eternal life.

Copia Sulam's letter, then, expresses unequivocally materialist and clearly heretical notions of body and soul. As discussed above, similar notions that challenged both Christian and Jewish orthodoxy were circulating widely in these years in Venice. Nevertheless, Copia Sulam took a risk by committing these thoughts to paper. As mentioned above, even the well-connected Cremonini was under intense pressure from the Roman Inquisition during the same years to disavow his published views on materialism and the soul's mortality, and he felt enough at risk to make successive – if never sufficient – attempts to answer the Inquisition's objections. Within the Jewish community, too, these views were seen as heretical, as the backlash against da Costa demonstrated.

After having forthrightly pursued this line of argumentation, Copia Sulam makes some attempt to mitigate her claims in her letter's closing lines. She asks Bonifaccio to excuse her "weak doubts," which she hopes he and an associate – she likely intended Paluzzi – would resolve.[102] With this remark she suggests that she may not have argued sincerely. She also implies that she anticipated her associates – Bonifaccio and Paluzzi in synchrony – would respond to her arguments within the confines of their literary circle, where face-to-face discussions were complemented by narrowly circulated manuscript letters that advanced the conversation when members were absent.

Bonifaccio's *Dell'immortalità dell'anima*

Bonifaccio instead broadcast the debate publicly with his *Immortalità* (see figure 2.3), which had at its centre the accusation that Copia Sulam denied that the soul was immortal.[103] He published the work with the ducal printer Antonio Pinelli, who had already published several of Bonifaccio's works.

Pinelli was one of the most prolific printers of the period.[104] He became ducal printer in 1617, which allowed him the right to print official documents in the city and in the territories of *La Serenissima*. The Pinelli press functioned as a sort of press of record for the Republic and kept archives of decrees and other documents it published. Alongside official printing,

DELL' IMMORTALITA'

DELL' ANIMA,

Difcorfo

DI BALDASSARE

BONIFACCIO.

CON LICENZA DE' SVPERIORI.
Et Priuilegio.

IN VENETIA, M. DC. XXI.

Appreffo Antonio Pinelli,

Stampator Ducale.

2

2.3 The title page of Baldassare Bonifaccio's *Dell'immortalità dell'anima* (Venice: appresso Antonio Pinelli, 1621). By permission of the Ministero per i Beni e le Attività Culturale – Biblioteca Nazionale Marciana (Misc. 1377.2). Further reproduction is prohibited.

Pinelli published more than 250 books in Roman characters between 1609 and 1631, and many more in Greek, the larger part of his production. He also worked as a bookseller for a broader European market. The Pinelli press was likely close to the circles of the historian and statesman Paolo Sarpi (1552–1623), champion of Venetian independence from Rome, and printed at least two editions of works attributed to him (with false publishing information) in 1619 and 1624.[105] The press would later print the works of many members of the Accademia degli Incogniti.

Pinelli signed the 25 June 1621 dedication of the *Immortalità* to Marcantonio Cornaro (1583–1639). As *primicerio* of Venice (the chief officiating cleric of San Marco), Cornaro was one of the most highly placed ecclesiastical officials in the Republic.[106] He was also from a most powerful family: his father, Giovanni, would be elected doge in 1625; his brother Federico would become patriarch of Venice in 1632; and Marcantonio himself would become bishop of Padua that same year.[107] Alongside Cornaro, Pinelli's dedication invoked another formidable protector: Domenico Molino (1572–1635), who was closely tied to Bonifaccio[108] and was "one of the most powerful and well-known Venetian patricians of the first three decades of the seventeenth century."[109] Pinelli said Molino had submitted the *Immortalità* for publication. The use of Molino's name to authorize the volume associated it with the patrician's politics, which were distinctly pro-Sarpi and in opposition to Rome and Spain[110] – a choice that showcased Bonifaccio's connection to the centres of power in Venice rather than his orthodoxy. The dedication associated Bonifaccio's text – and his accusations against Copia Sulam – with Cornaro and Molino as it distanced the writer himself from the work's publication: not he but Molino had purportedly submitted it for publication and not he but his printer had signed the dedication.

Bonifaccio's *Immortalità* attempts to prove the doctrine of the soul's immortality using evidence mostly from classical and Old Testament sources. Laborious and pedantic, the text is nevertheless interesting for its treatment of Copia Sulam, who figures prominently in it: the treatise was explicitly directed to her and she appears as a frequent interlocutor. Her doubt propels the text forward as Bonifaccio shows her stubbornly resisting the growing mound of evidence in favour of the soul's immortality. For instance, after a long list of proofs, he predicts that a defiant Copia Sulam will still need more proof: "I am guessing, signora, that the reasons that I have thus far produced will not satisfy you."[111] After amassing further proofs, and sometimes positing her imagined objections, he again chides her for her imagined resistance: "Now have I not proved sufficiently above that the soul is not the body, nor taken from the body, and that it is substance? ... Nonetheless, if you still want other proofs that the soul can operate without the participation of the body, lend me your ear."[112] Even as Bonifaccio concludes his treatise, he still envisions her dissatisfied: "Do you want me to declare for you the limit of subsistence? ... Do you also want me to prove to you that the soul of man is a subsistent form, such that his being is not dependent on his body ..., as if I have not made this clear with a hundred proofs?"[113] Bonifaccio paraphrases some remarks Copia Sulam made in her letter and may have based others on discussions that took place in the salon. In that venue, Copia Sulam was in the powerful position of presider, but in the conversation he recreates in his text he presents himself in the superior position, as an enlightened philosopher who tries to convince an obdurate interlocutor.

Such fictional repartee is almost entirely absent in the middle portion of the *Immortalità*, which provides philosophic proofs of the soul's immortality. But even when Bonifaccio does not address her explicitly, Copia Sulam's presence is essential to his argument – and not only because her supposed disbelief in the soul's immortality drives the text. With this treatise, Bonifaccio prepares a pre-emptive defence from the antagonistic response he expects from Copia Sulam. He describes the expected conflict in both military and literary terms, as a "battle" and "tenson."[114] To defend his text prophylactically, he relies on the real-world authority of the powerful patricians invoked through the dedication as well as the intellectual authority of the authors he cites – foremost among them Aristotle. Though he mentions in passing famous doubters of the soul's immortality, including Alexander of Aphrodisias (second to third century CE),[115] Empedocles (ca. 492–432 BCE),[116] Epicurus (341–270 BCE),[117] and Galen (129–ca. 200 CE),[118] the target of Bonifaccio's remonstrances remains Copia Sulam. In contrast to the resistance he anticipates from her, Bonifaccio expects a sympathetic response from the male Christian readers he posits as his ideal readers and whom he refers to in the text as *noi* (us). His dialogue with this anticipated audience drives the work as a whole, to the extent that his explicit aim – to convince Copia Sulam of the soul's immortality and, correspondingly, to show her the "truth" of Christianity – is in fact completely secondary if not irrelevant. The salon forum would have provided a much more effective means for such goals than this printed attack on her orthodoxy. Instead, his goal is to humiliate Copia Sulam in front of the Christian male audience that his work presupposes. To this audience, he repeatedly presents negative images of Copia Sulam as a woman and a Jew, portraying her as both threatening and weak – a common inconsistency of the antiwoman arguments of the *querelle des femmes* – and as religiously "dark."

Bonifaccio opens his address to Copia Sulam by emphasizing the
gendered nature of their interaction, claiming he does not mind learning from a woman: "I am honored to have found such an erudite teacher
as you, and I am not scornful of learning from a female (*femina*), because
in intellect there is no distinction between sexes."[119] Comparing her to
Diotima,[120] he feigns to accept the salonnière as a full member – even
guide – of intellectual society, a begrudging acknowledgment of her
stewardship of the salon. At the same time, he patronizes her as a female
intellectual, a disparagement he makes clear by using the dismissive term
"femina" rather than "donna" or "signora."[121] His initial posture of flat-
tery in any case rapidly disappears as he immediately begins his attack on
her, laying out his claim that she denied the soul's immortality. He claims
that the denial makes her even more dangerous to humankind than
Eve, since Eve only caused the death of men's bodies while Copia Sulam,
"listening to the pestiferous doctrine of a poisonous teacher, seek[s] to
bring about the death of men's soul."[122] Bonifaccio's use of the Eve myth
at the beginning of his treatise was pregnant with meaning. An interpretation of the Old Testament figure as the ruin of mankind was common-
place in *querelle des femmes* arguments against women but was especially
significant in a discourse directed to a Jewish woman since it plainly connected Copia Sulam to her dangerous biblical foremother. The comparison, which self-servingly (and perhaps humorously) exaggerates
the stakes of the debate, also reveals the disquiet Bonifaccio felt in his
exchange with a female adversary whom he perceived as powerful.[123] In
addition to her control of the salon, other sources of her power were her
beauty, wealth, and renown. He confirms his discomfort at her authority
by seeking actively to undermine it, insinuating that Copia Sulam did
not reach her own conclusions but was under the sway of a teacher – a
reference probably to Modena.[124] This was the first of his many remarks
in the treatise that suggest her dependence on her male associates, and
specifically on Modena – an additional indication that his initial praise of
her teaching was insincere. The charge of intellectual fraudulence was a
common one against early modern women, who were frequently denied
ownership of their ideas.[125] Bonifaccio would later redouble his attack
on Copia Sulam's professional honesty, blatantly accusing her of signing
work that she had not written.[126]

Towards the close of his *Immortalità*, Bonifaccio's rhetoric grows increasingly aggressive as he returns to the story of Eve. He charges that Copia
Sulam robbed mankind of the hope for eternal salvation and therefore
was not only more threatening than Eve but more dangerous than the
snake itself.[127] Urging her to embrace a belief in the soul's immortality,
he offers examples from antiquity of men who had believed so strongly

in the notion that they had killed themselves to achieve it. With striking rhetorical violence, he urges her, too, to achieve immortality by turning a knife on herself:

> I am by no means saying that you kill all of yourself, but those parts that, without destroying the whole, can be separated ... I want you, signora, to be cruel to yourself, so that you can be more merciful. Heart, heart, and not of a female (*femina*), or even if of a female, of such a one who has surpassed all men in cruelty. I want you to become a Procne, a Medea, or, if you want one of your own kind, a Mary of Bethezuba. Bleed dry your affections, dismember your emotions, slaughter your children, which are your sins. Happy you, lucky you, fortunate you, generous and magnanimous you, more than Deborah and Judith, if you strangle these children of yours. Don't listen to me; listen to your greatest prophet: *Blessed be he that shall take and dash thy little ones against the rock.* The rock is JESUS, that cornerstone that makes of two one, joining the Old and the New Testament. Smash your little ones with that rock; but quick, hurry, because they are growing; kill them before they die so that they don't kill you like little snakes as soon as they are born.[128]

These lines again reveal the disingenuousness of Bonifaccio's opening, in which he voluntarily submits himself to the teaching of a "femina." Here he urges Copia Sulam not to be a faint-hearted "femina" but to summon the virile courage necessary to eradicate her sinful beliefs – her denial of the soul's immortality, but, implicitly, also her Jewish beliefs – and to convert: in other words, he asserts that remaining a Jew would be an act of womanish cowardice. To make this argument, Bonifaccio invoked the most frightening images of female violence from classical mythology and history, exorting Copia Sulam to follow the example of women who murdered their children – Procne, Medea, and Mary of Bethezuba[129] – in order that she might rid herself of her sins, her "children." The "models" that Bonifaccio offered would have been cruelly offensive to Copia Sulam, a woman who had lost a child in infancy and at least one other in utero. In the contorted logic of the passage, Copia Sulam, by killing her children – that is, abandoning her beliefs about the soul and her faith – would achieve even greater glory than had two Old Testament heroines, Judith and Deborah, women also associated with violence but in the service of the Jewish people.[130] Bonifaccio argues, paradoxically, that by violently rejecting her Jewish faith Copia Sulam would surpass these female redeemers of the Jewish people. For this concluding passage – part of his final exhortation that she convert – the priest piles violent word upon violent word: "kill," "bleed dry," "dismember," "slaughter," "strangle," "smash," "kill." Such rhetorical ferocity renders surprisingly explicit the violence of his demands that she demolish her beliefs and sever her Jewish identity.[131]

At the beginning of his treatise, Bonifaccio asserts that Copia Sulam's purported denial of the soul's immortality separated her from other Jews. He told her that "by casting doubt on the truth of the sacred text, you alone among the Jews after many thousands of years deny faith in the infallible covenant that God wrote in His own hand."[132] But in the aggressive conclusion to the treatise, Bonifaccio associates Judaism in general with this denial, suggesting that belief in the immortality of the soul was the path to Christianity and eternal salvation. He declares that his religion would be meaningless without the soul's immortality: "I, who am Christian, would want to declare myself a Jew (*giudeo*) if our soul were ephemeral. But since it is most certainly immortal, you, who are Jewish (*hebrea*), will declare yourself Christian. Yes, yes, you will free yourself from the bondage of this most despicable Synagogue."[133] Rhetorically certain of Copia Sulam's conversion, Bonifaccio transforms her from his spiritual opposite – a Jew who, he claims, believed in the soul's mortality – to a sort of pious partner, a *cristiana* who could meet a *cristiano* on equal spiritual footing. While he expresses confidence that she, in response to his reasoning, will convert, he implies that if she rejects Christianity and disavows the soul's immortality, she will be not just *hebrea* but a reviled *giudea*.[134]

The conversionist appeal Bonifaccio made to Copia Sulam echoes the one that Cebà had made when he sent her a poem that played on her name "Coppia" or "couple."[135] Cebà wrote that he hoped "we would make a couple as Christian man and Christian woman"[136] – one mention of the sexual relationship he imagined with her throughout his *Lettere a Sarra Copia*.[137] In his *Immortalità*, Bonifaccio proposes a (spiritual?) relationship with Copia Sulam as a Christian man with a Christian woman. Elsewhere, he explicitly casts himself in the role of her lover: he portrays himself as Orpheus trying to save the beautiful Sarra/Eurydice from hell and compares his interaction with her to the lovemaking of doves.[138] Like a lover who urges his beloved to submit before she is overcome by the ravages of time, Bonifaccio also warns Copia Sulam of the transience of her beauty, cautioning: "These sparkling eyes of yours will become rheumy, your breasts flabby, and your flesh wrinkled. Your body will become a cadaver, and will turn in the end to rot and mud."[139] Though purporting to seek her spiritual, not physical submission, he lingers on the image of her body, and, as though he were a lover spurned, takes a grotesque delight in imagining its ruin. But his language, though typical of misogynist tracts, has a double meaning since he accuses Copia Sulam of believing that the soul, along with the body, will perish.

The treatise concludes with a sonnet that again focuses on Copia Sulam's beauty but that emphasizes the spiritual rather than the physical ruin that her Judaism wrought. He writes, in the quatrains:

> SARA, la tua beltà cotanto audace
> che sdegna tra le prime esser seconda,
> è però più caduca assai che fronda,
> è però più che vento assai fugace.
> E, se potessi dir, ma con tua pace,
> ciò che la tua bellezza in sé nasconda,
> Io direi ch'ella è tomba, ov'alma, immonda
> Di colpa original, sepolta giace.[140]

> (SARA, your beauty which is so bold
> that it refuses to be second among firsts
> is however much more ephemeral than a frond,
> is however much more fleeting than wind.
> And if I could say, but with your permission,
> what your beauty hides within itself,
> I would say that it is a tomb, where your soul, stained
> with original sin, lies buried.)

Bonifaccio's renewed warning about Copia Sulam's bodily vulnerability reveals his anxiety at her beauty: a dangerous disguise, but also a clear marker of her dark soul; a siren's threat that pulled men towards her spiritual darkness. Pages before, he presses her to be baptized in order to wash away her spiritual stain: "Your soul, remaining on the dry ground of your native faith, will always be gloomy and dark. But separated from that continent and surrounded by the sea of baptism, it will become white and shining."[141] The disturbing geographic and racial dimensions of Bonifaccio's metaphor compound his religious bigotry. In the concluding tercet of his final sonnet, he again urges Copia Sulam to convert:

> Corri, corri al lavacro, ond'hor deriva
> La vita: CHRISTO è quell'augel sì pio,
> Che col suo sangue i morti figli avviva.[142]

> (Run, run to the font that gives
> new life. Christ is a bird so pious
> that his blood gives his dead children life.)

With this final exhortation to baptism, Bonifaccio enjoins Copia Sulam to cultivate her spiritual well-being rather than her bodily beauty. Earlier in the treatise he criticizes her for focusing on another earthly concern: putting "so much effort into eternalizing [her] honored name with the immortal works of [her] divine intellect."[143] But for the most part, he ignores her writing and dispossesses her of her ideas – even her supposed disbelief in the immortality of the soul.[144] By concluding his treatise with a warning that she cultivates her beauty at the risk of her spiritual health, Bonifaccio criticizes her not as an intellectual but only as a vain woman. In her response *per le rime* to this poem in her *Manifesto*, Copia Sulam will instead insist on the importance of her intellectual pursuits.

3
The Salon and the Venetian Presses (1621)

Overview

By 1621, Copia Sulam's salon was thriving as a hub of intellectual exchange between Christians and Jews when her close associate Baldassare Bonifaccio accused her in print of heresy, charging that she denied the immortality of the soul. The controversy he began would be fought in some of the highest-profile presses in Venice. As discussed above, the ducal printer Antonio Pinelli published Bonifaccio's text, *Immortalità*, in June 1621. Within a matter of weeks, the well-known printer Giovanni Alberti issued Copia Sulam's pointed defence, her *Manifesto*. Bonifaccio's attack gave her an opportunity to establish her name in print. On Alberti's presses, which a decade before had printed the monumental *Crusca* Italian language dictionary, the *Manifesto* was an immediate success: by early August, it was in its third edition.

In her treatise, Copia Sulam blunts the religious elements of Bonifaccio's attack by declaring her belief in the soul's immortality and arguing that Christian and Jewish beliefs on the soul are equivalent. She instead shifts her focus to two other aspects of Bonifaccio's polemic: that Bonifaccio, as a man, had attacked a woman, and that he had done so in print. Assailing him for ill-treating a woman and asserting her right, as a woman, to engage in intellectual inquiry, Copia Sulam pushed their debate into the territory of controversies over women's nature and role that captivated readers across Europe during these years. The texts of these disputes, many printed in Venice, sold briskly and often went into multiple editions. Copia Sulam's emphasis on the gendered elements of the debate drove the popularity of her own volume.

Even as the *Manifesto* created a publishing phenomenon, it urged restraint in the use of the presses. In fact, a centrepiece of Copia Sulam's counter-attack on Bonifaccio – and of her self-defence – involved her assertion that print publication should be used judiciously and for high-minded pursuits. In contrast, she claimed that the sort of character assassination in which Bonifaccio engaged by presuming to judge the beliefs of a close associate in the court of public opinion was an inexcusable abuse of the medium. In response to his attack, which was grounded in his authority as a Christian man, Copia Sulam claimed that she, as a Jewish woman, had a special right to engage in intellectual inquiry. The defence she broadcast in the presses of Venice was thus a plea for them to be moderated not only by restraint but also by tolerance. Bonifaccio's response, published shortly after by Pinelli and laced with vitriol against the salonnière as both woman and Jew, ignored her plea: he played again to the basest use of the medium, attempting not only to discredit her but to stir up ethnic hatred under the guise of piety.

Copia Sulam's *Manifesto*

Copia Sulam composed and printed her *Manifesto* (figure 3.1), which is a fraction of the length of the *Immortalità*, in a matter of weeks.[1] Copia Sulam made both the brevity and speed of her response part of her self-defence, telling her readers that "it wasn't wise for me to respond with delay or wordy arguments to this affront because of the potential harm that it could have caused for me."[2] The *Manifesto* contrasts sharply with Copia Sulam's 1620 letter to Bonifaccio in both approach and conclusions: it lacks the letter's courteous tone, its philosophical argumentation, and its materialist and heterodox ideas. The primary purpose of the *Manifesto*, instead, is to discredit Bonifaccio.

Giovanni Alberti

As noted above, Copia Sulam turned to the well-regarded and experienced printer Giovanni Alberti to issue her response. Alberti was active in Venice from at least 1585 to 1622 and issued over a hundred volumes in the city.[3] He played a major role in seventeenth-century intellectual society by printing the first comprehensive Italian language dictionary, the *Vocabolario degli Accademici della Crusca* (Dictionary of the Crusca Academy Members), in 1612.[4] With its graceful typography, this monumental dictionary – which spans some 960 folio pages, plus indices, and registers nearly 25,000 lemmata – set the standard for the nascent genre.[5] Alberti was also an important disseminator of vernacular texts, including Ludovico Ariosto's *Orlando furioso*, Sperone Speroni's *Canace* and *Discorsi*, and Jacopo Sannazaro's *Arcadia* and *Rime*, several of which went into multiple editions. The printer was also known for dramatic works and for texts that were particularly challenging from a typographical point of view.[6] Early in his career, he printed works by another Jewish writer (Leone Ebreo, ca. 1460–ca. 1530) and by another

MANIFESTO
DI
SARRA COPIA
SVLAM HEBREA.

Nel quale è da lei riprouata, e deteſtata l'opinione negante l'immortalità dell' Anima, falſamente attribuitale dal

SIG. BALDASSARE BONIFACCIO.

Con Licenza de' Superiori.

IN VENETIA, M· DCXXI·

Appreſſo Giouanni Alberti.

3.1 The title page of the first edition of Copia Sulam's *Manifesto* (Venice: appresso Giovanni Alberti, 1621). By permission of the Ministero per i Beni e le Attività Culturale – Biblioteca Nazionale Marciana (Misc. 2503.5). Further reproduction is prohibited.

female writer (Laura Terracina, 1519–ca. 1577).[7] In his later years, Alberti
had a sustained interest in publishing texts with a religious dimension,
including Johann Justus Lansperger's *La vita della b*[eata] *vergine Gertruda*
(The Life of the Blessed Virgin Gertrude, 1618) and Giovanni Bellarino's
Doctrina catholica, ex sacro concilio tridentino et catechismo romano (Catholic
Doctrine from the Sacred Council of Trent and Roman Catechism, 1620),
though he might have had links to circles that opposed the Roman Curia
and supported Paolo Sarpi.[8] Of particular interest in Alberti's production
is the account of the ancient Jews by the pro-Roman Jewish author Flavius
Josephus (CE 37–ca. 101), *Delle antichità e guerre giudaiche* (Antiquities
of the Jews and Wars of the Jews), of which he published two editions in
1619. Though Copia Sulam's and Josephus's texts are fundamentally different, both defend Judaism to a non-Jewish audience. Josephus was well
known to the participants in Copia Sulam's salon: she cites his work in her
Manifesto, as does Bonifaccio in his response. Modena, whose *Riti* was also
intended for a non-Jewish audience, knew the work well.[9] The 1626 "Avisi"
manuscript that came out of Copia Sulam's literary circle also mentions
Josephus.[10] In the same year that Alberti published Copia Sulam's tract,
he published two works by another writer who was admired in – and connected to – her literary circle: the libertine poet and librettist Giulio Strozzi
(1583–ca. 1650).[11] Strozzi's and Copia Sulam's texts were an important
part of Alberti's publications for the year.[12]

Beyond Alberti's reputation for quality and his publication of numerous works that would have been of great interest to Copia Sulam, she may
also have chosen to work with the printer because an associate recom-
mended him.[13] Alberti's shop was located relatively near the ghetto, in
the parish of Santa Fosca.[14] Copia Sulam likely financed the publication
herself and could therefore be considered not only the author of the
volume but its *editrice*.[15] Such an arrangement was typical for Alberti.[16]
She did not request a printing privilege for the work.[17]

Although the *Manifesto* was brief, Copia Sulam chose to publish it with
a high-profile press and considered it a lasting literary monument. In
terms of genre, the work must be considered a pamphlet because of its
polemical nature and the urgency with which it was issued. However, it
is highly atypical for pamphlets in the era, given both the formal aspects
of the text (as discussed below, the text featured a note to reader, dedication, and initial and concluding verse, in addition to the prose response
to Bonifaccio) and its typographical presentation, including the use of
attractive woodcut initials. The text was written and printed to last, much
as a book would have been.[18] The work is distinctly different from the
lower quality pamphlets or ephemera that were published in great number in Venice in the period and distributed at low cost.[19]

As noted, the *Manifesto* came out in three separate editions in 1621. Alberti printed two editions of the work while the other was printed by Antonio Pinelli – who published the *Immortalità* as well as *Risposta al Manifesto*, Bonifaccio's immediate response to the *Manifesto*. The Alberti editions feature his usual device of a sibyl, here seated and consulting the book of oracles (see figure 3.1).[20] The Pinelli text features the printer's self-referential pine tree device. Apart from certain typographical differences and a small number of corrections, the content of the three editions is nearly identical, except for the fact that one edition, here referred to as text *a*, includes Pietro Petracci's name above the first introductory poetic compositions, while the others do not mention him (see figure 3.2).[21] Text *a* is the first Alberti edition.[22] It displays significant differences in form from the other editions: it is in a smaller format with denser type. This first edition was corrected and reset; it then appeared in a new, more lavish edition (text *b*), still by Alberti.[23] The greater luxury of the second edition was another sign of the *Manifesto*'s success. Pinelli printed text *c*, the work's third edition, in a volume very similar to text *b*.[24] Text *c* is the most error-free, since it corrects several printing errors in Copia Sulam's sonnets (it also introduced new, but less serious errors).[25] Pinelli almost certainly published the work together with Bonifaccio's response, the *Risposta*. This early August Pinelli printing, the third edition of the *Manifesto* published in a matter of weeks,[26] made the work nothing short of a publishing phenomenon.

A Printing Error

The first edition (text *a*) of the *Manifesto* provides evidence – through a printing error – that at least one contemporary Christian male writer was prepared to offer Copia Sulam his public support in the controversy.[27] In this edition, the words "Del Signor Pietro Petracci" appear over the work's introductory poems (see figure 3.2).[28] The poems cannot be attributed to Petracci: not only do they reflect Copia Sulam's perspective and style, but her enemies – always eager to discredit her as the true author of her writings – never credit her verse to him. The erroneous inclusion of his name, as explained above, was corrected in subsequent editions.[29] The presence, then removal, of Petracci's name most likely indicates that he wrote an introductory sonnet for the volume that was slated for inclusion, even as the pages were being composed, but that was excluded before it went to press. Petracci collaborated with Giovanni Alberti and worked for him as a proofreader.[30] If Petracci was a supporter of Copia Sulam's, as seems likely from this printing error, it is possible that he functioned as an intermediary between her and Alberti

Del Signor Pietro Petracci.

Ignor, che dal mio petto arderti auanti
Mai sempre scorgi in holocausto il core,
E sai ch'altro desio, che frale honore
M'instiga a porger preghi, à versar pianti.

Deh volgi in me il tuo sguardo, e mira quanti
Strali m'auuenta il perfido liuore,
Sgombra da cieche menti il fosco errore
Nè d'oltraggiar il uer l'empio si uanti.

Ben sò ch'indegna di tue gratie io sono;
Ma l'alma che formasti a tua sembianza
Fia ch'ad esserle scudo ogn'hor ti moua.

Cessi d'audace lingua il falso suono,
E chi adombrarla uuol scorga per proua,
Che la mia fede ha in tè ferma possanza.

On la tua scorta, ecco, Signor, m'accingo
A la difesa, oue m'oltraggia, e sgrida
Guerrier, che ardisce querelar d'infida
L'alma, che, tua mercè, di fede i cingo.

Entro senz'armi in non usato aringo,
Ne guerra io prendo contra chi mi sfida,
Ma, perche tua pietà mio Dio m'affida,
Col petto ignudo i colpi suoi respingo.

Che se di polue già l'armi formasti
Al grand'Abram, contra i nemici Regi
Sì ch'ei di lor fe memorando scempio.

Rinoua in me, bench'inegual l'esempio,
E l'inchiostro ch'io spargo fà c'hor basti,
A dimostrar di tua possanza i pregi.

MA-

3.2 The introductory sonnets in the first edition (text *a*) of Copia Sulam's *Manifesto* (Venice: appresso Giovanni Alberti, 1621) appear under Pietro Petracci's name. By permission of the Ministero per i Beni e le Attività Culturale – Biblioteca Nazionale Marciana (Misc. 2503.5). Further reproduction is prohibited.

and may even have suggested the press to the salonnière. No mention of Petracci's involvement appears either in Bonifaccio's response to the *Manifesto* or in any other works that regard her.

A Dangerous Attack?

Copia Sulam bases her response to Bonifaccio on the claim that his charge put her at risk.[31] She did not further describe the harm (*danno*) his text could have caused, but she may have feared the attention of the Inquisition and of secular authorities in Venice as well as damage to her reputation.

Since the Venetian Inquisition did not systematically pursue cases against unbaptized Jews during the seventeenth century, it is unlikely that Copia Sulam would have encountered problems from religious authorities on the basis of Bonifaccio's accusation.[32] Neither was she in immediate danger from the two lay magistracies that, in addition to others, regulated such matters: the *Essecutori contro la Bestemmia*, which sought to suppress blasphemy (as distinct from heresy), and the *Ufficiali al Cattaver*, which sought to maintain social distance between Christians and Jews.[33] These magistracies would have been unlikely to become involved, since they largely regulated matters of a more blatant sort – overt blasphemy, for instance, or sexual relations between Christians and Jews. Copia Sulam might not, however, have felt certain of her security, which can be perceived most clearly with historical perspective: the mere existence of such magistracies, not to mention of the Inquisition, posed a threat to Venetian Jews. Modena's autobiography gives a measure of the fear that conditioned their existence: he frequently worried about danger from Christian authorities, included several reports of Jews being arrested and detained,[34] and feared reprisals after his *Historia de' riti hebraici* was published (which he worried would be perceived as anti-Christian).[35] Though Copia Sulam had strategic reasons for underscoring the danger that Bonifaccio had created since it justified the publication of her *Manifesto* and allowed her to vilify him publicly in turn, she nevertheless had ample reason to fear personal difficulties with religious or secular authorities as she faced Bonifaccio's published accusation of her heresy.

The charges Bonifaccio made against this one Jewish woman were also dangerous to her community. Because Venetian authorities often considered Jews en masse, any Jew's misconduct or misbelief was seen as a threat to the whole community. Modena describes in his autobiography his fear that he had created trouble for all Jews because he had espoused beliefs contrary to Christianity in an initial version of his *Riti*: "I said to myself, 'When this book is seen in Rome, it will become a stumbling block for all the Jews and for me, in particular. They will say, "How insolent are they to print in the vernacular, informing Christians not only of their laws, but

also of some matters contrary to our religion and beliefs.""[36] Modena
observes elsewhere that the whole Jewish community was blamed if one
member misbehaved.[37] In his autobiography, he describes a grave crisis that befell his community in 1636–1637 because of the illegal activities of a few Jews. Their thievery and corruption brought the threat of
expulsion upon the whole community.[38] Though Bonifaccio's charge
of heresy against Copia Sulam certainly fell far short of this, it had the
potential to create problems for the Jewish community because it sullied
the reputation of one of its prominent members. Moreover, Bonifaccio
himself more than once explicitly linked doubt of the soul's immortality
to Judaism, and therefore to the Jewish community as a whole. Copia
Sulam's emphasis in her *Manifesto* on gender, rather than on religious
difference, was designed to protect her community by deflecting the religious attack. Because of this orientation, the *Manifesto* must be read as
part of the tradition of apologist texts written by Venetian Jewish intellectuals.[39] The forum of print allowed Copia Sulam to defend her religion to the same lettered and influential Christian readers to whom her
detractor had appealed.[40]

Copia Sulam in Print

Copia Sulam begins the *Manifesto* with an introduction to readers in which
she alludes to the reputation she has already gained in Venice and beyond:

> I can imagine, dear readers, that it will seem strange to you that my name,
> by no means unknown in this city nor outside it, appears for the first time in
> print on a topic quite different from the one that might perhaps have been
> expected from my pen. But another's malice or ignorance or negligence
> has compelled me to do that which I was not easily inclined to do for just
> any occasion, even though I have some works that I could publish, which,
> if I am not mistaken, might be greeted more eagerly and perhaps better
> enjoyed by the world than this one will be.[41]

Here Copia Sulam sets herself up in a position of power within the literary
world by emphasizing her agency and her control over her public persona. She had held off from publishing by choice – not for lack of works
or of access to the presses. The print medium, as she describes it, was one
to be used strategically and sparingly, and not "for just any occasion." She
now resorts to the medium, she claims, because "another" has forced her
hand to publish – and to publish a polemic work rather than the poetry
or perhaps letters that contemporary readers might have expected from
her. Her move into print, she declares, was nothing short of compulsory.

The fame Copia Sulam advertised in her address to readers – her name was "by no means unknown in this city nor outside it" – was not built around the presses. By the time of Bonifaccio's attack, the only mention of her in print was Modena's dedication of *L'Ester* to her in 1619.[42] Even that dedication, which compliments her on writing that had never been published and refers to her correspondence with Cebà, fed an interest in her manuscript works. By her own account, the limited circulation of her writing – available only to the exclusive coterie of her salon associates[43] – had created a demand for her works that only grew as they resisted inscription into print.

In the dedication to her work, which immediately follows the note to readers, Copia Sulam moves from discussing her decision to print to defending her beliefs. She dedicates the work to her deceased father, acting out her belief in the afterlife as she expresses to him her enduring filial devotion. In this touching frame of familial love, Copia Sulam acknowledges her desire for fame from this publication. She does not want such fame for herself, however, but for her father.[44] She expresses to him the hope that,

> with the small achievement of fame that you may see in my name ... you will appreciate having produced a woman for the perpetuation of your name no less than you would have appreciated producing a man, as you showed a great desire to do in this life.[45]

If, in the introduction to readers, Copia Sulam suggests the importance of the manuscript circulation of her writing, the dedication recognizes the enduring power of print. Immortalizing the Copio name with this print publication, the author exercises a power usually reserved for men: the propagation of the family name.[46] More than a "small achievement of fame," she anticipates a recognition that would last for generations.[47] But since such renown is only a secondary result of her necessary self-defence, and she bequeaths her fame to her father, Copia Sulam seeks to insulate herself from the negative impression a more open quest for fame might create, especially in a religious debate.[48] Though she does not mention it, Copia Sulam also immortalizes the Sulam name through her publication: the title pages of all editions list her as Sarra Copia Sulam (though Copia is always printed more prominently than Sulam). Her failure to mention her perpetuation of her husband's name is striking when one considers the case of Vittoria Colonna, for example, whose primary task as a poet was to immortalize her husband.[49] Copia Sulam's silence here regarding Giacob Sulam is part of his puzzling role in her literary career.[50]

The dedication Copia Sulam uses to preface her *Manifesto* contrasts sharply with the one used for Bonifaccio's *Immortalità*. Whereas the latter advertised a powerful dedicatee – Cornaro, whose subvention could have helped to finance the publication – the salonnière dedicated the book to her deceased father. While the dedication had strategic purposes, it did not bring outside financial backing to the project.[51]

Two sonnets addressed to God follow the dedication. These private conversations allow Copia Sulam another forum in which to set out her agenda, while their intimate tone distracts from their strategic purpose. As in her dedicatory conversation with her deceased father, in these sonnets she again acts out her religious devotion. While she humbly addresses God, her literary agenda is less overt but no less important: she makes it clear in the note to readers that it was not as a polemicist that she hoped to create her enduring fame, and the opening sonnets allow her prominently to display her poetic skill. The compositions foreground Copia Sulam's intimate relationship with God while marginalizing her aggressor, who remains unnamed and ultimately insignificant in comparison with her powerful faith and powerful God (the term *possanza* [power] is used in the last verse of each poem to describe these concepts in turn). In the sonnets, Copia Sulam offers her own soul as a reflection of God and repository of faith, in obvious counterpoint to Bonifaccio's closing sonnet of the *Immortalità*, where he insists that her soul, "stained / with original sin," lies buried in the tomb of her body.[52]

In the first sonnet, Copia Sulam asks God to help her respond to the unjust attack made upon her, his deeply devoted servant:

> Signor, che dal mio petto arderti avanti
> Mai sempre scorgi in holocausto il core,
> E sai ch'altro desio che frale honore
> M'instiga a porger preghi, a versar pianti,
> Deh volgi in me il tuo sguardo e mira quanti
> Strali m'avventa il perfido livore;
> Sgombra da cieche menti il fosco errore,
> Né d'oltraggiar il ver l'empio si vanti.
> Ben so ch'indegna di tue gratie io sono,
> Ma l'alma che formasti a tua sembianza
> Fia ch'ad esserle scudo ogn'hor ti mova.
> Cessi d'audace lingua il falso suono
> E chi adombrarla vuol scorga per prova
> Che la mia fede ha in te ferma possanza.[53]

> (Lord, you who always see in my chest
> a heart burning before you in sacrifice,

and who know that a desire beyond frail honor
drives me to offer prayers, to shed tears,
Oh, turn your gaze upon me and behold how many
arrows perfidious malice looses against me;
lift the cloud of dark error from blind minds
and let not the impious one boast of having insulted truth.
I know well that I am unworthy of your graces
but may the soul you formed in your image
compel you to shield it at all times.
May the false sound of a shameless tongue cease,
and may he who wishes to cast doubt
see as proof, that my faith gains unyielding power in you.)

Copia Sulam depicts her defence against Bonifaccio's attack not as personally driven (it is not her "frail honor" that spurs her to write) but instead as motivated by a desire to combat the lies spread by her adversary, whose impious disregard for the truth has allowed a "cloud of dark error" to descend on "blind minds." (By "dark error," Copia Sulam seems to intend not a misconception regarding her views on the immortality of the soul [since she claims she is not defending herself], but a more general misunderstanding of the tenet as gleaned from Bonifaccio's tract, whose content, argumentation, and efficacy Copia Sulam will harshly criticize in the *Manifesto*'s prose portion.) Copia Sulam here does not place herself in active combat with her adversary but suggests that her unshakeable faith in God will shield her from his attacks.

The second sonnet is instead rife with military language, as Copia Sulam imagines a more literal battle with her adversary:

Con la tua scorta, ecco, Signor, m'accingo
A la difesa, ove m'oltraggia, e sgrida
Guerrier, che ardisce querelar d'infida
L'alma che, tua mercè, di fede i' cingo.
Entro senza armi in non usato aringo,
Né guerra io prendo contra chi mi sfida,
Ma perché tua pietà, mio Dio, m'affida,
Col petto ignudo i colpi suoi respingo.
Che se di polve già l'armi formasti
Al gran Abram, contra i nemici regi,
Sì ch'ei di lor fe memorando scempio.
Rinova in me, bench'inegual l'esempio,
E l'inchiostro ch'io spargo fa c'hor basti,
A dimostrar di tua possanza i pregi.[54]

(With you as guide, Lord, behold, I prepare
To defend myself, since a warrior
Insults and harangues me, daring to call infidel
My soul which, by your grace, I gird with faith.
I enter unarmed into the unfamiliar arena
and make no war against the one who challenges me,
yet because your mercy, my God, secures me,
with a bare breast I repel his blows.
For if you formed arms out of dust
that the great Abraham used against the hostile royal troops
whom he slaughtered so famously,[55]
help me repeat the example (although I am unequal)
And ensure that the ink I spill will be sufficient
to show the merits of your power.)

Copia Sulam has been forced by her rival – who launched a sort of religious war against her as an "infidel" – to enter the "unfamiliar arena" of religious and literary combat. Though unarmed (because inexperienced in this sort of conflict), Copia Sulam predicts that she, rendered invincible by God's help, will fend off her adversary. The final lines of the poem transfer the military conflict to the written page, as Copia Sulam prays that her weapons – that is, the ink of her words – will reveal God's power and, implicitly, destroy her hostile rival.

Alongside such military discourse, the sonnets also continue the polemic on the proper use of the press that dominates her response. Rather than employing the presses as a tool to spread "perfidious malice"[56] – shorthand for the sort of character assassination in which Bonifaccio engaged – Copia Sulam suggests that she will use print ("the ink I spill")[57] for more high-minded pursuits and in particular for the celebration of God. Though in her treatise, as suggested above, she in fact largely downplays religious issues, the poems portray her publishing efforts as a righteous response to an impious adversary – impious not because he adheres to Catholicism but because he doubts her true religious faith.

Having carefully framed the debate with introductory prose and poetry, Copia Sulam undertakes a sharply worded response to Bonifaccio that stands at the heart of her *Manifesto*. She opens her direct address to her antagonist by advertising her familiarity with the intellectual and publishing landscape in Venice. Recounting her initial encounter with Bonifaccio's *Immortalità*, she reports that when she received the volume – she clearly kept abreast of books recently published in the city – she was merely surprised that he had undertaken to write on the immortality of the soul.[58] She claims that her surprise turned to shock when she saw that he had accused *her* of denying the tenet: "When I read on and found that the discourse was directed to me ... I could not help but feel great surprise, mixed with scorn, for the extreme boldness of the calumny."[59] She tells her detractor that she is publishing her response to make it known "publicly to the world, by means of the present document, that most false, unjust, and beyond any reason is the charge you made against me in your treatise, that I deny the immortality of the soul. I do this only to justify myself before and to convince all those who, not knowing me, might give some credence to your accusation, thinking it part of the religion that I profess."[60] Specifying her intended audience as readers who did not know her and were unfamiliar with her religion (in other words, Christians), Copia Sulam provides another reason for her use of print: the wider and more impersonal distribution it allowed. She tells Bonifaccio he was lucky she chose this course of action, rather than bringing him to court on libel charges, and says she let him off lightly because "the compassion my religion teaches makes me pity your simple-mindedness."[61] Putting herself in a position of both intellectual and religious superiority, Copia Sulam depicts her printed response as an act of clemency towards her slanderer.

Although she carefully justifies and discusses in detail her use of print to counter Bonifaccio's claims, Copia Sulam's prose response itself has all the attributes of a spoken, not written, exchange.[62] More than once she explicitly calls Bonifaccio – with whom she had conversed in person many times at her salon – into conversation. She invites him, for instance, to "discuss this issue, just the two of us, a little bit more freely and informally."[63] She turns to him with frequent apostrophe, uses interjections (*ah, orsù* [come on], *eh* [come now]), asks him probing questions, at times responds to his imagined answers, and throughout uses a colloquial tone. These conversational markers convey a sense of familiarity between the interlocutors, a familiarity that makes his printed accusation against her seem all the more treacherous. In contrast, the paratextual materials that introduce her address to Bonifaccio – including the note to readers, dedication, and opening sonnets – while always in dialogue with others (the reader, her father, God), do not have a spoken feel. The greater formality of these other exchanges lends the *Manifesto* as a whole a refined quality appropriate for the first published work of a writer who aimed to solidify her literary reputation. Their elevated tone also distinguishes them from her textual "conversation" with Bonifaccio, whose disloyalty rendered him unworthy of the respect she shows to others.

Bonifaccio's Abuse of the Presses

Copia Sulam's careful justification of her use of print sharply contrasts with her blistering criticism of Bonifaccio's use of the presses. Taking as much offence at the method of distribution as at the attack itself, she mentions several times not merely that he wrote his calumnious treatise but that he printed it. She questions her antagonist, for instance: "Kindly tell me, then, signor Baldassare, what moved you to compose that treatise, to print it, and to mix my name up with it?"[64] She claims that her opponent did not have the credentials to tackle the weighty topic he had chosen: "You're neither a philosopher nor a theologian ... yet you dared to print your discourse with such a sublime title?"[65] In her most direct condemnation, Copia Sulam examines Bonifaccio's motivations for printing his "noble" work. She explicitly rules out – but implicitly suggests – malice as a motive, saying her friendship with him precluded such a possibility. She speculates that misguided arrogance might have driven him to compose the treatise: as the *Galateo* shows, she writes, many commit incivilities in "wanting to show off in something they have no talent for."[66] But she finds the underlying reason elsewhere. She tells him:

> Nothing else has prompted you to undertake such a long and vain effort but that vain and small-minded ambition of yours which makes you run eagerly to the presses, believing that fame consists in having many volumes out, without thinking about the opinion that the world has of them. I think you know from experience how dissatisfied people are by things that are only moderately good, not to mention those that are shoddy and stupidly composed, and therefore Horace's *Art of Poetry* itself warns us not to run so easily to the presses.[67]

Copia Sulam charges Bonifaccio with seeking to rack up publications regardless of their merit, upending what would have been one of Bonifaccio's main advantages: his literary fame bolstered by his publications, which numbered six by the time of her response.[68] She instead offers his copious publications, which she implies found little favour because they were only "moderately good," as evidence of a sort of intellectual profligacy: they spoke against – not *to* – his literary merit, testifying instead to his "vain and immoderate thirst for glory."[69] The charge of vanity – in the sense both of uselessness and of egotism – lies at the core of Copia Sulam's criticism of her antagonist: she uses the word "vain" against him three times in one short section.

Copia Sulam criticizes other aspects of Bonifaccio's diatribe, including his ignorance and his lack of chivalry in assailing a woman. But she does

not enter into a point-by-point refutation of his work, she says, lest anyone think she opposed his premise, that the soul is immortal. As Copia
Sulam brings the tract to a swift close, she emphasizes that she is putting
an end to her printed exchange with Bonifaccio. She writes:

> This is not a formal response to your challenge, but a simple statement
> to excuse myself for not appearing, since there is no reason to fight when
> there is no conflict of opinions, neither in words nor in acts. Therefore, as
> far as I'm concerned, you can put down your arms, since, even if you pro-
> voked me again with a thousand insults, I will no longer counter you with
> any response so as not to waste my time, above all because I am as averse to
> placing myself beneath the world's gaze by means of the presses as you show
> yourself to be desirous.[70]

Copia Sulam ends her treatise as she began it, making her reticence to
publish a cornerstone of her print defence. She summarily dismisses the
possibility of any further response, even if (as her treatise prepares readers to expect) her antagonist again rushes to the presses to defame her.
With this declaration, she sought pre-emptively to weaken Bonifaccio's
hand, since another print publication would only confirm her charge
of his reckless use of the press. As mentioned, he did in fact print a
response mere weeks after the *Manifesto*'s issue.

Gender Wars

In criticizing Bonifaccio for his misuse of the press, Copia Sulam adopted the
rhetoric and subject matter of the debates about women that were fought
out in the commercial presses in these years. Bonifaccio had, of course,
invited a discussion of gender with his patronizing assault on Copia Sulam,
which began by mocking her as a female intellectual. As we have seen, his
claim to accept her as his teacher and women as men's intellectual equals
was belied by his condescension and disparagement.[71] In her response,
however, she takes his offer at face value and, seizing upon the opportunity
to instruct him, points out his many errors. For example, she provides a
long list of Bonifaccio's rhetorical missteps, claiming that his writing

> does not have a good thing about it other than the cause it defends. As
> for the rest, it is so jampacked with poorly understood terms, warped and
> misguided ideas of writing, with false forms of syllogisms, bad transitions,
> and strange leaps from one topic to another, with inappropriate citation of
> authors and, finally, with linguistic errors, that no one can read it through
> without cursing the author.[72]

She also mocks him for his philosophic and theological speculation, recalling that he had once claimed ignorance in these areas, and she argues that only foolish arrogance allowed him to "touch such a lofty matter with [his] little fingers!"[73] In her reckoning, his ignorance was matched only by his plodding slow-wittedness, which allows her easily to defeat him. She claims that he had long laboured over his treatise against her while she makes quick work of destroying it: "I set out, with the brief work of two days, to knock to the ground what you schemed against me in nearly two years of useless vigils."[74]

Even if, in the *Manifesto*, Copia Sulam assumes the position of teacher, she explicitly dismisses claims to authority. She tells her opponent: "I, for my part, am not addressing you in this way to instruct you as a school-mistress or a lady philosopher, as you derisively say to me while, like a pedant, you come to lecture me, because I confess that I am much more ignorant than you are in these disciplines."[75] While pointing out the discrepancy between his words and actions, she feigns her own ignorance. She goes on to claim that, in censuring his text, she merely reports the comments she has heard from others ("from all those who see your book").[76] Thus distancing herself from the criticism she levels against him, Copia Sulam here plays to both sides of the *querelle des femmes*. She highlights the bias against women inherent in Bonifaccio's mocking offer to accept her as his teacher, and throughout the treatise ridicules her opponent. But when she explicitly acknowledges the male-female dynamics at work, she pretends to submit to her male opponent's intellectual superiority – or to challenge him only on the basis of others' critiques. However, her outspoken self-assurance throughout the text and her relentless attack on his ignorance and incompetence belie such modesty. Despite her occasional denials, Copia Sulam's arguments in the *Manifesto* are based upon the presumption that she was intellectually superior to her opponent.

Using to her advantage a pose of weakness, however, she more than once suggests that men know more than women. She charges her opponent with cowardice, for instance, not only for assailing a woman, but for doing so on the unfair ground of learning. She asks: "Why would you challenge a woman? And a woman who, though she enjoys learning, does not pursue such study by profession?"[77] Were he brave, she argues, he would have targeted not her but famous defenders of the soul's mortality. But instead, he turned to a weaker female opponent, believing that this ploy would ensure his victory. She mocks him: "In this way, O valorous challenger of women, the field is all yours. Walk through it proudly nonetheless, striking blows to the air, O valorous champion, O generous warrior. And with no other blare but that of your rasping trumpet, go ahead and yell out to yourself 'Victory, Victory.'"[78] Depicting Bonifaccio's attack on *her* as a general attack on *women* ("O valorous challenger of *women*"),[79] she situates her debate with him firmly in the contemporary *querelles des femmes*, taking advantage of the ambiguous notions about women on which such debates often turned. By criticizing her opponent for a craven attack on the female sex, she appeals to a chivalrous code that would protect though disempower her. At the same time she subverts this code, more than ably defending herself with her own pen in this war of words even as she feigns feminine reserve. Using military language to ridicule him and his overweening masculinity, she portrays her aggressor as a soldier with no battle and urges him to lay down his arms.

By emphasizing gender conflict rather than doctrinal disagreement, Copia Sulam neither elides the religious element of the debate nor denies her Jewish identity. In fact, her defence of her faith is a cornerstone of the treatise. As much as she portrays their contest as gendered, she also acknowledges that Bonifaccio attacked her as a *Jewish* woman, and it is as a Jewish woman that she defends herself.[80] At the very beginning of her response, she acknowledges that she and Bonifaccio had exchanged views on philosophical and theological matters and that she had raised thorny questions. She denies, however, that such exchanges meant that her faith had wavered. Instead, she says, she was merely interested in hearing his answers. Asserting her own intellectual freedom, she claims she thought such inquiry was allowed to anyone who pursued learning, and especially to her as a Jewish woman constantly subject to conversionist pressure.[81] Copia Sulam affirms, that is, that she had the right to engage in intellectual inquiry not despite the fact that she was a woman, and a Jewish woman, but precisely because of it. She counters Bonifaccio's notion that her religion and sex were a double deficiency in intellectual matters and she recasts them as a double strength. Moreover, she argues that the conversionist pressure she faced – of which the priest, her former intimate, was well aware – strengthened her right to freedom of inquiry. She had just noted the Venetian setting for their debate, asking why he found it necessary to publish a text on the immortality of the soul "above all in Venice."[82] In defending her right to intellectual inquiry, she makes use of the city's favoured image of itself, in these post-Interdict years, as a bastion for free thought and independence. In her formulation, a woman – and especially a Jewish woman – would have a special privilege within this open-minded society. She suggests Bonifaccio violated this Venetian civic principle with the intolerance and chauvinism to which he had given public display in the presses.

Judaism Defended to a Christian Public

Although the *Manifesto* seeks in several ways to downplay the religious elements of the polemic, it was impossible, because of the nature of Bonifaccio's charges, for religion not to play a central role in the debate. Copia Sulam sought in two ways to win the religious argument: by criticizing her opponent's credentials in religious matters and by presenting a vision of Judaism that appealed to a Catholic readership.

To discredit the priest, she declares that his legal education did not prepare him for the topic he tackles in his *Immortalità*: "Much more is needed, my signore, than the title of 'Doctor of Both Laws' to be able to discuss the immortality of the soul."[83] She says his blunders, therefore, are many. He misses pertinent information in the New Testament, for example, and does not know which part of the Old Testament was written by the hand of God.[84] Bonifaccio's discussion of a Hebrew term in his treatise draws her greatest derision. He interprets the Hebrew word *ruah* as "soul," an interpretation Copia Sulam disputes, claiming that the word actually means "breath."[85] Again claiming her intellectual superiority over her rival, the salonnière says that what she calls his misinterpretation entirely undercuts his credibility, since he knew no Hebrew:

> Because I know that you have never seen the Hebrew language and that it was puffed into your blowgun by others, I will only tell you that by this you make it most clear that all the other things you said you dared to say without understanding them. At least on this point, since you were speaking with a Jew, you should have had someone who better understood the properties of the language feed you your words.[86]

Copia Sulam here paints her adversary as a foolish dilettante in matters of faith, fully incapable of understanding theological subtleties in Hebrew. Moreover, twice in this short passage she lodges against him the charge of intellectual dishonesty that women writers frequently faced and that Bonifaccio makes against her in his *Immortalità*.

She also criticizes him as if from *within* his tradition by taking issue with his joking manner, admonishing that it was inappropriate for a priest to adopt such a tone.[87] She questions the firmness of his own belief in the immortality of the soul, censuring him, for instance, for stating in the *Immortalità* "I wish to God that death were a joke rather than a serious matter."[88] Why did he say this, she asks, if he believed the soul immortal?: "Come now, signor Bonifaccio, what game are we playing at? Do you believe firmly in what you preach or not? ... Where does your affection for life on earth rather than the afterlife come from?"[89] She addresses him again informally and again with the impatience of a teacher exasperated at her student's hopelessly tangled thoughts. Since he also writes in *Immortalità* that death is sometimes preferable to life,[90] she argues that his inconsistencies threw the orthodoxy of *his* beliefs into question and she warns him: "Watch out because this self-contradiction is a bad sign."[91]

Copia Sulam also takes Bonifaccio to task for accusing her of being the only Jew to deny the soul's immortality, saying that both Jewish and Christian texts belie this allegation. Pardoning his ignorance of Jewish sources, she points out that the Gospels mention the case of a Jewish sect that denied the soul's immortality.[92] Lecturing her adversary, a priest, on the New Testament, Copia Sulam calls into question his most basic credentials. At the conclusion of her treatise, she highlights her own religious devotion and questions his faith one final time: "Live happily and nurture the hope that you will benefit from the immortality you preach, if you are as observant of your Christian religion as I declare to be of my Jewish one."[93] Casting doubt on Bonifaccio's adherence to the Christian faith, Copia Sulam distinguishes her opponent's beliefs from those of his religion so that it was clear that her pointed critique of him was not an attack on Christianity. Her distinction between the individual and his faith stands in contrast to Bonifaccio's confusion between her supposed views and Jewish belief.[94]

The other, and more subtle, technique that Copia Sulam uses to deflect Bonifaccio's religious attack was to suggest consonance between Judaism and Christianity. She employs this technique in the very first words she addresses to Bonifaccio in the *Manifesto*, as she unequivocally refutes his accusation that she did not believe in the soul's immortality: "The soul of man, signor Baldassare, is incorruptible, immortal, and divine, created and infused by GOD into our body at that moment that the fetus is rendered able, in the maternal womb, to receive it. And this truth is as certain, infallible, and beyond doubt with me as I believe that it is with every Jew and Christian."[95] Here she asserts that Jews and Christians share the same beliefs regarding the soul, a claim she also makes in her note to her readers, where she states that the doctrine of the soul's immortality is one "no Jew or Christian may contradict."[96] With such declarations, Copia Sulam highlights the similarity between Judaism and Christianity on matters of the soul, distancing not only herself but her entire community from the heresy with which Bonifaccio has charged her.

This claim of similarity was, however, merely tactical. Appealing to a Catholic audience, Copia Sulam describes the contemporary Christian view on the soul's infusion into the body – a view that was not completely in harmony with Jewish beliefs. Christian theologians agreed that a fetus was endowed with an immortal soul, and some even argued that the soul entered the body at conception. In the Jewish context, rabbinic responsa established no clear moment when the soul entered the body or when it became immortal. Various readings of the Talmud and Midrashic sources locate the infusion of life into a human being at far ends of the spectrum – from the moment of conception to the moment of birth. And "life" in this sense may or may not be equivalent to "soul." According to the rabbinic outlook, "The time of 'ensoulment' and the nature of that soul ... belong to those 'secrets of God.'"[97] Endowment with a soul is also, in the Jewish tradition, not the same as endowment with immortal life – another of the "secrets of God" with no doctrinal certainty.[98] Howard Adelman argues that Copia Sulam's statement on ensoulment is one of two affirmations she makes in the *Manifesto* that are "contrary to basic Jewish tenets"[99] – affirmations that suggest its authorship cannot be ascribed to the rabbi Modena, as Bonifaccio would later assert. The view on ensoulment that Copia Sulam sets forth was one "with which Modena would not have associated himself."[100] Yet Modena understood religious apology, too, and likely appreciated her oblique plea for sympathy from a Christian readership.

Copia Sulam uses this same technique to counter Bonifaccio's claim that God gave written proof of the soul's immortality. Asserting that God wrote only the Decalogue, she tells him: "If you have any other writing made by the hand of God on the topic of immortality, I would be anxious to see it."[101] Her assertion regarding God's limited authorship was not, however, standard Jewish belief. In fact, Adelman points out, the attribution of divine authorship only to the Ten Commandments and not to the entire Torah "would be considered absolute heresy by most Jews ... It was usually Christians who tried to reduce the divine authorship of the Torah to the Ten Commandments."[102] To argue against Bonifaccio, then, Copia Sulam creates a vision of Judaism that would have appealed to Christians even as it differed from her faith.

Copia Sulam here follows a path similar to the one Modena had traced in his *Riti*, composed in 1616 but printed in Venice by Colleoni more than two decades later, in 1638. Mark Cohen has shown that the *Riti* – which explained Jewish rites and customs to a non-Jewish audience – is an apologist tract along the same lines as the more overtly apologist *Discorso* by Luzzatto.[103] Modena's defence of Jewish law in terms familiar to Christians[104] may have provided a road map to Copia Sulam as she sought the same sympathy from her Christian readership. It is noteworthy in any case that Copia Sulam's is the first of these three apologist texts to be printed.

Copia Sulam's adoption of a perspective friendly to Catholicism in this debate does not imply, however, that she compromised her Jewish beliefs. If she consciously chose to depict Judaism in a way that was consonant with Catholicism (as is likely), it was a strategic choice, made as she faced down a dangerous adversary and meant to strengthen her defence of herself and her community before a Christian audience. A defence of her belief in the soul's immortality from within the Jewish tradition – for instance, along the lines of da Silva's treatise on the immortality of the soul[105] – would have weakened her appeal to a Catholic readership. If, in contrast, she adopted her position unintentionally, it shows a natural consonance of vision with her Catholic neighbours.[106] In either case, her strongly Catholicized vision of Judaism is evidence of the complicated relationship between the Christian and Jewish worlds.[107] Affirming her Jewish pride and insisting on Jewish difference while creating a vision of Judaism that was palatable to a Catholic audience, Copia Sulam constructed the sort of paradox that was central to the Italian Jewish experience in the early modern period.[108]

Copia Sulam Answers Bonifaccio's Verse

Copia Sulam concludes the *Manifesto* with two sonnets that depart from the urgency and combativeness of her prose address to Bonifaccio (see figure 3.3). In the first sonnet, she responds to the sonnet with which her detractor had concluded his own treatise, which urged her to set worldly beauty aside in search of spiritual perfection. Using the same rhyme, she answers:

> Ben so che la beltà ch'al mondo piace
> È fior caduco, e di superbia abonda:
> Ma de la spoglia fral che mi circonda,
> Qual si sia, stima in me l'alma non face.
>
> Per più nobil desio mio cor si sface,
> Baldassare, ond'ardita e sitibonda
> Quel fonte cerco, onde stillar suol l'onda
> Che rende ai nomi altrui fama verace.
>
> Né cercar dee altro fonte, od altro rio,
> chi di lasciar immortalmente viva
> La sua memoria al mondo ha pur desio.
>
> Che, s'a far l'alma in Ciel beata arriva
> Onda che bagni il volto o 'l petto mio,
> Di lacrime versar non sarò schiva. [109]

(Well do I know that the beauty the world enjoys
is but a delicate flower and abounds with pride:

> but my soul values not the mortal body
> that surrounds me, whatever it be.
>
> For a more noble desire does my heart come undone,
> Baldassare, whereby bold and eager,
> I seek that fount from which emerges the wave
> that brings true fame to others.[110]
>
> Nor need one who desires to leave
> memory forever alive in the world
> seek other source or other fount.
>
> Since if to bless my soul in Heaven
> a wave comes to bathe my face or breast,
> I will spare no tears.)

Copia Sulam uses simple syntax and a measured tone to counter Bonifaccio's claim (common against both women and Jews) that she focused too much on her exterior, physical being and too little on her spiritual one.[111] Yet she does not reject all worldly ambitions: she embraces the active search for earthly glory through her writing. Copia Sulam expresses this desire for fame – a motif throughout the *Manifesto* – most directly in this penultimate sonnet. She justified the pursuit of "true fame" – which stands in implicit contrast to the cheap sort of fame she accuses Bonifaccio of seeking through his unbridled use of the presses – by associating it with spiritual immortality.

In his concluding poem, Bonifaccio had urged Copia Sulam to seek out baptismal waters: "Run, run to the font that gives / Life."[112] Her sonnet of response is dominated by images of water – *fonte* (fount), *onda* (wave), *rio* (brook), *lacrime* (tears) – that substitute his immortalizing waters with her own: those of Parnassus that would bring her immortal fame,[113] and the waves of religious devotion and tears of gratitude that would grant her soul immortal life. Transforming Bonifaccio's literal water – the still liquid in the sacramental basin – into a powerful torrent, Copia Sulam offers a commanding metaphor for her literary and her spiritual worth.

Copia Sulam closes her treatise with a sonnet addressed to the human soul (see figure 3.3).

> Oh di vita mortal forma divina,
> e dell'opre di DIO meta sublime,
> in cui se stesso e 'l suo potere esprime,
> e di quanto ei creò ti fe' reina.

Rifpofta di Sarra Sulam.

En sò che la beltà ch' al mondo piace
E' fior caduco, e di fuperbia abonda:
Ma de la fpogliafral che mi circonda
Qual fi fia, ftima in me l' alma non face.
Per più nobil defio mio cor fi sface
Baldaffare, ond' ardita e fitibonda
Quel fonte cerco, onde ftillar fuol l' onda
Che rende a i nomi altrui fama verace.
Ne cercar dee altro Fonte, od altro Rio,
Chi di lafciar immortalmente viua
La fua memoria al mondo hà pur defio.
Che s' a far l' alma in Ciel beata arriua
Onde, che bagni il uolto, ò l petto mio
Di lacrime uerfar non farò fchiua.

Della medefima. Sonetto all'Anima humana.

O Di vita mortal forma diuina,
E dell' opre di Dio meta fublime,
In cui fe fteffo, e'l fuo potere efprime,
E di quanto ei creò ti fe Reina.
Mentre che l' huomo informi, in cui confina
L' immortal co'l mortale, e tra le prime
Effenze, hai fede nel volar da l' ime
Parti, là doue il Ciel a te s' inchina.
Stupido pur d' inueftigarti hor ceffi
Penfier che verfa tra caduchi oggetti,
Che fol ti fcopri allhor ch' a Dio t' appreffi,
E per far paghi qui gl' Humani petti,
Bafti faper che fon gl' Angeli fteffi
A cuftodirti, & a feruirti eletti.

3.3 The two sonnets with which Copia Sulam closes her *Manifesto* (Venice: appresso Giovanni Alberti, 1621). This image is from the first edition (text *a*). By permission of the Ministero per i Beni e le Attività Culturale – Biblioteca Nazionale Marciana (Misc. 2503.5). Further reproduction is prohibited.

Mente[114] che l'uomo informi, in cui confina
L'immortal col mortale, e tra le prime
Essenze hai sede nel volar da l'ime
Parti, là dove il Cielo a te s'inchina.
Stupido pur d'investigarti or cessi
Pensier, che versa tra caduchi oggetti,
che sol ti scopri allor ch'a DIO t'appressi,
e per far paghi qui gli umani petti,
Basti saper che son gli angeli stessi
A custodirti e a servirti eletti.

(O divine form of mortal life,
and sublime purpose of God's works,
in which he expresses himself and his power,
and made you queen of all he created.
You are the mind that forms man,
in which the immortal and the mortal join, and among the prime
essences you dwell, flying from the lowest
places, where Heaven bows to you.
Now may cease the thoughts that flow amid fleeting objects
and are bewildered just by considering you,
for you only reveal yourself as you approach God.
And to satisfy human hearts here,
may it be enough to know that angels themselves
are chosen to guard you and serve you.[115])

With this final poem, as with the opening dedication to her deceased
father, Copia Sulam does not merely state but demonstrates her belief in
the soul's immortality. She addresses the immortal soul directly, rejecting
reasoning about the soul in favour of faith, thus rebuffing Bonifaccio's bela-
boured point-by-point proof of the tenet. But in this intimate dialogue, she
makes no overt reference to her antagonist, whom she effaces as she shifts
her focus towards the divine. This erasure was strategic: by showcasing her
poetic talent with no reference to her adversary, she gives an example of the
sort of writing – poetic rather than polemic – that deserved her attention
and merited use of the presses. The poem, which celebrates piety based on
spiritual longing, resembles Catholic devotional poetry of the late-sixteenth
and seventeenth centuries. She thus ends her *Manifesto* with a poem that
fit reassuringly into Counter-Reformation notions of religious orthodoxy.

This spiritual conclusion is part of the remarkably careful structuring
of the *Manifesto*, achieved despite its hurried composition. Copia Sulam
frames her direct response to Bonifaccio – the text's prose centre and

the first poem after it – with other writing (the note to readers, the dedication, and the prefatory and concluding spiritual poetry) that strength-
ens her case against him. In the opening materials, Copia Sulam entices
her readers with her coy discussion (in print) of her reticence to print,
and she prepares the ground for a direct attack against her adversary
with martial introductory sonnets. These sonnets, addressed to God, also
show her religious piety, which is further demonstrated in the dedication
to her deceased father. When she finally turns to Bonifaccio, therefore,
she no longer needs to prove her beliefs but only to denounce the opponent who unjustly assailed her. Once she answers him, she turns her gaze
back to heaven with the pious poem that closes the tract and elides, as
does every other section of the *Manifesto*, Jewish–Catholic differences.

Bonifaccio Responds

Bonifaccio published his brief *Risposta* (figure 3.4), in early August 1621.
In it, he makes a vicious personal attack against Copia Sulam that he no
longer cloaks, as he did in the *Immortalità*, with theological concerns. He
predicates his scathing reply on the friendship he feigns with the salonnière, which he says he hoped to strengthen by his *Immortalità*, written
"with the most noble purpose and the constant intention of earning your
love and good favor."[116] He represents his treatise against Copia Sulam as
a token of his affection, ignoring the dangers he posed to her in publishing it, not to mention his disparagement of her within it. While depicting
his *Immortalità* as innocent, Bonifaccio portrays her *Manifesto* as malicious,
positioning her as the aggressor. He angrily catalogues the *Manifesto*'s
many charges against him and dismisses them, one by one, as ignorant
and petty, though he claims up front that "you aren't able to respond to
my reasoning, and I don't want to respond to your insults."[117] Despite
his palpable anger – more of which we will witness below – he writes that
she had offended not him but the notion of friendship. Nevertheless,
he claims that their friendship would continue: "Since I have not been
insulted by you, even if you call me your adversary, nothing you can do
would divert me from being your true friend. And so you will be to me, if
I have not misunderstood the kindness of your nature."[118]

   Bonifaccio, then, emphasizes the strength of his friendship with Copia
Sulam even as he defames her anew. The most damning aspect of the
Risposta by far was her 1620 letter, which he published as an appendix.
That letter, which shows the warmly cordial relationship they had enjoyed
in the past, does not so much prove the friendship that Bonifaccio
claims still existed but rather its betrayal: by bringing to press a private
letter that had been exchanged as part of an ongoing correspondence

RISPOSTA
AL MANIFESTO
Della Signora
SARA COPIA.
Del Signor
BALDASSARE BONIFACCIO.
Con Licenza de'Superiori, & Priuilegio.

IN VENETIA,

Appreſſo Antonio Pinelli.

M DC XXI.   5ª

3.4 Baldassare Bonifaccio's *Risposta al Manifesto* (Venice: appresso Antonio Pinelli, 1621). By permission of the Ministero per i Beni e le Attività Culturale – Biblioteca Nazionale Marciana (Misc. 2503.5.A). Further reproduction is prohibited.

between friends, Bonifaccio violated the bonds of trust that should have governed salon discussions whether in conversation or in correspondence. As discussed above, Copia Sulam's letter articulated a materialist viewpoint and argued that the soul was mortal. While his publication of the letter provided clear evidence that Copia Sulam had set forth these views, Copia Sulam herself had already explained them away in the *Manifesto*, stating that she had voiced such sceptical thoughts in order to hear how he responded to them, not because they represented her true beliefs.[119] Bonifaccio suggests that the views she expressed in the letter were erroneous enough to require his intervention, writing that "I was, I say, not only invited by you but pushed and compelled to respond to you with what I wrote."[120] He does not otherwise comment on the letter, letting its scandalous content speak for itself.

The publication of this letter continued the assault on Copia Sulam's orthodoxy that Bonifaccio had launched in the *Immortalità*. In his *Risposta*, he pairs this attack with one on her intellectual honesty, repeatedly accusing her of plagiarism.[121] He claims that "the rabbi"[122] – clearly a reference to Modena – was the real author of two important pieces of writing that she had signed: the letter that had prompted his *Immortalità* in the first place and the entire *Manifesto*. While categorically denying Copia Sulam authorship of both pieces of writing, he makes no attempt to explain why, if he believed the 1620 letter was Modena's, he directed his *Immortalità* to Copia Sulam. Instead, he lashes out against Modena for his supposed participation, but makes these attacks, too, under the guise of friendship. Having expressed his affectionate friendship for Copia Sulam, he writes: "With the same affection I will always love him who, just as he dictated to you the first letter, which prompted my discourse on immortality, also fed you the work you call '*Manifesto*' ... He, I say, and not you, because I recognize the strange idioms of his speech and those conceits that always spill out of his mouth."[123] Bonifaccio advertises his previous intimacy with Copia Sulam and Modena by claiming to know their way of speaking and style of reasoning, gained through personal interaction.[124] He likely professes to have this intimate knowledge to bolster the credibility of his claims and to showcase his participation in Copia Sulam's exclusive coterie. But at the same time that he reveals the close bonds that had developed between the participants in Copia Sulam's salon, he destroys them.

It is not incidental that Bonifaccio charges Modena, rather than Copia Sulam's Christian associates, with authoring the *Manifesto*. His response features the same thinly disguised anti-Jewish sentiment of his original tract, which he here directs against both Copia Sulam and Modena. Tapping into Christian fears of Jewish conspiracy, he suggests that the two had colluded to misrepresent her authorship. He also makes use of

stereotypical notions about Jewish superstition to criticize her for seeking to explain his hidden motivation for publishing the *Immortalità*: if
some pagan men examined animals' internal organs in order to foretell
the future, he says, "I see that among the Jews [*giudei*] there are women
who quite confidently investigate the internal organs of men."[125] His use
of the disparaging term *giudei* here was no accident.[126] Elsewhere, he
expresses outrage that Modena defaulted on a debt to him, a laden metaphor in a time when Christian resentment against Jewish moneylending
was rife.[127] He claims that while he had promoted Modena's interests
and fortunes, Modena, "spending that coin that only can be struck in
his mint, repays me with bitter invective."[128] In case these asides did not
make his feelings clear, Bonifaccio closes his *Risposta* by insisting on the
inferiority of Jews. He mocks Copia Sulam for her belief in heaven, "[t]o
which it seems you wish to believe that I, as a Christian man, and you, as
a Jewish woman [*giudea*], can equally aspire."[129] Bonifaccio suggests, in
fact, that the opposite was true: heaven was only for Christians. His conclusion thus emphasizes what he proposes to be a fundamental difference between Christianity and Judaism, whose consonance was instead a
centrepiece of Copia Sulam's *Manifesto*.

Bonifaccio paired his revilement of Copia Sulam as a Jew with his
revilement of her as a woman, a two-pronged offensive that is exemplified by these concluding remarks: as a Jewish woman she was doubly
inferior to him, a Christian man. At the start of the *Risposta*, he affects
backing away from the fight since his opponent was a woman, claiming
that "such a contest, since you are a female [*femina*], would be disad-
vantageous to me."[130] And yet he uses the work to disparage her specifically as a woman. In addition to the charge of plagiarism discussed
above, he mocks her pretensions of learning, sarcastically crediting her
for teaching him basic concepts: "I also understand from your lessons
that knowledge is the basis of good writing."[131] He offers this false gratitude amid a litany of what he claims are errors in the *Manifesto*. He also
suggests that she – whom he had feigned to celebrate in his *Immortalità*
as "such an erudite teacher"[132] – was entirely dependent on her male
associates. It is hard to argue against her, Bonifaccio mocks: "I, unlike
you, do not have such a copiousness of great teachers, under whose guidance you suddenly reached such perfection that you offer to teach me
not only the most recondite learning but our vernacular language."[133]
Although he denies her credit for her writing and ideas, he simultaneously criticizes her for them: he expresses resentment that she dares to
correct him, while at the same time depicting her as nothing more than
a puppet of her male associates. As the charge of intellectual dishonesty intensifies his religious diatribe, as seen above, so it also feeds his

gendered attack. Where some of his anti-Jewish sentiment is oblique – he employs anti-Jewish stereotypes without explicitly mentioning them – his disparagement of Copia Sulam as a woman and as a female intellectual is obvious. In a letter written a few months after his *Risposta*, Bonifaccio pairs such attacks on her religious and intellectual integrity with a patent suggestion – recalling Cebà's – of Copia Sulam's sexual misconduct: in the more intimate forum of the letter, with no pretense of friendship to uphold, Bonifaccio refers to Copia Sulam as "Jezabel," a woman represented in the Bible as a figure of intellectual, religious, and sexual depravity.[134] He flagrantly accuses Copia Sulam of heresy and suggests that because of her "unchastity" (*impudicitia*), she ("Jezabel") had become an outcast in the Jewish community, on which she had brought disgrace.[135] In his *Risposta*, such suggestions of sexual impropriety hover beneath the surface, implicit in the insistence on the close and morally suspect connection between Copia Sulam and her male associates.

In the *Risposta*, Bonifaccio ignores almost entirely the questions regarding the press that Copia Sulam had raised in her *Manifesto*. He was offended that she accused him of printing in haste (which, he notes, contradicted her claim that he had spent two years preparing the treatise),[136] but he does not otherwise comment on the appropriate use of print. Such questions were surely difficult for him to tackle, since by rushing to print his *Risposta* – as Copia Sulam had anticipated – he clearly demonstrated his precipitousness. As if to defend himself against that charge, he accuses her (or, in fact, "the Rabbi")[137] of haste in composing the *Manifesto* – a crime of which Copia Sulam had already declared herself guilty by proudly claiming in the work that she had written it in two days. He does not, however, criticize her for hurrying her treatise to press – or indeed for committing it to print at all. For Bonifaccio, it seems, print was the perfect forum for this controversy, which he sought to stoke, not put to rest, by foregrounding the most sensational aspects of the conflict – gender and religious polemics. It was a conflict in which he assumed that he, as a Christian man, had the natural advantage. He feigns retreat from the fight, however, claiming that "it would be an indecent spectacle to see, on this side of an arena a priest, and on that side a Jewish woman, compete in tumbling and falling."[138] But he seems instead to relish the fight, perhaps exactly because it was a spectacle he could display before all of Venice by means of the presses. Indeed, the *Risposta* begins to map out his next entry against Copia Sulam.[139]

But Copia Sulam never answered him, refusing to perpetuate the self-promotional print battle into which he tried to bait her. Her refusal to respond was in accordance with the scrupulous vision of publishing presented in the *Manifesto*, where she rejects the notion that "fame consists in having many volumes out."[140] Bonifaccio's *Risposta* – with its new and unsavoury attacks on her beliefs and integrity, not to mention on her as both woman and Jew – would only have increased her distaste for the sort of hasty, careless publishing that a continued controversy would fuel as it ravaged her reputation. With her silence, she turned away from publishing polemics and treated Bonifaccio's insults against her as unworthy of response. But her readers, who had quickly bought up multiple editions of the *Manifesto*, could still expect – as Copia Sulam had intimated – other works that "might be greeted more eagerly and perhaps better enjoyed by the world."[141]

4
Copia Sulam Compromised (1622–1623)

ᙏᙏᙏ

Overview

After Copia Sulam wrote and published her *Manifesto* in the summer of 1621 in response to Bonifaccio's attack on her religious beliefs, her correspondence with Cebà – according to the published record – immediately trailed off. In a letter of 17 July, Cebà told her of "a tribulation that is currently piercing me through" that would prevent him from writing "for some time."[1] The exchange that had been monthly and sometimes weekly suddenly came to a halt for six months. In January 1622, Cebà sent Copia Sulam an extremely brief letter. He then put an end to the correspondence with two letters dated March and April 1622. During this period, as we have seen, Cebà was fighting his own battle against charges of religious irregularity: in March 1621, the Congregation of the Index had asserted that his epic poem *La reina Esther* was unorthodox. While defending himself against this charge, he all but ceased his correspondence with the Jewish woman whose orthodoxy Bonifaccio had publicly thrown into doubt.

Cebà died in October of 1622, anguished to the very end by the censure of his epic poem. His friend and literary executor Marcantonio Doria continued to fight for that work's exoneration. He also took on the task of publishing Cebà's letters to Copia Sulam, which were issued in 1623 as *Lettere a Sarra Copia* (see figure 4.1). The volume was unflattering to Copia Sulam in many ways. It is unclear whether she sanctioned its publication.

The End of the Copia Sulam–Cebà Correspondence

The change in the Copia Sulam–Cebà correspondence after the *Manifesto* crisis is startling. In June 1621 – before the controversy exploded – Cebà wrote four solicitous letters to Copia Sulam, fearing for her health after

LETTERE
D'ANSALDO
CEBÀ
Scritte
A SARRA COPIA
E DEDICATE
A
MARC'ANTONIO DORIA.

IN GENOVA,
PER GIUSEPPE PAVONI.
MDCXXIII.
CON LICENZA DE' SVPERIORI.

4.1 The title page of Cebà's book of letters to Copia Sulam (Genoa: per Giuseppe Pavoni, 1623). Courtesy of Beinecke Rare Book and Manuscript Library, Yale University.

she reported a serious illness.[2] She notified him in a letter of 9 July of Bonifaccio's treatise and of her intention to respond, from which Cebà tried to dissuade her in a letter of 17 July.[3] She sent him a printed copy of her *Manifesto*, along with a letter, on 8 August, by which time Bonifaccio had published his *Risposta*. The intense personal vitriol Bonifaccio expressed against Copia Sulam in this response – not to mention the compromising letter of hers he published with it – provided new urgency for Cebà's backing. Yet such support never came. Cebà later wrote that her letter and the *Manifesto* took some seven months to come to him, finally arriving 1 March 1622.[4] He responded nearly three weeks after that date, mentioning the receipt of her parcel only offhandedly towards the end of a letter dated 19 March 1622: "I do acknowledge the receipt of your Apology, which together with your letter of 8 August was brought to me on the first of this month."[5] With these few words, Cebà dismisses Copia Sulam's most important literary accomplishment.

He makes no other comment on her work, but concludes the letter by warning her to "remember that it is not enough for you to believe that the soul is immortal if you don't also follow the path to render it blessed."[6] In this oblique reference to the *Manifesto*, he makes yet another plea for her to embrace Christianity. Her conversion would have been especially welcome to him in this period, since it could have proven that his *La reina Esther*, the text that drew her to him, was serving a Christian purpose. But his letter suggests that he no longer expected her to follow his advice and that he had, in essence, given up on her ever becoming a Christian. Indeed, Cebà asks Copia Sulam to stop writing him since he needs to leave his earthly affections, pleading, "Let me die without tormenting me anymore with your letters."[7]

In his last published letter to Copia Sulam, dated a month and a half later (30 April 1622), Cebà describes what he imagined was her endless desire for his writings, a yearning he depicts throughout his letters as an almost boundless sexual appetite.[8] Here he defends, in blatantly sexual terms, his ability to fulfill her: "I know everything that you are and that you want from me, and I repeatedly satisfy your desire with my pen."[9] Using the common double entendre between pen (*penna*) and penis (*pene*),[10] he claims to have discharged his duty to a lustful Copia Sulam. Cebà's pointed defence of his ability to satisfy her, however, betrays frustration at his inability to penetrate her in either amorous or spiritual ways. He asserts in the same letter that Copia Sulam was using him.[11] Claiming that a thirst for fame drove her self-interested relationship with him, he writes: "Worldly glory is what you seek, while you try by means of literary study to separate yourself from the common masses of females (*femine*). But the world, as you know, can provide nothing stable, and, even if it could, little would it matter that your name were remembered for many centuries while your soul were tortured for centuries without end."[12] Cebà highlights a tension between worldly glory and eternal salvation that had been a theme in Italian letters since the time of Petrarch.[13] But it is not the struggle of a Christian man that Cebà describes; instead, in his framing, Copia Sulam enters the battle with a double deficiency as a woman and a Jew. As regards the former, this last letter is a palinode of the first, in which Cebà praises Copia Sulam's literary interests, saying that they separated her from her sex.[14] He now belittles these pursuits as her calculated but ultimately futile attempt to separate herself from the "common masses of females." But the risk to Copia Sulam is not just the mediocrity of womanhood; as a Jew, she faced torment to her soul "for centuries without end" because her pursuit of glory distracted her from converting. He makes a lukewarm declaration of love and a halfhearted last plea for her conversion, but then gives up his attempts to bend her to his will: "If you don't plan to convert, please suspend your pen, since without this purpose, I do not plan to employ mine."[15] Without her conversion, Cebà was no longer interested in a correspondence with Copia Sulam, especially while facing a challenge to his own orthodoxy. During this very same month, his friend Doria reported that Cebà was "dismayed and afflicted because of this wretched poem," his *La reina Esther*.[16]

Cebà Defends Himself to the Church

When Cebà counselled Copia Sulam to remain silent in the face of Bonifaccio's attack on her orthodoxy, he admitted that he himself would not be able to follow this advice.[17] In fact, during the same period in which the Copia Sulam–Cebà correspondence disintegrated in the wake of the *Manifesto* controversy, Cebà dedicated himself to mounting a defence against the Congregation of the Index's censure of his work.

When Cebà learned that his work had been suspended until revised, he received no details about the charges against it.[18] Only with some insistence did he learn that these had to do with the work's "obscenity" (*oscenità*). He defended his work against these charges in a letter dated 20 August 1621 to Cardinal Alessandro d'Este, a well-known patron of the arts and a powerful figure in Rome whom Cebà had met during his studies in Padua.[19] Cebà's patron, Marcantonio Doria, who was in close touch with Este and regularly traded letters and gifts with him,[20] had explained Cebà's troubles to Este and asked him to intervene on the writer's behalf.[21] In his own letter to Este, Cebà addressed the charge of obscenity, describing it as "more in words than in meaning."[22] He also mentioned the other main criticism against the work: the presence of "a few small contradictions that can be noted between the text of the poem and that of Scripture."[23] Cebà promised to prepare a letter defending the work against this charge. In the meantime, he asked Este to try to ensure that the Church's actions were fair since, he suspected, the charges may have been a personally motivated attack. Indeed, Cebà believed that *La reina Esther* had been represented as "much more licentious" than it was:[24]

> The inquisition [*inquisitione*] that I hear being made into this poem, almost seven years after it was published, and the similarity that I find between the objections of the Congregation and those of some others make me suspect that someone went to Rome and persuaded a minister of the Tribunal to claim that I compiled a book that – with most obscene descriptions of sacred stories and with scandalous contradictions of these, made of profane lies – might contaminate minds with lasciviousness and sow the Church with errors. Who this minister is I have no idea ... but I am just saying what I suspect.[25]

Cebà focuses less on debunking the charges of lasciviousness and more on the conspiracy that, he suggests, lay behind them. A week later, he wrote another letter to Este that expressed even more strongly his belief that a personal vendetta stood behind the Congregation's actions.[26] His suspicion is validated by a contemporary account.[27]

The letters Cebà wrote to Este were part of his intensive effort to defend his *La reina Esther* throughout the summer and fall of 1621. He also wrote directly to the members of the Congregation of the Index, imploring them to stop short of demanding that he revise and reprint his poem – which, he wrote, "because of the wretched state in which I find myself, I know is beyond my ability."[28] He offered instead to write a preface that would correct the offending passages and he eventually wrote a lengthy Latin defence, in which he answered in great detail all of the charges against his work.[29] Marcantonio Doria also worked tirelessly to free *La reina Esther* from the Congregation's censure, writing as often as weekly to Este to remind him of the urgency of the affair.[30] Thanks to Este's intervention, Cebà made some inroads with the Congregation. In particular, Este gained Cebà the backing of an influential member: the erudite Genoese Dominican theologian Niccolò Riccardi (1585–1639),[31] who would later help clear the path to publication for Galileo's *Dialogo sopra i due massimi sistemi del mondo* (Dialogue Concerning the Two Chief World Systems).[32] The head of the Congregation, Bonifazio Bevilaqua (1571–1627), was also sympathetic.[33] However, the work also had powerful opponents, such as Maffeo Barberini (1568–1644),[34] who would ascend to the papacy as Urban VIII in 1623 (pope 1623–1644) and would later condemn Galileo.[35]

Cebà died in October 1622, suffering to the last under the heavy weight of *La reina Esther*'s censure,[36] but even after his death his friends persisted in fighting for his vindication, and Doria continued to write frequently to Este to advocate for the "liberation" of Cebà's work.[37] Este's own death in May 1624, however, deprived the work of one of its most important defenders, and the suspension was never lifted.[38]

Cebà's censure by the Congregation of the Index cast a long shadow over the last year of the Copia Sulam–Cebà correspondence. Facing charges centring around lasciviousness and religious irregularity, Cebà began to sever his ties to his correspondent who had faced – from him and then from Bonifaccio – accusations of the same. These charges were redoubled in Cebà's *Lettere a Sarra Copia* (1623), a collection whose framing may well have been determined by the ongoing controversy over *La reina Esther*.

The *Lettere a Sarra Copia*

As noted above, it was Marcantonio Doria, Cebà's patron and friend, who arranged the publication of Cebà's letters to Copia Sulam in 1623, the year after the writer's death. Her letters were not included. Cebà was far enough along in the planning of the collection before he died to dedicate it to Doria. The work was issued on the prestigious presses of Giuseppe Pavoni – Cebà's usual printer.[39] The *Lettere a Sarra Copia* participated in the letterbook vogue in sixteenth- and seventeenth-century Italy, a fashion that was born with the 1538 publication of the first volume of Pietro Aretino's *De le lettere* and that saw some 540 vernacular letterbooks published by the 1620s.[40] But while Cebà's collection fit into this popular genre, his volume was atypical within it since letterbooks rarely included letters to only one addressee.[41] Such a singular focus highlighted the salonnière's exceptionality and the special status of the Copia Sulam–Cebà correspondence. The Genoese writer underscored this distinction by publishing the letters to Copia Sulam separately from his general letter collection, *Lettere a Pallavicino*, which was also printed in 1623.[42]

In his dedication to the *Lettere a Sarra Copia*, Cebà presents the collection as a generous memorial to the Venetian writer: the volume was published out of gratitude for Copia Sulam's love, he claims, so that "some memory of her is preserved by means of these letters."[43] But he also uses the dedication – and the *Lettere* volume itself – to create a monument to his own literary works and life. The first line of his dedication touts the appeal of his embattled *Esther* poem, which had "prompted a noble Jewish woman (*hebrea*) to seek my friendship."[44] The relationship that resulted, he takes pains to underscore, had a Christian purpose: to improve Copia Sulam's and his own spiritual health.[45] Her conversion, he believed, would have aided both. Acknowledging that he had failed to win her to Christianity, he bequeaths the effort, along with the collection, to Doria, who could assure, he hopes, that "the Jewish woman (*giudea*), whom my letters advertised as generous, be known by means of your prayers as Christian."[46] The credit for such a conversion, in Cebà's account, would trace back to *La reina Esther*.

Another important element of the volume's front matter even more strongly affirmed Cebà's religious orthodoxy: an assurance from a named official of the Sant'Uffizio of Genoa (Giovan Vincenzo Bottazzini) that Cebà's letters did not contain "anything contrary to the Holy Faith nor to sound morals."[47] The Inquisitor of Genoa, Eliseus Masinius (Eliseo Masini, d. 1627), who had been involved with Cebà on other occasions, including over the censure of *La reina Esther*, signed the declaration.[48] Such imprimaturs were rare in Cebà's works that predated his trouble with the Inquisition. This imprimatur, along with the dedication it faced – which requested Doria's help in converting Copia Sulam – gave every appearance that Cebà was a devoutly religious man who planned the collection as a means to advance a Catholic purpose. This carefully crafted front matter also framed the reception of the religious debates in the *Lettere a Sarra Copia*, sanctioning Cebà's theological arguments against Copia Sulam.

The Copia Sulam–Cebà Exchange versus the Lettere a Sarra Copia

The calculated framing of this volume raises the question of its relationship to the original Copia Sulam–Cebà correspondence. Modern scholarship has clearly demonstrated that published letter collections are highly codified and meticulously crafted literary creations rather than faithful transcriptions of past epistolary exchanges.[49] For a letterbook, an author's own exigencies in creating a public literary persona naturally trumped loyalty to fact, and it was common for letterbooks to contain letters, or even whole correspondences, that were fabricated.[50] A writer could also, of course, choose to suppress a letter or several letters that were actually exchanged. We do know from an autograph letter by Copia Sulam – in addition to other contemporary accounts – that Cebà and Copia Sulam in fact carried on an ongoing epistolary relationship. The published correspondence, therefore, was rooted in an actual exchange. The 1623 collection indicates that Cebà retained copies of letters in anticipation of their eventual publication, a sign (in his published account) of his interest in documenting the actual epistolary exchange.[51] Though he based his volume on letters actually exchanged, it is almost certain that he altered them for publication. Such alterations could include minor amendments like small grammatical or orthographic interventions; they could also involve fundamental changes like the suppression of certain letters or the fabrication of others. The degree to which Cebà reshaped his letters for publication remains an open – and probably unanswerable – question, but it is one that cannot be left aside in a consideration of the published correspondence.

The very fact of the letters' publication fundamentally changed the nature of the exchange. Not only was one side of the correspondence missing from the collection, but the published volume included extensive paratextual material that shaped the letters' reception. This material includes not only the imprimatur of the Genoese Inquisitor and the dedication to Doria discussed above, but also the volume's material aspect, its publishing information, the letters' numbering, and prefatory notes that profess to explain certain statements from Copia Sulam's absent letters. The elegant publication of the text in quarto, the well-produced engravings on the frontispiece and colophon, the striking engraving of the author, the text's graceful italic type, and the relatively error-free copy all contribute to the impressive – and convincing – nature of the text. The publication of the text in Genoa, with Cebà's long-time publisher, placed the text in an environment as familiar to Cebà as it was alien to Copia Sulam, while the dedication to Doria not only touted the author's connection to this powerful man but implied the latter's support of the text's Christianizing mission that, in fact, Cebà entrusted to Doria to carry on.

The dedication also tells readers that the Copia Sulam–Cebà correspondence ended in failure because of Copia Sulam's refusal to convert, in effect (by anticipating this final result) removing the central narrative tension from the epistolary story. In other words, the dedication, as much as it attests to the author's orthodox Catholic motives, also suggests his correspondent's resistance to the Christian message. This impression is intensified in the prefatory notes that purportedly paraphrase some of Copia Sulam's statements from her letters. Many of her reported remarks are inflammatory, including several anti-Christian comments detailed below. In combination with the other paratextual materials, these notes act to reinforce the strength of the author's rhetorical position while undermining the salonnière's already inherently weak one.

Beyond the paratext that shaped the letters' reception, Cebà also had free rein over the letters themselves, and did not lack for motivation to alter them. As the dedication reveals, and as the published letters themselves recount, his correspondence with Copia Sulam ended after their increasingly tense confrontation over her refusal to convert. The situation escalated along with Cebà's problems with the Inquisition, and, as we have seen, he eventually ended the correspondence since, he says, his letters had failed to bring about her conversion. If he genuinely deemed the correspondence a failure – and if he in fact felt the increasing animosity towards his correspondent that he expresses in later letters – he would hardly have gone to special lengths to flatter her with the letter collection. Rather, it seems natural that he would have made changes, either small or large, to flatter himself or to slight her. Moreover, Cebà – as keenly aware of his mortality as he was of his fragile literary reputation and damaged religious credentials – would also have had reason to make such alterations to the correspondence as he believed would bolster his posthumous reputation. For instance, the more zeal the text showed him to have in his effort to convert Copia Sulam, the more pious and orthodox he would appear, contradicting unwelcome perceptions of religious irregularity created by *La reina Esther*'s censure. His goals were surely quite at odds with any goals that Copia Sulam had, primary among which was her quest to establish her literary reputation, a pursuit Cebà portrays in his published collection as a grave distraction from her spiritual health.[52]

But Cebà's own illness – along with his ambitious late publishing agenda – limited his ability to reshape the correspondence for publication. He suffered from failing health during the final years of his life and complained throughout the letters that illness interfered with his writing.[53] Yet he published five works in 1621, the year before he died, and left five other works to be published after his death in October 1622, less than six months after he ended the correspondence with Copia Sulam.[54] He was, moreover, engaged in the battle to defend *La reina Esther*, his most important last cause – and even that, he said, was impeded by his failing health.[55]

In addition to the health-related circumstances that limited Cebà's ability to intervene, the overall reliability of the *Lettere a Sarra Copia* as a transcript of the Copia Sulam–Cebà correspondence is bolstered by the fact that the collection's faithfulness was never questioned in contemporary accounts, although we know that associates in Genoa and Venice followed the manuscript exchange closely. Moreover, there are several instances in which we have other sources that confirm the content of Cebà's letters.[56] There are other elements of the correspondence – most notably, his insinuations about Copia Sulam's inappropriate contact with men and intimations of his own sexual desire for her – which it is quite difficult to believe he would have invented for publication. This specific element of the exchange, which was of course highly problematic for her, would also have been problematic for him at a moment when he was facing charges from the Inquisition about the lasciviousness of *La reina Esther*. It seems much more likely that Cebà, had he had time to edit the letters more carefully, would have downplayed or eliminated these sexual suggestions.

At his death, Cebà left the Copia Sulam letter volume to Doria not only as dedicatee but also as the party responsible for its publication. Because Cebà wrote the dedication before his death, we might assume that the volume was finished and that Doria had only to usher the work into print. Doria, however, made at least one substantive change to the volume: he removed a letter, dated 1 November 1619, at Copia Sulam's behest. She wrote both to him and to his wife to request the change. The letter may have regarded the discussion on the immortality of the soul that was unfolding in her salon during that period.[57] Doria's willingness to accommodate this change indicates that he was not completely loyal to the text that Cebà left. It is possible that he made other alterations to the correspondence that seemed expedient, eliminating information that was uncomfortable or unflattering to Cebà, to Copia Sulam, or to the many other people who are mentioned. A natural area of interest for Doria would have been the depiction of his wife, Isabella della Tolfa, whose role he might have wanted to highlight – or downplay – in the published collection.

Looking at the volume as a whole, then, it is clear that the extensive paratext – the frontispiece, the inquisitor's imprimatur, the dedication, the prefatory notes, and the engravings discussed above – as well as one major editorial change distance the published correspondence from the letter exchange upon which it was based. At the level of the individual published missives, however, several indices – the lack of contemporary objection regarding the accuracy of the letters; the external validation of facts presented in several letters; the presence of elements that would have been problematic for Cebà himself; and his lack of opportunity to make changes because of his compromised health and distraction by the controversy over *La reina Esther*, not to mention his ambitious publishing agenda – may indicate a substantial similarity between the actual letters Cebà sent and those that were published. Nevertheless, we must be careful to keep in mind that we are using a published volume to interpret Cebà's letters to Copia Sulam, rather than the letters that were sent.

The Absence of Copia Sulam's Letters

An issue central to the reception of the Copia Sulam–Cebà exchange is the absence of her letters from his published volume. These letters have not been found, and scholars generally conclude that Cebà destroyed them. The exclusion of her letters from the published collection has been variously interpreted either as his attempt to protect Copia Sulam from trouble with religious authorities or as his effort to silence her. Whatever his purpose in omitting them, the volume's perspective, in their absence, is necessarily lopsided.

Nevertheless, however frustrating it might be to readers, Cebà's decision to exclude Copia Sulam's letters cannot in itself be considered a slight. In fact, contemporary letterbooks almost always featured just the author's side of a correspondence. This construction allowed an author's voice – and self-portraiture – to remain front and centre while correspondents were addressed but not permitted to respond. The triangulated relationship with the reader, who was allowed to eavesdrop, gave letterbook authors additional power as they broadcast their side of purportedly private conversations to another audience. These elements were an integral part of the letterbook's appeal to both authors and readers.[58] Thus Cebà, in including only his side of the exchange (as he also did in his general letterbook of the same year) was simply following standard conventions.[59]

What was unusual, however – and what would have been particularly problematic for Copia Sulam – were the prefatory notes on her statements that prefaced the published letters. Cebà presents the notes as part of his address to readers, explaining that "because some things are addressed in these letters that might not be fully understood if one did not know the reason why they were said, certain statements from those letters of signora Sarra have been noted here, in order to help the reader understand these."[60] Far from an attempt to communicate Copia Sulam's point of view, Cebà declares that his notes on her letters only appear in order to make his more intelligible. He admits that even this effort may have failed, however, since "some statements might have been overlooked that would be necessary to the purposes mentioned above."[61] Though he does not explain her letters' exclusion (surely in part because this was standard practice), he acknowledges that their absence would frustrate a clear understanding of the text, a difficulty that the notes, he acknowledges, do not fully solve.

Copia Sulam's Anti-Christian Polemic

The notes on Copia Sulam's statements – which appear immediately after the dedication, in the note to readers (figure 4.2) – attribute to her several provocative anti-Christian statements. Cebà includes just enough of what she wrote to associate her with controversial ideas without, however, giving her the chance to make her own case. The notes, which capture the back-and-forth nature of the correspondence, also bolster the *Lettere a Sarra*

AL LETTORE.

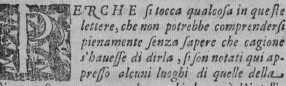

E*RCHE* *ſi tocca qualcoſa in queſte lettere, che non potrebbe comprenderſi pienamente ſenza ſapere che cagione s'haueſſe di dirla , ſi ſon notati qui ap- preſſo alcuni luoghi di quelle della* Signora Sarra *per ageuolar a chi leggerà l'intelli- genza di queſte . E però , quand'egli vedrà nella mar- gine qualche ſegno numerale , potrà cercare qui il ſuo riſcontro , e prendere la cognitione , che gli farà di bi ſogno : preſupponendo con tutto ciò , che non ſi ſia fat ta ne anche in queſto tutta la diligenza, che ſarebbe conuenuta ; e che perciò ſi poſſano eſſere tralaſciati qualch'altri luoghi neceſſarij per la dichiaratione ſopradetta . 1. la Signora Sarra , ſotto metafora di frutto , che naſce tardo , s'era ſcuſata d'hauer tar- dato a ſcriuere . 2. s'era doluta d'eſſere ſtata vici- na a morte per parto abortiuo . 3. hauea dannata la nouità della legge Chriſtiana col ſeguente prouer- bio . Che chi'l vecchio camin pel nouo laſcia , Speſſo s'inganna , e poi ne ſente ambaſcia . 4. hauea detto d'hauer occhi Lincei in materia di Religione . 5. hauea ſcritto d'hauer allogato nel ſuo cuore il libro del Cittadino . 6. hauea detto , che tenea ſul guan- ciale del ſuo letto il Poema d'Eſther . 7. hauea mandata vna pettiniera lauorata di ſua mano , e chiamatala con nome di fiori , e ſomigliatala all'ac- qua , che ſù donata ad Artaſſerſe &c. 8. hauea ſcrit- to, che*

4.2 The first page of the *Lettere a Sarra Copia*'s note to readers (1623), which includes numbered references to statements Copia Sulam supposedly made in her letters to Cebà. Cebà's published letters include cross-references to these notes. Courtesy of Beinecke Rare Book and Manuscript Library, Yale University.

Copia's impression of veracity. We cannot know if the notes faithfully report the contents of Copia Sulam's manuscript letters, but at a minimum they show the sorts of ideas her contemporaries attributed to her. They also suggest – with many degrees of possible distortion – that she was a clever, at times downright funny, religious pugilist (her sense of humour also comes through in the *Manifesto*) who went toe-to-toe with the humourless Cebà. But if Copia Sulam bested him with some retorts in their exchange, as these notes suggest, the *Lettere a Sarra Copia*'s advertisement of such victories might have harmed her cause with a Christian readership.

Many of the notes document Copia Sulam's justification of her decision to retain her Jewish faith, for instance:

> She had condemned the newness of the Christian faith with the following proverb: "Whoever leaves the old path for the new frequently is misled and later regrets it."

> She had said she was a Jew (*hebrea*) and not a Gentile, and she raised up the dignity of her faith.

> She said she wanted her tomb in the same place she had had her cradle, that is, that since she was born a Jew (*hebrea*), she wanted to die a Jew (*hebrea*).

> She had complained about the fact that it was held to be a vice of hers that she was born a Jew (*giudea*).[62]

These affirmations were only implicitly anti-Christian, as Copia Sulam upheld (according to Cebà) the dignity of the Jewish law in order to justify her decision not to convert. Nevertheless, her defence of the Jewish faith had as its corollary a rejection of the Christian one.

Other statements entered more directly into fraught religious territory. Cebà relates, for instance, two exchanges in which Copia Sulam jocularly rejected the baptism he urged on her. He reports:

> She had said that she yearned more for the waters of Parnassus than those of baptism.

> She had written ... that she had no need of water, since she was born in the middle of the sea, meaning that she didn't need baptism.[63]

Copia Sulam rebuffed the sacrament of baptism as part of her defence of her Jewish faith. However, the offhand humour ascribed to her in the second instance dismissed the gravity of this sacred rite that represented a basic division between Christians and Jews. Indeed, as Brian Pullan notes, the rite of baptism was a guiding factor in the Inquisition's interactions with Jews, and with the exception of a short period in the 1580s, the Inquisition did not make concerted efforts to judge and punish Jews who had not been baptized.[64] The question of baptism took on additional gravity in Counter-Reformation Europe since it was contested by Protestants as well: most radically, Anabaptists questioned the validity of infant baptism, while other Protestants redefined the Catholic ritual. The jokes Cebà attributed to Copia Sulam about the rite thus risked touching a raw nerve.

Cebà credits to Copia Sulam another statement that was especially fraught because of the Protestant threat: "She had written that God cannot be represented on earth since he cannot be materially formed."[65] Copia Sulam, in other words, defended the Jewish rejection of sacred images.[66] The defence recalled a central point of tension between Catholics and Protestants: as Pullan notes, Jewish prohibitions of images and other practices "at times overlapped perilously with those of Protestant heresy."[67] Her supposed affirmation of this principle risked stirring the deep anxieties that the Jewish presence provoked in a Catholic population still reeling in the face of the religious rebellion of fellow Christians. Even more damning, mention of the Jewish rejection of incarnation (God "cannot be materially formed") highlighted a fundamental point of difference between Judaism and Christianity.[68]

Other statements that Cebà attributes to her were even more directly hostile to the Christian faith. He reports that "she had said that she could not speak against our faith except when she was alone in her room" and that "she had refused the prayers for her conversion unless they could be reciprocal."[69] Rather than merely defending Judaism, she here appears as actively contesting Catholicism both by maligning it (supposedly in private, though Cebà makes public the fact if not the content of her objection) and by suggesting (even if in jest) that she would seek his conversion to Judaism. A final statement that the note to readers attributes to her – that she "had said she was sharp-sighted in religious matters"[70] – suggests a haughtiness in Copia Sulam's attitude towards Christianity. From Cebà's letters themselves, many other anti-Christian comments can be inferred: that she disdained the New Testament as beneath her,[71] characterized Christ as a "mere man,"[72] sought "to demean the Christian faith,"[73] and sought Cebà's circumcision.[74]

Potential for Danger from Authorities

That Cebà quoted Copia Sulam (accurately or not) on such contested religious points raises the question of whether he was trying to create difficulties for her with religious or lay authorities. As Brian Pullan notes, the Venetian Inquisition had jurisdiction mostly over baptized Christians "who flirted with Judaism, who mingled Judaism with Christianity, who alternated between Christianity and Judaism, or who withdrew from Christianity altogether and transferred their allegiance to the Jewish faith."[75] None of these categories would have applied to Copia Sulam, whose firm adherence to Judaism protected her from such trouble even as it frustrated Cebà and other associates. It was the people who hesitated on the line between Judaism and Christianity – largely but not exclusively Portuguese New Christians, or conversos – who were at much greater direct risk.

Pullan observes, however, that inquisitors could also claim jurisdiction over professing Jews, never baptized, who offended against the "law," a common Jewish–Christian code of religious belief and observance. He adds: "In principle their jurisdiction further extended to Jews who attacked, insulted or otherwise harmed Christians and the Christian Church."[76] Gregory XIII's 1581 bull "Antiqua iudaeorum improbitas" (On the Ancient Evil of the Jews) authorized the inquisitions to judge Jews in ten cases, including those involving blasphemy or attempts to convince Christians to embrace Judaism. If substantiated, some of Copia Sulam's reported criticisms of Christianity, as well as her purported attempts to convert Cebà, were acts that technically fell under the Inquisition's purview. Legislation passed in 1593 under Clement VIII extended the Inquisition's jurisdiction by authorizing it to judge Jews who, among other things, held or circulated works forbidden to Christians on grounds of heterodoxy, scandal, or obscenity.[77] Cebà suggested that Copia Sulam's salon was a hotbed for "speculations," or heterodoxy,[78] that could easily have included the discussion of prohibited works – for example, Cesare Cremonini's *Disputatio* (prohibited in 1622), which would have been of clear interest in discussions regarding the immortality of the soul[79] – or even Cebà's own ill-fated *La reina Esther*, suspended for obscenity in 1621, which his letter collection shows to have been one of Copia Sulam's favourite texts. However, as noted above, except for a brief period in the late sixteenth century, the Inquisition did not systematically pursue cases against unbaptized Jews. Therefore the *Lettere a Sarra Copia* – even with the scandalous statements on faith attributed to her – did not put Copia Sulam in any real danger from religious authorities.

Lack of repercussions from religious authorities did not necessarily mean impunity, however: in fact, the contest between religious and secular authorities to regulate unwanted behaviour in these post-Interdict years was hard fought, and the Venetian government – bolstered in its approach by the writings of Paolo Sarpi – sought to assert its sovereignty through its own actions in this area. The line between the jurisdictions of Church and state was not, however, always easy to trace. Pullan notes: "In principle, no unbaptized Jew could be charged with heresy or suspicion of it. But the Inquisition claimed the right to judge crimes other than heresy ... However, the need for an inquisitor's expertise was reduced where Jews or infidels were being accused of simple disrespect for Christianity ... Hence, there would always be an argument for leaving such matters to the lay magistrate, as defender of the Church."[80] In addition to other bodies, two lay magistracies in particular regulated such behaviours, but they usually sought to control the most egregious behaviour rather than the sort of incidental remarks that Cebà's *Lettere a Sarra Copia* attributed to Copia Sulam.[81] In any case, we have no evidence that she ran into trouble with any lay authorities: there is no trace of difficulties either in the archives (in which there are lacunae) or, more convincingly, in contemporary accounts, where her enemies would surely have trumpeted this sort of information.

However, the controversial statements that Cebà attributes to Copia Sulam were not without consequence. The disdainful attitude they suggest she held towards the Christian religion would surely have rankled a Catholic readership. They might also have irritated her co-religionists, who could justly have feared that her reported disdain for Christianity would be interpreted as the community's perspective rather than hers alone.[82] The attitudes that the *Lettere a Sarra Copia* associated with Copia Sulam were problematic therefore more in terms of public perception than the actual danger they represented for the salonnière herself.

Whether or not Copia Sulam actually expressed the thoughts that Cebà attributed to her, the fact that he advertised them so prominently – and out of context – meant that they were among the most notable elements of the *Lettere a Sarra Copia*. They functioned, much like the accusations against her reputation that he made with increasing forcefulness throughout the volume, to turn sympathies against her – and therefore, naturally, towards Cebà. But unlike the charges about her sexual availability to her male associates, which were buried in the text and obscured behind repeated denials, the religious polemic functioned as the entrée into the volume.

Copia Sulam's Shifting Stance towards Christianity

The difference in attitudes towards Christianity that Copia Sulam articulates in the 1621 *Manifesto* and that Cebà attributes her in the 1623 *Lettere a Sarra Copia* is astounding. In the *Manifesto*, while she proudly defends her Jewish faith, she presents a Christianized view of Judaism and accentuates the similarities between the two faiths. She behaved, as discussed in chapter three, as a religious apologist – a defender of Judaism who was determined to engage Christian sympathies. In the *Lettere a Sarra Copia*, on the other hand, she appears to be an anti-Christian polemicist. The fundamental difference between the two works was of course Copia Sulam's degree of editorial control. Whereas she wrote every line of the *Manifesto* and carefully fashioned its presentation, she wielded very little power over the *Lettere a Sarra Copia*.

Questions nevertheless arise over the sharp differences between the two works. It seems obvious to note that the statements attributed to Copia Sulam in the *Lettere a Sarra Copia* suggest that she felt a greater freedom of expression in the informal (and initially unpublished) medium of the manuscript epistle than she did in the more formal, and public, medium of the published *Manifesto*. As we know, the letter collection has as its nucleus an exchange that, while not private per se (the letters were widely shared with associates in both Genoa and Venice), had limited dissemination. The back-and-forth nature of the letter exchange also freed the correspondents to set forth ideas that they knew they would be able to qualify or expound upon in subsequent letters.[83] When the original exchange was transformed into a published volume with wide distribution, however, the nature of the exchange fundamentally changed, and many of the freedoms that the original manuscript correspondence offered translated into permanent provocation or indiscretion.

It would be a mistake to interpret as deliberate the shift from the *Manifesto*'s more conciliatory stance towards Christianity to the *Lettere a Sarra Copia*'s more aggressive one. As discussed below, Copia Sulam's relationship to the published volume of the *Lettere a Sarra Copia* remains ambiguous: it is not clear that she sanctioned the publication, and her editorial input on the volume was only marginal. The initiative to print the collection came from Cebà and Doria, who, as noted, thoroughly controlled the text's presentation. Regardless of her intentions, Copia Sulam had little chance to harmonize her discourse between the two volumes, a task that would have been difficult in any case since her original letters were written over a four-year-long period that overlapped with the *Manifesto*'s publication.[84] Rather than intentions, then, we must consider results: the 1621 *Manifesto* was a veritable bestseller that poised Copia Sulam for future literary success; the *Lettere a Sarra Copia* instead began the unravelling of her literary career.

Copia Sulam's Sanction of the Lettere a Sarra Copia's Publication

The *Lettere a Sarra Copia* collection as a whole paints an unflattering portrait of the salonnière. Cebà's denigration of her falls into three major categories: he condemns her literary vanity and pursuit of fame, he attacks her faith and her beliefs (and suggests a tendency towards heterodoxy, though he does not term it as such), and – most damning – he assails her reputation with insinuations about her inappropriate contact with male associates. Given the view of her that emerges in the publication, therefore, it is puzzling that Copia Sulam wrote a letter in which she voices some support for his letters' publication. This apparent approval appears in an autograph letter dated 8 January 1623 (1622 Venetian style), in which she asks Isabella della Tolfa to ensure the suppression of one letter (dated 1 November 1619) that Cebà had addressed to Copia Sulam (see figure 4.3).[85] She does not explain her request, only saying that she is moved by "a very pressing interest."[86] His letter may have been compromising enough to her, probably in religious terms, that she did not need to elaborate.[87]

In her letter to della Tolfa, Copia Sulam said she was repeating a request already made to Doria, who had not responded. Cebà had died less than three months before Copia Sulam wrote della Tolfa; the letter to della Tolfa likely followed the one to Doria by several weeks.[88] Copia Sulam, therefore, sprang to action barely two months after Cebà's death to influence his letters' publication. It is not clear if she made her request only after his death because his absence offered her an opening to assert a degree of editorial control, or if the project was languishing during his infirmity and only when Doria assumed charge of it did its publication seem likely enough to merit intervention. In any case, she would have been well apprised of the letter collection's imminent publication through the Genoese network her correspondence with Cebà had allowed her to build.[89] Neither his cessation of correspondence with her the previous spring nor his death in the fall had ruptured the other relationships she had built around this exchange, which were in fact crucial to her remaining abreast of literary developments. She here used these connections to achieve an important, if narrow, goal.

Copia Sulam's urgent request to della Tolfa indicates her intense interest in the story that Cebà's letters would tell when published and was her clear attempt to shape an aspect of the narrative. But with the exception of the one letter to which Copia Sulam objects – which in fact does not appear in the printed volume – she voices no other hesitations about the volume. She indeed urges della Tolfa to assure her husband Doria, the *Lettere a Sarra Copia*'s editor, that "if he were worried that he was doing something that went against the reputation and will of signor Ansaldo, ... that the blessed soul arranged this printing more to honor me, his servant, than out of his own ambition."[90] Copia Sulam, who may have anticipated Doria's objection to altering the volume that Cebà had left, asserts that its author considered the project as a final act

4.3 Copia Sulam's autograph letter to Isabella della Tolfa (1623). Archivio di Stato di Napoli, Fondo Doria D'Angri, parte 2, busta 688, "Lettere senza nome di destinatario," 1609–98, c. 12 [1623].

of generosity to her: a literary tribute to a devoted admirer. Copia Sulam implies that, as the recipient of this yet unseen gift, she should have a say – at least in this extreme instance – in its content.

This argument – or perhaps the scandalous nature of the letter she brought to Doria's attention – evidently convinced della Tolfa or Doria to disobey what even Copia Sulam portrays as Cebà's final literary will. The fact that he might have included a letter overtly compromising to her does not come as a surprise, in light of the rest of the volume's content. However, it is surprising that his patron(s) would – seemingly on the basis of her plea – remove it. Also surprising in Copia Sulam's manuscript letter to della Tolfa – given our record of the Copia Sulam–Cebà exchange – is Copia Sulam's positive representation of her relationship with Cebà and the pleasure she voices at the gift that he had bequeathed her. The delicate nature of the request she makes, however, through which she sought to sway Cebà's close friend and literary executor, clouds the sincerity of her portrayal. The letter proves neither that she retained a positive view of her late correspondent nor that she welcomed the letter collection's publication. Her written request indicates only that she knew of the forthcoming publication and that her attempt to censor it remained narrow. It could be that, to achieve her most important goal – the suppression of the most compromising letter – she feigned acceptance of the collection as a whole.

It is nevertheless possible that Copia Sulam sincerely supported the publication of Cebà's letters to her, though it is unlikely she knew the full contours of the volume as it would appear. After all, Cebà had literally written her off and Doria did not answer her one attempt at editorial intervention. It is unlikely, in particular, that she knew about the volume's paratext, including the notes that decontextualize and sensationalize some of her anti-Christian statements. Her expressed support of the letters' publication, therefore, whether it was sincere or not, was not an endorsement of the actual volume that was printed.

Copia Sulam would have had some reason to embrace the publication of the letters, since it did offer potential benefits. It promised to advertise her connection to a widely published author and to show her to be a prolific writer, a talented poet (the volume includes four of her sonnets), a literary critic whose opinion and editorial assistance were sought by an established writer, and an intellectual with a loyal group of followers. The work, published in Genoa and documenting her important contacts in the city, would in addition establish her as a writer whose appeal was not merely local. The exchange also cast her in the role of muse to Cebà, allowing her to take her place next to the Beatrices and Lauras of the Italian literary tradition, who wielded their influence through inspiration. But she was author as well as inspiration – writing her way into current literary society while spurring Cebà to write as well.

If Copia Sulam truly endorsed this publication, she must have thought that the religious dimension of the letter exchange – its most overt element – would not have negative repercussions for her. (As mentioned, she would not have known how the paratext would highlight her controversial religious statements). Most important, she must have assumed (and rightly, all indications show) that the letter exchange would not create trouble for her with the Inquisition. Perhaps her experience in her debate with Bonifaccio, where his charges of heresy against her provoked no reaction from Christian religious authorities, reassured her of some safety from religious censorship.

The battle with Bonifaccio could also have favoured her acceptance of the letters' publication for other reasons. Although the letters were frequently critical of her, she may have thought them more flattering than Bonifaccio's writings, and thus welcomed the new publication as an antidote – however imperfect – to his poisonous 1621 attacks. She may also have believed that Cebà's letters, which showed her repeatedly fighting off Cebà's conversionist attempts, would prove her orthodoxy to members of her own community. At the same time, the letters would demonstrate to a Christian readership that she was open to dialogue across faiths.

More puzzling to explain would be Copia Sulam's sanction of a volume that included compromising charges about her intimate contact with other Christian men. The *Lettere a Sarra Copia* collection traces her growing alarm, as reported by Cebà, at this increasingly blatant aspect of Cebà's missives. She could have judged, however, that the many positive aspects of Cebà's correspondence with her would counterbalance this unflattering element. But if she sanctioned the volume in the hope that the letters' publication would propel her career upwards, she was disappointed, since the very literary society that had grown up around the correspondence unravelled in an unseemly scandal shortly after the *Lettere a Sarra Copia* came off the presses.

5
Friends and Enemies (1621–1626)

Overview

Between spring 1621 and spring 1622, the two most important literary relationships Copia Sulam had forged – with Baldassare Bonifaccio and with Ansaldo Cebà – collapsed. Bonifaccio had been her salon's most well-established writer, with valuable academy memberships as well as literary and editorial contacts. He had also played an important role in salon discussions, where she looked to him – as she reported in her *Manifesto* – for spirited conversation on controversial, at times heterodox, topics. Her relationship with Bonifaccio disintegrated in their public debate over the summer of 1621, and her connection to Cebà cooled immediately thereafter: their correspondence, which had provided an important focal point for salon activities since spring 1618, was over by April 1622.

Upon the departure of these two well-known and well-connected figures from Copia Sulam's literary circle, her associates Numidio Paluzzi and Alessandro Berardelli, who were eking out a living at the edges of the Venetian publishing world, assumed a more central importance. The two men, both dependent on Copia Sulam for financial support, conspired to defraud her in a sordid scheme they used to enrich themselves and to humiliate her. When she discovered and punished their dishonesty, the men brutally defamed her. Their treachery and slander convinced her to give up her public literary life.

This chapter traces the collapse of Copia Sulam's literary career. After recounting the initial stages of the falling out between Paluzzi, Berardelli, and Copia Sulam, the narrative moves on to examine Paluzzi's *Rime*, a 1626 volume edited and issued by Berardelli that shamelessly slanders the salonnière. Since this was the work that sank Copia Sulam's literary career, its various dimensions are considered through an assessment of the role the work's prominent publisher played in providing authority to the volume and an examination of the connections between publisher, author, editor, and contemporary literary academies. This external perspective is complemented by a careful look inside the volume to examine first its poetry, then – in some detail – the volume's vituperative representation of Copia Sulam, and finally, the work's celebration of Berardelli's loyalty to Paluzzi in the context of the contemporary craze over male friendship.

As a counterpoint to the analysis of the *Rime*, this chapter concludes with a detailed consideration of a manuscript response to Paluzzi's volume entitled "Avisi di Parnaso." This manuscript, a collaborative work between several writers – including Copia Sulam – circulated shortly after the *Rime* volume was published. The "Avisi" manuscript not only pillories Copia Sulam's detractors but also provides evidence that she maintained a robust literary network even after her row with Paluzzi and Berardelli. Nonetheless, that public confrontation, which is rehashed in the *Rime*'s pages, convinced her to give up her literary career. She explains this decision in five sonnets included in the "Avisi"; the poems are Copia Sulam's last known writing.

The Betrayal and Its Punishment

Before examining the events that precipitated the disintegration of Copia Sulam's salon, we must pause to consider our sources. The account that follows is based on the blow-by-blow reports given in the "Avisi" manuscript, which is the last major contemporary work that discusses the salonnière and is essential to understanding the final years of her salon.[1] It is certainly not an unbiased account, since it aims to repair Copia Sulam's reputation by denouncing her enemies. However, its meticulous detail bolsters its credibility, as does the fact that other sources corroborate several of the manuscript's reports. That the "Avisi" manuscript is relatively reliable is important, since it is the only source available for many of the events that shaped Copia Sulam's career during these years.

The story the "Avisi" manuscript reports begins with Copia Sulam's generosity to Paluzzi, who had long suffered from the "French disease."[2] As the condition began to handicap him around the time of the *Manifesto* controversy, he became increasingly dependent on Copia Sulam for material and practical support. This was support that she liberally offered, perhaps in part to repay him for his backing during that controversy.[3] When his health worsened in spring 1622, she financed his cure at a steam bath (*stufa*), one of several in the city where the population of syphilitics burgeoned during the seventeenth century (6v–7r).[4] After his disease went into remission in mid-August 1622, she transferred him to the home of her longtime laundress, Paola Furlana. Copia Sulam rented and comfortably furnished a room for him there, fed him (7v), and provided him a five-*scudi* monthly salary and other gifts (33v).[5]

After only four days in these new quarters, Paluzzi learned of Furlana's ongoing plot to swindle Copia Sulam, which the laundress had contrived along with Copia Sulam's Moorish scullery maid Arnolfa (8r).[6] The plot involved attempts to convince Copia Sulam that aerial spirits were whisking off items from her household (8v). Paluzzi immediately joined in on the scheme and played a crucial role in convincing his patron to lend credence to the supernatural events (9r). Since he was too sick to act himself, Paluzzi sought help from Berardelli, who became a willing co-conspirator and in fact seems to have quickly become the ringleader in the efforts to fleece the Sulams (9r–9v and passim). The laundress's three sons were also involved (9v). The band worked together to steal numerous household articles, necklaces, rings, a gold belt fob and other accessories, sheets, underwear, candlesticks, food, and wine (9r–10r and passim).

In early July 1624, Giacomo Rosa – who had been Cebà's agent in Venice and had become a close associate of Copia Sulam – discovered the deception and informed the salonnière (28r–29r).[7] She took immediate action against the conspirators (11v), who had robbed her of some 400 golden *scudi*, or around 520 ducats (15r).[8] She abrogated her relationship with Paluzzi, cutting off her assistance to him, and denounced Berardelli, the principal thief, to judicial authorities (11v).[9] The Signori di Notte al Criminal, the Venetian judicial body that investigated most person-on-person crime in the city, prosecuted the case (15v) and found Berardelli guilty, sentencing him to a prison term and to the galleys (57v).[10] He was free by summer 1626.[11]

Within a month of Copia Sulam's discovery of the conspiracy, that is, in late summer 1624, Berardelli (and perhaps Paluzzi) wrote and circulated a defamatory pamphlet about her – it is unclear whether it was printed or manuscript – called "Le Sareide," probably written in verse.[12] The "Avisi" manuscript states that the pamphlet – which was read aloud around the city and, to shame Copia Sulam among her co-religionists, in the ghetto (49r) – was of breathtaking vulgarity and vitriol. These "most disgraceful writings"[13] occasioned angry controversy, the manuscript states: at their reading in the ghetto, "insults were traded, slurs unleashed, and threats to cut and burn were thrown back and forth."[14] In short, since Berardelli was no longer able to defraud Copia Sulam, he instead defamed her. The slander against her may have in part motivated Berardelli's punishment by the Signori di Notte al Criminal.[15] Yet, however intense the campaign to humiliate her, which played out in the *campi* of the city, the 1624 "Sareide" did not exhaust Berardelli's desire to denigrate her. Two other events intensified his anger: Paluzzi died of syphilis in abject poverty in July 1625[16] and Berardelli himself was punished for his crimes. The enraged Berardelli was no longer satisfied with the ragtag attack of the pamphlet; he instead defamed Copia Sulam in a 1626 work published with one of the best-known presses in Venice.

Numidio Paluzzi's *Rime*

Giovanni Battista Ciotti, Publisher

As noted in chapter one, Berardelli published his posthumous edition of Paluzzi's *Rime* with Giovanni Battista Ciotti. Since Ciotti and Paluzzi had known each other for some time and the poet likely worked for Ciotti's press,[17] the publisher may have intended to pay homage to his late associate with this publication. Ciotti issued the *Rime* towards the end of his nearly half-century-long career in the publishing industry in Venice, where he had worked variously since the early 1580s as a publisher, printer, and bookseller.[18] He had published at least 58 books in Venice by 1600,[19] and another 105 through 1625.[20] He also wrote several presentations to works he published, showing himself to be a man of some culture.[21]

Around the turn of the century, Ciotti ran afoul of the Inquisition for his association with Giordano Bruno, who was burned at the stake for heresy in 1600.[22] In 1599, Ciotti was arrested and fined by the Inquisition for importing forbidden books from Germany; in 1607, after he and some associates printed a suspect work, the Congregation of the Index issued an excommunication *latae sententiae* that made it a crime to possess or buy any of their books in the future[23] – a prohibition that would have included Paluzzi's *Rime*. A scholar has recently termed Ciotti one of "Venice's primary suppliers and publishers of heretical texts."[24] Despite Ciotti's prominence, his press's production was "qualitatively not of the highest level."[25] The acclaimed poet Giambattista Marino, who frequently published with Ciotti, complained to him of his press's 1619 issue of *La Galleria* (The Gallery), writing that "never – either from your presses or from others – has a book that is more error-filled and disjointed been published."[26] Ciotti's edition of Paluzzi's *Rime* is also riddled with errors.

In the context of women's writing in particular, it is worth noting that Ciotti had an important role in launching the career of Lucrezia Marinella, the only other published female Venetian writer of the period. He published several of her early works, including her first, *La Colomba sacra, poema eroico* (Holy Columba, Heroic Poem, 1595); the pastoral novel *Arcadia felice* (Happy Arcadia, 1605); and, most notably, her *Nobiltà* (1600, figure 5.1), which he had commissioned to respond to the publication in Venice of Passi's *Diffetti* (1599).[27] Marinella's *Nobiltà* was successful enough that Ciotti issued it in a much expanded edition the next year. The author

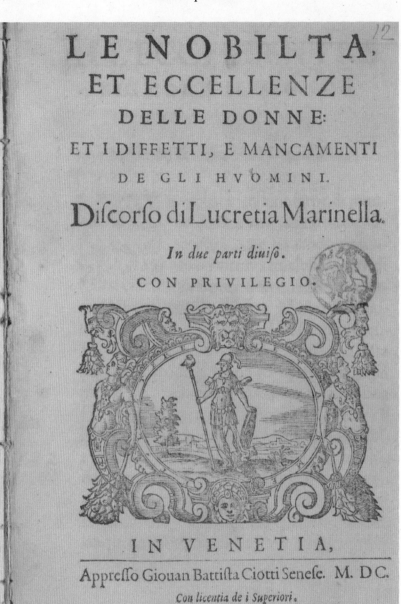

5.1 The title page of the first edition of Lucrezia Marinella's *Le nobiltà et eccellenze delle donne et i diffetti e mancamenti de gli huomini* (Venice: appresso Giovanni Battista Ciotti senese, 1600). By permission of the Ministero per i Beni e le Attività Culturale – Biblioteca Nazionale Marciana (Misc. Teza 709.12). Further reproduction is prohibited.

and publisher seem to have been well acquainted: Ciotti wrote a prefatory letter to readers for *Arcadia felice* in which, in addition to praising Marinella's productivity, he defends her against charges that she had plagiarized another of her works, a life of the Virgin Mary. He declares that the work "has been recognized by an eminent person as the true offspring of her mind, as it certainly is, much to the shame of slanderers."[28]

Ciotti's support for Marinella at the turn of the century – and in particular his defence of her against charges of plagiarism – are particularly striking since, a quarter century later, he published Paluzzi's *Rime* volume, which repeatedly defames Copia Sulam with similar charges. Her supporters were especially offended that the poetry collection was issued by this well-known publisher.[29] His involvement, however, likely did not stem from any personal animus against Copia Sulam nor from a shift towards a more misogynistic stance, but rather from his loyalty to Paluzzi and from changes in the cultural landscape.

Paluzzi's Rime, Ciotti, and Contemporary Literary Academies

Early in his career, Ciotti was the official printer of the second Accademia Veneziana, a group founded in 1593 that flourished until 1609 and aimed to guide Venetian intellectual life.[30] Marinella had strong ties to this group as did her father, a doctor and writer.[31] The academy had a markedly philogynist tendency: members supported Marinella's *Nobiltà* as well as Fonte's *Il merito delle donne* (also published in 1600).[32]

By the 1620s, however, Ciotti was linked to the writers and intellectuals coalescing into the Accademia degli Incogniti, a group that would grow to include more than 300 writers from around Italy and by the 1640s would dominate the literary and cultural landscape in Venice.[33] Members of the academy supported religious freedom and an unfettered press, and they backed a libertine political dissident in his confrontation with the Church.[34] Yet despite certain progressive tendencies, members would later produce virulently antifeminist works[35] and clash with another female Venetian polemicist, Arcangela Tarabotti (1604–1652),[36] whose fearless critiques of the Church and Venetian state and defence of women's human rights were famous in European intellectual circles.[37] Marinella would lament the intellectual climate of mid-century Venice that the academy controlled, where women writers encountered ceaseless hostility.[38] The *Rime* edition, which (as discussed below) came out of incipient Incogniti circles, is an early example of this misogynistic tendency.

Despite the changing intellectual climate, Ciotti's earlier association with the second Accademia Veneziana remained relevant into the 1620s. Some of the leading figures of that turn-of-the-century academy were later involved in founding the Accademia degli Incogniti: most important, the writer Guido Casoni (1561–1642) was deeply involved in both academies.[39] Ciotti's publishing activity is part of this continuity: during the years of his work with the Accademia Veneziana, he published one of Casoni's most important works, his *Ode* (Odes), which came out in the same year (1601) as the second edition of Marinella's *Nobiltà*. In the early to mid-1620s Ciotti issued works by several writers who would become important Incogniti members, including Giulio Strozzi.[40] He also published a play by Cesare Cremonini, a guiding spirit of the academy,[41] along with numerous editions of Marino's works.[42] Support for the celebrated Neapolitan writer (and disparagement of his rival Tommaso Stigliani [1573–1651]) was a key tenet of the Incogniti's cultural politics.

Ciotti's publication of Paluzzi's *Rime* also demonstrates the press's connection to the nascent academy. The contributors to the volume read like an early who's who of the Incogniti. The volume features verse from many who would later become academy members, including Pietro Michiele (1603–1651), Claudio Achillini (1574–1640), Gaspare Bonifaccio, Baldassare Bonifaccio, and Giacomo Litegati (b. sixteenth century, fl. early seventeenth century). Gabriele Zinano may have been an academy member, and Paluzzi directed poems to academy members Giulio Strozzi and Giovan Battista Lalli (1572–1637). Berardelli – the *Rime*'s editor – would be an academy member too; he was considered significant enough to contribute to the group's *Novelle amorose* (Novellas on Love), a bawdy collection published in 1642.[43] Several other writers of the period who had ties to the academy but do not seem to have been official members, including Pier Francesco Paoli and Pietro Petracci, also contributed to Paluzzi's *Rime*. Several of these men – Zinano, Baldassare Bonifaccio, and perhaps Gaspare Bonifaccio and Petracci – alongside Berardelli and Paluzzi, had been associates of Copia Sulam. Berardelli dedicated the *Rime* to Giovanni Soranzo (1600–1665), then Venetian ambassador to Holland, whose connection to the incipient academy could also be seen in the dedication to him the preceding year of a work Casoni edited.[44] By the 1630s, Soranzo was "one of the principal protectors of the Accademia degli Incogniti and its members."[45]

According to customary dating, the connection between Ciotti and the Incogniti would be anachronistic. Ciotti moved around Italy between 1621 and 1625[46] and may have left Venice around the time he published Paluzzi's *Rime*.[47] His work in the city certainly trailed off after these years. The academy's formation has traditionally been dated to 1630, after Ciotti's importance as a publisher had diminished. But new evidence has led one scholar to date the academy's founding to between 1623 and 1626[48] – or in the very years Berardelli prepared and published Paluzzi's *Rime* with Ciotti.

The Rime: Format and Themes

The *Rime* volume was long considered lost but in recent years two separate copies have been located (figure 5.2).[49] The collection, poorly printed in duodecimo, does not show great editorial care: the front matter is not factually consistent and it excuses the work's "many errors,"[50] in truth numerous and significant, which are highlighted also in a front-of-volume errata sheet. Paluzzi's writing in the *Rime* consists largely of traditional love poetry addressed to a beloved named Filli.[51] The love story, recounted episodically, conforms to the initial claim Berardelli makes that the writing he offers is incomplete. Indeed, the collection shows no narrative arc. The poems feature the beloved glimpsed in fleeting moments, pointing out a shooting star or admiring Roman ruins – or, in more pedestrian occasions, writing or sneezing[52] – and describe other women as well. The sexual imagery in the *Rime* is sometimes overt – a poem early in the collection, for instance, features a woman who, under the veil of night, bares her breasts to her lover[53] – and the influence of Marino is patent.

The collection advertises a bland Petrarchan imitation in its opening sonnet:

> Queste, ch'al Tempio de la Fama appendo
> In mal vergate carte accolte rime,
> Son del mio vaneggiar le spoglie opime;
> A l'otio già le tolsi, a lui le rendo.[54]

> (These rhymes that, gathered on these humble sheets,
> I hang at the Temple of Fame,
> Are the rich spoils of my vain pursuits.
> I robbed them from leisure; I now return them to the same.)

or in other sonnets such as "Standing in a Theater":

> "Stando in un teatro"
> Per incerta cagion piango, e sospiro.
> Così ardo, e non ardo, amo, e non amo.
> Né sciolto vive, né legato il core.
> Ho perpetuo desio, né so che bramo.[55]

> (For an unknown reason do I weep and sigh.
> I burn so, and burn not, I love, and love not.
> My heart lives neither free nor bound.
> I am always yearning, yet know not what I desire.)

5.2 The title page of Numidio Paluzzi's *Rime*, edited by Alessandro Berardelli (Venice: dal Ciotti, 1626). Courtesy of Beinecke Rare Book and Manuscript Library, Yale University.

Other poems indulged the contemporary taste for the deformed or the exotic. Two poems, for instance, feature a woman (probably Filli) disfigured by pox;[56] a sonnet entitled "Turban Wrapped around His Lady's Head"[57] describes the beloved in orientalized dress while "The Beautiful Turkish Woman"[58] suggests the allure of a woman from the East. The "Avisi" manuscript claims that this poem was originally entitled "In Praise of a Beautiful Jewish Woman"[59] and described Copia Sulam. The substitution of a Turkish woman for a Jewish one would hardly have been innocent during the years in which the Ottoman threat hung over Venice and would have implied an equivalence between these non-Christian female figures.[60] Such a substitution also suggests that the volume, which suppresses Copia Sulam's name even as it slanders her, effaces her presence in other ways.

In addition to the love poetry, Berardelli intersperses occasional encomiastic or elegiac poems that Paluzzi wrote to potential patrons, including Louis XIII of France (1601–1643), the Duke of Parma (Odoardo Farnese [1612–1646], but not named in the collection), Giovanni de' Medici (1567–1621), and Cardinal (Giannettino) Doria (1573–1642).[61] A number of poems also weave both author and editor into the fabric of contemporary literary society. Berardelli reprints a poem that Paluzzi had contributed to a collection published by Ciotti memorializing the death of Battista Guarini;[62] he also printed another poem of Paluzzi's that celebrated Giovanbattista Lalli's recently published mock epic *Moscheide ouero Domiziano il moschicida* (The Epopee of the Fly or Domitian the Fly Killer).[63]

The Rime*: Copia Sulam Defamed*

The most striking feature of Paluzzi's *Rime* is Berardelli's unremitting attack on the character and credibility of Copia Sulam. The 4 August 1626 dedication he signs to Soranzo, for instance, claims that the talented but hapless Paluzzi wrote much more than he chose to publish, allowing "a Jewish woman" – unnamed, but unmistakably Copia Sulam – to claim his unpublished writings for her own. Specifically, Berardelli asserts that Paluzzi's illness "presented a Jewish woman the opportunity to steal the biggest and best part [of his poetry] together with many other compositions in two big wrapped bundles, which netted her the reward of many works that Paluzzi had written for her."[64] An infuriated Paluzzi would have burned the rest of his writings, Berardelli claims, but was prevented from doing so. Portraying himself as the hero of this textual rescue, the editor reports, "I found a way, even if to my own detriment, to pull [these writings] out of the jaws of oblivion."[65] The published volume of Paluzzi's poetry was, in Berardelli's account, the product of this act of valour. It is not clear what detriment he may have suffered as a result, unless this incident factored into the punishment Berardelli received from the Signori di Notte al Criminal.[66]

Berardelli's version of the events is clearly distorted. Blurring the concepts of literary theft (plagiarism) and physical theft, he alleges that Copia Sulam took "the opportunity to steal" many of Paluzzi's writings – that is, physically stole them. But he suggests in the same sentence that these works belonged to her – she took "many works that Paluzzi had written for her" – which would mean that her alleged crime was not theft but plagiarism, claiming works written by another as her own. Anomalous as well is Berardelli's description of Paluzzi's writing. He praises Paluzzi's poetry "for its sweetness, for its style, for the novelty of its witty conceits, expressed with ease and grace"[67] – qualities that, the editor writes, placed his friend second to none in lyrical poetry. Perhaps worried that Paluzzi's *Rime* would not support these claims, however, Berardelli pre-emptively excuses not only the paucity of this production but also its quality by suggesting that the poems Copia Sulam took were "the biggest and best part" of Paluzzi's poetry. In this account, then, the poetry (purportedly written by Paluzzi) that went under Copia Sulam's name – perhaps he intends her verse in the *Manifesto* and her poems published in *Lettere a Sarra Copia*, as well as other poetry that circulated in manuscript – was superior to the verse published in the *Rime*.

Another noteworthy aspect of Berardelli's dedication is his failure to use Copia Sulam's name, which – as mentioned – he suppresses throughout the volume. This omission was likely motivated by his fear of repercussions: he had already been punished for defrauding and/or defaming her[68] and may have been concerned that she could have brought new charges against him, akin to the charge of libel that, as she wrote in her *Manifesto*, Bonifaccio's attack on her merited.[69] But there was no mistaking which "Jewish woman" Berardelli intended – beyond the fact that her history with both author and editor was well known, she was the only Jewish woman leading a public literary career in Venice at the time. But as Berardelli levelled accusations of theft at a woman clearly identifiable as Copia Sulam – turning against her the very charge that she seems successfully to have proven against him – he sought retribution only in the court of public opinion, not of law. In the latter arena, he knew based on bitter past experience that Copia Sulam had the upper hand. She had money, was backed by powerful people – not least of whom Senator Giovanni Basadonna – and had succeeded in securing Berardelli's punishment once before.

In the prefatory note addressed to "kind readers,"[70] Berardelli returns again to the ostensible theft of Paluzzi's writings, an episode whose importance the editor emphasizes by recounting it twice in the volume's first five pages.[71] But in its second iteration he changes some details, again avoiding Copia Sulam's name but referring to her as "a little female."[72] (He uses the derogatory term *femina*[73] and pretends to dismiss her power with the diminutive ending [*feminella*]). If the dedication associates her thievery with her Jewish identity (the crimes were committed by "a Jewish woman"), here he links her dishonesty only with her female identity. He claims that Paluzzi wrote, for this *feminella*,

> many poems, two books of paradoxes in praise of women and against men, and a great number of letters, and a manifesto on the immortality of the soul. She took from him in two big wrapped bundles the biggest and best part of his verse, his "On Politics," a tragedy, and his "Pamphlets" – the fragments of which, gathered by me, will soon be published. And these will make it clear how skilled he was in all branches of knowledge.[74]

The dedication had claimed that the unnamed Copia Sulam had *stolen* the author's poetry "together with many other compositions." The vague term "compositions" could refer to all the writing that had earned Copia Sulam fame, including her well-known poems and letters to Cebà as well as the published *Manifesto*. Here, instead, Berardelli contends that she *plagiarized* these noted writings ("many poems, ... a great number of letters, and a manifesto on the immortality of the soul") along with two books of prowoman paradoxes that evidently went under her name but have not survived – a very interesting detail that suggests her active participation in the contemporary *querelle des femmes*.[75] In addition to this alleged plagiarism, he states that she *stole* specific works that have not traditionally been ascribed to her, including a political discourse, a tragedy, and a series of pamphlets. In a backhanded way, then, Berardelli compliments Copia Sulam's versatility and fecundity – attributing to her an oeuvre that was much more developed than future generations have known – even if he simultaneously accuses her of resorting to dishonest means to produce it.

Although the most obvious attacks on Copia Sulam appear in the dedication and prefatory note to the *Rime*, the editor continues to defame her within the volume itself. He includes a poem in the collection that had been published earlier under Copia Sulam's name: her sonnet to the human soul,[76] which appears at the end of the *Manifesto*.[77] Its inclusion in the *Rime* constitutes an implicit charge of plagiarism against Copia Sulam. Berardelli publishes this poem without reference to her and does not explain his decision to include this poem but not others from the *Manifesto*, whose entire authorship he attributes to Paluzzi. The sonnet differs from others in Paluzzi's *Rime* for its spiritual subject matter and more complex syntax. Elsewhere, the editor introduces poetry fragments with the provocative statement that "the complete original versions were stolen by the Jewish woman mentioned before."[78] He prefaces the fragment of the tragedy that he publishes by again claiming (as in the note to readers) that the work had been stolen: "among the other writings that were stolen from the author there was a tragedy, which was almost completed, of which only this scene was recovered."[79] At his most vituperative, he alleges that only a handful of the sonnets written to Paluzzi by other authors were found – and these mostly without the authors' names – since these poems and the poet's responses "were stolen from him by that perfidious Jewish woman" (see figure 5.3).[80] Because Copia Sulam's purported theft is the organizing narrative behind Paluzzi's *Rime*, the numerous insertions of ellipses and notations stating "the rest is missing" (*manca il resto*) stand as implicit indictments of her.[81] Additionally, one sonnet contains a thinly veiled attack: though unnamed, Copia Sulam is clearly represented in the figure of "impious envy" responsible for the "false charge" that Berardelli faced.[82] Even the editor's expressed hope to polish the poet's posthumous reputation ("to revive the name of the author")[83] aims to discredit Copia Sulam, since his reputation could not improve without harming hers.

While reserving actual slander for Copia Sulam, Berardelli does not exempt Paluzzi from criticism. The editor opens the note to readers (see figure 5.4) by bemoaning the sad fate of the poet's works, which were "born beneath the same unhappy constellation under which he was born, since they suffered some of the same troubles that beset him at the end of his life."[84] But Berardelli himself contributes to Paluzzi's unhappy reputation, charging him with intellectual carelessness and attributing his lack of success – "for which he himself was to blame"[85] – to the fact that he wrote for another person (the unnamed *feminella*, but clearly Copia Sulam) and failed to publish his own works. The editor also presents some of the *Rime*'s verse as mediocre[86] and touts as more interesting the writing he claims had been taken by Copia Sulam (it was the "biggest and best part"). If the poet had had any talent, this framing suggests, Copia Sulam was successful in appropriating it. Moreover, Copia Sulam's starring role in the volume's storyline – even if in the role of villainess – casts her shadow over the literary memorial Berardelli built for his friend. The editor never issued the second volume of Paluzzi's writings that he promised would "soon come out,"[87] a sign perhaps that his eagerness to memorialize the poet waned or that the *Rime* collection, which interweaves conventional verse and confusing fragments of other works with repeated defamation of Copia Sulam, was not well received. The work was never reprinted.

120   *Rime del Sig.*

D'vn gran numero di Sonetti da diuerfi
perfonaggi fcritti all'Autore appena
fi fon trouati quefti pochi, & la maggior parte fenza nome, perche ha-
uendoli egli pofti infieme con le fue
rifpoftegli fono con l'altre ftate rubate da quella perfida Hebrea.

Del Sig. Claudio Achillini.

Augura perpetui honori all'Autore per
le fue Rime.

Correte lauri, e le fue chiome ombrofe
Fatte de voftri rami, ond'ei s'adori,
Apriteui al fuo crin rofe amorofe
Poiche fcriue la man teneri amori.
bellifimo Cintio a lui propofe
Quefti fioriti, e quefti verdi honori,
Sù baciateui infieme allori, e rofe
Sù ftringeteui in vn rofe, ed Allori,
d ecco pur de le mie note al fine
Rofa, ch'à te deuota in vn baleno
Vaga del Lauro fuo lafcia le fpine.
ofi già mai non mora, ò venga meno,
Fatto Imeneo de le fue nozze vn crine,
L'odorata conforte al lauro in feno.

Del

CORTESI
LETTORI.

PAr che le Rime, e le altre opere
del Signor Numidio Paluzzi fiano
nate fotto l'iftefa cattiua coftel-
latione, ch'egli nacque, hauendo
patito parte delle iftefe miferie ch'e-
gli ha fofferto nel fine della fua vita, e
di ciò ne ha hauuto, egli fteffo la colpa
per hauer fempre tenute oppreffe quel
le, che per fe hauea fatte, & hauendo
compofto per vna feminella molte rime, dui libri di Paradofi in lode delle
Donne contro gli huomini, & vn numero grande di Lettere. & vn mani-
fefto dell'Imortalita dell'anima. Ella
gli hà tolti in dui groffi inuogli la maggior, e miglior parte delle Rime. Della Politica, vna Tragedia, & li Opuf-
coli, i fragmenti delle quali da me adunati preffo verranno fuori. Et in quefti fi fcorgerà quanto egli valeffe in
tutte le fcienze. In quefte Rime ve ne
fon molte, che egli le rifiutaua, pure vi
fi fon pofte per effer fue. Le voci di Pa-
radifo, Dea, Angelo, Diuino, Fato, De-
A 4   ftino,

The introduction to Claudio Achillini's
net in Paluzzi's *Rime* (120) (1626) terms
ia Sulam "that perfidious Jewish woman"
uella perfida hebrea"). Courtesy of
necke Rare Book and Manuscript Library,
e University.

5.4 The opening page of Berardelli's note to
readers in Paluzzi's *Rime* (A4r) (1626) charges a
"*feminella*" (a "little female," clearly Copia Sulam)
with plagiarizing and stealing Paluzzi's writings.
Courtesy of Beinecke Rare Book and Manuscript
Library, Yale University.

The Rime *and Heroic Friendship*

Though in the *Rime* Berardelli spares no effort in touting his efforts to commemorate his luckless friend Paluzzi and in disparaging Copia Sulam, the volume demonstrates that his main hope was to improve his own standing. In the front matter, Berardelli blatantly seeks reward for his dedication to Soranzo,[88] which the editor implies would be proper repayment for the "detriment"[89] he endured for bringing the *Rime* to press. He includes flattering poems from the well-known writers Michiele and Zinano that praise Berardelli for his sacrifices for and immortalization of Paluzzi. These poems appear before Latin compositions in praise of Paluzzi written by Baldassare Bonifaccio – Copia Sulam's old nemesis who had privately expressed scorn for Paluzzi[90] – and by Claudio Achillini. Not only do the poems that laud Berardelli come first, but his name appears in a significantly larger and bolder typeface with respect to Paluzzi's (figures 5.5 and 5.6). It is likely that Berardelli, who was reported to have haunted Venetian printshops,[91] did not leave these elements to the printer's discretion. In addition to trumpeting Berardelli's role, the introductory poems also advertise the strength of his connections, showcasing his ability to marshal well-known writers to glorify himself and to memorialize his friend.

At the end of the *Rime*, Berardelli included a sort of anthology of verse that Paluzzi had exchanged with other writers: Claudio Achillini, Pier Francesco Paoli, Romolo Paradiso (b. sixteenth century),[92] Giovan Battista Bellaver (fl. seventeenth century), Pietro Petracci, Giacomo Litegati, Sebastiano Andrantonelli (or Andreantonelli, d. 1643), and Gaspare Bonifaccio. The volume concludes with an elegiac poem by Michiele on Paluzzi's death.[93] As Paluzzi's literary executor, Berardelli solidifies (and displays) his own relationships with these writers by including their verse, using their conventional praise of Paluzzi to re-establish, in (male) literary society, not only Paluzzi's credibility but also his own, which had been damaged by his fraudulent dealings with Copia Sulam.

At the centre of the male literary society created by Paluzzi's *Rime* stands the author and editor's friendship – or, more accurately, Berardelli's friendship towards Paluzzi: as we have seen, the volume publicizes the sacrifices the editor made for his friend and showcases the continuing loyalty that led Berardelli, after Paluzzi's death, to construct a literary memorial to him. This promotion of a strong male friendship bond had special resonance in Venice during these years, where a more famous male friendship was attracting clamorous attention and scandal: the so-called "heroic friendship" between Nicolò Barbarigo (1579–1644) and Marco Trevisan (1588–1674) (figure 5.7).[94] Barbarigo and Trevisan, both members of powerful noble families, came into contact

AL SIGNOR

ALESSANDRO

BERARDELLI,

Che oltre hauer sofferti danni, e perigli per l'amico suo Signor Numidio
Paluzzi,mentreche era in vita,dopò
la sua morte da molte parti raccolse
le presenti Rime.

DEL S. GABRIEL ZINANO.

Orse l'Asia Aleßãdro e i piani,e i mõti
    Empì di strage,a le Città diè morte,
I Rè spogliò de la real lor sorte,
E se d'amico sangue horridi fonti.
S'Alessandro maggior con modi conti
Tu,aperte ad opre pie più degne porte,
Cerchi l'amico trar di man di morte,
E contro gl'anni à suo fauor t'affronti.
Poi che sofferti pria danni,e pergli,
Et altri guai,d'onde la vita è carca,
Volgi à pietà più cara i tuoi consigli.
mentre il buon Paluzzi à morte varca
T'ingegni porre,(e che faran più i figli?)
Il nome suo d'eternità ne l'arca.

Al-

AD NVMIDIVM
PALVTIVM.

Vmen eris ; sentis ipsum id portende-
    re nomen ;
Quis Deus esse velis,elige; Numen eris .
Abdita naturæ pandens,Physis altera fies ;
Altera Suada loquès,altera Apollo canes.
Elige;ne incipias tantùm Deus esse Deorum,
Qui nihil humanæ conditionis habet.
Interea si fas homines imponere Diuis
Nomina, dû statuis quis Deus esse velit;
Corpore mortalem, diuinum mente, vocabo
Semideumq; virum,semiuirumq; Deum.
Balthassaris Bonifacij .

DE CARMINIBVS

ELEGANTISSIMIS,
Et Argutissimis Paluti.

Audete,ò Veneres,Veneres,quas Mu-
    sa Paluti ,
    Iussit in Etruscos molliter ire pedes;
Gaudete, ò Charites, Charites, quas blanda
    Paluti
    Fecit in Etruscos currere Musa pedes;
Vos etiam gaudete Sales, gaudete Lepores,
    Gaudete Etrusco nunc saliente pede ;
Sub luce in Delfos, Dafnis Romana,virores,
    Dum rigua in lacrimas , Laurus Etrusca
    subit .

Claudij Achillini.

The introductory poetry in Paluzzi's *Rime*
(1626) in celebration of Alessandro Berardelli
(A5v). Courtesy of Beinecke Rare Book and
Manuscript Library, Yale University.

5.6 The introductory poetry in Paluzzi's *Rime*
(1626) in celebration of Numidio Paluzzi
(A6v). Courtesy of Beinecke Rare Book and
Manuscript Library, Yale University.

around 1618 or 1619 when both were down on their luck: Barbarigo
had fallen into deep disgrace for unknown reasons, while Trevisan had
alienated his family and others with spendthrift ways that squandered
his family's patrimony.[95] When Barbarigo heard that Trevisan had defended him – or perhaps another ostracized man – against defamatory
remarks, he invited the younger nobleman to his house to thank or com-
pliment him for his action. From their initial meeting a friendship was
born. In the close-knit political and social climate of Venice, Trevisan's
engagement with the dishonoured Barbarigo troubled the former's family and friends, yet he chose nevertheless to continue the relationship,
eventually even going to live with Barbarigo and his family. The friendship grew out of Barbarigo's gratitude for Trevisan's loyalty, which was
generously remunerated: the wealthy Barbarigo not only supported his
friend but paid 5,700 ducats to free him of debt. As the friendship continued, they made increasingly dramatic gestures to demonstrate their
loyalty to one another. First, in 1624–1625, Barbarigo made Trevisan
his legal representative in charge of all his personal property and real
estate. Then, in March 1626, the two friends made out their wills: Barbarigo made Trevisan his general executor, mentioned him first among
his heirs, provided generously for his maintenance, and allowed him to
make decisions regarding the Barbarigo daughters (Barbarigo was married with children, Trevisan unmarried), specifying that Trevisan could
"rule over these daughters of mine, and money, as he pleases, without
the slightest obligation ever to justify his actions in any way, either with
regard to my above-mentioned daughters, or regarding the use of the
money."[96] Barbarigo didn't mention his wife, whose power this formula
sought to abrogate. Trevisan, who had little to bequeath, nonetheless
made the symbolic gesture of stipulating that nearly everything go to his
friend. Despite the disparity between the friends' material investments,
the celebrations of the friendship that would follow praised Trevisan's
contribution to the relationship: the lavish material support that Barbarigo showered upon Trevisan was nothing in comparison with the honour
that Trevisan helped Barbarigo to regain.[97]

   This showy, even theatrical, friendship – dubbed by contemporaries as
"heroic" – drew increasing attention, even internationally, throughout
the rest of the decade for what amounted to a series of publicity stunts:
the friends' publication of their wills in 1627 and a series of encomiastic
texts issued from then on.[98] Already earlier in the decade (and certainly
by mid-1626, when Berardelli published Paluzzi's *Rime*), the friendship
was well known in Venice. Its first indirect echo can be heard in a dialogue
on friendship in Ludovico Zuccolo's *Dialoghi* (Dialogues), which was dedicated in 1623 and published in 1625.[99] Zuccolo published another work

5.7 Nicolò Barbarigo and Marco Trevisan in *L'heroica e incomparabile amicitia de gl'illustriss. signori Nicolò Barbarigo e Marco Trivisano ... celebrata ... da molti eccellenti ingegni del nostro secolo* (Venice: Marco Ginammi, 1628), 2. By permission of the British Library, General Reference Collection DRT Digital Store 11427.de.30. © The British Library Board.

in 1625, *Nobiltà commune et heroica* (On Common and Heroic Nobility),
which praised the "nobility" of the friends in two chapters, and he
promised another discourse entirely focused on the friendship itself.[100]
A translation of a work by the Spaniard Bartolomé de Las Casas published
in Venice in 1626, *Istoria o Breuissima relatione della distruttione dell'Indie
Occidentali* (A History or Brief Report on the Destruction of the West
Indies),[101] featured a dedication to friendship, offering Barbarigo and
Trevisan as its most current and noble expression. Giacomo Castellani,
the volume's translator, extolled friendship in general as the "binding
together of hearts, the happiness of souls, the spice of human life, an
incomparable and priceless gift that defies understanding."[102]

It would have been difficult for these publications to escape the
notice of Berardelli, a man who eagerly sought opportunities in the
publishing industry and who, the "Avisi" manuscript reports, was wont
to "stroll through the streets of Venice and enter into printshops."[103]
Of even greater interest to him would have been the epic poem in
five cantos on the heroic friendship, *Il Barbarigo, overo L'amico sollevato*
(Barbarigo, or The Friend Comforted, figure 5.8), which was composed
by Giulio Strozzi – a writer whom Paluzzi (and Berardelli) admired, as
two poems of praise to Strozzi in the *Rime* attest.[104] *Il Barbarigo* was
a clamorous success that was published again and again.[105] Though
the volume's October 1626 dedication indicates that it came out after
the *Rime* (dedicated in August), Strozzi reports in his note to readers that his poem had been eagerly anticipated during its composition and that its first canto, which circulated separately, had already
invited praise.[106] He describes the clamour that the heroic friendship
had already created:

> I wish I were able to record here all the homage that the farthest flung
> foreign princes offer, and all of the praise, honorifics and encomia that are
> spontaneously generated by the most renowned foreign pens in their letters
> and tracts, and even by the most important and famous academies in Italy,
> all inspired by the splendor and utmost marvel of this phenomenon and of
> this celebrated friendship. If I were able to record these I could let shine
> forth the universal admiration that this friendship encounters.[107]

Strozzi's hyperbole describes a cultural spectacle that his own work in-
vigorated. Even the most serious scholars had to take notice: Nicolò
Contarini (1553–1631), who was writing the official history of Venice,
promised to mention the friendship.[108] It was so much in the public eye
by 1626 that it would have been a natural point of reference for Berardelli as he proclaimed his own loyal friendship for Paluzzi.[109] It is even

5.8 Giulio Strozzi's *Il Barbarigo* (Venice: appresso Girolamo Piuti, 1626). By permission of the British Library, General Reference Collection DRT Digital Store 11427.e.19. © The British Library Board.

possible that the Barbarigo–Trevisan friendship not only influenced the presentation of the *Rime* but inspired the editor to publish the work, and that the polemic against Copia Sulam, which became a focus of the text, was not the original spark that led to its creation.

Given the clamour over the heroic friendship, it is not surprising that the *Rime* volume employs some of the tropes of that famous friendship. Berardelli highlights his selfless sacrifices for his friend and the difficult odds they faced; he describes their friendship as a refuge from hostile outsiders, who, despite their ill intentions, were unable to disrupt it; and he employs the presses to advertise the importance of the relationship, whose private dimensions were dwarfed by its public celebration. Additionally, both the Barbarigo–Trevisan and the Berardelli–Paluzzi friendships gloried in the connection that endured beyond the grave. The wills of Barbarigo and Trevisan describe a relationship that death could not destroy, and the latter even requested in his will that he be buried together with his friend.[110] The *Rime* collection is (in a reading generous to Berardelli's motives) a funerary monument to Paluzzi. Moreover, the Berardelli–Paluzzi friendship involved similar issues of honour. For redeeming his honour, Barbarigo paid Trevisan in material ways; Berardelli claimed to redeem Paluzzi's honour, and also sought repayment.[111] And the *Rime*, like the heroic friendship and the works that glorified it, celebrated the homosocial bond of friendship between men that pushed women to the margins: the heroic friendship imperilled Barbarigo's wife and daughters' financial future,[112] while the *Rime* jeopardized Copia Sulam's honour and credibility.

Despite these numerous parallels, however, something rings false in Berardelli's construction of his friendship with Paluzzi. As self-interested as the more famous friendship was – despite all the panegyrics, the Barbarigo–Trevisan friendship pivoted upon a crass notion of exchange – it seems noble, indeed even "heroic," in comparison with the debased model of friendship that Berardelli showcases in the *Rime*. Many aspects of the volume actively damage Paluzzi when they don't simply disregard him. These include Berardelli's unflattering portrayal of Paluzzi's character and writing, his self-interested attempts to coopt Paluzzi's literary legacy, his complaints about the sacrifices he made for Paluzzi, and his focus on Copia Sulam rather than on Paluzzi himself. Far from a tender tribute to a dearly departed friend, the volume seems instead to be Berardelli's attempt to settle scores and to propel his own career upward by capitalizing on the current fashion for male friendship.

Issues of gender and sexuality in both of these friendships cannot be ignored. Both present a ready instance of Eve Sedgwick's male homosociality, a theory of men's relations with other men centred around the notion of desire and imagined as a continuum that includes all forms of exclusively male interaction.[113] This does not imply that their practice of homosociality necessarily included "genital homosexual desire," as Sedgwick terms it,[114] or physical sexual relations between these friends, though certain aspects of the relationships, for example, the yearning for union after death, are erotically charged.[115] Instead, these relationships were structured *textually* to focus on bonds among men. David LaGuardia has pointed out the continuity between social and textual realities for men, noting that social roles and rules for men both determined and were determined by texts: "Reading and writing for men throughout the Middle Ages and Renaissance was in large part both a continuous reflection upon the relation of texts to other texts, and a constant consideration of what it meant to *be* a man and to *read* as a man within the social context that was defined by those texts."[116] Of interest here is specifically what these textual relations among men meant for the women who were drawn into them, quite against their will. As Sedgwick notes, "the status of women ... is deeply and inescapably inscribed in the structure even of relationships that seem to exclude women – even in male homosocial/homosexual relationships."[117]

Of particular interest to the Berardelli–Paluzzi "friendship," and its effect on Copia Sulam, is the model of triangulation that Sedgwick proposes, where men bond with one another through the involvement of a woman, as in a classic love triangle, but that Sedgwick warns must be examined with careful attention to asymmetries produced by gender and other factors;[118] here, of course, religious difference is important. Even if Paluzzi–Berardelli–Copia Sulam hardly seems a "love triangle," but rather a triangle formed around dishonesty and disrespect, the model still illuminates important aspects of their relationship. Courtney Quaintance has recently noted that "the power dynamic in the erotic triangle is even more asymmetrical ... when the female mediator between men appears in the guise of a whore."[119] The same can be said, certainly, when the female mediator appears as a "perfidious Jewish woman," especially since Jews and prostitutes were frequently associated with one another in culture and law.[120] Quaintance looks at what she calls "literary fraternity," that is, "relationships between men that were constituted through literary and social gatherings, companionship and conversation, and, especially, the practice of exchanging texts about women."[121] She notes that "as they tell and retell stories of men who judge and then dominate prostitutes, [the texts] affirm and strengthen the bonds between men."[122] Berardelli certainly used the revilement of Copia Sulam, denigrated as both a woman and a Jew within the *Rime's* pages, alongside his "friendship" with Paluzzi, to strengthen the bonds of the Christian literary fraternity he was seeking quite publicly to build – a fraternity that was at direct odds with the sort of literary society that nurtured dialogue between genders and across faiths that Copia Sulam had tried to build through her salon. Though the *Rime* volume rips apart the final strands of this literary society, the "Avisi" manuscript provides one final testament to the enterprise the salon had undertaken – as well as a counter-attack against Berardelli and his abuse of friendship and friends.

The "Avisi di Parnaso": Copia Sulam and the Barbarigo–Trevisan Friendship

Berardelli's careless and mercenary handling of Paluzzi's literary legacy, along with his dishonesty and immorality, is savagely pilloried in the "Avisi" manuscript, which as we have seen was written and then circulated in defence of Copia Sulam shortly after the *Rime*'s publication. Like the *Rime*, the collaborative "Avisi" text maps the confrontation between the former associates onto the terrain of "heroic" friendship – most obviously through the dedication of the work to one of those heroic friends, Marco Trevisan. The manuscript also uses the yardstick of friendship and fidelity to contrast the actions of Berardelli, shown to have failed sorely as a friend, and those of Copia Sulam, a model of loyalty and honour.

This story of friendship upheld and betrayed plays an important role in the "Avisi," a long and often internally contradictory manuscript.[123] Giulia Solinga, who signed the dedication and the note to readers (figure 5.9), is often given credit for the work, which gives an angry and at times vulgar account, in poetry and prose, of Paluzzi and Berardelli's betrayal of Copia Sulam. Aiming to debunk the *Rime*, the varied writings of the "Avisi" display an intense intertextuality with Paluzzi's volume, referring to it – often with specific page references – more than forty times.

The central portion of the "Avisi" is an intricate narrative on the model of Traiano Boccalini's enormously successful *De' ragguagli di Parnaso*. The *Ragguagli*'s publication in Venice in 1612 and 1613 popularized a fanciful hybrid genre that uses poetry and prose to recount and comment on current and past events.[124] The importance of these events is amplified when they reach Mount Parnassus as news reports, which gods, goddesses, and historical figures from different eras debate in proceedings presided over by Apollo. Boccalini's work, often with additional *ragguagli*, was reprinted repeatedly in Venice during the decade and a half after its first appearance;[125] a 1619 edition was published with the title *Avvisi di Parnaso*. The fashionable *ragguagli* genre provided an easily digestible and entertaining format in which to address the literary controversy that surrounded Copia Sulam.

5.9 The note to readers signed by Giulia Solinga in the "Avisi di Parnaso" manuscript (5r) (1626). Correr Library, Venice (Ms. Cicogna 270). 2018 © Biblioteca Correr – Fondazione Musei Civici di Venezia.

The "Avisi" manuscript opens, as mentioned, with a dedication to Marco Trevisan. The dedication contrasts friendship, virtue, and loyalty – embodied by Trevisan and by Copia Sulam – with ingratitude and vice. The dedication reports that Trevisan, like Copia Sulam, had been the victim of ingratitude – in his case when Giulio Strozzi violently betrayed him.[126] This report is perplexing, since it describes an intense antagonism between Trevisan and Strozzi during the very same months in which the latter was finalizing *Il Barbarigo*, which celebrated "the splendor and utmost marvel" of the Barbarigo–Trevisan friendship.[127] In other words, the "Avisi" account suggests that the relationship between one of the heroic friendship's protagonists (Trevisan) and one of its proponents (Strozzi) was collapsing at the same moment as each was capitalizing on the cachet of that famed male friendship. Again, as with Berardelli, ill-will, self-interest, and betrayal are seen lurking around the edges of the heroic friendship, sullying the honour and generosity it was supposed to embody.

The dedication of the "Avisi" is followed by a sonnet addressed to Trevisan and written from Copia Sulam's perspective ("in the person of the Jewish woman").[128] In the poem, the figure of Copia Sulam bemoans the episode of ingratitude Trevisan suffered at Strozzi's hand. The sonnet claimed that Trevisan's was

> Caso che ben pareggia, anzi ch'adombra,
> Signor, le mie sventure e in via maggiore
> Pelago d'acque ingrate le sommerge. (3r)

> (An incident that certainly equals, or rather overshadows,
> signor, my troubles and sinks them
> in a much wider sea of ungrateful waters.)

The dedication and opening sonnet draw Copia Sulam into close relation with one of the celebrities of the heroic friendship and associate Copia Sulam with the nobility and liberality that the famous friendship had come to symbolize. The manuscript seeks, in other words, just like the *Rime*, to capitalize on the heroic friendship's cultural cachet. It is equally important that the "Avisi" account proposes, though never explicitly mentions, a female version of heroic friendship between the two women who figure prominently in it: Giulia Solinga, who signs the manuscript dedication, and Copia Sulam, whom she defends. As Trevisan tried to restore Barbarigo's honour, so Solinga tried to restore Copia Sulam's.

A lengthy note to readers, signed by Solinga, gives a chronological account of the events that precipitated Copia Sulam's break with Paluzzi and those that followed it. Again repeating the tropes of the heroic friendship, this account insists on the magnanimity and nobility of Copia Sulam's spirit, which were exemplified by her loyalty to Paluzzi – to whom she showed "the greatest compassion" – and by her open-handed maintenance of her household staff, whom "she bankrolled generously."[129] In stark contrast stands the perfidy of the schemers, who repaid her munificence with "shameful ingratitude."[130] That she received no loyalty for her noble generosity recalls the depiction of Trevisan in the "Avisi" as a victim of ignoble friendship.

The note to readers is followed by the first of the manuscript's five poetic exchanges between various writers and Copia Sulam. An "uncertain" author addresses a sonnet (*sonetto de incerto*) to her that decries her enemies' actions, which were driven by "Every excess that renders a heart wicked / Every disloyalty that derives from cowardice."[131] She responds *per le rime* with a sonnet that expresses hope that her story will warn those who have "the serpent in their breast to drive it out / before it sprays them with poisonous rage."[132] If the idealized Barbarigo–Trevisan friendship offers an inspirational model of extreme self-sacrifice to other aspiring friends, this sonnet provides an antimodel, warning that what masquerades as friendship might instead conceal noxious enmity.

These extensive introductory materials lead into the "Avisi" proper, where – as the locus shifts from contemporary Venice to a timeless Mount Parnassus – friendship betrayed is still a dominant theme. The "Avisi" account pits the former friends Paluzzi and Berardelli against one another. A fictionalized Paluzzi, now in Parnassus (a device allowed by his 1625 death), inveighs against Berardelli's misuse of his writing, claiming that Berardelli deliberately took "anything that was good among those fragments [of Paluzzi's writing] ... and he disfigured it, ... in order to bolster his heinous accusations."[133] This fictional Paluzzi takes repeated umbrage at Berardelli's attempts to capitalize on their friendship. He criticizes, for instance, the fact that his editor claims to have endured "harm and peril for his friend signor Numidio Paluzzi"[134] when he really suffered punishment "for his outrageous thievery."[135] He charges that one of Berardelli's primary motives in the *Rime* was to appear to be a good friend: "Indeed that scoundrel thought he could with one shot strike many targets: to seem zealously protective of his friend, to take revenge against the Jewish woman by defaming her with lies, and to cover up his own abominations."[136] On the pages of the "Avisi," Paluzzi depicts Berardelli's edition of the *Rime* as a simultaneous attack on his own and on Copia Sulam's honour – a tool Berardelli uses to feign friendship in order to advance the basest of personal motives.

The "Avisi di Parnaso" and the Italian Literary Tradition

The use in the "Avisi" of Boccalini's flexible and fashionable genre gave cultural currency to Copia Sulam's story. This currency is just one of the ways in which the manuscript positioned her in the Italian literary and cultural tradition. At the centre of the manuscript is the fictional trial of Paluzzi and Berardelli – a proceeding occasioned, the text explains, by the arrival in Parnassus of the *Rime*, in which "the reputation of a virtuous woman was torn apart with the most bald-faced lies and with abominable slander."[137] Alerted to this, Apollo assigns to judicial inquiry female poets of recent memory – Vittoria Colonna, Veronica Gambara, and Isabella Andreini (1562–1604) – together with poets of antiquity – Corinna and Sappho.[138] Beyond these writers, who become Copia Sulam's champions after hearing all the evidence, dozens of other luminaries of the Italian literary tradition support her, including the unlikely defender of women, Pietro Aretino (1492–1556), who prosecutes her nemeses.[139] As discussed in greater detail below, both Paluzzi and Berardelli are in the end found guilty.

Aretino takes up his case against the defendants in response to Paluzzi, who attempts to exonerate himself by blaming his erstwhile friend. Though Paluzzi's crimes are considered less grave, in the fictionalized account he is punished bodily, since he already inhabits Parnassus, while Berardelli, who is still among the living, is hanged in effigy. This outcome relies on Aretino's merciless prosecution: he dismisses Paluzzi's protestations and claims that the defendant was guilty not only of stealing from Copia Sulam but of having slandered her as well (26r). As evidence of these wrongdoings, Aretino presents a letter from Giacomo Rosa, Cebà's agent in Venice, who had become friends with Copia Sulam (26r–34v). The manuscript presents the document as an authentic letter actually exchanged. Though its appearance in the fictionalized and polemical "Avisi" account certainly makes the letter's veracity questionable, the intricate account – including specific dates – that it gives of Paluzzi's betrayals of Copia Sulam and the fact that it is said to have been widely circulated in Venice (34r) suggest that the document may not be a literary invention but instead the transcript of a letter Rosa sent to Paluzzi in 1624. As noted above, such a mixture of fact and fiction was intrinsic to the *ragguagli* genre. Rosa's letter, beyond exposing Paluzzi as an unpleasant and arrogant social climber, suggests that he was an integral part of the scheming against Copia Sulam.

But as much as the manuscript reviles Paluzzi by means of Rosa's letter and Aretino's attacks, its true target is Berardelli. Unlike Paluzzi, Berardelli is given no chance to defend himself, and while Aretino criticizes and condemns Paluzzi, mocks his writing, and blames him for the wrongs committed against Copia Sulam,[140] the prosecutor seethes with loathing for Berardelli, describing him as "that stinking scullery boy, that filthy ruffian, that scofflaw, that incestuous ox, that obscene stallion, that cupbearer to the dregs of society, ... that herald of infamy, that witness for falsehood, that hostel of evil, that portrait of shamelessness ... that chiromancer, that pyromancer able to control spirits ... that ghastly wizard, worthy pupil of the black scullery maid!"[141] The string of insults reveals a rage that the page can barely contain and casts Berardelli as the true villain of the story.

The manuscript weaves into its case against Paluzzi and Berardelli other documents that are presented as factual. These include an anonymous letter (43r–49r), said to have been written to Berardelli, that provides counterpoint to and affirmation of Rosa's letter. The anonymous letter, which is even more vitriolic than Rosa's, focuses its attack on Berardelli's dedication of the *Rime* to Soranzo, charging that the editor tried to use his dedicatee's position of distinction to cover a vile attack (44v): "You [Berardelli] have the nerve to appear before a man of the utmost integrity [Soranzo], whose dignity buttresses Justice, whose heart nests all heroic virtues, to whose judgment such a great Republic entrusts itself ... And a man of your standing tries to swathe himself with *his* reputation? You dare to go that far, a scoundrel like you?"[142] This withering address attempts to draw a very clear distinction between the editor and the powerful man he tried to court through this dedication. It is impossible to know whether the letter was in fact sent to Berardelli, as the manuscript suggests, but its inclusion contributes in any case to the text's lively, variegated nature and – since it was clearly written by a knowledgeable insider while the sting of the *Rime* was still fresh – to the immediacy and intimacy it proffers in its account of events.

Even more prominent than these letters in the multiform attack on Paluzzi and Berardelli are the more than seventy poems, attributed to various writers, included in the manuscript. Giulia Solinga is given credit for at least some of them (51r, 53v–55r), though the attributions are not always clear. The poems, which focus on the defendants' petty thievery and their slanderous tongues, use violent images and vulgar language to denounce the pair. Standing in a long tradition of comic-realist poetry – which, unlike idealized Petrarchan poetry, confronts readers with an often brutal reality – the poems present direct and angry dialogues with the reprobates for whom they imagine gruesome punishment. One particularly explicit example is a sonnet that describes Berardelli's lynching:

Sì, vedrem spinta da vindice corda
Di bocca a forza la essecrabil lingua,
Sporca di schiume, schernir l'aere e i venti. (53v)

(Yes, we will see his detestable tongue, dirty with froth
and thrust out of his mouth by an avenging rope,
scorn the air and wind.)

This envisaging of Berardelli's punishment centres on his tongue, which
even in death remains contemptuous. Other poems return to the image
of his hanging, using grotesque metaphors of the theatre stage for the
scaffolds and of dance for the writhing body of the hanged man.

The anthology of poetry includes, as mentioned above, five poems addressed to Copia Sulam and her five poems of response: her last extant
writing. Her poetry closely associates the manuscript with her literary enterprise and showcases the remarkable versatility of her verse, with which
she addresses such sublime subjects as the human soul (as in her debate
with Bonifaccio), but also the ignoble matters of this late controversy. All
of the poems addressed to her in the manuscript have as their subject the
defendants' betrayals. Whereas in certain responses Copia Sulam avoids
direct censure of her enemies, in others she openly denounces Paluzzi
and Berardelli. In one of her most explicit condemnations, composed in
response to a poem by a certain Annibale Grimaldo,[143] she writes:

Se può vil nube anco adombrar del cielo
a le più chiare stelle i suoi orizonti,
perch'a vil bue vietar sorga o tramonti
il sol ch'ei non rimuggi e al caldo e al gelo?
Non fia che adduggi al verde del mio stello
livor d'infame mostro, monti a monti
inalzi, ch'ivi al mondo pur son conti
suoi indegni vanti e non gli adombra velo.
Ma che? vil core d'ignominia al pondo
forsi pon cura? se in sozzi costumi
gode qual entro al lezzo porco immondo?
Quindi è signor ch'ai fiati odiosi, ai fumi
D'empie fauci non bado: a più secondo
Spirar d'aura hor m'avvien che i vanni impiumi. (85r)

(If even a vile cloud can darken
the most radiant stars in the sky's horizons
why prevent a vile ox from mooing

in summer or winter, when the sun rises or sets?
Let not the spite of a defaming monster
wither the green of my stalk, even if he piles mountains upon
    mountains,[144]
since there, revealed to the world,
are his baseless claims, and no veil hides them.
But what does it matter? Does a vile heart
perchance care if it is dragged down by ignominy?
If it wallows in filthy habits like a dirty pig in muck?
Thus it is, signor, that I pay no mind
to the poisonous breath, to the smoke of impious jaws.
Now I sprout wings to ride the wind to greater heights.)

Here Copia Sulam adopts a register that suited the loathsome conduct of her opponents – the term "vile" (*vil*) is repeated three times – and their brute nature. The poem is in fact a small bestiary in which the author employs images of repulsive animals – vile oxen, dirty pigs, and wicked monsters – to portray the baseness of her enemies. The coarseness of Copia Sulam's word choice and imagery, which exceeds that of the poem she was answering and is reinforced in the jarring rhythm created by the repeated use of enjambment, reveals not only the depth of her disgust, but also her ability to capture it in verse. Indeed, her creation of a clear contrast between herself and her enemies is a measure of her versatility as a poet: while she uses rough language to describe their contemptible conduct, she creates an idealized image of herself rising above it as a winged bird, riding a breeze that allows her to soar above her enemies' poisonous stench. This versatility is typical of her "Avisi" sonnets, in which she discusses Paluzzi's and Berardelli's misdeeds alongside her own nobility.

The manuscript intersperses poetry with Aretino's assault on Paluzzi, which includes an accusation that he was godless and denied the soul's immortality (55v). This accusation, which echoed the one Bonifaccio made against Copia Sulam, shows how much the literary landscape had shifted for her in the five years since he had accused her of heresy in print. In that battle, she had support and advice from Paluzzi to defend herself, in a printed forum, against her former associate's charge. Now her allies – probably with her support, as discussed below – turned the same charge against her former supporter in a manuscript that, if anything, might even be said to be flattering to Bonifaccio (51v).

Also recalling the *Manifesto* controversy, where Copia Sulam used a vernacular literary tradition to mock Bonifaccio, the "Avisi" account shows famous vernacular writers scorning Paluzzi.[145] This contempt stands in stark contrast to the fervent support Copia Sulam receives, in the

Parnassian fiction, from numerous illustrious writers who by their solidarity affirm the Jewish writer's place within the Italian literary tradition.

The "Avisi di Parnaso" and Venetian Justice

In a Parnassus that the "Avisi" manuscript models on Venice, justice – a key
component of Venetian civic ideology – must be fairly rendered. Paluzzi,
in the "Avisi," therefore receives a defence attorney: the medieval poet
Cino da Pistoia (1270–1336). Cino's defence, however, is interrupted
by a scuffle precisely over the issue of the Venetian justice system –
the manuscript's clear indication that the judicial, editorial, and literary
issues that it addresses pertained not only to Copia Sulam's case but to
larger issues of press freedom and judicial fairness in the city. Earlier
in the manuscript, Aretino suggests that the *Rime*'s use of the Venetian
presses to defame an innocent woman had shamed the whole city, saying:
"Oh Venice, Venice, I turn to you, how clear are ... their false claims and
with what shamelessness do they appear marked on paper and printed
on your presses!"[146] The text goes on to present the Spanish poet Don
Garcilaso de la Vega (ca. 1501–1536), who pushes the argument even
further. He points out flaws in the Venetian system of justice, which he
criticizes not only for letting Berardelli off lightly – saying that in Spain
he would have been strung up – but also for the unreasonably free publishing environment that allowed a text as vituperative as the *Rime* to be
printed and even dedicated to a venerated senator (Soranzo) (57v–58r).
Boccalini – a figure of some authority in this text that imitates his own –
rises up in Venice's defence and challenges the Spaniard to a duel. Boccalini, who was clearly meant to garner a Venetian audience's sympathy
against his Spanish rival in a period when anti-Spanish sentiment was
strong, defends Italy's and Venice's judicial systems while also criticizing
the *Rime*'s dedication to Soranzo. He contends that Soranzo "never knew
the perfidy of the [*Rime*'s] author [Paluzzi], nor the detestable wickedness of the servant [Berardelli]."[147] This account uses Berardelli's low
social status as part of the case against him, while Soranzo's distinguished
position places him above reproach. Boccalini's defence of the Venetian
judicial system includes a sharp critique of Copia Sulam's attempts to
bring Berardelli to justice, charging that she did not understand legal
procedures nor did she receive proper counsel since she rashly changed
lawyers repeatedly. Boccalini suggests that her imprudence allowed
Berardelli to get off lightly (60r–60v), since Venice's justice system, like
all others, demanded a shrewd and cunning lawyer of the sort that Copia
Sulam, because of her impatience, was not able to retain. Boccalini's
defence of the Venetian legal system is ambivalent, suggesting that it was

a vicious system in which justice did not triumph so much as craft. De la Vega rejects Boccalini's apologetics and, continuing to criticize Venice, recalls that Boccaccio disparaged the city (62r);[148] Boccalini counters by recalling the esteem that Petrarch and others had for the city (62v–63r). The two fail to find a compromise, and a battle nearly breaks out between their supporters until a brigade of other prominent writers, led by Baldassare Castiglione (1478–1529), intervenes to keep the peace. In the end, Boccalini and de la Vega make peace offerings in the form of verse that denounces the *Rime*, sometimes in vulgar terms.

This highly symbolic scene – the most critical of Copia Sulam in the manuscript – places the writer at the centre of questions regarding both literary and judicial power in Venice. While Boccalini and de la Vega disagree on why Berardelli got off with a light sentence (whether because of Copia Sulam's imprudence or because of more fundamental flaws in the Venetian system of justice), they concur that he deserved a stiffer punishment, which they mete out in this literary venue. The rest of the volume enacts his punishment in verse (some by Copia Sulam) that answers the *Rime*'s charges against her (66r–99r). In Boccalini and de la Vega's confrontation, Venice's position as a publishing capital and the city's reputation as a centre for justice come into conflict since unregulated presses could create injustices that the government could not or did not control. But the manuscript suggests that literature could provide justice where the law did not. The literary court featured in the "Avisi" properly punishes Berardelli in poetry and prose. Such a literary punishment did not of course address his crimes against the Sulams' property, but it seeks in some measure to address the literary (and perhaps more grave) crime: his defamation of Copia Sulam in print.

After this literary and judiciary controversy is quelled, Cino is finally able to take up his defence of Paluzzi. He makes a plea for clemency, saying that Paluzzi had already in part admitted his fault and that it was Berardelli who was responsible for most of the wrongs committed against Copia Sulam (70v–71v). Paluzzi's attorney charges that Berardelli authored and circulated "Le Sareide" and was responsible for editing the *Rime* collection, which discredits Paluzzi as well as Copia Sulam (74r–74v). Cino takes particular umbrage at Berardelli's repeated attacks against Copia Sulam as well as his suggestion that Paluzzi authored the *Manifesto*: "And apart from that thief [Berardelli], who else contends that [Paluzzi] ever bragged of having composed the *Manifesto*, a work put together with no attention, only written by the Jewish woman to clear her name before the public (*sencierarsi col mondo*) of that accusation that was wrongly made against her?"[149] If this depiction of the work seems dismissive, it is worth noting that it echoes Copia Sulam's own description

of it in the *Manifesto* itself, where she insists that she would not descend
into philosophical or religious arguments but wants only to clear her
name (she also used the verb "sincerarsi") of the charge made against
her. Because of Berardelli's false attribution of the *Manifesto* and many
other misdeeds that also harmed Paluzzi, Cino pleads for clemency.

Having heard all the testimony, the women responsible for deciding the
case – Colonna, Gambara, Andreini, Corinna, and Sappho – quickly issue
their sentence. They order that Paluzzi be publicly humiliated by brand-
ing, among other punishments, and that Berardelli be hanged in effigy
(77r–77v). As mentioned above, only Paluzzi is physically disciplined in
this fictional account, since the still-living Berardelli is absent from the proceedings in Parnassus. But the latter's virtual punishment is much more
violent, just as the rhetoric against him is notably more vitriolic in the
manuscript as a whole. In fact, Berardelli's guilt is never presented as an
open question at the Parnassian trial: it is assumed. The "Avisi" manuscript
turns instead on Paluzzi's guilt or innocence, and although he is found
guilty to some extent, he is partially absolved by Berardelli's greater guilt.
The reports suggest that Berardelli was the mastermind of the crimes –
material and literary – that the manuscript describes and propose that he
was also the more dangerous enemy. The deceased Paluzzi was already
weakened by the publication of the *Rime* volume, whose contents showed
him to be ineffective and his writing to be erratic. His editor, in contrast,
was still living and seeking to establish his own mark on the Italian literary
tradition by capitalizing on Paluzzi's name and by defaming Copia Sulam.
Berardelli's punishment within the confines of Parnassus, assigned at the
hands of female intellectuals, seeks to re-establish a sense of justice within
Venetian letters that had been missing in the city's presses and in its courts.

The Dating and Authorship of the "Avisi" Manuscript

Critics have not resolved with certainty either the dating or the attribution of the "Avisi" manuscript. I suggest that Copia Sulam, along with
Leon Modena and other close associates, may have been involved in its
preparation, and that the manuscript circulated within a month of the
publication of the *Rime*, in August or September 1626. Since few of her
works survive, the salonnière's involvement in this manuscript would be of
great interest. Nevertheless, critics have overlooked the possibility for several reasons.[150] Since Giulia Solinga signed the manuscript's dedication
and note to readers, scholars have generally attributed authorship to her.
However, neither I nor other researchers have found a trace of a Giulia
Solinga in libraries or archives, despite extensive searching. The manuscript itself uses her name inconsistently: the note to readers she ostensibly

wrote, for example, refers to her twice in the third person (10r, 11v). I contend that the name, which could be translated as "Julia Alone," was a pseudonym for a member or members of Copia Sulam's inner circle. Poems in the volume are attributed to more than a dozen other writers never before associated with Copia Sulam. Critics have largely assumed these names were real, and therefore that a group of writers not closely connected to her took up her defence.[151] The manuscript also takes its distance from the salonnière by referring to her always in the third person (except in her own poems) and by including some elements in the manuscript that were decidedly unflattering to her. These criticisms are discussed in further detail in the next section, but for present purposes it suffices to say that, despite them, the manuscript unequivocally contradicts the attacks on Copia Sulam's honesty and honour that had been made in print and in no uncertain terms defends Copia Sulam as the true author of all the writings that appeared under her name.

Several elements suggest Copia Sulam's possible involvement in the "Avisi" manuscript's preparation. First, the inclusion of five of her poems – which critics agree are hers – point to her participation in and support of the project. Beyond this, the prose portions of the manuscript betray an intimate knowledge of her personal and literary affairs. For example, the manuscript offers details about the Sulam household and describes with precision what Berardelli and his accomplices stole and how they circulated within the house. The central presence of women writers in the manuscript's prose portions – from the famous female literary luminaries on Parnassus to the "Giulia Solinga" who dedicated the manuscript – also suggest the involvement of Copia Sulam, who adopted *querelle des femmes* tropes in her *Manifesto* and was associated with two books of prowoman paradoxes.[152] Additionally, certain prose sections of the manuscript recall Copia Sulam's style in the *Manifesto* as well as its subject matter. For example, in both works her male antagonists are mocked for going to battle against a woman.[153] More generally, the text of the "Avisi" showcases the same sharp polemical skills, laced with biting sarcasm, that Copia Sulam had exercised in her contest with Bonifaccio. Thus the tenor, content, and aspects of the "Avisi" manuscript's style may all reflect the salonnière's influence. Additionally, the fact that this work remained manuscript, rather than being printed, could point to the involvement of Copia Sulam, who told her antagonist Bonifaccio in her *Manifesto*, "I am as averse to placing myself beneath the world's gaze by means of the presses as you show yourself to be desirous."[154] Her hesitation to publish is discussed in further depth below. I hypothesize that Copia Sulam was responsible for the document's master plan: the choice of the Parnassian genre, which was the perfect space in which to ridicule her enemies; the centrality of the female investigators, who hold men accountable for their misdeeds to women; the overall structure, which includes an end-of-volume anthology of occasional poetry, with almost fifty poems attributed to over a dozen different writers; and the choice to use pseudonyms (discussed further below). In addition, I suggest that Copia Sulam wrote and edited certain parts of the manuscript's prose sections. It is in this manuscript, whose contours and content I suggest she shaped, that she chose to place the last attributed poetry of her career.[155]

Many aspects of the manuscript's prose indicate that it was collectively authored. Though it was recopied in a single hand,[156] "Solinga" states that she compiled the writings from "various original copies."[157] The note to readers uses the first-person plural to describe the manuscript's composition.[158] The diverse styles, tones, and perspectives of its prose sections also indicate that many people were involved. The manuscript also suggests that such collective action on Copia Sulam's behalf was not new: associates had previously banded together to defend her after Bonifaccio's attack.[159] Elements in the prose portion that reveal an intimate knowledge of Copia Sulam's literary salon[160] and specific details about how she composed and circulated her works[161] suggest they were written by members of her inner circle, if not in places by the author herself. At a global level, the manuscript's angry tone and its hasty issue (discussed below) also show the involvement of this intimate group, since Copia Sulam's closest associates would have been those most offended by the *Rime*'s defamation and would have felt an urgent need to clear her name. The group authorship of this document suggests the sort of collective production that Joan DeJean has termed "salon writing."[162]

The writers who banded together to create this document show a familiarity with Jewish customs and perspectives as well as with events that occurred within the ghetto. The manuscript refers courteously to Copia Sulam's religion[163] and to her husband;[164] it includes in its Parnassus the Jewish historian Flavius Josephus (38r–38v);[165] and, significantly, it completely avoids anti-Jewish tropes, even if certain elements – for instance, its focus on the Sulams' wealth, targeted by the band of thieves – provided ample material for such bigotry.

As a Jewish writer who had been in close contact with Copia Sulam for years, Modena was the most likely of her associates to have been involved along with the salonnière herself in the manuscript's preparation. In seeking to resolve the question of attribution for the "Avisi" manuscript, several other critics have proposed him as its scribe or author.[166] Among her Christian associates, many betrayed her by associating their names with Paluzzi's *Rime*, but among those in her inner circle still loyal to and able to contribute materially to the manuscript's narrative were Giovanni Basadonna, who is praised in the manuscript,[167] and Giacomo Rosa, who played an active role in the events narrated, since he is reported to have discovered and revealed the crimes being committed against the Sulams. He is also praised in the manuscript and, as we have seen, a letter he purportedly wrote is included.

As mentioned briefly above, the manuscript attributes the poetry it includes to more than a dozen writers, but extensive bibliographic and archival research has not uncovered information on any of these writers – with the exception of Copia Sulam herself.[168] I argue that the other names were pseudonyms.[169] Many of the pseudonymic poems, particularly those among the nearly fifty poems at the manuscript's end, show a Jewish perspective: they address "Jewish brothers,"[170] refer to the ghetto as Jerusalem,[171] and describe the general fear of Berardelli that Jews in the ghetto felt.[172] Though the poems appear under a dozen different pseudonyms, fewer writers were probably involved. It would have been important, however, to create the appearance of a broad chorus of support for Copia Sulam to counter the symphony of derision that Berardelli had orchestrated against her in the *Rime*.

As discussed, the manuscript was prepared with haste to quickly rebut the charges that had been levelled against Copia Sulam. In the earlier controversies that beset her, both she and her enemies rapidly produced and circulated texts in order to control public perceptions and to limit the damage of negative portrayals. In the *Manifesto* controversy, for example, as detailed previously, Copia Sulam said it took her two days to compose her response to Bonifaccio's defamation, and she certainly published her final product within a matter of weeks. Her detractor responded in print with similar speed.[173] Berardelli (and perhaps Paluzzi) wrote and circulated "Le Sareide" only a month after Copia Sulam broke off ties with them in 1624.[174] The salonnière and her allies would certainly have felt such urgency in the 1626 controversy, since the *Rime*'s depiction of her as a plagiarist and a thief gravely threatened her reputation.

If Copia Sulam was, as evidence suggests, involved in the manuscript's preparation, its contents provide clues about her state of mind at the end of her literary career. In this light, it is important to consider the fact that this work was not printed, though publishers would certainly have been most anxious to print a response to an attack on Copia Sulam. The *Manifesto* had convincingly demonstrated the profitability of such a publication, and the "Avisi" would have been even more interesting to readers because of the personal information the manuscript provided about the salonnière, who had gained prominence both with her *Manifesto* and her well-known salon – as well as infamy at the hands of Bonifaccio, Cebà, and Berardelli.

But the decision to avoid the presses indicates that Copia Sulam was reticent to broadcast the details of this latest controversy. In the *Manifesto* conflict, she had expressed a high-minded vision of the print medium, stating that authors should only publish carefully prepared works rather than "run[ning] eagerly to the presses" with works that were "shoddy and stupidly composed,"[175] as she accused Bonifaccio of doing. She went on to tempt readers with a description of other writing that she might publish: if the *Manifesto* was on a "topic quite different from the one that might perhaps have been expected from [her] pen,"[176] she had other, even more compelling works that the reading public would embrace. Copia Sulam surely referred to her poetry and may also have intended other prose writings, such as her letters or the prowoman paradoxes Berardelli mentioned in connection to her. It was on the basis of such works, composed with care and published without haste, that Copia Sulam hoped to secure her reputation.

By the time of the *Rime*'s publication, however, she had not yet seen fit to publish any other works. Her attention was likely diverted by the end of the Cebà correspondence in 1622, its publication in 1623, and the row with Paluzzi and Berardelli that started in 1624. And yet none of these events altered her conception of the proper uses of the presses that she had articulated in the *Manifesto*. If anything, the three works maligning her that had been issued in the meantime (Bonifaccio's *Risposta*, Cebà's *Lettere a Sarra Copia*, and Paluzzi's *Rime*) would only have strengthened her convictions about the dangers of abusing the print medium. She would therefore have been loath to have the next work she committed to print be one that she was compelled to publish quickly in order to respond, as she said in her *Manifesto*, to "another's malice or ignorance or negligence."[177] Copia Sulam would have been especially reluctant to print the sordid details of the Berardelli–Paluzzi betrayals that were a necessary part of her defence. Additionally, in contrast to the *Manifesto* controversy, where charges of religious irregularity forced her to defend publicly her own and her community's beliefs, a print response to the *Rime* was not necessary since the volume's accusations, however unsavoury, were strictly personal. It is not surprising, then, that she and her allies would have chosen to respond through the more controlled channels of manuscript circulation, where only a targeted audience – for example, of more distant literary associates and key members of the Venetian literary establishment, as well as the educated elite within the Jewish community – would have had easy access to her defence. The manuscript circulation of her text may have indeed cemented ties among these important allies. One of the functions of such exchange, as Harold Love has observed, "was that of bonding groups of like-minded individuals into a community, sect, or political faction, with the exchange of texts in manuscript serving to nourish a shared set of values and to enrich personal allegiances."[178] Such bonds would have been crucial for Copia Sulam in this moment of crisis. Contrarily, print, whose enduring power Copia Sulam emphasized in her *Manifesto*,[179] would only have immortalized a sordid scandal. This was not a controversy upon which Copia Sulam could have hoped to build her literary reputation. As she wrote in one of her last known sonnets, a "proud mind ... / does not hope ... / to awaken illustrious fame from a vile dispute."[180]

Representations of Copia Sulam in the "Avisi" Manuscript

As we have seen, certain aspects of the "Avisi" are unflattering to Copia Sulam. The description of the *Manifesto*, for instance, is not wholly positive, and some sections of the manuscript – most prominently its front matter – suggest that the salonnière was lacking in judgment. The note to readers implies that Paluzzi tricked a woman who was "attracted by the false sound of his learning" and "lured by that shell of knowledge which he seemed to demonstrate because of his animated way of speaking";[181] it goes on to call her "imprudent."[182] But the note to readers also touts the loyalty, generosity, and virtue she displayed by helping Paluzzi "with an open heart" and "with utmost compassion."[183] These qualities – however vulnerable they left her – recalled those that were being lauded, during these very same years, in the Barbarigo–Trevisan heroic friendship. As noted above, the manuscript's dedication to Trevisan explicitly connects Copia Sulam with his finest characteristics and reminds readers that she, like he, was a victim of ingratitude and that she, like he, was guided by virtues that exposed her to evildoers. The dedication states that only Trevisan could understand how her associates' wickedness "almost drove to destruction a lady who, because of the loyalty of her heart and the affection she always showed to those who profess virtue, certainly did not deserve to fall into such evil hands."[184] The comparison between these two friends invokes the values of heroic friendship, around which contemporary rhetoric celebrated not a cunning and clever protection of one's self-interests, but rather a selfless generosity of spirit. Both Trevisan and Barbarigo could certainly have been condemned for being "imprudent" in their friendship, but (in the friendship's mythology) they – like Copia Sulam – were guided by higher ideals. In this context, it becomes clear that the criticisms levelled against Copia Sulam in the note to readers and dedication in the "Avisi" were not serious: any missteps she may have taken derived, like those of Trevisan, from the generous inclination of her spirit. Such a defence admitted only the fault of virtue, yet by admitting some fault – and in this way taking distance from the salonnière – these accounts seem to offer an impartial, and therefore more reliable, account.

One of the manuscript's most serious criticisms of Copia Sulam revolves around her pursuit of her legal case, as described above. While less than flattering, the discussion criticizes Copia Sulam for the relatively minor offences of impatience and inexperience. By doing so, the reports blame procedural error – rather than blatant unfairness in the Venetian legal system and, in particular, specific unfairness against Jews – for the unreasonably light sentence the manuscript says Berardelli received. The "Avisi" manuscript succeeds, that is, in protesting this sentence without indicting the Venetian judicial system – a recasting that is part of the manuscript's general effort not to offend powerful forces in Venice. Other examples of this tendency include the manuscript's avoidance of any criticism of Christianity – another similarity the manuscript shares with the *Manifesto*[185] – and its praise for Giovanni Soranzo and the other powerful figures whose names appear in the *Rime*.

Another serious criticism of Copia Sulam regards suggestions that she superstitiously believed her associates' tricks. Virginia Cox sees such portrayals of Copia Sulam as the controlling ones in the manuscript, showing her "in an undignified light as foolishly credulous and superstitious," a representation so damning that Cox interprets the text of the "Avisi" as "a satirically inflected exercise in character defamation."[186] The manuscript's organizers may have felt compelled to include these details, since the unseemly story of Copia Sulam's falling out with Paluzzi and Berardelli had certainly circulated via "Le Sareide" as well as by rumour. The reports were intended to set the record straight, to "reveal to the world the truth, so that everybody knows why that thief [Berardelli] was driven to slander the Jewish woman's good name."[187] In this statement, we perhaps have the key to the manuscript's inclusion of such unflattering information: her supporters believed that the best way to defend Copia Sulam was with a truthful account that revealed Berardelli's motivations.

By discussing rather than ignoring the tale of her deception, the reports were also able to shape perception of it, strongly defending Copia Sulam for falling into such thinking by emphasizing that the elaborately orchestrated deception to which she was subjected justified her belief:

This situation may make one wonder how a person known for her judgment allowed herself to be caught in these snares. But if one considers how artfully fraud can be cloaked and how easily deceit can be achieved by those who, beneath a mantle of false learning, lying semblances, assumed manners, fake declarations and fictitious zeal, hide in their foul

hearts the strongly rooted vines of the most abominable impiety on which
... the ripe fruits of treachery are always found – then perhaps will wonder
cease, all the more so since all seven of the people who were involved in
that sordid conspiracy owed their lives to that honorable woman for the
considerable help she had always given them over a long span of time –
a circumstance that helped that loathsome rabble doggedly to continue
their deceit for two years.[188]

The "Avisi" manuscript thus argues, in the strongest of terms, that Copia
Sulam's lapse in judgment should be excused because of the extreme cunning of her deceivers, whom she had every reason to trust since they relied on her for their well-being, to which she, in turn, solicitously tended.

Even taking such criticisms fully into account, the representation of
Copia Sulam in the manuscript is overwhelmingly positive. The note
to readers, in which some of the criticism appears, underscores Copia
Sulam's strength more than once, giving proof of her fortitude with a
detailed account of her unstinting assistance for Paluzzi. The account
goes so far to emphasize her righteousness that it compares her with
the Virgin protector[189] and calls the refuge she created for Paluzzi the
"Promised Land."[190] Her endless patience, loyalty, and generosity in the
face of ingratitude and treachery seem almost Christ-like – a representation that, along with the absence of any hostility towards Christianity,
would have resonated with Christian readers alongside the Jewish readers
who were also courted.

The "Avisi" account always highlights Copia Sulam's virtue, calling
her "honourable" and "virtuous" dozens of times and referring to her
frequently as "illustrious," "worthy," "good," and "esteemed."[191] These
descriptors contrast her in the starkest terms not only with Berardelli
and Paluzzi, who are described as "nefarious," "wicked," and "evil,"[192]
but also with the portrayals that Bonifaccio, Cebà, and Berardelli had
offered of her in print. Bonifaccio and Berardelli blatantly attacked her
intellectual and personal honesty, while Cebà had obliquely questioned
her intellectual honesty and, more damning still, raised the spectre of
sexual impropriety in her relations with her male associates. In fact, the
"Avisi" could have reinforced this latter impression by showing how thoroughly her male literary associates had penetrated her domestic space to
perpetrate their crimes, had the manuscript not underscored her virtue
so emphatically. Proving Copia Sulam's honour and virtue was a major
thrust of the manuscript.

The repeated representation of Copia Sulam as an "honorable and
virtuous woman" clearly foregrounds her faithfulness to her husband
as well as her intellectual honesty – her respectability, in other words,

in a society where women's sexual virtue was of paramount importance. As a foil to Copia Sulam's purity of mind and body, the manuscript criticizes not only the literary but also the sexual activities of Berardelli and Paluzzi, repeatedly suggesting that Berardelli had sexual relations with the Sulams' Moorish scullery maid Arnolfa and stressing the religious and racial transgression such a union presented: an "illicit commerce that the servant had with the Moorish girl ... because of his impious habits, which always disregarded the law."[193] The critique goes yet further, calling Berardelli "a servile soul, the beloved darling of that filthy black girl,"[194] and an "incestuous ox."[195] The troubling racial and sexual dimensions of the manuscript's attack on Arnolfa show a bigotry that was rooted in widely held stereotypes of Africans, including belief in their promiscuity.[196] Paluzzi, on the other hand, is reviled as hermaphroditical (16r, 38v) and is accused of committing sodomy: the reports attribute to him the "wicked vice" and state that he would "violate the laws of love and nature."[197] As portrayed by the manuscript, Berardelli's and Paluzzi's vices combine to suggest their utter moral depravity, putting into starker relief Copia Sulam's virtue and honour.

Copia Sulam's Poetic Retrospective

Notions of virtue and honour also guided Copia Sulam's representation in the "Avisi" of her own literary career, upon which she casts a backward gaze in several of the collection's sonnets. As in the *Manifesto*, she proposes an ideal of noble intellectual pursuits in contrast to the dishonesty and slander that she encountered. In the first of these poems, she defends her association with her ignoble associates by saying that she was misled by her intellectual curiosity:

> Quel desio di saper ch'in cor gentile
> sovente alberga ad ingannevol luce
> mi trasse, indi seguendo infido duce
> tardi di cor vilan scorgei lo stile. (83r)

> (That desire for knowledge that in a noble heart
> often resides drew me toward a deceptive light
> by which, following a treacherous leader,
> only too late did I make out the markings of a loutish heart.)

To describe her associates' betrayal of her desire for knowledge, she uses language that immediately connects her to the Italian literary tradition.

The "cor gentile" she ascribes herself recalls the central notion of the medieval Dolce Stil Novo poetic school to which Dante belonged.[198] Her phrasing also recalls his *Inferno*, where Dante the pilgrim expressed his "great desire to know" ("gran disio ... di savere" [VI.83]). The eminent tradition that she invokes to explain her devotion to knowledge justifies it implicitly, even if it left her vulnerable to deception. This insistence on her thirst for knowledge recalls her debate five years earlier with Bonifaccio, where she explains in her *Manifesto* in response to Bonifaccio's accusations that she had posed difficult philosophical and theological questions in their conversations because she was eager for "curious and rare knowledge."[199] In this late poem in the "Avisi," Copia Sulam still affirms the nobility of such pursuits, despite their costs.

In the *Manifesto*, as we have seen, Copia Sulam expresses distaste for the literary battle that Bonifaccio forced her to enter with his calumnious attack. Nevertheless, she embraces the fame that he offered her through conflict. The *Manifesto* shows her to be a skilled polemicist even as she claims, in one of its sonnets, to enter "unarmed into the unfamiliar arena" (*Entro senz'armi in non usato aringo*).[200] In the "Avisi," Copia Sulam refers again to the "arena" of the literary battle, but this time she does not deign to enter:

> Se con armi in aringo si de' entrare
> conformi al vil nimico, ah, che dispera
> ch'in alto aspira: e sdegna uscir di schiera
> Per ignobil trofeo scuro e volgare. (84r)

> (If one must enter armed into the arena
> like one's vile enemy, ah, one who aspires to reach great heights
> will despair and refuse to break rank
> for a trophy that is ignoble, dark, and crass.)

Here the salonnière contrasts pure intellectual pursuits – "great heights" – with the sort of battles into which her "vile" enemies baited her. The "ignoble, dark, and crass" trophy of these conflicts – the fame earned through fighting them – is a prize that she rejects out of hand. In the final tercet of the poem, she hints at the ugly aftereffects of such contests:

> Ma per il più (qui vaglia il ver) si pente
> d'aver mai da faretra schiuso strale
> né affisso a infame segno illustre telo.[201] (84r)

(But for the most part, may the truth be clear: one regrets
ever having taken an arrow from the quiver
or having shot a noble shaft at a foul target.)

These battles, whose "foul target" defiles any arrow aimed against it,
leave virtuous combatants only the regret of having entered the arena.

As Copia Sulam justifies her decision not to pursue literary war with
Berardelli, she also reflects retrospectively – and regretfully – on her
literary career that included high-profile contests with Bonifaccio and
Cebà, whose costs, she seems to indicate, were too high. She argues that
an intellectual life that does not aim for "great heights" and instead looks
downward towards base enemies frustrates rather than fulfills the aspi-
rations of an honourable writer. Her own literary career, in which she
was constantly beset by hostile attacks, did not foreclose the possibility
of fame, yet it did not offer the sort of fame that Copia Sulam sought – a
fame earned on her terms, by means of worthy texts published sparingly,
rather than one gained solely by means of the conflicts into which her
enemies baited her.

By claiming to turn away from a new, unworthy battle, Copia Sulam of
course fights back against her enemies, as she and her associates do in
the "Avisi" manuscript as a whole. This defence could not be more different from the one she mounted with the *Manifesto*. There, she responded
to an attack on her reputation with a sharply worded treatise, which she
alone signed and published under her own name, and in which she
openly espoused a quest for fame. Here, she responds, alongside other
writers, with a work left manuscript, in which she conceals her involvement and in which she rejects the fame won through polemics that she
had embraced in the *Manifesto*. Though she does not back away from
conflict altogether and in fact fires back with the "Avisi," her approach
and attitude towards polemics have fundamentally changed.

In her final sonnet of the collection (figure 5.10), Copia Sulam discusses her pursuit of writing as a thing of the past:

> Tace è gran tempo qual pose la cetra
> onde sen gio talhor mia fama intorno;
> noiose cure al bel desio troncorno
> l'ali onde s'alza il canto e vita impetra. (86r)

> (Having set down the lyre which once sounded my fame
> I have been silent for some time.
> Vexing troubles clipped the wings of the noble desire
> on which poetry takes flight and seeks life.[202])

5.10 Copia Sulam's final sonnet in the "Avisi di Parnaso" manuscript (86r) (1626). Correr Library, Venice (Ms. Cicogna 270). 2018 © Biblioteca Correr – Fondazione Musei Civici di Venezia.

In this final extant poem, Copia Sulam upholds the value of her poetic endeavours, which she describes in lofty terms. Yet "vexing troubles" destroyed her ability – or will – to pursue them. Since constant controversies rendered it impossible for her to pursue poetry as she wished, and since she had no interest in building her reputation on defamatory polemics, Copia Sulam rested her pen.

6
The Salon's Afterlife (Post-1626)

~~~~~

Overview

Copia Sulam ended her literary career after her last public row with Berardelli, which dragged on through 1626. But she didn't immediately disappear from the literary stage. The next year, Zinano advertised his connection to her in four poems included in his 1627 *Rime diverse*. After this, she all but disappeared from view until her death in 1641.

Berardelli, on the other hand, went on to a career of moderate prominence in the same literary society that had reviled Copia Sulam. He shared membership in the Accademia degli Incogniti with the Agostinian friar and literary adventurer Angelico Aprosio, who defamed the salonnière in an account that was published towards the end of the seventeenth century. The literary historian Giovanni Cinelli Calvoli defended Copia Sulam against Aprosio's charges, but his text was not circulated widely until well into the eighteenth century. Much literary criticism from the eighteenth through the twenty-first century has continued to be unflattering to Copia Sulam, but scholarship focused on women writers or on Jewish writers has tended to be an exception. Over the last several decades, the salonnière has been the object of increasing scholarly attention.

Gabriele Zinano's *Rime diverse*

The *Rime diverse* volume was one of more than a dozen works that Zinano published in Venice between 1623 and 1627, and one of eight that he published in 1627 alone.[1] Copia Sulam's appearance in the volume and its publication of one of her poems gave her a small role in the publishing phenomenon that Zinano created that year. But while he disseminated her poetry, he made no attempt to resuscitate her reputation or to help her relaunch her literary career. The poems by or

about Copia Sulam were, at the time of the publication, three to four
years old, written during or shortly after Zinano's stay in Venice in late
1623.[2] They document the philosophical exchanges and religious debates that took place at the salon. But the active literary society that animated these poems could only be seen here in retrospective, since the
salon that had fostered such exchanges had in the meantime collapsed.
The volume also acknowledges this collapse by including a poem to
Berardelli that postdates the latter's break with Copia Sulam, to which
Zinano refers obliquely.[3] That poem had been published the year before in Paluzzi's *Rime*.[4]

While documenting a literary sensation that had already passed,
Zinano's poems still cast Copia Sulam in a problematic light. His sonnet to Geronimo Bembo, "a Venetian gentleman who was visiting the
young Jewish woman called signora Sarra Copia when the author was
also there,"[5] for instance, shows her freely consorting with male associates who were drawn to her by sexual desire: the poem, titled "La bella di
Giesù nemica, e nostra" (Jesus's Beautiful Enemy, and Ours), describes
habitual salon gatherings where

> Spesso di fiamme le sue guancie mostra,
> e d'accesi coralli arma la bocca
> onde nel dolce incendio[6] ognun trabocca.
> Amanti ov'è più la speranza vostra?[7]

> (She often shows her cheeks aflame
> and she arms her mouth with burning coral,
> whence everyone falls into the sweet fire.
> Lovers, where more is your hope?)

The poem depicts Copia Sulam as surrounded by men who threatened
her honour and, along with an exchange of poems between Zinano and
the salonnière (discussed below), also shows her resisting her associates'
conversionist appeals (she remains, that is, "Jesus's beautiful enemy"). The
sexual and religious dimensions of this portrayal are unflattering in much
the same way as is Cebà's portrait of her in his *Lettere a Sarra Copia*, whose
publication in 1623 may have shaped Zinano's approach in these 1623–
1624 poems. Zinano's publication of them several years later, therefore,
reprised the destructive attacks in Cebà's letters that had cast suspicion on
Copia Sulam's salon, but after the salon had already been shuttered.

At the same time, the *Rime diverse* collection does showcase Copia
Sulam as a writer of some importance. The sonnet exchange with
Zinano reveals the strength of her literary network, highlighting her

connections both to him and to Cebà. Zinano addresses his sonnet "To a Jewish woman called signora Sarra Copia who loved the virtues of Signor Anselmo [*sic*] Cebà despite his death."[8] Comparing his own sorrow at the death of his beloved to Sarra's sorrow at Cebà's passing, Zinano writes "Sarra, mort'è il tuo bene, e morto il mio" (Sarra, your treasure has died and died has mine, figure 6.1). This poem invited Copia Sulam's "Amai Zinan qui il ben d'ogni ben mio," (On earth, Zinano, I loved the treasure of all my treasures, figure 6.2), a sonnet of response in which she sums up some of the most important tropes of her literary life. She highlights her connection to Cebà, around which she had built her literary career, and proclaims her certainty that she was bound for enduring literary fame and eternal spiritual glory:

> Amai Zinan qui il ben d'ogni ben mio,
> Ma l'amo or più, che sta beato in Cielo,
> Perché spogliato del terren suo velo
> Fatt'è più bel ne le beltà di Dio.
> E crescendo l'amor, cresce il desio
> Di gire a lui con più devoto zelo,
> Ché dove non può entrare caldo né gelo,
> Se speri tu d'andar, no'l despero io.
> E se tu aspiri a uscir di man di morte
> Co 'l favor de le Muse, io porre il piede
> Con maggior forza ne l'eterna stanza,
> Ché s'apre la virtù del Ciel le porte,
> De le virtù d'Anselmo io fatta erede,
> D'andarlo ivi a goder prendo speranza.

> (On earth, Zinano, I loved the treasure of all my treasures,
> But I love him more now that he lives blessed in Heaven,
> Since, stripped of his earthly veil,
> His beauty has grown in the beauty of God.
> And as my love grows, so does my desire
> To go to him with more devout zeal,
> Since if you hope to go where neither ice nor cold can enter
> Neither do I lack hope of going there.
> And if you aspire to escape the hand of death
> By the favor of the Muses, I will place my foot
> Even more firmly in the eternal hall,
> Since if virtue opens the doors of Heaven
> I, heir to the virtues of Anselmo,
> Take heart that I will go there to exult.)

46   R I M E

Ad vn'Ebrea detta la Signora Sarra Copia
che amaua le virtù del Signor Anfelmo Cebà ancor che morto .
Sonetto. 385.

Sarra, mort'è il tuo bene, e morto il mio .,
   Ah non fon morti, viui andaro al Cielo
   Par ver morir, ma fù fquarciar il velo,
   Che gli impedia la via di gire à Dio.
E fpero iui falir , come hò defio
   Vittoria mia à goder con dolce zelo ,
   S'offefo hò Dio con troppo ardore, o Zelo ,
   Ei può perdonar più che peccar' io.
La Bontà, che per noi lo fpinfe à morte
   Sempre aperfe le porte à vitra fede ,
   Del Ciel. Qual maggior vò defio, e fperäza?
Ma fe quefta Bontà chiude le porte
   A quel fuperbo cor, ch'à lei non crede,
   Doue sëza il tuo Anfelmo haurai tu ftäza?

Ad vn'Ebreo detto il Signor Giacob V-
riel , che cantaua il Seren ifs. Dauite.
Sonetto. 386.

Canti l' Eroe, ch'or co'l valor de l'armi
   Fieri domando, ancor deftruffe gli empi,
   Or con la cetra, e con pietofi carmi
   De le glorie di Dio fonar fe i Tempi .
Grande four'ogni ardir quafto tuo parmi,
   Ma fegui pur, che fe'l difegno adempi ,
   Moftrerai come il Mondo, ò canti, ò s'armi
                Poffa

D I V E R S E: 47

Poffa il Ciel guadagnar, vincere i tempi .
Come vinceffe Eroi, forti, e giganti
   Non cantar fol. Ne la tua penna fdegni
   D'annouerarlo pur fra gli altri amanti .
Peccò, ma vien che nel peccar n'infegni
   Quefto gran Re co' i fuoi deuoti pianti
   A meritar il Ciel fra errori indegni .

Rifpofta della predetta,
       Son. 387.

Amai Zinan qui il ben d'ogni ben mio,
   Ma l'amo or più, che ftà beato in Cielo,
   Perche fpogliato del terren fuo veloce
   Fatt'è più bel ne la beltà di Dio .
E crefcendo l' amor, crefce il defio
   Di gire à lui con più deuoto zelo,
   Che doue non può entrar caldo, ne gelo ,
   Se fperi tu d'andar, no'l defpero io,
E fe tu afpiri à vfcir di man di morte
   Co'l fauor de le Mufe, io porre il piede
   Con maggior forza ne l'eterna ftanza,
   Che s'apre la virtù del Ciel le porte
   De le virtù d' Anfelmo, io fatta crede,
   D'andarlo iui à goder prendo fepranza.

Al Sig. Aleff. Bernard .   Son. 388.

Corfe l' Afia Aleffandro e i piani, e i monti
   Empì di ftrage, à le Città die morte,
   I Rè fpogliò de la real lor forte,
   E fè d'amico fangue orridi fonti .
                   D' A-

6.1–6.2 Zinano and Copia Sulam's exchange in Zinano's *Rime diverse* (Venice:
appresso Evangelista Deuchino, 1627), 46–7. Copia Sulam's poem is her last
that would be published in her lifetime. By permission of the British Library,
General Reference Collection 839.a.23.(4). © The British Library Board.

In his sonnet to Copia Sulam, Zinano asserts that she was lost because of Cebà's death since, as a Jew, she had no access to heaven.[9] In her response, Copia Sulam instead places herself on an equal spiritual footing with Zinano: she has no less hope of enjoying eternal life than he. Her simple assertion that Jews and Christians have the same spiritual worth contradicted the assumption of inferiority that informed the attitude of the Church – and of broader Catholic culture – towards Jews, the very attitude that conditioned many of her associates' interactions with her. It also echoes her assertion in the *Manifesto* of the consonance between the Christian and Jewish faiths, and her vindication of the dignity of Jewish beliefs in both the *Manifesto* and (as reported by Cebà) in the *Lettere a Sarra Copia.* In literary matters, however, Copia Sulam does not claim mere equality with Zinano – instead, she boasts of her greater chances for poetic immortality. She maintains that Cebà's death did not deprive her of her literary and spiritual identity, as Zinano suggests, but rather that it empowered her as the heir to his literary and spiritual qualities. She thus recasts the difficult legacy of Cebà's original letters as well as their 1623 publication (which, as we have seen, were both deeply problematic for her) as a positive inheritance that ensured her success both in this world and the next.

Although Copia Sulam's exchange with Zinano likely dates to 1624, its 1627 publication allowed her voice to be heard directly one final time. She may not have meant this sonnet to be her final literary statement, yet it functions as such, providing a distilled manifesto of her religious and literary ideals. "Amai Zinan" was the last piece of writing printed under her name during the seventeenth century. By 1629, she had disappeared from the literary stage. Agostino Superbi (d. 1634), in his *Trionfo glorioso d'heroi illustri et eminenti dell'inclita, & maravigliosa città di Venetia, li quali nelle lettere fiorirono,* lauds Moderata Fonte and Lucrezia Marinella in a section entitled "Donne nelle lettere singolari" (Exceptional Women of Letters), but makes no mention of Copia Sulam.[10] The 1630 plague that ravaged Venice may have prevented a comeback, had she desired it, since at least one loyal ally, her associate Giacomo Rosa, died in the outbreak.[11] At her death in 1641, her close literary associate Leon Modena wrote an epitaph that did not mention her writing.[12]

A Resuscitated Reputation: Alessandro Berardelli

As Copia Sulam disappeared from public view, her enemy Alessandro Berardelli became more prominent. Through his 1626 edition of Paluzzi's *Rime,* with its open advertisement of its editor's connections to powerful members of contemporary literary society, Berardelli, who was a painter, had some success establishing himself in Venice as a writer and as an editor of poetry. He shared a close friendship with the successful patrician writer Pietro Michiele, author of the licentious *Arte de gli amanti* (The Art of Lovers),[13] who was a key figure in the Accademia degli Incogniti as it coalesced during these years. Agostino Superbi highlighted Michiele's powerful position in Venetian letters by including him in his *Trionfo glorioso*, calling him "quite wise, with a noble and clever intellect."[14] Berardelli was in touch with Michiele by 1626 at the latest: the latter contributed a sonnet in praise of the former to Paluzzi's *Rime*.[15] Michiele included this composition as well as another to Berardelli in his own 1642 *Rime*,[16] and wrote five other flattering compositions later published in his 1671 *Delle poesie postume* (Posthumous Verse).[17] For his part, Berardelli dedicated a 1635 poetry collection that he edited to Michiele: Giovanni Battista Manso's *Poesie nomiche* (Gnomic Verse).[18] This exchange of writing and compliments demonstrates Michiele's esteem for Berardelli, with whom he associated over many years, as both an artist and a writer.[19] Berardelli attracted other praise as well. In addition to Zinano, who commended Berardelli in the composition published in Paluzzi's *Rime* and in his own *Rime diverse*,[20] the famed contemporary poet Ciro di Pers (1599–1663) lauded Berardelli's artistic skill in a sonnet addressed to him.[21] Even his critics begrudgingly acknowledged his shrewdness, calling him "quite well-known for the cunning of his intellect."[22]

For the next two decades, Berardelli remained an active member of contemporary literary society, contributing his writings to several important collections that offered, along with the writing they assembled, unofficial surveys of writers à la mode. His participation in Copia Sulam's salon may have provided the connections he used to establish himself. He contributed two poems, for instance, to *Il teatro delle glorie della signora Adriana Basile* (Showcase of the Glories of signora Andreana Basile), a work in praise of the poet and singer (ca. 1580–ca. 1640), sister of the writer Giambattista Basile (1566–1632), that was organized by Strozzi and printed in Venice in 1623.[23] Strozzi was well known to Copia Sulam and her associates.[24] Berardelli continued to work his way into literary society after his break with Copia Sulam. His poetry was included in a celebration of the heroic friendship of Barbarigo and Trevisan published in 1628[25] and in Carlo Ridolfi's *Le maraviglie dell'arte, ouero Le vite de gl'illvstri pittori veneti, e dello stato* (Artistic Marvels, or Lives of the Illustrious Painters of the Veneto, and the State, 1648).[26] Berardelli also contributed to the Accademia degli Incogniti's racy collection of novellas issued in 1642, *Novelle amorose*. The inclusion of his novella in this important Academy publication showed that by the 1640s he had established himself in the group that dominated mid-seventeenth-century

6.3 Alessandro Berardelli's pledge of friendship to the classical scholar Johann Friedrich Gronovius in his *Album amicorum* (1634–1646). With permission of KB | National Library of the Netherlands: MS 130 E 32.

Venetian intellectual life. It is worth noting that his story presents its female protagonist as oversexed, scheming, and ruthless.[27]

Berardelli also had many ties to the publishing industry. The "Avisi" manuscript describes him as frequenting the printshops of Venice and working as a proofreader.[28] By the time he dedicated Manso's 1635 *Poesie nomiche*, Berardelli had solidified his position: the dedication indicates that he was a decision maker at the printing house of Francesco Baba.[29]

Some manuscript works of Berardelli's are extant. His inscription for the *Album amicorum* (Friendship Album) of the classical scholar Johann Friedrich Gronovius (1611–1671) (figure 6.3),[30] shows that Berardelli established a tie with the famed scholar during his 1641 visit to Venice.[31] In his inscription, Berardelli praises Gronovius's "virtues and merit" and pledges himself his "eternal friend and servant."[32] Also preserved in manuscript form is his sonnet in celebration of the 1644 appointment to cardinal of Pietro Ottobono (later Alexander VIII).[33] Although the Roman Berardelli never fully established himself in Venetian letters – he never, for instance, published his own free-standing work – he developed ties to those who were thriving, both financially and professionally, in the city.

A Renewed Attack against Copia Sulam, and a Defence

Berardelli's continued presence on the Venetian literary scene throughout the 1630s and into the 1640s stands in contrast to Copia Sulam's public silence until her death in 1641. No attributed works are known after
the five poems she circulated in the 1626 "Avisi" manuscript.[34] Virginia
Cox has recently proposed that a 1638 opera libretto by Benedetto Ferrari
(c. 1600–1681), *La maga fulminata* (The Thunderstruck Sorceress),
may include one of Copia Sulam's poems, a composition signed by a
"signora S.C."[35] It would be extremely interesting to be able to prove
that she continued writing – and maintained literary contacts – into the
1630s. If signora S.C. is indeed Copia Sulam, the encomiastic sonnet
included in Ferrari's work is more interesting for its date of composition – over a decade after Copia Sulam rejected a public literary life –
than for its themes. But at the current state of research it is not possible
to determine if the poem was in fact written by her. Speaking in favour
of an attribution might be the fact that the first word in rhyme in the
poem, "cetra" or lyre, is the same as in her last composition in the "Avisi"
manuscript[36] – possibly a self-referential gesture. Additionally, Ferrari,
like Copia Sulam herself, had connections to the Incogniti, though he
was not a member.[37] Speaking against attribution is the fact that there
is no information that she was in contact with Ferrari or any of the
other writers who contributed verse to *La maga fulminata*, nor is there
any evidence of Copia Sulam having any link to the printer Bariletti.
Additionally, there is no other trace of her having continued literary activities beyond the late 1620s.[38] We can say at a minimum that this poem,
if hers, shows her working in an entirely new literary circle; and that her
activity was sporadic or casual enough that it did not attract other notice.
It is also possible that the use of the name "signora S.C." was a hoax,
meant to refer to Copia Sulam but with a poem that she did not write – a
"joke" for literary insiders.

Copia Sulam was only explicitly mentioned in print one other time in
her contemporaries' lifetimes, and even then obliquely. The profile of
Cebà in the Accademia degli Incogniti's 1647 *Le glorie de gli Incogniti* (The
Glories of Incogniti Members) – a bio-bibliographical survey of the group's
most prominent members – listed his *Lettere a Sarra Copia* as one of his publications. Other than that title, the *Glorie* profile provides no information
about the letter collection or about Cebà and Copia Sulam's relationship.[39]

Contemporaries had not forgotten Copia Sulam, however. Later in the
century, Aprosio reprised with new intensity the vicious attacks against her
that had tainted her literary career. Aprosio, an Augustinian friar, wrote
an undated letter (probably from the last quarter of the seventeenth

century) to the Roman writer Prospero Mandosio (1643–1724), who was compiling a reference work on Roman writers.[40] Aprosio's report purports to be a biography of Copia Sulam's associate Paluzzi, who was from Rome, but it focuses mostly on the salonnière. The friar recounts the major episodes of her literary career, including her correspondence with Cebà, the controversy with Bonifaccio, her falling out with Paluzzi and Berardelli, and the publication of Paluzzi's *Rime*. Although Aprosio admits that Paluzzi treated the salonnière dishonourably, his report focuses mostly on discrediting her with charges against both her literary and her sexual reputation. Aprosio claims that Copia Sulam initially hired Paluzzi as her tutor because she was worried that her fame exceeded her skill and she needed his help. Regarding the Cebà correspondence, Aprosio alleges that "it was Paluzzi's job to play the part of the Jewish woman, nor did he lack for work. I who met her know that she wasn't that smart."[41] The friar attempts to give weight to the accusation of plagiarism by claiming to have met Copia Sulam, an assertion difficult to credit since he arrived in Venice around the beginning of 1640, a decade and a half after she had ended her public literary career and shortly before her death (she died in February 1641, after months of illness).[42] The events that Aprosio recounts with seeming authority occurred when he was between eleven and nineteen years of age. Other errors mar the account: for instance, he claims that Copia Sulam's father, Simon, was involved in founding her salon (which he terms an academy [*accademia*]), though it coalesced more than a decade after his death.

Such distance from Copia Sulam's story did not blunt the ill will Aprosio felt towards her. He attempts to strip her of any claim to her writing by asserting that her *Manifesto* was not "flour from Sarra's sack, however, but from Paluzzi's, who masqueraded as a Jewish woman."[43] The report also offers new and more scandalous stories about Copia Sulam's inappropriate contact with men at her salon, stories even more shocking than those intimated in Cebà's published letters a half-century earlier: Aprosio states quite explicitly that Copia Sulam, a married woman, desired another man. In the same period in which Paluzzi began to "use discourtesies toward her,"[44] Aprosio reports: "A powerful figure, French, came to Venice, and attracted by her fame, went to that house as well. He was most handsome in appearance, so that she could say, even though she was married to Giacob Sulam, *I looked and I was lost!*"[45] The friar (who simultaneously undertakes an attack on Giacob's honour, as Cebà had earlier done in his *Lettere a Sarra Copia*) claims that Paluzzi took advantage of this infatuation, thinking that he had "found the path to trick her."[46] Aprosio alleges that the Roman writer fooled her into believing that she could communicate with the Frenchman from a distance by magic, a story that "was not

difficult to get her to believe, since the Jews haven't stopped practicing
and believing in magic arts."[47] The friar's report, therefore, depicts Copia
Sulam as both an unfaithful wife and a superstitious Jew. The charges
Aprosio made against her sexual honour reinforce those made against
her professional integrity: in both her personal and literary dealings, he
portrays her as corrupt. Mandosio included this defamatory report in the
second volume of his *Bibliotheca romana* (Roman Library), which was published in Rome in 1692; Aprosio wrote another slanderous report about
Copia Sulam for the second part of *La Biblioteca aprosiana* (The Aprosian
Library), which circulated but was never published.[48]

Though Aprosio wrote towards the end of the seventeenth century,
his views were shaped by his involvement in mid-century Venetian literary society. In his account to Mandosio, Aprosio wrote that he had
based his information on a 1637 conversation held in Treviso with
Giovanni Maria Vanti, a good friend of Baldassare Bonifaccio and possibly a salon associate (Vanti would likely have left the circle at the time of
Bonifaccio's battle with the salonnière). Aprosio certainly learned more
about Copia Sulam in Venice, where he lived from 1641 to 1647.[49] He
was in direct touch with Baldassare and Gaspare Bonifaccio, and with
Berardelli's good friend Pietro Michiele.[50] Aprosio was also a member
of the Accademia degli Incogniti and moved in the same literary circles
in which Berardelli reinvented himself after his row with Copia Sulam.

Aprosio's accounts of Copia Sulam, then, essentially transmit the antagonistic perspective of his friends – Copia Sulam's enemies – and artic-
ulate the sorts of views that were rife in the literary society that had sought
to discredit her. That Aprosio was not merely parroting the anti-Copia
Sulam rhetoric of her detractors, however, may be borne out by the fact
that he also nurtured a long-lasting resentment against another female
writer of the period, the feminist polemicist Arcangela Tarabotti, who in
the mid-1640s blocked the publication of a work he wrote that slandered
her.[51] He succeeded in publishing a revised version of the work, in which
he removed overt slander but did not relent in his attack against the
writer, even going so far as to pit her against her contemporary, Lucrezia
Marinella.[52] He also sought mercilessly to discredit Tarabotti, most sting-
ingly by accusing her of plagiarism.[53] Attacks on female writers, as we
have seen repeatedly, were not unusual in mid-seventeenth-century
Venetian literary society – but the enduring nature of Aprosio's attacks is
remarkable. He continued to revile Tarabotti and Copia Sulam throughout the rest of his long life, seeking to settle scores in these decades-old
battles long after most of their protagonists had died.

Aprosio's accounts, however, were not the only ones available to readers in the latter part of the seventeenth century. The Florentine Cinelli

Calvoli was preparing a wide-ranging bibliographic repertory entitled *Biblioteca volante* (The Flying Library) during these years. Cinelli Calvoli wrote an entry on Leon Modena's *L'Ester* that focuses on Copia Sulam, the dedicatee, and casts doubt upon the attacks that Aprosio had made against her reputation:

> Leon Modana [*sic*] dedicates [*L'Ester*] to signora Sarra Copio Sullam [*sic*], that woman who is so renowned and famous. Father Angelico Aprosio, in the second part of his *Biblioteca Aprosiana* (whose manuscript I saw), speaks quite badly of this same signora Sarra Copio Sullam, but I strongly suspect that Father Aprosio was misled by someone spiteful and envious of the above-mentioned signora, since there is a great abundance of this type of men even outside of my home city. It is certain that Leon Modana was most learned, nor can that be put into question. Moreover, he did not only know Sarra Copio Sullam by her reputation ... Since he knew her directly he couldn't be fooled, as might have happened to others.[54]

Cinelli Calvoli contends that Modena's admiration of Copia Sulam, based on his direct experience with her, was much more reliable than Aprosio's denigration based on hearsay. He therefore accepts Modena's praise of "her exceptional attributes, many virtues, and great learning, with which she exceeded both her age and her sex."[55] Cinelli Calvoli's report is notable not only for what it says, but what it does not: it does not mention her beauty, the allegations of plagiarism, or the correspondence with Cebà, nor does it make suggestions about her having inappropriate contact with men. By the same token, it also does not mention her writing. Although significant because of its positive tone, Cinelli Calvoli's report is similar to those of Aprosio and of subsequent authors in that it discusses Copia Sulam only as part of an entry on one of her male associates.

Cinelli Calvoli's *Biblioteca* was published in installments – twenty-three separate *scanzie* – between 1677 and 1739 (two editors continued the work after his death in 1706). His assessments of Modena and of Copia Sulam appeared in the fourth *scanzia*, published in Naples in 1682,[56] ten years before Aprosio's vitriolic report would be published by Mandosio in Rome. Cinelli Calvoli's text, however, had limited initial circulation,[57] and it would take until the middle of the next century, when the *Biblioteca* was republished in four volumes, for his reassessment of Copia Sulam to be available to a wide audience.[58] His was the first to question both the motives and the reliability of those who reviled her; it was the only positive assessment of her that would appear in the first century after her death.

Eighteenth-Century Literary Histories

With the exception of Cinelli Calvoli, other late seventeenth- and early eighteenth-century critics returned to the aspects of Copia Sulam's story – her tie with Cebà, her religious difference, and the charges of plagiarism against her – that had dominated her contemporaries' views. (While the reports at times sexualize the tie with Cebà, they do not mention the reports about her inappropriate contact with other men at her salon). All of these reports consider her only in relation to her male associates and none take her writing seriously. They are, however, notable for including Copia Sulam in general histories of Italian literature, whereas later histories – from Girolamo Tiraboschi's *Storia della letteratura italiana* (History of Italian Literature, 1772–1782) through twentieth-century accounts – fail to mention her.[59]

At the close of the seventeenth century, the literary historian Giovanni Mario Crescimbeni (1663–1728) provided an ambivalent report on Copia Sulam in his entry on Cebà for *L'istoria della vulgar poesia* (History of Vernacular Poetry, 1698), claiming that Copia Sulam "lacked nothing but the light of faith" to be worthy of Cebà's love.[60] (He, like many subsequent literary historians, tended to read the love rhetoric in the Copia Sulam–Cebà correspondence literally). But his more extended discussion of her in the fourth volume of his *Commentari intorno alla sua istoria della vulgar poesia* (Commentary Regarding His History of Vernacular Poetry), originally published in 1711, was dismissive.[61] He focuses on her relationship with Cebà, whom he says she loved "most intensely"[62] and could have married had she converted. He discounts her writing, saying she was "quite enchanted by our poetry, which she almost wrote well."[63] The "our" presumably means that, in his reckoning, the poetic tradition belonged to Christian men. While dismissing her writing's merit, however, it is notable that Crescimbeni did not deny Copia Sulam's authorship.

Francesco Saverio Quadrio (1695–1756) closely follows some aspects of Crescimbeni's report in his *Della storia e della ragione di ogni poesia* (History and Rationale for All Poetry, 1741), calling Copia Sulam again "quite enchanted by our poetry" and focusing on what he portrays as her love affair with Cebà, "with whom she was taken."[64] Giovanni Maria Mazzucchelli (1707–1765) instead considers her relationship with Bonifaccio, calling her "a witty young woman, dilettante of literature" and, following Aprosio, reports that "it is said that [her *Manifesto*] was not her own work, but rather the work of the Roman Numidio Paluzzi."[65] Such doubts about her authorship have persisted even in modern scholarship. For example, in the 1981 entry on Copia Sulam for the *Dizionario biografico degli italiani* (Biographical Dictionary of Italians) – the key biographical reference work for modern scholarship on Italy – Giorgio Busetto states that it is "not difficult to believe" that Modena authored the *Manifesto* or the 1619 letter to Bonifaccio. Busetto also reports, without providing details, that "according to some accounts ... Paluzzi gave no little assistance to Copia Sulam in her composition of letters to Cebà and her sonnets."[66] These scholars' claims, taken together, are contradictory – sceptics variously attribute her works to Paluzzi or to Modena, two writers with entirely different formations and worldviews. Nonetheless, the charges of plagiarism against Copia Sulam continue to echo nearly 400 years after they were first made. In a 2004 article, Giuseppe Veltri questions whether Copia Sulam wrote the 1619 letter to Bonifaccio, wondering "how much is her own and how much contributed by others."[67] He also casts doubt upon her authorship of the *Manifesto*, saying that the work was "composed, or at least 'signed' by the female poet from the Ghetto."[68]

The Roots of Modern Scholarship

While some of the major works of eighteenth-century literary history fault Copia Sulam for her continuing adherence to the Jewish faith and consider her only in relation to male writers, it was as a woman and as a Jew that she began to attract positive critical attention in that century. Luisa Bergalli (1703–1779) includes three sonnets by Copia Sulam in her *Componimenti poetici delle più illustri rimatrici d'ogni secolo* (Poetic Compositions of the Most Illustrious Female Poets of Every Century, 1726).[69] Francesco Pentolini (1702–1787) included Copia Sulam in his 1776–1777 poetic celebration of *Le donne illustri* (Illustrious Women) and, while focusing on what he also portrayed as the failed love affair with Cebà, calls her "famous and no less learned."[70] This interest in her as a female writer continued into the nineteenth century. In an 1824 survey of lettered women, Ginevra Canonici Fachini (1779–1870) praised Copia Sulam's "delicate verse" as one of the bright spots in a century "of darkness and wretched squalor."[71] Bartolommeo Gamba (1766–1841) includes her *Manifesto* (reprinted without the sonnets or introductory prose) in his anthology of *Lettere di donne italiane del secolo decimo sesto* (Letters of Italian Women of the Sixteenth Century, 1832), ignoring his title's temporal and generic constraints to do so and calling her "a learned woman, skilled musician, talented poet and worthy of admiration for her epistolary style."[72] Pietro Leopoldo Ferri (1786–1847) mentioned several of Copia Sulam's works, including her *Manifesto* and some of her sonnets, in his *Biblioteca femminile italiana* (Bibliography of Works by Italian Women, 1842).[73] Domenico Legrenzi included one of her sonnets in his *Galleria poetica di donne veneziane* (Poetic Gallery of Venetian

Women, 1852).[74] Legrenzi, like his predecessors in this line of criticism, takes for granted Copia Sulam's authorship and ignores the defamatory information that circulated in earlier accounts.

While Copia Sulam attracted attention as part of the growing interest in women writers throughout the eighteenth and nineteenth centuries, she also benefitted from a movement to catalogue and recognize Jewish writers. Christian Hebraists Johann Christoph Wolf (1683–1739) and Giovanni Bernardo De Rossi (1742–1831), for instance, included her in their bio-bibliographic repertories on Jewish writers (in 1732 and 1802 respectively).[75] Calling her a "learned woman,"[76] Wolf focuses mostly on Cinelli Calvoli's defence of Copia Sulam against Aprosio's attack and on Modena's description of her in his dedication to L'Ester, while also mentioning that she had a debate with Bonifaccio and wrote on the immortality of the soul. He introduces no doubts as to her authorship. De Rossi writes that Copia Sulam "cultivated poetry and learning and made a name for herself in her own time,"[77] mentions her tract on the immortality of the soul (the Manifesto) and scattered poems, and also does not question her authorship.

Interest in Copia Sulam as a Jewish writer intensified during the middle of the nineteenth century as the foundations were laid for the discipline of Jewish studies. In a movement known as the "Science of Judaism" (Wissenschaft des Judentums), Jewish historians and writers sought to record and codify a cultural heritage as part of a larger project of philology and cataloguing in mid- to late-nineteenth-century scholarship.[78] Julius Fürst (1805–1873) includes Copia Sulam in the first volume of his Bibliotheca Judaica (Judaic Bibliography, 1849), which mentions Bergalli's report and Copia Sulam's work on the immortality of the soul (again, the Manifesto).[79] Heinrich Graetz (1817–1891) discusses her in his Geschichte der Juden (History of the Jews) and praises her writing.[80] More detailed accounts appeared during the late nineteenth century in studies by scholars including Abraham Geiger (1810–1874), Moritz Abraham Levy (1817–1872), Moisé Soave (1820–1882), Ernest David (1824–1886), and Meyer Kayserling (1829–1905).[81] These scholars present important new biographic and bibliographic information on Copia Sulam in portrayals that often laud her as a Jewish "heroine."[82] In a similar vein, Nahida Remy Lazarus (1849–1928) celebrates Copia Sulam's adherence to her faith and her "moral purity" in her work, Das jüdische Weib (The Jewish Woman, 1891).[83] Kayserling and Remy Lazarus appeal to Jewish women in particular, whom they saw as custodians of the faith. This focus on women, whom these authors insist were highly valued in Judaism, was part of a complicated attempt, in a German context, to affirm Jewish difference while also demonstrating Jewish integration into modern national society.[84] The ideological interests of these studies sometimes cloud their scholarly accuracy.

Another influential work of the period was *Les quatre martyrs* (The Four Martyrs, 1856) by Alexis-François Rio (1797–1874),[85] who also authored the influential art history tract *De la poésie chrétienne* (The Poetry of Christian Art, 1836), later expanded and published as *De l'art chrétien* (Christian Art, 1861–1867).[86] Rio, an art historian who viewed his subject through a Roman Catholic lens, profiles Cebà as a "martyr of charity." Rio's narration of Cebà and Copia Sulam's relationship, written in an almost novel-like style, is based on the *Lettere a Sarra Copia* and depicts with pathos Cebà's suffering at Copia Sulam's continued adherence to Judaism. Nevertheless, Rio, a devout Roman Catholic author, also provides an extremely sympathetic portrayal of the salonnière, whom he represents as keenly intelligent and constant in her Jewish faith. This positive characterization persuaded certain German scholars associated with the Wissenschaft des Judentums to consider Copia Sulam's life and work.[87] Rio ignores, or did not know about, the negative accounts of her literary career, casts no aspersion upon her artistic and personal integrity, and recounts with relish her besting of Bonifaccio in the *Manifesto* debate. For all his sympathy, however, Rio's account is deeply romanticized and lacks in scholarly rigour what it offers in narrative force.

Two other studies from the latter half of the nineteenth century have, in contrast, remained important reference works for modern scholars. The first is an 1865 study by the Venetian historian and antiquarian Emmanuele Antonio Cicogna (1789–1868),[88] who provides a systematic and well-annotated study of Copia Sulam along with a history of the criticism. He also includes the first mention of the "Avisi" manuscript, whose only known copy he possessed and bequeathed to the Biblioteca del Museo Correr in Venice.[89] The librarian and Hebraist Leonello Modona (1841–1902) built on Cicogna's work to present an 1887 edition of Copia Sulam's poetry,[90] which was the first to publish all fourteen of her known poetic compositions, together with biographical and bibliographical information, including a relatively detailed account of her career from the correspondence with Cebà to the late controversy with Paluzzi and Berardelli.

Few studies appeared on Copia Sulam in the early to mid-twentieth century.[91] During the last three decades, however, as the fields of both gender studies and Jewish studies have burgeoned, she has attracted increasing attention in both Italian and anglophone scholarship.[92] This first biography of her life – published at the 400th anniversary of her salon's 1620 apex – showcases her exceptional role not only as a Jewish woman writer but also as an early advocate for tolerance. This book aims to broadcast her clarion call for cross-faith understanding, intellectual freedom, respect for women, and judicious use of media. Much more than the "small achievement of fame" she hoped for in her *Manifesto*, this appeal is her legacy.

BIOGRAPHICAL NOTE:
SARRA COPIA SULAM IN THE VENETIAN GHETTO

Overview

Copia Sulam was in her day – and has remained – the most famous early modern Italian Jewish woman. Nevertheless, many aspects of her biography have remained perplexing, and scholars disagree even on the most basic biographical facts. Information about her family has also been scarce. The following biographical note, based on a series of documents on the Copio family from the Archivio di Stato di Venezia, provides a clearer record of Copia Sulam's life, including a more definitive dating of her birth and marriage. It also traces the wealth of the Copio family, which Simon Copio – Sarra's father – left in usufructuary to his wife upon his death, to be passed down upon her death to his daughters (see Appendix A). By fleshing out our understanding of Copia Sulam and her family, these documents also provide clues as to how Copia Sulam succeeded, despite numerous proscriptions, in leading a public literary life.

The Copio Family

Sarra Copia was born in Venice around 1592 to a prominent family in the ghetto.[1] She was the eldest of three daughters.[2] Her father, Simon Copio, was a successful businessman: he was a merchant, an insurer of cargo on boats sailing throughout Europe and the Mediterranean, a dealer in agricultural goods, an owner of lands in the Eastern Mediterranean, and a moneylender in the ghetto.[3] Although Simon calls himself only "banchier ebreo" ("Jewish banker") in his will,[4] he likely made his money through trade.[5] He was an important member of the Jewish community, as his signature on the pan-ethnic conventions in 1603 demonstrates.[6] While he encouraged his co-religionists to renew biblical and rabbinical studies that they had left "because of the heavy yoke imposed on them by various states and princes,"[7] he also favoured ties with the Christian world. He had a strong interest in the arts and in culture, as demonstrated by the broad education he provided to his daughter as well as his patronage of the famed rabbi and polymath Leon Modena, who dedicated a work to Simon and Simon's brother Moisè in 1602.[8] Simon, whom a contemporary account described as tall, handsome, and generous,[9] was also prosperous. At his death on 26 August 1606, he had 10,000 ducats in his loanbank, plus "other goods, gold, silver, jewels and various sorts of things."[10] An inventory of Simon's household goods shows numerous pieces of jewellery made of gold and precious stones, strands of pearls, dozens of silver objects, and valuable linens, cloth, furs, other clothing, furnishings and cash, all together estimated to be worth 6,275 ducats.[11] (It is not clear why Simon's inventory does not list any books, which, given his interest in culture and education, he certainly possessed. It is possible that his books were handled separately or that their mention is avoided.)[12] Rent from lands in Zante and other items were worth another 2,250 ducats.[13] The money and goods that the Copios possessed – worth over 18,500 ducats, in addition to Copia Sulam's 3,500-ducat dowry[14] – plus improvements on a dwelling (presumably the family dwelling) in the Ghetto Nuovo, which are listed as an asset but without a valuation[15] – distinguished the family as affluent not only in the ghetto but also in the city as a whole.[16]

Simon and at least three brothers, Moisè, Patiel, and Michiel,[17] were probably born in Zante and maintained strong ties to the area. Simon's presence in Zante is confirmed in a 1567 document that shows him engaged in shipping merchandise to Venice.[18] Simon and his brother Moisè moved to Venice in the mid-1580s,[19] but Michiel continued to live on the Ionian island into the seventeenth century and Patiel likely lived there until his death sometime in the late sixteenth century.

A small Jewish community had inhabited Zante since at least the early sixteenth century. Some of these Jews were refugees from Venetian territory in the Peloponnesus that had been conquered by the Ottomans at the beginning of the century.[20] Zante was also home to Romaniot Jews,[21] as was common throughout the Venetian Mediterranean.[22] Others had come to the area after the Jewish expulsions from Spanish territories in the late fifteenth and early sixteenth centuries.[23] The Jewish community in Zante grew along with commercial opportunities during the first half of the sixteenth century; the island became a major emporium for Venice after it had lost other important trade centres like Coron and Modon to the Ottomans.[24] Zante was also an appealing place for Jews to settle because it offered them the chance to live freely: Jews and Christians lived side by side.[25] Jews in Zante engaged in agrarian credit – advancing money to be redeemed for future crop yields – and in many other activities, including commerce and artisanal work of various kinds:[26] such artisanal trades were forbidden to Jews in Venice. Despite the numerous advantages of life in Zante, however, Simon and Moisè likely considered a move to Venice financially advantageous, especially since the Venetian colonies in the Eastern Mediterranean became marginalized after the loss of Cyprus in 1573.[27]

Even after Simon and Moisè Copio left Zante, they and their brothers continued to control crop-producing land there whose produce they exported. One parcel of land that the brothers shared produced around 1,500 ducats a year in currants,[28] a crop for which Zante was famous.

Michiel and Simon, who were in partnership together until the latter's
1606 death, conducted other business in Zante and in northern Africa,[29]
while Moisè was also active in the Venetian colony of Ceffalonia and in
many cities on the Italian peninsula including Ferrara and Verona.[30]
Despite his and his brothers' numerous business dealings outside Venice,
Simon Copio seems to have considered his money safest in that city: his
will required that his capital remain in Venice for his daughters' benefit.[31]

The ethnic identity of the Copio family is not clear. As noted in the
introduction to this book, the Jewish ghetto was home to Jews of different ethnic backgrounds, including German and Italian Jews; *ponentini*, or Spanish (Sephardic) Jews; and *levantini*, or Levantine Jews from
Ottoman territories. Some important evidence suggests that the Copios
were *ponentini*.[32] The nineteenth-century scholar Moisè Soave reports that
Simon left a sizeable bequest to the Scuola Spagnola, the synagogue of
the *ponentini* in Venice.[33] Umberto Fortis lists Simon among the leaders
of the Sephardic community.[34] It is possible that the Copios' ancestors
were Marranos or Crypto-Jews (the Jews on the Iberian Peninsula who
were forced to convert to Christianity but continued to practise Judaism
secretly), who after leaving the Iberian Peninsula settled in Zante, where
they returned openly to Judaism. Usually such Marranos were considered
ponentini. Another Copio, seemingly a relative, left money to the Venetian
Levantine synagogue.[35] A Levantine identity would suggest the Copios
were either Romaniot Jews or Marranos who had judaized themselves
thoroughly once they left Spain.[36] If the Copio brothers were either *ponentini* or *levantini*, they would have benefitted from the 1589 charter,
adopted shortly after they arrived in Venice, which allowed *ponentini*, like
levantini, to engage in international trade, and allowed both groups to settle in the city with their families.[37] Copia Sulam was born in the city shortly
after the charter's issue.

There are other indications, however, that the Copios were considered
part of the Italian-German Jewish communities, often grouped together for
administrative purposes. Simon is reported to have represented the German
community in 1603[38] and his brother Moisè was an official of the *italiani*
community in 1606.[39] The different ethnic communities in the ghetto were
distinct from one another in their business activities: moneylenders of this
period were predominantly Italian and German (Ashkenazi) Jews, though
Spanish and Levantine Jews were also eligible,[40] and the *levantini* and *ponentini* engaged in international trade. But in the Copios' case, the nature of
their business dealings does not clarify the matter, since the brothers were
both moneylenders and international merchants. And although the Ghetto
Nuovo – where the Copios lived – had originally been home to Italian and
German Jews,[41] while the Ghetto Vecchio was traditionally for the *levantini*

and *ponentini*, both areas were mixed by the seventeenth century.[42] Sarra
Copia Sulam and her husband Giacob Sulam lived in the Ghetto Nuovo
in 1615 but would later move to the Ghetto Vecchio.[43] As Benjamin Ravid
observed, the Copios' case would "seem to attest to at least a certain degree
of fluidity of affiliation in the Jewish community."[44]

Ricca or Richa (Rebecca) Grassini in Copio (Ricca Copia) was Simon's
wife and Sarra's mother. A member of another prominent family in the
ghetto,[45] Ricca was empowered by her husband's will to conduct the
family's affairs after his death: making her executor of his estate, Simon
called her "my agent and the sole governess of everything I am leaving."[46]
He stipulated that his estate would go evenly to his three daughters upon
Ricca's death, but he named his wife "the proprietress, possessor, and
usufructuary of everything I own so long as she lives and does not remarry."[47] Although Ricca had full use of Simon's estate during her life
as a widow, she was not his heir. It was in fact rare for widows in Italian
Jewish communities to inherit their husbands' full estates.[48] Ricca was almost certainly involved in Simon's loanbank before his death, especially
since Simon had long suffered from failing health.[49] It was typical for
women to be involved in the lending activities of their husbands[50] and it
was also not unheard of, as in Ricca's case, for Jewish women to be made
usufructuaries of estates, one of the best outcomes for a widow: less for-
tunate widows became dependent on family members or even on public
assistance after their husbands' deaths.[51] Simon may additionally have
sought to ensure the financial well-being of his wife and daughters by
filing his will with Christian notary Giovan Andrea Trevisan.[52] In the will,
Simon also sought to protect Ricca's interests from those of his brothers.[53] She had many years to exercise her role as usufructuary of Simon's
sizeable estate: she died in 1645, nearly forty years after Simon and four
years after Sarra.[54]

For at least a decade and a half after Simon's death in 1606, Ricca
actively carried on the family's business.[55] The complex business transactions she arranged in Venice and abroad, including intricate contractual
negotiations, demonstrated a high degree of literacy and business skill.
It was common (especially in Venice) for Jewish women to act in business matters after their husbands died,[56] and widows often had greater
autonomy in Jewish communities than did wives or unwed daughters.[57]
After Simon's death, Ricca maintained active relationships with her
brothers-in-law. She had close business dealings with Moisè, with whom
she entered into partnership,[58] and she negotiated the 1612 marriage of
Sarra's sister Ster (Ester) to Michiel's son Gabriel.[59]

Simon Copio and his family lived in the Ghetto Nuovo, the oldest
part of the ghetto, where Ricca continued to reside after her husband's

death; they rented their home from the Michieli.[60] Jews were technically prohibited from owning property in Venice but in practice had property rights, were able to rent out and pass down properties, and were able to claim credit for improvements they made upon their dwellings.[61] As mentioned, improvements made to her dwelling were listed as one of Ricca's assets in 1607.[62] The rent for her dwelling in 1616, which included a wine cellar (caneva) and was located beneath the Italian synagogue (Scuola Italiana), was 68 ducats per year, with a 200-ducat deposit,[63] at the higher end of rents in the ghetto.[64] Records show that, at least in the year 1619, her brother-in-law Moisè paid this rent, probably as an arrangement of their partnership.[65]

Simon Copio, who had no sons, invested resources in the education of his daughter Sarra (and perhaps of his other daughters as well) that might otherwise have gone to a boy. In the Jewish as well as the Christian world, well-educated girls were likely the daughters of well-educated and prosperous men, who at times taught their daughters themselves.[66] It is likely that Ricca also played a role in her daughter's early instruction and continued Sarra's education after Simon's death.[67] Sarra had great affection for her father, to whom she dedicated her one published work, the *Manifesto*, calling him a "most adoring parent" who bore her "inexpressible love."[68] She acknowledged that her father had been disappointed in his desire for a son but hoped the fame she acquired by publishing might help to preserve the family name as a boy would have.[69]

Marriage to Giacob Sulam

Sarra Copia married Giacob Sulam after her father's death. Simon Copio's will shows that he had stipulated his eldest daughter's 3,000-scudo dowry but not yet married her off.[70] Her youngest sister Ster was married in 1612 with a 3,500 ducat dowry,[71] an approximately equal sum.[72] Sarra's cousin Diana, daughter of Moisè, had a dowry of 3,300 ducats when she married in 1619.[73] The dowries recorded for the Copio girls were considerable for Jewish girls of the era: though dowries in the Venetian Jewish community could run as high as 12,000 ducats and as low as 10 to 18 ducats for the poor, the usual amount was 500 to 1,000 ducats for families with annual income of about 200 ducats.[74] Modena married his daughter Diana with a dowry of 450 ducats in cash and 200 ducats in clothing in 1611, a sum he had difficulty producing.[75]

Sarra and Giacob were certainly married by 1609,[76] probably by 1608,[77] years earlier than scholars have generally assumed.[78] The usual age for betrothal and marriage for Jewish women was between fourteen and eighteen.[79] Since Sarra was married by 1609, she was likely born in the early 1590s.[80] Sarra and Giacob settled in the Ghetto Nuovo, where she had grown up and where her mother still lived.[81]

Sarra almost certainly had a part in choosing her husband. Her father indicates in his will that he considered his daughters' satisfaction with their spouses of paramount importance. He asks his wife to ensure that his daughters "have husbands to their liking, so long as they are upstanding, honest, and honourable."[82] Many women in early modern Venice did not have such choice, as the writings of Arcangela Tarabotti clearly demonstrate. Tarabotti decried the widespread practice in the Christian world whereby families decided daughters' fates with little regard for their wishes, forcing them into convents or marriages regardless of their own desires.[83] There were also forced marriages among Jews in Italy, but in general Jewish men and women had some say about the unions they entered into. The settling of young men and women was simpler in the Jewish community than it was in the Christian world since, in the absence of monachization, marriage was the only expected outcome. Nonetheless, fathers often sought a match based on financial advantage rather than compatibility.[84] It is notable, therefore, that Simon Copio sought to ensure his daughters' approval of their husbands. Since Simon was still living when Sarra's marriage was contracted, he would have been personally able to ensure her satisfaction with her future spouse.

Simon was likely also pleased with the match from a financial standpoint – as Sarra herself might well have been – since she married a man of means. Upon his wedding, Giacob Sulam received from his father 5,300 ducats in cash and 1,213 ducats worth of other goods, including gold and jewels, as payment for his portion of his father's estate. He also received 500 ducats from his mother's dowry. Giacob later declared that this money and these goods satisfied his claims on his family's estate. The Sulam estate was sizeable, especially given the fact that Giacob had four brothers.[85] In 1611 he had enough cash on hand to repay outright a 3,500-ducat debt on his brothers' behalf.[86]

Sarra's dowry granted her economic power that was no doubt important in her marriage and in her literary career.[87] Stanley Chojnacki has long argued that dowries empowered Christian women in early modern Venice within marriages and families, and Howard Adelman suggests a parallel with Jewish women as well.[88] Simon arranged to leave his daughters even greater financial means: after his wife's death, his estate was to be divided equally among the three girls and each would have full control of her portion. Simon wrote:

> After [my wife Ricca's] death, I want everything I own to go in equal share to my above-mentioned three daughters.[89] I desire and decree that, when

it is time, these daughters of mine be freely able to bequeath and to spend
what they receive after the death of their above-mentioned mother, as each
best sees fit, and to bequeath and to donate as they wish and to whom they
want the above-mentioned inheritance that will be returned to them after
[the death of] their above-mentioned mother, so that they always retain
absolute control of the said inheritance, so long as they continue to follow
and to abide by our Jewish law.[90]

Upon their mother's death, each Copio girl would have inherited almost 4,000 additional ducats from Simon's estate, more than doubling
their dowries;[91] they would also have divided among themselves the
worth of real estate improvements on their family dwelling.[92] Simon
thus provided great financial security to his daughters and tried to ensure their marital satisfaction through the instrument of his will; he
also sought by financial means to ensure that they would stay within the
Jewish faith by stipulating in his will that they would lose control of their
inheritance if they converted. All told, Sarra's claim upon her father's
estate was greater than Giacob's was upon his own father's. Between
her dowry and the additional inheritance promised her, Sarra's father
arranged to leave her more than 7,300 ducats, plus her portion of the
value of the real estate improvements on their property.[93] Giacob's full
claim on his father's estate and mother's dowry amounted to 7,013
ducats.

Giacob's family lived in Mantua. The famous musician and composer
Salamone de Rossi dedicated a collection of synagogue music to Moisè
Sulam, perhaps Giacob's brother – an indication of the family's culture
and standing.[94] Giacob came to Venice on his own around the time of
his marriage.[95] It was not uncommon for children of privileged Jewish
families to find spouses in different cities, given the small number of
elite families in any one ghetto.[96] Because of his distance from his family,
Giacob separated his economic interests from his brothers in 1611.[97]

A series of notarial acts over more than a decade show the numerous
business ties and deep trust that linked Giacob to Sarra's mother, Ricca,
her paternal uncle Moisè Copio, and her sister Ster. These three blood
relatives of Sarra appointed Giacob to act in their name in business matters, and Giacob also repeatedly appointed Moisè to act in his name.[98]
In October 1613, when the Venetian *condotta* with the Jews was renewed,
Moisè and Giacob were together appointed by the Jewish community to
run a loanbank.[99] These two relatives by marriage had been involved in
lending – separately, together, and sometimes with Ricca – during the
previous half-dozen years, continuing the activity of Sarra's father.[100] In
1617, Giacob and Ricca were involved together in lending.[101] Giacob

dealt with Christians as a normal part of his banking business and had other business connections with Christians; for example, he assigned Giovan Battista Cattan as his *procuratore e commesso* in July 1614[102] and used a Christian notary extensively (as the documents in this biographical note show). Because of his business interests, Sarra's husband lived in a world in which contact with Christians was both frequent and necessary.

In addition to his business activities, Giacob was an important figure within the ghetto. He was a leader in the *scuola italiana*, the synagogue that followed Italian Jewish rites. In 1621–1622, he was a tax assessor, one of the most difficult and sensitive positions in the ghetto.[103] He was one of the heads of the *italiani* community in 1639 and again in 1650.[104]

Sarra and Giacob may have had trouble conceiving children and did not have any offspring who lived beyond infancy. Their daughter Rica (Rebecca), who was born at the beginning of 1614 – some five years after their marriage – died around a year later in January 1615.[105] In 1618, nearly a decade into Sarra's marriage, when she was around 26 years old, she wrote to Cebà about a miscarriage or still birth ("parto abortivo").[106] Her lack of children, during an era in which Jewish women, like Christian women, were valued in large part for childbearing and childrearing, separated her from other women.[107] On the other hand, the absence of ongoing childrearing duties freed her for literary pursuits. In fact, her literary career became serious immediately after her 1618 miscarriage.

Sarra Copia Sulam's Exceptionality

Copia Sulam's intellectual endeavours were highly unusual. For Jewish (as for Christian) women, marriage usually precluded sustained intellectual activity.[108] The salonnière, however, was able to devote considerable time to study – achieving renown for her erudition and keeping abreast of current cultural developments. Her close interaction with numerous men outside her family, both Christian and Jewish, was also exceptional. A behaviour manual for Jewish women, *Precetti da esser imparati dalle donne hebree* (Rules Jewish Women Must Learn) – published in translation in Venice in 1616 – censures women for this type of contact.[109] The author, Rabbi Biniamin d'Harodono, contends that a woman "must not joke around with, nor be friendly with other men."[110] Copia Sulam's associates frequently praised her beauty and admired her tresses; d'Harodono urges women not to show their hair and criticizes those who seek attention for their appearance and adornments ("Woe betide them. How much better would it be if outside of the home they wore a nightcap and no adornment, and at home they adorned themselves to satisfy their husbands, to seem beautiful to them, and not to outside men?"[111])

D'Haradono's generalized complaints suggest that it was not uncommon for Jewish women to associate with men outside the family, nor to reveal their beauty to others. Nevertheless, Copia Sulam's frequent and close interaction with her many male associates violated norms that regulated Jewish women's lives as well as norms common among Christians. Cebà, for example, repeatedly criticized Copia Sulam for interacting freely with men and for not devoting herself to her duties in the home; Baldassare Bonifaccio publicly rebuked her for focusing too much on her physical appearance.

Several factors in Copia Sulam's family background and marital circumstance favoured her ability to flout many of the proscriptions placed on Jewish women in the era. As mentioned above, the lack of sons in her natal family was decisive in shaping her education. Also critical was her father Simon's advocacy for her and her sisters' interests, which is attested in his will and remembered with fondness in the dedication Copia Sulam penned to him in her *Manifesto*. Her ability to choose a husband to her satisfaction – expressly safeguarded by her father[112] – also set her apart. She was certainly successful in choosing a husband who allowed her intellectual pursuits: Giacob lent at least tacit support to these and permitted her salon, since within Jewish tradition and law women were bound to their husbands' will.[113] Copia Sulam's financial means may have allowed her greater autonomy than Jewish wives generally had. Giacob may also have encouraged his wife's unusual occupation since a woman's learnedness could be a prestigious sign of a family's status and wealth: few families had the resources to allow daughters and wives the luxury of time for study. In Copia Sulam's case, her and her husband's combined assets allowed them to employ a household staff that freed her from the chores that ordinarily structured Jewish women's lives.[114] Her public display of exceptional learnedness thus emphasized the Sulams' economic comfort. This same desire for status may have led Giacob to condone Sarra's literary interaction with Christian men – an absolutely extraordinary degree of contact that he might have believed would add additional lustre to the family name. He may also have been led by open-mindedness towards the Christian world, conditioned by his frequent contact with Christians in his business activities.

There are scattered indications about how Copia Sulam's literary activities were perceived in the ghetto. Her prominence may initially have benefitted Giacob's standing, or at the very least does not seem to have harmed it: his appointment as tax assessor occurred after she had already established herself as a well-known intellectual in the ghetto. Over the next five years, when she was embroiled in continual controversies, and indeed for another decade afterward, we do not have any record of Giacob holding leadership positions in the ghetto,[115] perhaps a sign that the scandals that dogged Copia Sulam impacted his standing.[116] As for the perception in the ghetto of Copia Sulam herself, we must consider as unreliable Bonifaccio's 1621 report that Copia Sulam had "become odious" within the Jewish community.[117] Nevertheless, Copia Sulam's prominence as a public intellectual may have been troubling to many of her co-religionists, and the high-profile controversies surrounding her were certainly as unwelcome to her community as they were to her.[118] But a report indicates that when her erstwhile associates sought publicly to humiliate her within the ghetto, crowds vigorously defended her,[119] and while the actions against her kindled fear within her community, they also created a sense of solidarity.[120]

Pressure to Convert

Many of the Christian men who surrounded Copia Sulam forcefully pressed her to convert to Christianity. Cebà relentlessly sought, through his correspondence, to convert her; the exchange disintegrated, in his telling, when he realized his efforts were in vain. Bonifaccio also urged Copia Sulam to convert, suggesting that Judaism led her to unorthodox beliefs. Other associates are reported to have pleaded in private for her conversion.

Conversion was fairly common in the era, largely due to the extensive social and economic rewards that the turn to Christianity could bring.[121] Simon Copio sought to counterbalance these rewards, however, when he set his daughters' continued adherence to Judaism as a precondition of his bequest to them. Nevertheless, in her *Manifesto*, Copia Sulam recalls the heavy pressure she faced and hints that the lures she was offered for her conversion would have outweighed any losses: "I would not have lacked opportunities, by changing my faith, to improve my status: something that is well known to people of much authority, who have insistently sought and tried for my conversion."[122] Only her belief in the eternal rewards Judaism would bring, she argues, allowed her to resist such attempts: proof, as she says, that she believed in the soul's immortality.

Moisè Copio

The possibility of conversion was vividly presented to Copia Sulam not only by her Christian literary contacts, but also by a close relative who converted in the mid-1620s. Moisè Copio, her father's brother and a close business associate of her mother and husband, converted to

Christianity sometime between 1621 and 1625.[123] Moisè's conversion, through which he adopted the name Francesco Zacchia, was likely a great shock to the whole Jewish community. For years he had been a prominent businessman: in addition to his work in moneylending, he was a cargo insurer, a merchant, a broker of agricultural goods, and a real-estate entrepreneur.[124] He was also a leader in the ghetto: he was an official of the *italiani* community in 1606, one of the three heads of the *Università degli Ebrei* in 1609, and an assessor in this same year.[125] Like his brother Simon, Moisè was a patron to the rabbi Modena and may have shared his brother's cultural interests.[126] As mentioned above, he was also named banker (moneylender) in 1613,[127] a position that indicated the community's trust.[128] From 1608 through 1617, he was frequently named as an arbiter in disputes.[129] His role within the Jewish community, however, was not without controversy: he was involved in frequent disputes,[130] and Modena – whose wife was related to Moisè[131] – portrays him as deeply disagreeable, remembering that in fall 1607: "I went to live in the house of a very unpleasant person, my wife's relative Moses Copio ... in order to teach his son Abraham Copio, a regular chip off the old block, and four other students, and to board at his table. And because no one could live cooped up with such a wild person, the following Tammuz [June–July 1608] I left his house."[132] Appearing after Moisé's name is the annotation "may his name be blotted out," written in another ink and afterwards,[133] probably after Moisé's conversion. Jews were discouraged from pursuing some of business activities in which he engaged: a 1607 document, for instance, suggests non-Christians may have been banned from insuring cargo;[134] Moisè's real estate activities were also technically off-limits.[135] Moisè's conversion to Christianity would have allowed him to engage freely in such business pursuits. Copia Sulam's uncle lived a long life as Francesco Zacchia, outliving his brother Simon by a half century. He remained active in business deals in the ghetto until at least 1650[136] and was still alive when his son Abraham, who was also a moneylender but did not convert, wrote his own will in 1655.[137]

Moisé's conversion was surely deeply disconcerting to his family, especially given the close business and personal associations family members had shared with him over a number of years. Moreover, Moisé/Francesco continued to occasion scandal as a convert, repeatedly running into trouble with Christian authorities. A 1625 document reports that his Christian wife brought a complaint against him, claiming that he was a man of "such an evil nature" that he ruined and bilked her until she was forced to enter the convent of the Convertite (Santa Maria Maddalena) on the Giudecca, where he then proceeded to harass and bring shame upon the nuns.[138] The same document casts doubt on the sincerity of

his conversion, calling him "the Jew Moisè Coppio, now outwardly a
Christian under the name Francesco Zachia."[139] The complaint about
Moisé's scandalous misbehaviour occurred the year after some of Copia
Sulam's Christian associates shamed and humiliated her by circulating
a scurrilous pamphlet about her, "Le Sareide"; as mentioned, they specifically targeted her reputation within the Jewish community by reading the leaflet in the ghetto.[140] The familial humiliation could only have
worsened the effects of the professional one: within the ghetto and beyond, both Copia Sulam's enemies and Moisé/Francesco himself sullied
the Copio name. As we have seen, Copia Sulam withdrew from the public arena shortly after these controversies, blaming "vexing troubles."[141]

The Final Years

Copia Sulam and her husband both survived the plague of 1630–1631,
in which over a quarter of the city's residents died.[142] At least one of her
strong supporters, Giacomo Rosa, Cebà's agent in Venice who stayed in
touch with her after Cebà's death, died in the scourge.[143] We have scant
information from the last dozen years of her life. Only a faint echo of her
name can be found in the numerous texts reviewed for this study that
were published in Venice during the second quarter of the century.[144]
Copia Sulam died 15 February 1641 in the Ghetto Vecchio after languishing three months with a fever.[145] Outlived by her husband,[146] she
did not leave a will in Venice.[147] Modena, her close associate who had
faithfully participated in her salon and dedicated a book to her based
on their similar literary interests,[148] remembers her in an epitaph for her
wisdom and her charity but does not mention her literary activities.[149]

APPENDIX A: LAST WILL AND TESTAMENT OF SIMON COPIO[1]

Transcription criteria: To facilitate comprehension of the Italian transcription of this document, I have spelled out abbreviations and modernized capitalization, punctuation, accents, paragraph divisions, and the distinctions u/v and i/j. I have retained all other elements of the document, including variations in spelling. There are two copies of the will, the *cedola* (the sealed copy filed with the ducal chancellory) and the *protocollo* (the copy the notary kept for his records) found in the same busta in the archive.[2] They are almost identical, except in the signatures that appear and the placement of the death notice. Copy *a* (the *cedola*) includes two witnesses' signatures followed by the death notice; copy *b* includes the death notice followed by the notary's signature. I have transcribed from copy *a* but I include (with explanatory notes) the signatures and death notices for both copy *a* and copy *b*. See figures A.1 and A.2.

1606 adí 18 agosto Inditione quarta
Io Simon Copio banchier ebreo
  quondam ser Abram, considerando
  non esser cosa alcuna piú certa della
  morte, nè piú incerta dell'hora di
  essa; nè volendo quando mi ocorerà
  passar di questa a miglior vitta lassar
  le cose mie inordinate, attrovandomi
  massime infermo del corpo, ma per
  la gracia de Dio sano della mente et
  inteleto, giacendo nel letto in casa
  della mia habitazione in Ghetto
  Novo, ho fatto chiamar et venir a
  mi Zuanandrea Trivisan nodaro di
  Venetia et quello ho pregato voglia
  scriver questo mio testamento et
  ultima voluntà, et quello doppo la
  morte mia compisca et robori giusta
  le leze di Venetia, nel qual prima
  racomando l'anima mia al mio
  creator Iddio.
Prima lasso per l'anima mia [che] sia
  datto a sei orfane al tempo del suo
  maritar ducati 25 per una, nelle
  quali sii inclusa una figliola de ser
  Lazaro Colombin ebreo. Piú lasso
  che sia mandato in Terra Santa alli

1606, 18 August, in the fourth indiction
Since I, Simon Copio, Jewish banker[3]
  and son of the late *messer* Abram, know
  that there is nothing more certain
  than death, nor more uncertain than
  its hour; and since, when[4] I must
  pass from this life to the better one,
  I do not want to leave my affairs in
  disarray; and since I am most infirm
  of body, but by the grace of God of
  sound mind and intellect, I have
  called and summoned Zuanandrea
  [Giovanni Andrea] Trivisan, notary in
  Venice, to my sickbed in my dwelling
  in the Ghetto Nuovo. I entreated
  him kindly to write this last will and
  testament of mine, and after my death
  to register and validate it according
  to the laws of Venice. Herein first and
  foremost do I commend my soul to
  God my creator.
First, I will that, for the good of my soul,
  six orphan girls be given 25 ducats
  each at the time of their marriage.
  May a daughter of the Jew messer
  Lazaro Colombini be among these.
  Likewise, I will that, for as long as

poveri nostri ogni anno persino che
la mia comissaria viverà ducati 25
all'anno, con questo che ogni anno
sia mandato de qui la fede della
riceputa di essi ducati 25 all'anno.
Lasso alla mia massara de casa oltra
il suo salario nominata Stella ducati
25 per l'anima mia per una volta.
Similmente a Abaam Todesco servitor
di casa oltra il suo salario li lasso
ducati 25 per l'anima mia per una
volta ut supra.
Voglio sia mia comissaria et sola
governatrice de quanto lasso la
mia carissima consorte, madonna
Ricca, qual prego a esequir quanto
ordinerò, et questo vedoando essa.
Et dechiaro che mi attrovo investiti
nel mio banco, che serve la povertà
per mano del mio fator Samuel
Spera, ducati vintitremille incirca
come per li registri del ditto Spera
appare. Ittem mi atrovo delle altre
mercantie, ori, arzenti, zoglie, et
robbe de diverse sorte, de qualche
summa che la quantità non so,
delle quali tutte cose, occorendo
la mia morte, che Dio guardi, essa
mia commissaria debba farne far
inventario per mano de nodaro come
si osserva. Et debbi governar il tutto
con diligentia et buona custodia,
et non voglio che in nessun modo
la mandi alcuno delli mei cavedali
fuori di Venetia, nè per mar nè per
terra, ma il tutto sia traficato in
questa città, per beneficio et utile de
mie figliole.
Voglio che sia datto di dotte a ogni una
de mie figliole scudi tremille per
una, sí come è statto promesso alla
prima mia fiola nominata Sara, et
cossí voglio che habbino Rachel et
Ster, sue sorelle, per dotte, et prego
che la mia consorte facia che le ditte
mie fiole habbino li sui maritti di loro
satisfatione, però nelle cose licite et
honeste et honorate.

my agent lives, 25 ducats be sent
every year to our poor in the holy
land, on the condition that every
year a certificate of receipt for these
25 ducats is sent back here. For my
soul I leave a one-time bequest of 25
ducats, in addition to her salary, to
my housekeeper Stella. Similarly, I
leave my household servant Abraam
Todesco, in addition to his salary, a
one-time bequest of 25 ducats, for my
soul, as above.
I want my dearest wife, madonna Ricca,
to be my agent and the sole governess
of everything I am leaving, so long as
she does not remarry, and I entreat
her to execute what I will lay out.
I declare that I have around 23,000
ducats[5] invested in my loanbank,
which serves the poor under the
guidance of my manager Samuel
Spera, as it appears in the registers of
the above-mentioned Spera. Likewise
I have other goods, gold, silver,
jewels, and various sorts of things,
whose exact value I do not know.
Should I die, God forbid, my above-
mentioned agent [Ricca] must have
a notary prepare an inventory of all
of these things, as is customary[6]; and
she must administer all of this with
diligence and good care. I do not
want her, under any circumstances,
to send any of my capital out of
Venice, either by sea or by land, but
instead want all of it to be used in
this city, for the benefit and use of my
daughters.
I want each of my daughters to receive
a 3,000-scudo dowry, as has been
promised to my first daughter, named
Sara, and I want Rachel and Ster,
her sisters, to have the same for their
dowry.[7] I pray my wife to see to it
that these daughters of mine have
husbands to their liking, so long as
they are upstanding, honest, and
honourable.

Lasso la sopraditta madonna Ricca
mia consorte, dona, madona et
usufrutuaria de tutto il mio in vitta
sua vedoando, et che la non possi
esser molestata da alcuno, et dapoi
la sua morte voglio che tutto il mio
haver vada in le preditte tre mie
figliole equalmente. Le qual mie
figliole voglio et ordino che al tempo
debito le possino testar et disponer
de quanto che in esse pervenirà
doppo la morte de ditta sua madre
liberamente, come a cadauna di
esse meglio parerà, et lassarla et
donarla come a esse piacerà et a chi
esse vorano la preditta dimissoria
che in esse ha da tornare doppo
ditta sua madre cossí che le siano
patrone sempre absolute de ditta
dimissoria, perseverando sempre nella
legge nostra ebraica, et stando alla
obedientia de quella.
Ittem dechiaro che tutto quello che mi
atrovo in questa città et tutti li beni
che si atrovano al Zante cossí anco
fuora del Zante, il tutto è pro indiviso
tra ser Michiel Copio mio fratello
et me, che il tutto è di ragione de
noi dui soli, del che tutti duí deveno
haver la parte sua, dovendo cadauno
de noi dui render conto all'altro
de buona administration et reffarsi,
come è honesto, di quanto si andasse
creditore, cossí che cadauno habbi il
fatto suo.
Lasso per segno d'amor a cadauno de
mei nepotti maschi, zoè; alli dui fioli
di esso ser Michiel et alli dui fioli di
ser Moyse Copio, etiam mio fratello,
uno diamante de scudi cinquanta
a cadauno di essi quatro nepotti
mei, che lo godino per amor mio.
Nel resto racomando l'anima mia al
signor Dio.
Interogatus de luochi pii, responde non
voglio ordinar altro. Preterea etc. si
quis etc. igitur etc. signum etc.

I appoint the above-mentioned madonna
Ricca, my wife, as the proprietress,
possessor and usufructuary of
everything I own so long as she lives
and does not remarry, and may no
one bother her.[8] After her death, I
want everything I own to go in equal
share to my above-mentioned three
daughters. I desire and decree that,
when it is time, these daughters of
mine be freely able to bequeath and to
spend what they receive after the death
of their above-mentioned mother, as
each best sees fit, and to bequeath
and to donate as they wish and to
whom they want the above-mentioned
inheritance[9] that will be returned to
them after [the death of] their above-
mentioned mother, so that they always
retain absolute control of the said
inheritance, so long as they continue to
follow and to abide by our Jewish law.
Likewise I declare that everything I
possess in this city, and all the assets in
Zante as well as outside of Zante, are
all common property of my brother
messer Michiel Copio and me, and
that it all rightfully belongs only to the
two of us, and each of us must have his
share, since each one of us is obliged
to give the other recognition for good
management and to take for himself,
as is honest, as much credit as he has
earned, in such a way that each one of
us has what he deserves.[10]
As a token of my love I leave jewels to
each of my nephews; to each of the two
sons of the above-mentioned messer
Michiel and the two sons of messer
Moyse [Moisè] Copio, also my brother,
I leave a diamond worth fifty scudi.
May these four nephews of mine enjoy
these with my love. As for the rest, I
commend my soul to the Lord God.
Asked about charitable institutions, he
responds "I do not wish to arrange
anything else." In addition etc. if
someone etc. therefore etc. sign etc.

°°[Mano diversa]
Io Zuane quondam Armanin squerariol
   al ponte de l'Aseo fui testimonio
   pregado et zurado
[Altra mano diversa]
Io Lorenco del conda [quondam]
   Fransceco [*sic*] Tineli tiraoro fui
   testimonio pregado et zurado
[Di nuovo mano del notaio]
1606 die 26 Augusti nocte. Publicatum
   viso cadavere°°
**1606 adi 26 Augusti nocte. Publicatum
   viso cadavere
[Signum tabellionis]
Ego Joannesandreas Trivisano quondam
   domini Johannismariae publicus
   imperialis ac Venetiarum notarius
   complevi et roboravi**

°° [11][In a different hand]
I Zuane [Giovanni], son of the deceased
   Armanin, gondola-maker at the bridge
   of Aseo, give my sworn witness as asked.
[In yet another hand]
I Lorenco, son of the deceased Fransceco
   Tineli, gold-wire drawer, give my sworn
   witness as asked.
[Again in the notary's hand]
26 August 1606, evening. Made public
   after corpse was seen.°°
**[12]26 August 1606, evening. Made
   public after corpse was seen.
[Official symbol of the notary]
I, Giovanni Andrea Trevisan (son
   of the deceased Giovanni Maria),
   imperial and Venetian public notary,[13]
   registered and validated [this]**

A.1 A page from Simon Copio's will (copy *a*). He mentions Sarra (spelled here "Sara") at the bottom of the page. ASV, Sezione notarile, Testamenti, b. 962.387.

A.2 The final page of Simon Copio's will (copy *a*), with the witnesses' signatures. ASV, Sezione notarile, Testamenti, b. 962.387.

APPENDIX B: INVENTORY OF SIMON COPIO'S HOUSE AT HIS DEATH

The following inventory of Simon Copio's household goods, completed shortly after his death on 26 August 1606, shows numerous pieces of jewellery of gold and precious stones and strands of pearls, dozens of silver objects, and valuable linens, cloth, furs, vestments, furnishings, and cash.[1] See figures B.1 and B.2. Another notarial document estimates the worth of these items at 6,275 ducats.[2]

Die 3 septembris 1606 Inventario di beni mobili, ori, et zoglie, et altro de ragion del q[uondam] m[agnifi]co D[on] Simon Copio ebreo q[uondam] m[agnifi]co Abram, attrovatti nella casa della sua habitation in Ghetto Novo, fatto ad Instancia della magnifica signora Ricca olim sua consorte, comissaria et usufructuaria, come nel suo testamento rogato per me infrascritto nodaro sotto dí 18 Agosto prossimo passatto et prima.	3 September 1606 Inventory of the furniture, gold, jewels, and other things belonging to the honourable late messer Simon Copio of the honourable late Abram, found in the house in which he resided in the Ghetto Nuovo. Made at the behest of the honourable signora Ricca his wife, agent, and usufructuary, as specified in the will he drew up with me, the notary of these rolls, registered the 18th day of this past August, and beforehand.
Ori diversi, zoè, cadene, manini, rechini, anelli, broche, et altro in tutto onze cinquanta.	Various objects of gold, jewels, chains, bracelets, earrings, rings, brooches, and other, totaling 50 ounces.
Zoè onze 50	Jewels: 50 ounces
Un filetto de perle numero 63 sono per pegno per ducati 40	Small string of 63 pearls, in pawn for 40 ducats
Un altro fillo simile de numero 66	Another similar string of 66
Un altro fillo de numero 56	Another string of 56
Un bacil de arzento et il suo bocal	A silver basin and its pitcher
Una concheta d'arzento	A small silver bowl
Tre sotto coppe d'arzento	Three silver coasters
Due sechialetti d'arzento ed sue cazette	Two small silver buckets and their servers
Tre confitiere d'arzento	Three silver candy dishes
Quatro candelieri d'arzento	Four silver candlesticks
Gotti d'arzento doradi numero tre	Three gilded silver cups
Un tazzon d'arzento dorado	A large gilded silver mug
Due profumiere d'arzento	Two silver perfumers
Dui pomoli d'arzento che serve alla sinagoga	Two silver knobs used in the synagogue
Una zogieleria d'oro con pietrie [sic] false in pegno per ducati 50	A gold jewellery box with fake jewels, in pawn for 50 ducats
Un pugnal alla turchesca con finimenti de arzento doradi	A Turkish-style dagger with gilded silver decorations
Tagieri d'arzento numero sei	Six silver knives
Un scatolin con ori in pegno per ducati 26	A small box with gold pieces, in pawn for 26 ducats
Un altro pegno sopra ori per ducati 19	Another pawn on gold pieces for 19 ducats
Una conccheta de arzento dorada	A small gilded silver bowl

Sei pironi d'arzento doradi	Six gilded silver forks
Sei cuchieri d'arzento doradi	Six gilded silver spoons
Sei cortelli col manego d'arzento doradi	Six knives with gilded silver handles
Un altro pegno sopra ori et arzenti per ducati 50	Another pawn on gold and silver pieces for 50 ducats
Tazze d'arzento numero 8	8 silver cups
Cortelli d'arzento zoè il manego numero 9	9 silver knives with jewelled handles
Pironi d'arzento numero 25	25 silver forks
Cuchieri d'arzento dozine una	One dozen silver spoons
Un fornimento de cuori d'oro usadi nella sala	A gold-stamped used leather accessory set in the drawing room
Un altro simile fornimento de cuori nella camera	Another similar leather accessory set in the master bedroom
Due altri fornimenti de cuori d'oro vechi per le altre due camere	Two other gold-stamped leather accessory sets (old) for the other two bedrooms
Tovagioli de piú sorte usadi numero 100	100 assorted napkins, used
Tovagioli grezi boni numero 38	38 rough napkins, serviceable
Linzuoli de piú sorte, compresi doi para lavoradi in tutto para numero 29	29 assorted pairs of sheets, including two embroidered pairs
Tovaglie da tavola diverse numero 18	18 various tablecloths
Fazuoli da man numero sei grezi	Six rough handkerchiefs
Un panier de mussolo bianco	A basket of white muslin
Quatro pezze de mussolo grosse	Four large pieces of white muslin
Camisi da homo de piú sorte numero 31	31 assorted men's shirts
Braghesse de tella bianche para numero sei	Six pairs of white cloth socks[3]
Fazuoli da man usadi numero 10	10 kerchiefs (for hands), used
Fazoletti da naso numero 25	25 kerchiefs (for nose)
Una pretina de damascheto negro fodra de felpa	A short jacket of black damask lined with plush
Una romana de damascheto fodra de veludo negro	A robe of damask lined with black velvet
Calzete de seda colorade para numero 17 nove	17 pairs of coloured silk hose, new
Una muda de drapi de veludo rizzo negro	A bunch of black pile-on-pile velvet cloth
Una muda de drapi de ormesin negro	A bunch of black armozeen
Un'altra muda simile de damascheto	Another similar bunch of damask
Un feriariol de ferandina	A cloak of farandine
Un altro feriariol de manto negro usado	Another black mantle cloak, used
Una romana de ormesin negro	A robe of black armozeen
Damasco cremesin braza 63	63 *braccia* of crimson damask
Una pezza de raso zallo in pegno, per ducati ottanta	A piece of yellow satin, in pawn for 80 ducats
Camise da d[onn]a de piú sorte, numero 84	84 assorted women's shirts
Fazuoli da man diversi numero 24	24 assorted kerchiefs (for hands)
Meze traverse numero 24	24 waist aprons
Dui rochetti de seda	Two spools of silk
Un pavion de seda bianco et uno safil legado in oro in pegno per ducati 130	A tester of white silk and a sapphire set in gold, in pawn for 130 ducats
Una sponza da letto lavorada	A decorated headboard for the bed
Una pezza de renso	A piece of white Rheims linen[4]
Dui cavezzi de tella de Alessandria	Two remnants of Alexandrian cloth
Dui fazuoli da testa	Two head scarves
Un tazzon d'arzento in pegno per ducati 15	A large silver cup, in pawn for 15 ducats
Due vesture de ormesin ganzante [*cangiante*] da donna	Two women's gowns of iridescent armozeen
Una vestura de veludo sguardo et bianco	A gown of scarlet and white velvet
Un'altra de veludo verde et zallo	Another of green and yellow velvet
Un'altra de veludo verde et vinado	Another of green and burgundy velvet

Una vestura de damascheto verde	A gown of green damask
Una carpeta de ormesin zallo	A petticoat of yellow armozeen
Una carpeta de raso cremesin	A petticoat of crimson satin
Una ruba de veludo negro da donna	A women's dress[5] of black velvet
Una ruba de ormesin negro	A dress of black armozeen
Una ruba de veludo fiocado	A dress of flocked velvet
Un rubon de tabì franzà	A fringed dress of tabby[6]
Una vesta de tabì vinado	A burgundy garment of tabby
Casse de noghera, ritagiade e schiete, numero 9	9 walnut chests, carved and plain
Una vesta de brocadello de piú colori	A garment of multi-coloured brocatelle[7]
Carieghe de bulgaro alla pretina usade numero 10	10 simple leather chairs, used
Stagin de noghera da pozo numero 8	8 walnut well buckets
Un farro dorado con sua coverta de tella	Gilded lamp with its cloth shade
Due tavole de noghera con sui telerii	Two walnut tables with their tablecloths
Dui tavolinii de noghera doradi	Two small gilded walnut tables
Lettine de ferro dorade numero 4 vechie	4 small old gilded iron beds
Un pavion de damasco verde et	A tester of green damask and
Uno pavion de ormesin verde	A tester of green armozeen
Stramazi de piú sorte numero otto	Eight assorted mattresses
Pagiarizzi numero dui	Two straw mattresses
Uno paro de cavedoni de laton con li sui fornimenti	A pair of brass andirons (with their accessories)
Cinque lume de laton	Five brass lanterns
Candelieri de laton numero quatro	Four brass candlesticks
Sechieleti de latton numero 4	4 small brass buckets
Un bacil con suo ramin de latton	A brass basin with its ladle
Un pelizo de volpe coperto de zambelotto	A fox pelt covered with cloth woven from goat hair
Una pretina de volpe coperta da zambelotto	A short jacket of fox fur covered with cloth woven from goat hair
Due scaldavivande de laton	Two brass chafing dishes
Peltrii de piú sorte pezze numero 200 (ducento)	200 (two hundred) assorted pewter objects
Una coltra da letto de seda e d'oro	A bedspread of silk and gold
Un'altra de ormesin e dimitto	Another of armozeen and dimity[8]
Quatro felzade bianche	Four white cloth covers for gondola cabin
4 coltre usade de rassa de piú sorte	4 used bedspreads of coarse wool, assorted
Penachi balle numero tre	Three balls of plumes
Fangotti [=fagotti] de penachi numero do	Two bundles[9] of plumes
Dui saffili bianchi ligadi in oro	Two white sapphires set in gold
Una meza casseta de barete da Verona	A half chest of hats from Verona
Sechi de rame grandi numero cinque	Five big copper buckets
Altri sechi de rame piú picoli numero 8	8 smaller copper buckets
Una credenza de noghera	A walnut sideboard
4 conche de rame de piú sorte	4 assorted copper bowls
Una caldiera de rame	A copper cauldron
Danari contadi ducati cintocinquata (numero 150)	Cash currency, one hundred and fifty (150) ducats
Actum in domo habitationis dicte donna Richae in Ghetto Novo, presentibus ser Francisco de Gaggis filio de Nicolai de Muriano, et messer Joanne quondam Nicolai de Dulcinio, marangono [sic] in Arsenatu [sic], Testibus vocatis etc.	Drawn up in the residence of the above-named donna Ricca in the Ghetto Nuovo, in the presence of messer Francisco [Francesco] de Gaggis son of Nicolai [Nicolò] of Murano, and messer Joanne [Giovanni] son of the deceased Nicolai [Nicolò] of Ulcinj,[10] carpenter in the Arsenale, called as witnesses, etc.

B.1 The penultimate page of the post-mortem inventory of Simon Copio's household goods. "Inventory of Simon Copio's House at His Death," 140v.

B.2 The final page of the post-mortem inventory of Simon Copio's household
goods. "Inventory of Simon Copio's House at His Death," 141r.

APPENDIX C: CURRENCY VALUES

Simon Copio specifies his daughters' dowries in *scudi*, whereas the other sums in his will and in the household inventory done shortly after his death are in *ducati*.[1] It is tricky to understand the precise relative value of these currencies, since the terms *scudo* and *ducato* described several different monies minted in the era, whose relationship depended on the volatile rate of exchange between gold and silver. In a 1606 publication, Galileo Galilei provides an exchange rate of 186 golden *scudi* to approximately 240 *ducati*.[2] According to that rate, the dowry promised to each of Simon Copio's three daughters equalled roughly 3,900 *ducati*. A 1611 document, on the other hand, records a 3,500-ducat dowry for the marriage of Sarra's youngest sister Ster (Ester).[3] The differing rates likely reflect the fluctuations of these currencies during this period.[4] For our purposes, we will consider the value of Copia Sulam's dowry as 3,500 ducats.

At his death, Simon Copio had 10,000 ducats in his loanbank in Venice,[5] his household goods were worth an estimated 6,275 ducats,[6] and his brother Michiel owed his estate approximately 2,250 ducats.[7] The total value of his holdings in Venice, calculated after Sarra's dowry had been paid,[8] was therefore over 18,500 ducats.[9] The worth of a 3,500-ducat dowry – and of Simon Copio's 18,500-ducat holdings – can be surmised by some relative points of measure in the era. Daily wages paid in the middle of the first decade of the century to master masons and carpenters working for the Scuola Grande di San Rocco, for which meticulous records exist, were just over 60 *soldi* a day, or around half a ducat of account.[10] (A ducat of account's actual value in gold or silver varied, but it retained a fixed exchange of 1 ducat to 6 *lire* and 4 *soldi*. One *lira* equalled 20 *soldi*.) In 1607, the price for a *staio* (almost two-and-a-half bushels) of wheat – enough to make 200 loaves of bread – was a little over 20 *lire*.[11] A 1618 document suggests that a series of items – a copper bucket, two pewter plates, two shirts, and a pair of pants – would have been worth 10 to 12 *lire* if offered in pledge for a loan.[12] In contrast, we can see the pledge value of some luxury items as attested in Simon Copio's 1606 household inventory; for example, a string of 63 pearls was left in pawn to his loanbank for 40 ducats; a piece of yellow satin for 80 ducats; and a tester of white silk and a sapphire set in gold for 130 ducats.[13] A 1616 document shows that the rent for Ricca Copia's dwelling in the Ghetto Nuovo was 68 ducats.[14]

Notes

Introduction

1 Infelise, *I padroni dei libri*, 131–2.
2 These include two recent books on Copia Sulam: Umberto Fortis's *La "bella ebrea": Sara Copio Sullam, poetessa nel ghetto di Venezia del '600*, an illuminating study that focuses on her poetry, and Don Harrán's comprehensive edition and translation of all known primary-source writings by and about the writer that includes extensive biographical information and analysis of her works – Copia Sulam, *Jewish Poet and Intellectual in Seventeenth-Century Venice.*
3 On the close links between women writers and the presses, see for example J.D. Campbell, *Literary Circles*; Ray, *Margherita Sarrocchi's Letters*; Robin, *Publishing Women*; Ross, *The Birth of Feminism*. See also Victoria Kirkham's edition and translation of Battiferra degli Ammannati, *Laura Battiferra*; Pal, *Republic of Women.*
4 Jews had been allowed to live in the city since the 1509 League of Cambrai War, during which Jews from the mainland had sought refuge in the city; the legislation of 1516 that established the ghetto sought to separate Jews living in the city from Christians. On Jews in Venice, a broad perspective is offered in Calabi, Galeazzo, and Massaro, *Venice, the Jews and Europe*; Davis and Ravid, *The Jews of Early Modern Venice*; Cozzi, *Gli ebrei e Venezia*. See also Mark R. Cohen's critical edition and translation entitled *The Autobiography of a Seventeenth-Century Venetian Rabbi: Leon Modena's Life of Judah*, with essays and apparatus by Theodore Rabb, Howard Adelman, Natalie Zemon Davis, and Benjamin Ravid (hereafter Modena, *Autobiography*). On Jews in Italy, see also the numerous studies by Roberto Bonfil, especially *Jewish Life in Renaissance Italy*, and the many works of David Ruderman.
5 One study estimates the Jewish population to have been 1,043 in 1581 and 5,000 in 1630. Calimani, *Storia del ghetto di Venezia*, 185. Ravid ("Venice

and Its Minorities," 456) instead estimates 2,500 to 3,000 ghetto residents
in the first half of the seventeenth century and states that, over time, Jews
made up between 1 and 2 per cent of the total population of the city.

6 The word "ghetto" (*gheto, getto, geto*, from *gettare*, to cast or throw) originally designated the copper foundry in Venice where cannon balls were
cast (Ghetto Vecchio was the foundry itself and Ghetto Nuovo the adja-
cent island where waste products from the foundry were left); after the
foundry was abandoned in the fourteenth century, the term was used to
refer to the former foundry location. With the segregation of Jews to this
part of the city, though, the term over time came to denote, elsewhere
and in Venice, the "compulsory, segregated, and enclosed Jewish quarter."
A demonstration of this is the use of the term Ghetto Nuovissimo for
the new part of the Jewish quarter established in 1633, though the land
it was situated on had not been part of the foundry. See Ravid, "Ghetto:
Etymology," 24–5, 28.

7 See Katz, *The Jewish Ghetto*, 1–2: "Ghetto architecture, rising high above the
horizon line, placed Jews in the position of urban onlookers whose viewing
point did not necessarily degrade them to passive objects but rather animated the Jews' status as observing subjects. Through its vertical ascend-
ancy, the Venice ghetto inadvertently granted its Jewish inhabitants visual
recognition in a city that required their marginalization."

8 Ravid, "New Light," 152.

9 Calabi, "Il ghetto e la città," 235.

10 The practice of usury (conceived of as lending money at interest) is
condemned in several places in the Old and New Testament, including
Exodus 22:25; Leviticus 25:35–7; Psalms 14:5 (Latin Vulgate/DR)/15:5
(King James). Deuteronomy 23:19–20 is more ambiguous: "Thou shalt
not lend to thy brother money to usury, nor corn, nor any other thing:
But to the stranger. To thy brother thou shalt lend that which he wanteth,
without usury." The verse was used to justify Jewish lending at interest
to Christians. See Todeschini, "Franciscan Economics," 106–8; Penslar,
Shylock's Children, 53–4. Some Christians maintained the verse was a Jewish
perversion of the authentic text. Todeschini, "Franciscan Economics,"
108. In addition to the use of Deutoronomy 23, Penslar (*Shylock's Children*,
18) also notes, "it was commonly argued that because the Jews were already damned, they may be left to commit the sin of usury, thereby saving
the souls of Christians who might otherwise engage in this activity." The
Talmud encouraged lending as an aid to commerce but forbade usury as
it is meant in a modern definition (charging exorbitant interest). See also
Dimont, *Jews, God and History*, 264–5. The idea that profit from the use of
money (i.e., interest) was unnatural was anchored in Roman law and in
Aristotelian thought; Aquinas combined the two to create "a compelling,

and what became the traditional, argument on the nature of money. For the saint, money had no intrinsic value; it was essentially sterile; and it was not a natural source of profit." Kirshner, "Raymond de Roover," 28.

11 In 1635–1636, the entire community came close to expulsion because of serious crimes committed by several Jews. See Ravid, *Economics and Toleration*, 10. See also Modena, *Autobiography*, 143–6.

12 Malkiel, *A Separate Republic*, 149. See also Modena, *Autobiography*, 144.

13 See chapter three, 81–2, 92–5.

14 On this issue, see Katz, *The Jewish Ghetto*, 48–83, esp. 63. Such fear of the reciprocal gaze also guided similar restrictions on the Fondaco dei Turchi, where itinerant Turkish (Muslim) merchants were required to lodge. Ibid., 76–7.

15 See Ravid, "From Yellow to Red." In the early seventeenth century, Venetian Jews were required to wear yellow or red hats, though there were both exemptions and frequent infractions; the colour changed from yellow to red across the seventeenth century. Regarding Venetian Jewish women, a traveller in 1664–1665 noted that "women have a head-dress hanging backward in their necks, and some of them wear red head-dresses." Ibid., 180. Elsewhere, Jews were required to wear badges, overclothes, or veils. Hughes, "Distinguishing Signs," 21–2. It was common throughout early modern Italy for members of other groups considered destabilizing to political, religious, or social order (such as prostitutes) to be required via sumptuary laws to wear distinguishing dress. See ibid., 25; Hughes, "Sumptuary Law," 92–3. In some cities, the distinguishing dress Jewish women were forced to wear was similar to that of prostitutes. Hughes, "Distinguishing Signs," 30, 46–7.

16 On the slight variations in the closing time and the violations for transgressing it, see Ravid, "New Light," 164–5.

17 Doctors and merchants often received special permission for nighttime excursions, and other individuals like glass workers and printers, as well as those acting for their own or the community's welfare, would occasionally get standing exemptions; frequent one-time permission was also granted for urgent errands. At times, especially during Carnival, permission was granted even for such reasons as musical or dance performances that the Jews were presenting. Ibid., 166–8. Ravid (ibid., 170–1) notes that these special permits indicate that the regulations on movement were otherwise in force, and that in the middle part of the seventeenth century the government tried to tighten the controls and to stop suspected violations. See also Siegmund, "La vita nei ghetti," 858; Katz, *The Jewish Ghetto*, 101–2.

18 "The members of the elite class – the small world of families of bankers [moneylenders] and merchants, doctors and rabbis – were surprisingly

mobile, since they were able both to stay out late at night in the city and to travel frequently." Siegmund, "La vita nei ghetti," 856.

19 This report comes from a manuscript defence of Copia Sulam. See "Avisi di Parnaso," 6or–6ov.

20 Adelman, "Success and Failure," 619–20. On Copia Sulam's cousin Diana, see the biographical note, 191, 296n73, 296n76.

21 Christians sometimes stayed in the ghetto even after its gates were locked for the evening: for example, in 1628 the gates were opened for many noble gentlemen and ladies who had come to witness a festival that lasted into the night, and in 1644 a Christian was granted permission to enter the ghetto at night to pick up Jews' correspondence for delivery elsewhere, a task deemed necessary possibly because it involved commercial matters that could not wait. Ravid, "New Light," 171–2.

22 See Adelman's several articles on Italian Jewish women and Italian Jewish women's intellectual lives.

23 For excellent overviews of women's writing in Italy, see Virginia Cox's *Women's Writing in Italy* and *The Prodigious Muse*.

24 King and Robin, "Volume Editor's Introduction," 6–8.

25 Robin, "Editor's Introduction," 6.

26 In 1547, the pope secured Fedele an appointment as the prioress of a Venetian orphanage; in 1556, the doge invited her to deliver an oration in honour of the queen of Poland, Bona Sforza. Ibid.

27 The bulk of Colonna's poetry published in the sixteenth century came to press in the city, including one of the earliest printed editions of her poetry (Zoppino, 1540). The first edition of her *Rime*, however, was printed in Parma. Her poems were published both as freestanding works and as parts of anthologies. For this publishing history, see Robin, *Publishing Women*, 260–1.

28 Ibid., 219–42.

29 Quaintance, *Textual Masculinity*, 144–5.

30 Ibid., 158–64. See also Rosenthal, *The Honest Courtesan*, 17–19, 49–57.

31 Ibid., 153–7, 161–76. See also Ray, *Writing Gender*, 129.

32 Quaintance, *Textual Masculinities*, 141.

33 Carinci, "Una lettera autografa," 679.

34 See Westwater, "The Disquieting Voice," 107–9; See also the discussion in the introduction, 11.

35 Boccalini, *Advices from Parnassus*, 32; I have modernized the capitalization, punctuation, and spelling in this excerpt and provide my own translation of the final clause. "Gli eccellentissimi signori Intronati, contro i loro antichi instituti, alcuni mesi sono ammisero nella loro Accademia le virtuosissime Donna Vittoria Colonna, Veronica Gambera [*sic*], Laura Terracina, e altre dame poetesse più segnalate di Parnaso ... Ma poco

tempo passò che alle nare [*sic*] di Sua Maestà giunse certo odore molto spiacevole, per lo quale comandò all'Archintronato, che in tutti i modi dismettesse quella pratica: percioché si era finalmente avveduto che la vera poetica delle donne era l'aco e il fuso, e che gli esercitij letterari delle dame co' virtuosi somigliavano gli scherzi e i giuochi che tra loro fanno i cani, i quali, dopo brieve tempo, tutti forniscono alla fine in montarsi addosso l'un l'altro." Boccalini, *De' ragguagli di Parnaso. Centuria prima,* 73–4.

36 See Cox, *Women's Writing in Italy,* 64–79.

37 For excellent summaries of these well-studied debates, see J.D. Campbell, "The *Querelle des femmes*"; Robin, "Gender."

38 The ostensible celebrations of women could be as unflattering as the attacks.

39 For a recent discussion and partial translation of the *Diffetti,* see Magnanini, "Giuseppe Passi's Attacks," 143–94.

40 Westwater, "Disquieting Voice," 1–3. Critics have long noticed the exceptional flourishing of women's writing in the period. See for example Labalme, "Venetian Women on Women."

41 See the modern English editions for synthetic introductions to the works: Cox, "Moderata Fonte and *The Worth of Women*"; Panizza, "Introduction to the Translation."

42 See Cox, *Women's Writing in Italy,* 174.

43 *Nobiltà* publisher Giovanni Battista Ciotti competed against *Merito* publisher Domenico Imberti to issue the first printed response to Passi. Ciotti edged out Imberti by three months. Zanette, *Suor Arcangela,* 218.

44 See chapter five, 137.

45 On the *Essortazioni,* see Westwater, "Disquieting Voice," 111–62, esp. 113–19; Price and Ristaino, *Lucrezia Marinella and the "Querelle des Femmes,"* 154. See also the modern English edition and translation by Laura Benedetti: *Exhortations to Women and to Others If They Please.* The text is an ambiguous one, as Benedetti ("Introduction," 34) notes, calling it a "complex and sometimes contradictory work"; she nevertheless reads it primarily as a recantation of Marinella's earlier prowoman positions.

46 She articulated this view most clearly in her *Tirannia paterna* (Paternal Tyranny), published (against Tarabotti's wishes) under the title *Semplicità ingannata* (Innocence Deceived). The text – which charged that Church and state colluded to compel girls with no religious calling to become nuns – was unpublishable in a Catholic country. She therefore used a transnational network of free-thinking intellectuals to publish the work in Leiden. Regarding the work's path to publication and its title, see Westwater, "A Rediscovered Friendship."

47 Benzoni, *Gli affanni della cultura,* 69.

48 On the academy, see Zanette, *Suor Arcangela*; Ulvioni, "Stampa e censura"; Spini, *Ricerca dei libertini*; Mancini, "La narrativa libertina"; Rosand, *Opera in Seventeenth-Century Venice*, esp. 37–40; Miato, *L'Accademia degli Incogniti*; the several studies of Cannizzaro, especially "Studies on Guido Casoni"; Heller, *Emblems of Eloquence*, esp. 47–81; Infelise, "Ex ignoto notus?" and "Libri e politica"; Muir, *The Culture Wars*.

49 There is evidence, however, that some women (though not the writers here under consideration) did attend meetings. See Rosand, "Barbara Strozzi," 245–52.

50 Cannizzaro, "Studies on Guido Casoni," 309 and Cannizzaro, "Surpassing the Maestro," 369, 387–9, 389n77. See also Fulco, "Introduction," xx–xxi. Others doubt this claim: see for example Carminati, "La prima edizione della *Messalina*," 338.

51 Heller, *Emblems of Eloquence*, 52. For a discussion of Incogniti attitudes to women, especially as reflected in the academy's involvement with opera, see ibid., 47–81.

52 Rosand, *Opera*, 38.

53 Loredano, *Bizzarrie accademiche parte prima*, 17–21. He (ibid., 20) writes: "Waiting for gifts and favors from a beloved is a result of fear and diffidence; snatching them is an act of courage and daring; whence, as much greater is the latter than the former, that much happier is the lover who steals than the one who receives a gift" (L'attendere i doni e i favori dall'amata è un effetto di timore e di modestia; rapirli è un atto di animosità e d'ardire; onde quanto più è degno in amore questo di quello, tanto è più felice l'amante che rubba che quello che riceve in dono). On Loredan's public discourses in the Accademia on women – presented before an audience of men (and sometimes women) and striking for their "inherent theatricality" – see Heller, *Emblems of Eloquence*, 53.

54 "un male così grande che non si può descrivere." Loredano, *Delle bizzarrie academiche parte seconda*, 167. Both the first (1638) and second (1646) parts of the *Bizzarrie* contain numerous negative portrayals of women.

55 On the various editions of the clamorously successful *Bizzarrie*, see Menegatti, *"Ex ignoto notus,"* 151–73.

56 See Cosentino, "Dee, imperatrici, cortigiane."

57 An autograph letter from Loredano suggests the work was by Rocco and provides the approximate date of composition; see Neri, "Il vero autore," 221–2.

58 Coci, "Nota introduttiva," 8.

59 A synthetic overview of the life of this most controversial Incognito is offered in Infelise, "Pallavicino, Ferrante."

60 For a description of this parody, see Coci, "Introduzione." See also Muir, *The Culture Wars*, 90–4.

61 Pallavicino, *La retorica delle puttane*, 8.

62 *Che le donne non siano della specie degli huomini, discorso piacevole tradotto da Orazio Plata romano* (That Women Are Not of Mankind, a Pleasant Discourse Translated by the Roman Orazio Plata). On the Incogniti's and Loredano's involvement in this work and its publishing history, see Infelise, "Libri e politica" (available also in English: "Books and Politics").

63 See Rosand, "Barbara Strozzi," 249. She also states that Loredano took Tarabotti seriously and that "Barbara Strozzi may well have enjoyed a similar respect." Ibid.

64 Ibid., 249–52.

65 "come que' segni che servono a' saggittari, li quali sono percossi e lacerati da ognuno e da ogni parte." Marinella, *Essortazioni*, 2.

66 See Westwater, "Disquieting Voice," 6–16.

67 On the academy's ambivalent views on women, see Heller, *Emblems of Eloquence*, 49–52.

68 For a recent discussion of the issue, see Katz, *The Jewish Ghetto*, 103–10, esp. 106: "The barriers established around the ghetto consigned sex to a patrolled status contained behind brick walls. Those walls, nonetheless, did not abate the fear of the Jews' sexuality in Venice or in early modern Europe more generally. The Jews' sexualized bodies aroused constant scrutiny. For instance, Jewish women were thought to be sexually suspicious with enhanced libidos that triggered an uncontrollable attraction to Christian men ... [M]edieval theologians rendered Synagoga, the collective image of the Jewish community, as a personified woman seducing Christianity ... The seductive qualities of Synagoga render her a shameful temptress difficult to repress in the sexual imagination of Christian society." Katz notes the prevalence of these stereotypes in seventeenth-century Venice.

69 Copia Sulam, *Manifesto*, A2r, C3v. Unless otherwise specified, all quotations from the *Manifesto* are from the Pinelli edition. See chapter three, 79, 252–3nn24–5. For Copia Sulam's views on the proper use of the presses, see chapter three, 82–9.

70 For the nomenclature of and relation between these bodies, see Black, *The Italian Inquisition*, 24, 161–2.

71 Terminology for works in the *querelle des femmes* is tricky. Here I use the interrelated terms "feminist" and "antifeminist," to show how the prowoman and misogynist arguments in these debates were often bound up with one another. By "feminist" I mean the expression of belief in the dignity and merit of women, not (as in a modern conception) a political program for women's social advancement. By "antifeminist" I mean an expression of hostility to women that exceeded the general cultural belief that women were subordinate to men. I should emphasize the term *expression*, since I mean to distinguish the antifeminism I discuss from violent manifestations of hostility to women, such as wife-beating or witch hunts, even though I believe, with many others, that the two phenomena are interrelated. In discussing

misogyny, Bloch (*Medieval Misogyny*, 4) notes, for instance, that "speech can be a form of action and even of social practice, or at least its ideological component." Bonifaccio's vicious attack on Copia Sulam's orthodoxy exceeded the bounds of antifeminism since it could have affected her bodily safety. In this book, I use the terms "antifeminist," "antiwoman," and "misogynist" interchangeably. For the other side of the debates, I use the term feminist or prowoman. On the matter, see Cox, *Women's Writing in Italy*, xxvii.

72 Hereafter referred to as *Lettere a Sarra Copia*.

73 Ascarelli and Menato (*La tipografia del' 500*, 430) as well as Contò ("Ciotti, Giovanni Battista," 293) thus list Ciotti's birth year. Rhodes ("Some Neglected Aspects," 225) gives it as ca. 1560 and states that his publishing activity trailed off dramatically a decade before it ceased in 1635, presumably with his death. Contò ("Ciotti, Giovanni Battista," 295) also gives 1635 as the last possible date for Ciotti's publishing activity.

74 These dates differ from those offered in other studies, most recently Harrán, "Introduction," 16–19. See the biographical note, 191–2, 296nn76–80.

1 The Birth of a Salon (1618–1621)

1 "d'incerto autore hebreo ad instanza della signora Sarra Coppia." Ansaldo Cebà, *Lettere a Sarra Copia*, 4.

2 Fonseca-Wollheim ("Faith and Fame," 62, 136) convincingly proposes Uziel's involvement based on Gabriele Zinano's inclusion, one after the other, of poetry exchanges with Copia Sulam and with Uziel in his 1627 *Rime diverse*. Zinano was a poet, playwright, and political theorist born in Reggio Emilia. On Uziel, see also Harrán's note in Copia Sulam, *Jewish Poet and Intellectual*, 117n27; Fürst, *Bibliotheca Judaica* (1960), 3:462.

3 Zinano, *Rime diverse*, 46–7.

4 Modena gives an account of the astonishing number of his manuscript and printed writings in his autobiography. See Modena, *Autobiography*, 121–7. Alongside Cohen's critical edition of Modena's *Autobiography*, the definitive work on Modena is Adelman, "Success and Failure."

5 On Modena's tie to and stay with Moisè Copio, see Modena, *Autobiography*, 104–5. See also the biographical note, 187, 197, 300n131.

6 See Modena, *L'Ester*, 3–6. Modena's *L'Ester* revised a version by the author Salomone Ulsque. See Soave, "Sara Copia Sullam," 15 (1876–1877), 198n2.

7 "siamo più volte caduti in ragionamento." Ibid., 3.

8 Cebà, *Lettere a Sarra Copia*, 31–2 (30 March 1619).

9 Adelman, "Leon Modena: The Autobiography," 29; Cohen, "Leone da Modena's *Riti*" (1972), 289n14.

10 Ibid., 287. The work was a response to diatribes against Jews, particularly Johann Buxtorf the Elder's *Synagoga Judaica*. Cohen, "Plea for Toleration," 292–310. Adelman ("Leon Modena: The Autobiography," 29) notes that

Modena's *Riti* became "a major source of information for Christians about Judaism for many generations to come." The work circulated in manuscript form for many years before it was published; Modena long avoided printing it because he feared ecclesiastical censorship. When the work was published in Paris in 1637, he was so uneasy about the consequences from the Inquisition that he submitted the work to the Venetian Holy Office, which permitted it to be published in Venice in 1638 only after offending passages were removed. See Cohen, "Plea for Toleration," 290–2.

11 The literary production of the Accademia degli Incogniti foregrounded eroticism, representing a notable shift from the dominant sixteenth-century use of neoplatonic models. See Cosentino, "Dee, imperatrici, cortigiane," 292–3. The Neoplatonist tendency in Italian letters had tended to favour philogyny, whereas the erotic tendency grew hand in hand with hostile attitudes towards women. See also Cox, *Women's Writing in Italy*, 178–9.

12 Isabella della Tolfa – daughter of Carlo della Tolfa, count of San Valentino, and Livia Spinelli – was the second wife of Agostino Grimaldi, prince of Salerno, duke of Eboli, and marchese of Diano, to whom she was married by 1592. Widowed in 1594, she married Doria in 1598, bringing to the marriage considerable landholdings in the South and strengthening the Dorias' position there. On della Tolfa, see Campanile, *Notizie di nobiltà*, 168; Modestino, *Della dimora di Torquato Tasso*, 239n1; Reale Simioli, "Ansaldo Cebà," 99, 99n12; Storchi, "Formazione," 2:554–6.

13 On Castello, who in his long and prolific career painted (among numerous other works) portraits of many famous writers including Torquato Tasso, Gabriello Chiabrera, and Ansaldo Cebà, see Biavati, "Castello, Bernardo." Figure 1.2 shows an engraving of Cebà based on Castello's portrait. See Harrán's caption to figure 4 in Copia Sulam, *Jewish Poet and Intellectual*, 191.

14 See chapter one, 39–41.

15 On Copia Sulam's letters to della Tolfa and Doria, see chapter four, 122–4. Marcantonio Doria, from one of the most important Genoese families, was the firstborn son of Agostino Doria, doge from 1601 to 1603. Doria's interests were, unlike his father's, not political, and he lived much of his life in Naples, though he did serve as senator in Genoa in 1630. He was a major patron of the arts and a philanthropist who strongly supported Cebà both during his life and after his death. The two shared the ideal of "civil equality." By means of the land acquired by his marriage to della Tolfa and subsequent consolidation of his power, Doria became part of the Neapolitan feudal aristocracy. Storchi, "Formazione," 555. On Doria, see ibid., 554–5; Cavanna Ciappina, "Doria, Marcantonio." For his dates and an account of his art patronage, see Zafran, *Renaissance to Rococo*, 64. On Doria and Cebà, see also chapter four, 108–14. It was Doria who would prepare the posthumous edition of the *Lettere a Sarra Copia*, along with other posthumous editions of Cebà's works.

16 Cebà was the son of Nicolò Cebà (d. 1603); see "Albero genealogico della famiglia Cebà," 4. Most studies of Copia Sulam also include important information regarding Cebà. Additional biographical information can be found in Mutini, "Cebà, Ansaldo"; Vazzoler, "Le *Rime* di Ansaldo Cebà"; Cebà, *Tragedie.*

17 Spotorno, *Storia letteraria della Liguria*, 4:130–1.

18 See Cox, *Women's Writing in Italy*, 148. On the Spinolas, see also Cox, *The Prodigious Muse*, 268–9.

19 Pavoni's presses issued official documents for the Republic of Genoa and literary works by the most important Ligurian writers. See Ruffini, "Note su Giuseppe Pavoni." See also Ascarelli and Menato, *La tipografia del '500*, 140; Sartori, *Dizionario degli editori musicali*, 115–16.

20 His first collection (*Rime*, Padua and Antwerp, 1596; Padua 1601) was Petrarchan. Cebà later worried that these poems would reflect badly on his reputation and tried to "abolish them," perhaps by buying up extra copies. Reale Simioli, "Tracce di letteratura ligure," 116. His second collection (*Rime*, 1611) departed from the Petrarchan model to examine civic and moral issues. His first epic poem was the short *Lazaro il mendico* (The Beggar Lazarus, 1614); another epic poem was published posthumously, *Furio Camillo* (Marcus Furius Camillus, 1623).

21 Walfish, *Esther in Medieval Garb*, 1.

22 Jewish commentaries show ambivalence regarding this aspect of the tale, especially as regards the "mixed marriage" between Esther and the king. Ibid., 121–41.

23 "virtù de l'alma ... sì grande / Che soverchiava in lei l'etade, e 'l sesso." Cebà, *La reina Esther*, 3.

24 See Klein, *Portrait de la Juive*, 19–20. For its significance in a Jewish context, see Walfish, *Esther in Medieval Garb*, esp. 1, 121–41, 202; Cavarocchi Arbib, "Rivisitando la biblica Ester," 143–57.

25 See Fonseca-Wollheim, "Faith and Fame," 53–5.

26 Tornabuoni was the mother of Lorenzo "il Magnifico" de' Medici (1449–92). For a modern edition of her *Esther*, see "The Story of Queen Esther," in Tornabuoni de' Medici, *Sacred Narratives*, 163–215. This edition, by Jane Tylus, is based on Magliabechiano VII, the manuscript of Tornabuoni's sacred stories found at the Biblioteca Nazionale di Firenze. Milligan ("Unlikely Heroines," 548) says Tornabuoni likely wrote the *Sacred Narratives* after her husband's death in 1469.

27 See Tylus's introduction to "The Story of Queen Esther" in Tornabuoni de' Medici, *Sacred Narratives*, 166–7.

28 Spotorno, *Storia letteraria della Liguria*, 4:126.

29 This edition was published in the inferior duodecimo format.

30 He discussed his disappointment throughout his general letter collection: Cebà, *Lettere d'Ansaldo Cebà ad Agostino Pallavicino di Stefano* (Ansaldo Cebà's Letters to Agostino Pallavicino di Stefano; hereafter *Lettere a Pallavicino*), for example 148, 214, 241–3, 252–3, 267. Pallavicino would become doge of Genoa in 1637.

31 Cebà's friend Marcantonio Doria reported in 1622 that Cebà had 400 unsold copies of the book. See Reale Simioli, "Tracce di letteratura ligure," 116.

32 On the correspondence, see for instance Boccato, "Lettere di Ansaldo Cebà," 169–91; Rio, *Les quatre martyrs* (1856), 95–163; Fonseca-Wollheim, "Acque di Parnaso"; Ultsch, "Sara Copio Sullam"; Harrán, "Introduction," 38–45.

33 With her first letter she also included the poem by Uziel, as discussed above.

34 Cebà, *Lettere a Sarra Copia*, 3.

35 That is, heaven and earth. See Fortis, *La "bella ebrea,"* 103n8.

36 Fortis (ibid., 104) notes the striking use of the term "empyrean heaven," which he states is "one of many concessions in Copia Sulam's poetry to the culture outside the ghetto – a disinctive trait of her production."

37 "mi paio obligato a far di voi altro giudicio, che non si suole ordinariamente fare del vostro sesso." Cebà, *Lettere a Sarra Copia*, 1.

38 The works included a dialogue, *Il Gonzaga overo Del poema eroico* (Gonzaga, or On the Epic Poem), which responded to criticism about his *La reina Esther.*

39 For example see Cebà, *Lettere a Pallavicino*, 148, 156, 202, 212, 213–14, 224, 249, 264. Despite the sole addressee indicated in the title, the letters are directed to a wide variety of correspondents.

40 He had published a single composition entitled "Corona di Pietà" in a collection of writings published in Venice in 1605 (republished in 1610). See Gentile, *Della corona*, 41–8.

41 The title was slightly altered to *Il cittadino nobile di repvblica*. For Copia Sulam's praise of the work, see Cebà, *Lettere a Sarra Copia*, 9.

42 See *Le glorie de gli Incogniti*, 71–3.

43 "più benigno il cielo." From a letter cited in Mandosio, *Bibliotheca romana*, 2:112.

44 Ibid. On his lack of success in Tuscany, see the late manuscript ("Avisi," 6r) that regards Copia Sulam and her associates.

45 *Varie poesie di molti eccellenti autori in morte del m. illustre sig. cavalier Battista Guarini.* Paluzzi's poems appear at ibid., 18; poems to Paluzzi from Pier Francesco Paoli are at ibid., 20. On the *Varie Poesie*, see also 230n147.

46 Marino (*Lettere*, 226–7, 265) assumed they were in regular contact when he sent his greetings to Paluzzi through Ciotti. Harrán ("Introduction," 392n202) makes a similar point. On Paluzzi as a proofreader, see also below, n47 and n169.

47 Misserini was active in Venice from 1589 to 1635. Ascarelli and Menato, *La tipografia del '500*, 440. See also Pastorello, *Tipografi, editori, librai*, 55; Borsa, *Clavis typographorum librariorumque Italiae*, 1:223. The Misserini edition in quarto of the *Commentaries* was a re-edition of a well-known text with copper plates by Andrea Palladio, first printed in 1575. The frontispiece advertised this version of the commentaries as "newly corrected with diligence" – a description of Paluzzi's work. Paluzzi helped produce a volume of good quality: Melzi judges the 1619 edition superior to the 1598 one. See Melzi, Zardetti, and Melzi, *Dizionario di opere anonime e pseudonime*, 1:225. Haym (*Biblioteca italiana*, 1:29–30) says that the "first of 1575 and the latter one of 1619 are the best and the most useful editions of Caesar, other than those printed by Giolito."

48 See n45 above. Paoli was a writer of some acclaim from Pesaro; he published poetry in various collections, wrote some encomiastic works, and had ties in several cities, including Ferrara, Venice, and Rome, where he spent most of his literary career. See the entry on "Paoli, Pier Francesco" in Hainsworth and Robey, *The Oxford Companion to Italian Literature*, 433.

49 "Delle qualità del signor Numidio Paoluzzi io sono molto meglio informato di voi già molti anni fa: so il suo valore ed a quanto arriva il suo ingegno. Ho ambizione che parli onorevolmente di me e me ne glorio oltremodo, assicurandolo che non ne riceverà mal cambio." Marino, *Lettere*, 226–7.

50 Ibid., 265. In that same letter, he passes greetings to Pietro Petracci, whose name appears in one edition of Copia Sulam's *Manifesto*. On Petracci, see chapter three, 79–81.

51 The dating to 1618 of Copia Sulam's and Paluzzi's collaboration can be reconstructed from a late manuscript about Copia Sulam which indicates that, by 1624, she had employed Paluzzi for six years. See "Avisi," 5v, 34v.

52 Ibid., 5r.

53 Ibid., 5v, 21v.

54 See ibid., 71r.

55 On Berardelli as a painter, see Mandosio, *Bibliotheca romana*, 2:112; chapter six, 285n19. Berardelli would later become a writer and editor. See chapter five, 128–9 and 133–48, and chapter six, 175–7.

56 See Mandosio, *Bibliotheca romana*, 2:112–15.

57 "famiglio" or "guataro" (="sguattero"). See for example "Avisi," 15v, 17v, 34v, 35r.

58 Ibid., 36v.

59 The principal scholars of Copia Sulam tend to use this term: see for
example Harrán, "Introduction," 16, 34, 58; Fortis, *La "bella ebrea,"* 30–48;
Adelman, "Italian Jewish Women," 140; Boccato, "Lettere di Ansaldo
Cebà," 169; Boccato, "Le *Rime* postume," 114. Elsewhere Boccato ("Un
altro documento," 303) calls the group an academy, perhaps in keeping with more elastic contemporary terminology (see below, nn64–5).
Fonseca-Wollheim ("Faith and Fame," 47–9) terms the group a côterie,
but also notes the resemblance to a salon.

60 See Cox, "Members, Muses, Mascots," 132–45. See also Fahy, "Women and
Italian Cinquecento Literary Academies." Though it was relatively rare for
women to be members of academies in Italy, many cases do exist. Venice
was more conservative than other cities in this respect, and even well-
known writers like Lucrezia Marinella and Arcangela Tarabotti were not
apparently invited to join any of the city's academies. One Venetian academy, the Accademia dei Desiosi, did have a female member from 1626 to
1630, however: the artist Artemisia Gentileschi. See Cox, "Members, Muses,
Mascots," 134–42. Ray (*Daughters of Alchemy,* 135–6) notes Neapolitan
poet and scientist Margherita Sarrocchi's association with the Accademia
degli Umoristi and Accademia dei Lincei and her role in co-founding the
Accademia degli Ordinati in Rome. See also J.D. Campbell, *Literary Circles,*
26–7; Bettella, "Women and the Academies," esp. 103–5. Italy's, and perhaps Europe's, first female academy, the Accademia delle Assicurate, was
founded in 1654 in Siena. See McClure, *Parlour Games,* 119–58.

61 Benzoni, "Le accademie," 141. In total there were 107 academies in
Venice between the end of the fifteenth and the end of the seventeenth
century. Testa, *Italian Academies,* 81.

62 Benzoni, "Le accademie," 137–9, 146, 160–1. See the editors' introduc-
tion to Everson, Reidy, and Sampson, *The Italian Academies,* 4; Quaintance,
Textual Masculinity, 61; M. Feldman, *City Culture,* 22. Testa (*Italian
Academies,* 4) notes varied levels of formality in Italian academies. See also
Findlen, "Academies."

63 For a discussion of the relationship between academies and politics in
Venice in the mid- to late sixteenth century and early seventeenth century,
see Testa, *Italian Academies,* 80–124.

64 Angelico Aprosio used this term to describe the group. Mandosio,
Bibliotheca romana, 2:113.

65 M. Feldman, *City Culture,* 22. The Accademia della Crusca's 1612
Vocabolario (8) defines *accademia* as a "gathering of scholarly men"
(adunanza d'huomini studiosi).

66 Ray, *Daughters of Alchemy,* 135.

67 M. Feldman, *City Culture,* 21–2; Quaintance, *Textual Masculinity,* 68–9.

68 M. Feldman, *City Culture,* 21.

69 Robin, *Publishing Women*, 40. Robin contrasts this phenomenon to that observed by Landes (*Women and the Public Sphere*, 23) in France, where the salon "was displaced in part with the creation of a modern publishing apparatus."

70 "In Italy, reciprocity and dynamism characterized the relationship between the salons, the academies, and the presses." Robin, *Publishing Women*, 40.

71 For example, charges of unchastity were made against Sarrocchi (1560–1617), who was a member of academies in Rome. See Ray, *Daughters of Alchemy*, 132; Cox, *Women's Writing in Italy*, 201–2; Bettella, "Women and the Academies," 104: "Sarrocchi's participation in academic debates was a source not only of praise and admiration but also of accusations of vanity and sexual impropriety ... As Sarrocchi's case shows, the main obstacle to female membership was the question of decorum: respectable women could not attend academic meetings, or participate in debates and discussions where most participants were men."

72 Other texts that illuminate the workings of Copia Sulam's salon include Baldassare Bonifaccio's *Immortalità* and *Risposta al Manifesto*, as well as the writers' letter exchange (see chapter two, 60–72, and chapter three, 99–104); the "Avisi" (see chapter five, 160); Angelico Aprosio's account, published in Mandosio's *Bibliotheca romana* (see n150 below).

73 Cebà, *Lettere a Sarra Copia*, 28. Since there was no formal membership – in fact, participation seems to have been fairly fluid and open – the men Copia Sulam interacted with in the salon can be called either "participants" or "associates."

74 "trattano con esso voi per solo diletto della vostra conversatione." Ibid., 31.

75 Cebà (*Lettere a Sarra Copia*, 55–6) criticizes her writing style as too elaborate and suggests others helped her with it, using the metaphor of her hair: if he came to visit her, he writes, he would want to see her hair simply done and not arranged with the cunning of her maid. Cox (*Women's Writing in Italy*, 368n221) reads this insinuation similarly.

76 Copia Sulam and della Tolfa first exchanged letters in June 1619 (Cebà, *Lettere a Sarra Copia*, 37). On her possible correspondence with Doria, see Cebà, *Lettere a Pallavicino*, 191–2. On della Tolfa, see n12 above; on Doria, see n15.

77 Cebà, *Lettere a Sarra Copia*, 29. Cebà's sonnet of response (ibid.) is not only *per le rime*, as are his other responses to her poetry; here, every verse concludes with precisely the same word (Lanfranco, velo, etc.) as the corresponding verse in Copia Sulam's composition. This close adherence to her poem indicates that Cebà attributed special importance to it, perhaps because of its subject matter.

78 See chapter three, 93–5.

79 See Harrán's note in Copia Sulam, *Jewish Poet and Intellectual*, 148n123.

80 Cebà, *Lettere a Sarra Copia*, 29.
81 The location of the ancient region of Thrace fell within lands controlled
    by the Ottoman Empire in the seventeenth century.
82 Cebà, *Lettere a Sarra Copia*, 57.
83 Ibid., 58.
84 Bonifaccio had printed two works with Fioravante Prati by 1619. Prati
    collaborated with Ciotti to print a 1617 work, Giacomo Pergamini's *Il
    memoriale della lingua italiana*; Prati is mentioned in the colophon. (*Il
    memoriale* was the first modern European dictionary with definitions
    but was soon eclipsed by the Accademia della Crusca's *Vocabolario*. See
    Lubello, "Pergamini, Giacomo"; on the *Vocabolario*, see chapter three, 76).
    Bonifaccio's brother Gaspare also printed his *Amor venale, favola boscherec-
    cia* with Ciotti in 1616; as we have seen, the latter was in regular contact
    with Paluzzi.
85 Bonifaccio's mother and Corniani's father were siblings. The cousins
    had long collaborated, as their coauthored *Sinodia* from 1612 indicates;
    Bonifaccio said Corniani was the first to teach him poetry. See Cicogna,
    Delle iscrizioni veneziane, 5:341–2.
86 On Corniani's participation in the group, see Copia Sulam's letter printed
    in B. Bonifaccio, *Risposta al Manifesto*, A5r.
87 For Corniani's dates and his career, see Cicogna, *Delle iscrizioni veneziane*,
    5:341.
88 Gaspare became connected to other participants in the circle, exchanging
    poetry, for instance, with Paluzzi (*Rime*, 129). See also Soranzo, *Bibliografia
    veneziana*, 478. Baldassare and Gaspare, along with their brother
    Melchiore, were triplets named for the three wise men. Born, "Baldassare
    Bonifaccio," 222.
89 A member of the Accademia degli Incogniti, Vanti was praised for his liter-
    ary and mathematical skills in *Le glorie de gli Incogniti*, 252–5. At his death
    in 1641, he left several works unpublished, including an epic poem on the
    New World. Ibid., 254–5. Vanti also wrote the dedication and note to the
    reader in Baldassare's *Stichidion*. Vanti and Baldassare published works to-
    gether and were said to love each other like brothers. See B. Bonifaccio and
    Vanti, *Castore e Polluce*, +12r. Corniani contributed two sonnets to this work
    (ibid., +7v–8r) and Gaspare wrote nearly 100 pages of interpretation of his
    brother's and Vanti's verse (ibid., I1r–M12v [separately numbered pages
    1–96]). Many other manuscript works document the continuing close ties
    among these writers: see Cicogna, *Delle iscrizioni veneziane*, 5:340–2.
90 See Mandosio, *Bibliotheca romana*, 2:115. On Vanti's account as reported by
    Aprosio, see chapter one, 46, and chapter six, 178–80.
91 Bonifaccio (*Delle amene lettere*, fascicolo 21, 11r–12r) wrote a new year's
    greeting to Copia Sulam in late December 1619 or early January 1620

that took up the topic of mortality and immortality, which they had clearly already discussed. The undated letter is published in Boccato, "Una disputa secentesca," 603–4, and translated in Copia Sulam, *Jewish Poet and Intellectual*, 270–3. On Bonifaccio's use of the term Sabba to address Copia Sulam, see Harrán's note in ibid., 270n4.

92 "Se pure in alcun discorso io vi ho promossa alcuna difficultà filosofica o teologica, ciò … è stato … solo per curiosità d'intender da voi, con la soluzione de' miei argomenti, qualche curiosa e peregrina dottrina, stimando ciò esser concesso ad ogni persona che professi studi, nonché ad una donna, e donna hebrea, la quale continuamente vien posta in questi discorsi da persone che si affaticano di ridurla, come voi sapete, alla cristiana fede." Copia Sulam, *Manifesto*, B1v.

93 See chapter two, 62–6. In his *Risposta al Manifesto* (A5r–A6v), Bonifaccio printed Copia Sulam's January 1620 response to the letter he wrote in late 1619 or early 1620.

94 Ibid., A5r.

95 Cebà, *Lettere a Sarra Copia*, 67.

96 Ibid.

97 Published in Paluzzi, *Rime*, 48.

98 Though Bonifaccio's sonnets have been lost, Copia Sulam reports on their recitation in her letter to Bonifaccio, published in his *Risposta al Manifesto* (A5r). She may not have responded enthusiastically to his recitation; in her letter she explains the silence with which she greeted his compositions as awe.

99 In a letter acknowledging the poetry, Cebà (*Lettere a Sarra Copia*, 65–9) suggests that many different writers were involved.

100 Bonifaccio (*Delle amene lettere*, fascicolo 21, 12r) discussed one of these sonnets in the letter to Copia Sulam cited in n91 above.

101 "valorosi compagni." Cebà, *Lettere a Sarra Copia*, 67.

102 Ibid., 68.

103 Ibid.

104 Ibid., 70.

105 Ibid., 68–9. One of Copia Sulam's associates had warned Cebà that seeing Copia Sulam would make him an idolater. Ibid., 67.

106 See Boccato, "Il presunto ritratto di Sara Copio Sullam," 193–5; Harrán, "Introduction," 22–7. The portrait, now thought to be by Antonio Logorio (conjecturably copied from Castello's portrait of the salonnière), is held in a private collection. Ibid., 24–6.

107 Cebà, *Lettere a Sarra Copia*, 75.

108 Cf. for instance Petrarca, *Rerum vulgarium fragmenta*, 127 (RVF 155).

109 "Voi penerete a trarmi dalla polvere, signora Sarra, ancorché scriviate e facciate scrivere di me con tanta sollecitudine. Frenate però, vi priego, il vostro

stile e l'altrui; e provvedete, che chi ha tocco infino ad hor del mio nome si distenda per l'avvenire nel vostro; perché la maggior gratia che mi si possa fare è che voi siate lodata e riverita da tutti." Cebà, *Lettere a Sarra Copia*, 87.

110 Cebà (ibid.) claims he sends the originals of the writings back because they were in the author's hand.

111 Ibid., 95–6.

112 Harrán (Copia Sulam, *Jewish Poet and Intellectual*, 223n432) tentatively identifies the "Vicentine doctor" as Bonifaccio. Fonseca-Wollheim ("Faith and Fame," 64) believes the reference to be to Corniani. Neither of these writers, however, is from Vicenza. Bissari was a Vicentine writer who received his doctorate in law before 1620 and published his first work in 1619. He still lived in Vicenza during these years, but Venice was where he nurtured his most important literary ties – he would later become a member of the Accademia degli Incogniti – and where he published his best-known works. See Ballistreri, "Bissari, Pietro Paolo." By the mid-seventeenth century he was "resident or partially resident in Venice." Glixon and Glixon, *Inventing the Business of Opera*, 110. Bissari would later show positive interest in another woman writer, Arcangela Tarabotti. See Tarabotti, *Letters Familiar and Formal*, 53.

113 For Basadonna's dates, see Barbaro, "Genealogie delle famiglie patrizie venete," 92r; Cappellari, "Campidoglio veneto," 127r. There are two Giovanni Basadonnas in the period but in Cappellari, this Giovanni – son of Pietro – is listed as "doctissimo senatore" (most learned senator). I thank Stefano Trovato for consulting this source on my behalf.

114 See Soranzo, *Bibliografia veneziana*, 321.

115 Nani, *Historia della Republica Veneta* (1680), 66. See also Soranzo, *Bibliografia veneziana*, 321.

116 The role of *savio grande*, or "great sage," was one of the most prestigious posts in the Republic. See Grendler, "The Leaders of the Venetian State," section 11, 39–50.

117 See Nani, *Historia della Republica Veneta* (1662), 327–30.

118 Superbi, *Trionfo glorioso*, 93.

119 "nella gravità, nella prudenza, e nell'heroiche sue operationi, mostrasi amabile, singolare, & di gran senno. Nelle cose publiche indefesso, & nelle private mirabile. Nelle lettere latine eccellente, & e nelle volgari di molta intelligenza. Egli è ricco de beni di animo e di fortuna parimente, vivendo con molta riputatione, honorevolezza, & splendore presso ad ognuno nella sua gloriosa Patria." Ibid., 3:93–4.

120 Ferrari, *Prolusiones*, 386–7.

121 "I vostri versi mi piacciono, perché mi piace la vostra persona: ma quelli del Basadonna mi spaventano, perché mi spaventa il suo cognome: e però, se, quand'egli viene a visitarvi, potesse lasciarlo fuori dell'uscio, parmi che parlerei di lui con la bocca più dolce." Cebà, *Lettere a Sarra Copia*, 98.

122 See also Harrán's note in Copia Sulam, *Jewish Poet and Intellectual*, 226n444.

123 Cebà, *Lettere a Sarra Copia*, 99.

124 "molta gente ... , senza vostra colpa, vorrebbe peravventura dimesticarsi con voi"; "tanto rigida nel contrasto de gli amori lascivi, quanto vi reputo gratiosa nell'essercitio de' continenti." Ibid., 100.

125 A first mention of Giacob early in the letters seems initially less problematic. Cebà (*Lettere a Sarra Copia*, 20) writes to Copia Sulam that "I have ordered [my servant] to greet the signor your husband on my behalf; since he had the good fortune of having you for his wife, I cannot believe that he is anything but most courteous" (Al medesimo ho ordinato che saluti da parte mia il signor vostro marito, il quale, poic'ha havuto in sorte d'havervi per moglie, non credo che possa essere se non gentilissimo). Cebà will continue to tie Giacob's reputation to that of his wife even as he attacks the latter. See below, n137.

126 Ibid., 23.

127 "The rhetorical device of emphasizing or drawing attention to something by professing to say little or nothing about it, or affecting to dismiss it (usually with such phrases as *not to mention, to say nothing of*, etc.); an instance of this" (OED).

128 The implication of Giacob's cuckolding is particularly troubling (but was perhaps especially suggestive to Cebà) since from the Middle Ages onward Jews were equated with the devil and were considered horned. Poliakov, *The History of Anti-Semitism*, 1:142. Trachtenberg (*The Devil and the Jews*, 45) also points out that Michelangelo's Moses is horned, based perhaps on the mistranslation of Exod. 34.29 that appears in the Vulgate: "and he knew not that his face was horned from the conversation of the Lord" (ignorabat quod cornuta esset facies sua ex consortio sermonis Domini). On the equation of Jews with the devil, see also Bonfil, "The Devil and the Jews." On the figure of the cuckold, see LaGuardia, *Intertextual Masculinity*, 3–4: The cuckold is "transformed in the comic literature into a stingy, paranoid, stupid and often debauched buffoon ... [T]he cuckold literature helped to propagate a set of ideas that called on masculine subjects to perform their genders, and whose very meaning and structure was contingent upon the 'correct' performance of that gender as the essential condition of marriage at the very foundation of social structure."

129 "Ma, s'in noi la fede è doppia / non farem mai bella COPPIA." Cebà, *Lettere a Sarra Copia*, 24.

130 The exclusion of Giacob is additionally ironic since a few lines later Cebà (ibid.) tells Copia Sulam to "drag your husband with you" (tirar teco il tuo consorte) when she converts.

131 On Cebà's use of Copia Sulam's last name, see also below, n139.

132 "Felice augurio mi feci io sul principio dal vostro cognome, sperando di dovere fare con voi coppia di cristiano con cristiana; ma voi, togliendo ad esso assai tosto una consonante ... mi deste ad intendere che ricusavate di pareggiarvi meco in materia di fede." Cebà, *Lettere a Sarra Copia*, 59.

133 See the biographical note, 195, 299n113.

134 See the biographical note, 191–5.

135 In poems he published in 1627, Zinano (*Rime diverse*, 24–5) would say that at the salon, before a beautiful Copia Sulam depicted with flaming cheeks and red lips, "everyone falls into the sweet fire. / Lovers, where more is your hope?" See chapter six, 172. Many years later, Angelico Aprosio (without evidence) would claim that Copia Sulam, though married to Giacob, fell in love with another man. The passage appears in a letter from Aprosio. See Mandosio, *Bibliotheca romana*, 2:114. See also chapter six, 179, 287n45.

136 "non vegga troppo volentieri questo nostro traffico di lettere, non perché curi gli assalti d'un amante vecchio, ma perché teme gli assedij d'un huom christiano." Cebà, *Lettere a Sarra Copia*, 100.

137 Cebà (ibid., 104) tells Giacob: "You have by your own merit qualities that should please everyone; but even if you lacked them, the virtue alone of your consort can render you honourable everywhere" (Voi havete per voi stesso conditioni da piacer a tutti; e quando non l'haveste, la sola virtù della consorte vostra vi può rendere da ogni parte honorevole).

138 Other elements of the letter, as read in the *Lettere a Sarra Copia*, could be interpreted as insulting: Cebà only addresses Giacob after writing nearly three dozen letters to his wife (and includes no other missive to him in the published collection); accords him respect largely on the basis of his wife's virtue (elsewhere questioned); and condescends to him by asking for his conversion (after having long asked for his wife's) and calling him his son.

139 An additional insult to Giacob can be seen in the title of Cebà's *Lettere a Sarra Copia*. Since the volume was published by Marcantonio Doria after Cebà's death, it is not clear whether Cebà or Doria decided to leave off her husband's last name. Though we do not know how Copia Sulam signed her letters to Cebà, Copia Sulam's one extant autograph letter is signed "Sarra Copia Sulam" (see figure 4.3), the same name under which she published her *Manifesto*. Cf. Copia Sulam, "Lettera a Isabella della Tolfa." Leon Modena (*L'Ester*, 3) calls her "Sarra Copio Sullam."

140 A 1607 document (ASV Spinelli Records, 78or) lists a "Giacomo Rosa, merchant here in Venice" (Giacomo Rosa mercante qui in Venetia), though it is not clear that this is the same Giacomo Rosa. Later notarial documents list a Giacomo Rosa – certainly the correct one – as an organist. See Boccato, "Manoscritto," 110n14. Rosa was likely from Genoa since he was in contact with Cebà (and his family) and since he leaves money in his 1630 will to two people in Genoa, including Nicolo Grimaldo Cebà,

230 Notes to pages 45–6

perhaps Cebà's nephew. See ASV Will of Giacomo Rosa; Reale Simioli, "Tracce di letteratura ligure," 112. Harrán ("Introduction," 57) and Fonseca-Wollheim ("Faith and Fame," 55) call him Genoese.

141 Both Cebà's letters and the "Avisi" (chapter five, 161) document Rosa's frequent visits. For his close association with Paluzzi see, for example, "Avisi," 26r–34v.

142 Pagnoni's certification of Rosa's handwriting in his will demonstrates this close connection: "Having been sought out ... to testify under oath about whether I recognize the letters and characters written on this sheet, I say that I think and believe that this is written by the deceased signor Giacomo Rosa, because I recognize his handwriting since I have some things that he wrote to me. Thus I affirm under oath" (Essendo ricercato ... a dover deponer con giuramento sopra la ricognitione della lettera et carattera scritta nel presente foglio, dico che io tengo e credo che questa sia lettera scritta dal q. S. Giacamo Rosa per la cognitione della sua mano, havendo delle cose scrittemi da lui et così affermo con giuramento). See ASV Will of Giacomo Rosa. I thank Federico Barbierato for the information regarding Pagnoni.

143 "persona ecclesiastica." Sansovino and Martinioni, *Venetia*, 637.

144 Petracci edited *Le muse sacre*, a 1608 anthology of spiritual poetry by various authors, including Cebà, whose poems appear at ibid., 57–8. Petracci also edited several volumes of Angelo Grillo's letters that were repeatedly printed: volume 1, for instance, was printed for a fourth time in 1616 (by Ciotti). See Grillo, *Delle lettere*, Quondam, "Dal 'formulario' al 'formulario,'" 144–7.

145 Among Petracci's encomiastic works are a 1618 *Corona* for Antonio Priuli and a 1619 *Lode* of Giovanni Tiepolo.

146 Petracci and Paluzzi express their mutual admiration in verse in Paluzzi, *Rime*, 126.

147 Marino (*Lettere*, 226) complained of Petracci's verse in a 1619 letter to Ciotti, but he also asked Ciotti several times to give his regards to Petracci; see for example ibid., 306. Petracci published with Ciotti in 1616 (see above, n144) and contributed verse to (and proofread) the 1616 *Varie poesie* (47–9, 72), which was published and dedicated by Ciotti; Paluzzi contributed to the collection as well.

148 Petracci had worked with Alberti since 1607, when he edited and signed the dedication to Ralli d'Arezzo, *L'astrologo impazzito*, A2r–A3v.

149 Copia Sulam, *Manifesto*, A2v; see chapter three, 79–81, and figure 3.2.

150 "concorrevano a gara per sentirla discorrere non pure i vicini, ma anco da Trevigi, da Padova, da Vicenza, e luoghi più lontani i letterati." Mandosio, *Bibliotheca romana*, 2:113. Though Aprosio's account is marred by numerous inaccuracies (see chapter six, 179), this claim is supported by other sources that report the salon's renown.

151 See Cebà, *Lettere a Sarra Copia*, 116 (letter dated 12 April). The Spinola family was one of the most important in Genoa. On Cebà's ties with the family, see Harrán's note in Copia Sulam, *Jewish Poet and Intellectual*, 242n503.

152 Cebà, *Lettere a Pallavicino*, 192 (undated letter). See also the preceding note. The letter, to Marcantonio Doria, was written at Easter-time since Cebà (ibid., 191) refers to Doria's recitation the day before of the then-traditional Holy Friday prayer "let us pray for the perfidious [or unbelieving] Jews" ([oremus] et pro perfidis Judaeis). This visit probably occurred in spring 1620 or 1621, when her salon was well established. It is less likely that it took place in spring 1622, when Cebà and Copia Sulam's correspondence was trailing off (his last letter to her is dated 30 April 1622).

153 "poetessa ebrea di molto nome." Imperiale, *Viaggi di Gian Vincenzo*, 212.

154 Tiraboschi ("Zinani Gabriello Reggiano," 422) dates Zinano's 1623 stay in the city, where he had come to publish his works (including his *Eracleide*, which was printed in Venice in the same year).

155 Zinano, *Rime diverse*, 24–5, 46–8. The poetry exchange between Zinano and Copia Sulam included in the *Rime diverse*, which according to the title page ordered the poems chronologically, probably dates to 1624, since between Zinano's poem and Copia Sulam's response is one from Zinano to Giacob Uziel (written "Uriel"), congratulating him on his epic poem *David* (1624). Ibid., 46–7. Another poem by Zinano to Berardelli immediately following Copia Sulam's poem to Zinano, refers to Copia Sulam without naming her and probably dates to 1625 (see figure 6.2 and below, n158). Ibid., 47–8. A poem to Gironimo Bembo regarding Copia Sulam, located earlier in the collection, probably dates to 1623. Ibid., 24.

156 The first poem, entitled "La bella di Giesù nemica, e nostra" (Jesus's Beautiful Enemy, and Ours), indicates that Zinano frequently visited Copia Sulam's house. The poem was directed "To signor Gironimo Bembo, Venetian nobleman, who was visiting the young Jewish woman called Sarra Copia, at a time when the author was also there" (Al Sig. Gironimo Bembo Gentilhuomo Venetiano, che si trovò visitar una giovane ebrea detta la Sig. Sarra Copia, in in [=un] tempo, che c'era anche l'A.) and describes habitual situations at the salon, including Copia Sulam's "often" flaming cheeks. Ibid., 24–5.

157 The poetry exchange (ibid., 46–7) regarded Cebà's death. Zinano's lament suggests he shared the other associates' interest in the Cebà correspondence.

158 Ibid. Regarding the poem to Uziel, see n2 and n155 above. The poem to Berardelli (written "Bernard.") – "Corse l'Asia Alessandro e i piani e i monti" (Alexander travelled both the plains and mountains of Asia) – probably dates from 1625 and was also published prominently in Paluzzi's

Rime (A5v); it demonstrates that Zinano (*Rime diverse,* 47–8) knew both Paluzzi and Berardelli.

159 On the poem, see chapter six, 172.

160 Ravid (*New Light,* 166–73) notes the many instances of Jews gaining permission to leave the ghetto when the gates were closed (generally from one to two hours after sunset until sunrise), but usually for urgent matters such as to provide medical care or to conduct trade. Records also document numerous instances of Christians exiting the ghetto after the gates were closed, but their passage still required special permission.

161 Including, for 1618–22, Cebà's *Lettere a Sarra Copia;* for 1619–21, Aprosio in Mandosio's *Bibliotheca romana;* for 1623–24, Zinano's *Rime diverse;* for 1618–26, the "Avisi."

162 This estimate, which may be low, is based on her nine known associates, plus three probable associates, in addition to visitors to the salon.

163 The dynamics at Copia Sulam's salon recall the description by Robin (*Publishing Women,* 40) of sixteenth-century women-led literary salons as well as academies: "In the salons and academies, works in progress were performed, read, and critiqued in ways that were helpful to both fledgling and seasoned authors, while this kind of pre-publication screening fostered sales as well as interest in the literary works. The Italian salons also served as sites where friendships were forged between writers, editors, and publishers. Social interaction, whether at the salons or the academies of the peninsula, led ... to publication."

164 For example in Baldassare Castiglione's *Cortegiano.* As Schiesari ("In Praise of Virtuous Women?," 75) notes, "the women [in the *Cortegiano*] are accorded a marginal role. They speak very little and if they do speak, it is to adorn the discussion as the beautiful centerpiece around which (male) discourses are spoken."

165 J.D. Campbell, *Literary Circles,* 13.

166 See Robin, *Publishing Women.*

167 See Cebà, *Lettere a Sarra Copia,* 10, 25; "Avisi," 39v. On music in the salon, see Harrán, "Doubly Tainted."

168 See, for example, chapter one, 38.

169 Paluzzi is reported to have written scathing critiques in his copy of Bonifaccio's *Immortalità.* The "Avisi" (51v) implies that Paluzzi's actions were rooted in a more general hostility towards Bonifaccio than in a defence of Copia Sulam. Bonifaccio in response would call Paluzzi "Zoilus," after the Greek literary critic (ca. 400–320 BCE) reputed to harshly denigrate the work of others. Bonifaccio also calls Paluzzi "the scum of Venetian pedantry, and most contemptible proofreader" (feccia della pedanteria Vinitiana, et abiettissimo correttore di stampe). The comments

are in Bonifaccio's December 1621 letter to Uberto Manfredino: B.
Bonifaccio, *Delle amene lettere*, fascicolo 20, 5r.

170 Landes (*Women and the Public Sphere*, 24–8) describes the animus against
the power of salonnières in early modern France. See also DeJean, *Tender
Geographies*, 21–2.

171 In the controversy with Bonifaccio, for instance, Copia Sulam consulted with
"many honorable and virtuous men" who wrote works in her defence, which
included a "most learned discourse … of a most illustrious gentleman who
loved her as a daughter" (scritti di tanti honorati virtuosi che per quella degna s.ra allhora si mossero a scrivere, tra i quali un dottisimo discorso ci fu
de il.mo gentilhuomo che qual figliola amava quella). "Avisi," 73r. The discourse's author was surely Giovanni Basadonna, who was a generation older
than Copia Sulam. Other defenders may have included Modena or Petracci,
as well as these writers' literary associates. Giacomo Rosa was a faithful advocate for her interests who helped her in the debate with Bonifaccio and
later, in the controversy with Paluzzi and Berardelli, circulated a letter to defend her. See "Avisi," 26r–34r. The "Avisi" manuscript itself appears organized by close associates in Copia Sulam's defence (see chapter five, 158–63).

172 See Love, *The Culture and Commerce of Texts*, 183: "The handwritten text …
was … to be chosen in preference to other media … also because this was
usually privileged information, not meant to be available to all enquirers";
in contrast, "the printed text, being available as an article of commerce,
had no easy way of excluding readers."

173 See chapter one, 51–2. See also chapter four, 108–10.

174 Reports of Cebà's health appear in letters from spring 1621. See for example Cebà, *Lettere a Sarra Copia*, 110–11, 113, 117. On Copia Sulam's illness,
see chapter four, n2.

175 "con lineamenti troppo poetici." Cebà, *Lettere a Sarra Copia*, 110.

176 "licenza che faccia ancor esso l'amore con voi." Ibid.

177 "Gran galant'huomo son io veramente, che communico con tanta facilità
la mia padrona con tutti; ma non vi scandalezzate, signora Sarra, perché 'l
vostro thesoro non è fatto per arriccchire la povertà d'una persona sola. Il
bene è più bene quanto più si communica. Lasciate però che ciascun sia
partecipe delle vostre gratie e, poiché vedete che me ne contento, mettete
ancora me in dozzina con gli altri." Ibid.

178 "l'amor mio è tanto generoso ch'egli ha molto più riguardo alla vostra
ch'alla mia persona; della quale, s'havessi quella sollecitudine che forse ha
qualch'altro che vi corteggia, mi parrebbe d'essere troppo sventurato di
non poter venire a visitarvi e procurar da voi quel diletto che la virtù vostra
so che sarebbe duro a concedermi e la ragion mia è lontanissima da desiderare." Ibid., 114.

179 "I miei scherzi non son mai stati tali che v'habbiano intaccato (per usar le vostre parole) l'honore: leggete le mie lettere quanto vi piace, che vi vedrete ben sublimata quant'altra donna mai fossse, ma non troverete che, parlando di lascivie, io v'habbia mai giudicata se non continentissima ... E se vi debbo confessare la verità, io non son sì curioso, come credete, di far inquisitione se voi trattiate con Vinitiani e se scriviate a Genovesi, perché, oltre che vi tengo per pudicissima, l'infermità e l'occupatione mie non mi dan luogo d'ingelosire né mi lascian tempo da perdere. Ben è vero c'ho creduto poco che voi m'amiate molto; ma non ho però pensato che siate invaghita di qualch'altro: né m'è caduto in mente che teniate in casa altro traffico che di speculationi e di lettere." Ibid., 117.

180 "I hope to say of her things that were never yet written of any woman" (io spero di dicer di lei quello che mai non fue detto d'alcuna). Alighieri, *Vita nuova*, 74; Alighieri, *The Vita Nuova*, 114.

181 The Accademia della Crusca's 1612 *Vocabolario* (451) defines "inquisizione" as "diligent inquiry" (diligente rercamento) and states that "we more commonly use *inquisizione* today to refer to the Sant'Uffizio, where heretics are investigated" (inquisizione più comunemente diciamo oggi al Santo Ufizio, dove s'inquisiscon gli eretici).

182 The first instance of this word cited in the Accademia della Crusca's 1612 *Vocabolario* (829) underscores this negative acceptation of *speculazione*: Boccaccio's use of the term to describe Guido Cavalcanti's philosophic orientation in *Decameron* 6.9 (cited as 5.9). The dictionary cites a sanitized version of the quote: "All his speculating had no other goal than to search for what didn't exist" (Queste sue speculazioni eran solo in cercare, ciò che non fosse). Boccaccio's original reads: "All his speculating had no other goal than to see whether he could show that God did not exist" (Queste sue speculazioni erano solo in cercare se trovar si potesse che Iddio non fosse). My translation from the Crusca is based on Rebhorn's rendering in Boccaccio, *The Decameron*, 500. The Italian edition employed throughout is Branca's: Boccaccio, *Decameron*, 2:756. The "other sorts of 'trade'" that Cebà mentions seems to be a veiled reference to prostitution.

183 "Intorno a quel che toccate d'essere stata sanguinaria contro a chi ha havuto verso di voi men che honorata pretensione, per certo che m'havete non solamente dato inditio della vostra virilità ma m'havete anche ammonito di raffrenar la mia voglia, s'ella mai mi venisse (che non credo) di dimesticarmi con voi." Cebà, *Lettere a Sarra Copia*, 118.

184 "veggo, che voi guardate meco tutta la vostra riputazione." Ibid., 113.

185 For an intricate account of the suspension and of Cebà's response, see Reale Simioli, "Ansaldo Cebà."

186 Ibid., 157.

187 Ibid., 145–58.

188 His response to the secretary, acknowledging the action, is undated. On 16 July, Marcantonio Doria wrote a letter requesting the intervention of Alessandro d'Este to resolve the problem. Ibid., 165–7.

189 In later correspondence about the matter, Cebà said that the charges from the Congregation of the Index echoed those a malevolent critic had made and who, he suspected, had worked behind the scenes to influence the Congregation's actions against him. See chapter four, 109.

190 "tanto mortificato ... che più volentieri tollererebbe la morte che questa infamia." The quotation is from Cebà's friend Agostino Mascardi. Mannucci, *La vita e le opere di Agostino Mascardi*, 472.

191 Cebà dedicated his 1621 *Il Gonzaga overo Del poema eroico* to Este and corresponded regularly with him. On Este, see chapter four, n19. Este was also friends with Cebà's patron Doria, who immediately sent all of Cebà's posthumous works to the cardinal. Corradini, "Introduzione," xlii.

192 Reale Simioli, "Tracce di letteratura ligure," 165–7.

193 Mannucci, *La vita e le opere di Agostino Mascardi*, 472–3. Up until late June 1621, Este had employed Mascardi as a secretary.

194 In her response, Copia Sulam (*Manifesto*, B2r) mocked Bonifaccio for the fact that it had taken him nearly two years – since the time of their original debates on the nature of soul – to write his treatise.

195 "senza vostra colpa, voi siate stata incolpata." Cebà, *Lettere a Sarra Copia*, 125.

196 "Ridetevi però, signora mia, mentr'havete pura la coscienza, di chi si pruova d'intorbidarvi la fama; e sdegnatevi di rispondere a chi non è ragionevole ch'apriate neanche l'orecchie per ascoltare." Ibid., 126.

197 "Le difese che v'apparecchiate a fare contra chi v'ha chiamata infedele nelle leggi giudaica, riserbatevi a convertire in prediche quando combatterete per la christiana." Ibid., 125.

198 "v'assicuro che vi sarà più utile per haver pace con Dio che non vi sarà honorevole formare apologie per tener guerra con gli huomini." Ibid.

199 "tanta tenerezza." Ibid.

200 "Io vorrei saper far quel che dico, quando me ne viene l'occasione, ma m'avveggo in fatti che son più filosofo di parole che d'opere." Ibid., 126.

2 A Rupture in the Salon (1619–1621)

1 "difficultà filosofica o teologica." Copia Sulam, *Manifesto*, B1v.

2 The *Phaedo* is from Plato's middle period. A summary of ancient views on the soul can be found in Lorenz, "Ancient Theories of Soul." For a synthetic overview of the history of the belief, see Knox, "Immortality of the Soul." See also Salomon and Sassoon, "Introduction," 38–47.

3 A helpful overview of Aristotle's views on the soul is in Miller, "Aristotle's Philosophy of Soul." See also the variety of perspectives in Nussbaum and Rorty, *Essays on Aristotle's* De anima.

4 *De anima* 2.1.412a6–11. For the original Greek, see Aristotle, *De anima* (1907); translations are from the Shields edition: Aristotle, *De anima* (2016).

5 Ibid., 2.1.413a.

6 Ibid., 2.1.413a2–6.

7 Ibid., 2.1.413a6–8.

8 Ibid., 2.2.413b24–6.

9 On the ideological dimensions of interpreting Aristotle in the early modern period, see for example Martin, *Subverting Aristotle*, esp. 1–10.

10 Shields (in his introduction to Aristotle, *De anima* (2016), xviii) argues that the debate over Aristotle's views on the soul derives from the fact that he was "not content to reject Platonic dualism only to embrace an expedient form of reductive materialism ... Aristotle sees the virtues and vices of both poles; he seeks to craft a theory which embraces their strengths while eschewing their weaknesses without lapsing into the muddle of a blurry compromise ... Hylomorphism, as he sees it, is non-reductive but also non-Platonic: it is intended to embrace the insights of the materialists without accepting their view that the soul just is this or that element, and to join Plato in contrasting the soul and body, but without inferring on that basis that the soul can exist without being embodied."

11 See Nussbaum and Putnam, "Changing Aristotle's Mind," 51–2.

12 For an overview of the topic, see McInerny and O'Callaghan, "Saint Thomas Aquinas," esp. section 4 ("Thomas and Aristotle") and section 7 ("Perception and Thought"). See also Nussbaum and Putnam, "Changing Aristotle's Mind," 51–5.

13 Kraye, "Pietro Pomponazzi," 93; Kristeller, *Eight Philosophers*, 74.

14 Kraye, "Pietro Pomponazzi," 96. For the development of Nicoletto Vernia's views, see De Bellis, *Nicoletto Vernia*, esp. 94–6, 125–31.

15 Kraye, "Pietro Pomponazzi," 96–7. De Bellis, *Nicoletto Vernia*, 129.

16 A classic overview of Ficino's views on the soul is given in Kristeller, "The Theory of Immortality in Marsilio Ficino." See also Albertini, "Marsilio Ficino," 82–91.

17 The decree stated: "We condemn and reject all those who insist that the intellectual soul is mortal, or that it is only one among all human beings, and those who suggest doubts on this topic. For the soul not only truly exists of itself and essentially as the form of the human body, as is said in the canon of our predecessor of happy memory, pope Clement V, promulgated in the general council of Vienne, but it is also immortal." Tanner, *Decrees*, 1:605. See Kraye, "Pietro Pomponazzi,"

97. For a different interpretation of this decree, see Constant, "A Reinterpretation," 353–79.

18 The modern edition is by Gianfranco Morra: Pomponazzi, *Tractatus de immortalitate animae* (1954). See also Gilson, "L'affaire de l'immortalité." For helpful overviews of Pomponazzi's life and thought, see Kraye, "Pietro Pomponazzi"; Compagni, "Pomponazzi, Pietro."

19 Kraye, "Pietro Pomponazzi," 102.

20 As with the *Tractatus*, both were published in Bologna with Justinianum Leonardi Ruberiensem. On these works, see Gilson, "L'affaire de l'immortalité," 35–40; Gilson, "Autour de Pomponazzi," where there is in-depth discussion of the various works published against Pomponazzi as well as of his replies.

21 Kraye, "Pietro Pomponazzi," 102; Compagni, "Pomponazzi, Pietro," 708.

22 Knox, "Immortality of the Soul," 460; Compagni, "Pomponazzi, Pietro," 708.

23 Kraye ("Pietro Pomponazzi," 102) makes this suggestion.

24 Ibid., 103.

25 On the evolution in the interpretation of Aristotle across these years, see Martin, *Subverting Aristotle*, 1–10. On the use of Averroes in Pomponazzi and his detractor Girolamo Cardano, see Valverde, "Averroistic Themes."

26 Barbierato, *The Inquisitor*, 168. A common story narrates that Cremonini refused to look through Galileo's telescope, an anecdote often used as proof of his blind adherence to Aristotle. The story, however, is based on an imprecise reading of the account. See Forlivesi, "Cesare Cremonini," 251.

27 From 1598 to 1626 Cremonini was subjected to some dozen denunciations and charges of heresy from the Sant'Uffizio in Rome and from local Inquisitions. See Poppi's introductory remarks in Cremonini, *Le orazioni*, 99. For a 1604 denunciation of Cremonini, including the charge that he denied the immortality of the soul, see Poppi, *Cremonini e Galilei inquisiti a Padova nel 1604*, 41–9, esp. 43–4. For his defence against these charges, see "L'autoapologia presso la Signoria di Venezia (1604)" in Cremonini, *Le orazioni*, 103–8, esp. 105. In 1607–8, he was accused of spreading the doctrine of the soul's mortality among the Venetian nobility. Spini, *Ricerca dei libertini*, 155–6. In 1611, he was under surveillance along with Galileo. Schmitt, "Cremonini, Cesare," 620. Documents regarding Cremonini, the Inquistion, and the Venetian Senate are in Poppi, "Cremonini, Galilei e gli inquisitori," 81–109.

28 "Explicit denial of the existence of God could also be reached in degrees – the idea of progression from heresy to atheism was widespread ... In short, a fairly elastic concept was used to identify who did not believe in the existence of God and those who did not believe in something which made existence irrelevant, like the immortality of the soul." Barbierato, *The*

Inquisitor, 90. Boccalini (in an ASV manuscript translated and quoted in
ibid., 90n94) articulated this point of view: "Even in religious matters little
sparkles of superstition, of an almost imperceptible alteration, turn into
great fires, because as time passes superstitions change into heresies, heresies transform into unbelief, and the latter becomes atheism."

29 Cremonini (*Disputatio de coelo*, 113) wrote "the soul itself by virtue of its
own substance is a function of the body" (anima ipsa de sua substantia
est actus talis corporis), as cited in Berti, "Di Cesare Cremonino," 279n2.
Berti (ibid.) suggests that Cremonini therefore asserted that the soul is not
only mortal but material.

30 The secretary to the Venetian ambassador wrote in 1614 that Pope Paul V
was appalled that the local Inquisitor had approved the book without
realizing that it contained "evil teaching, and in particular that the soul is
mortal" (mala dottrina et particolarmente che l'anima sia mortale). See
Poppi, "Cremonini, Galilei e gli inquisitori," 89 ("Il segretario dell'ambas-
ciatore riprende la causa del Cremonini," dated 27 September 1614). The
Inquisitor had accepted Cremonini's preface to the work that clarified
he was explaining Aristotle historically, as a pagan philosopher, and not
through a Christian lens – the defence that Cremonini continued to make
for the work. Ibid., 89n5.

31 This account of Cremonini's interaction with the Roman Inquisition
follows Berti, "Di Cesare Cremonino," 279–80. See also Del Torre,
"La cosmologia di Cremonini"; Grendler, *The Universities*, 294–7.

32 On the teaching of the philosophy, the Fifth Lateran Council decreed:
"We strictly enjoin on each and every philosopher who teaches publicly in
the universities or elsewhere, that when they explain or address to their
audience the principles or conclusions of philosophers, where these are
known to deviate from the true faith – as in the assertion of the soul's mortality or of there being only one soul or of the eternity of the world and
other topics of this kind – they are obliged to devote their every effort to
clarify for their listeners the truth of the Christian religion, to teach it by
convincing arguments, so far as this is possible, and to apply themselves to
the full extent of their energies to refuting and disposing of the philosophers' opposing arguments, since all the solutions are available." Tanner,
Decrees, 1:606.

33 The letter is published in Poppi, "Cremonini, Galilei e gli inquisitori,"
102–3.

34 The documents from the Inquisition (published in Poppi, "Cremonini,
Galilei e gli inquisitori," 95–101) are "Observationes in *Apologiam dictorum
Aristotelis de quinta caeli substantia*" (Observations regarding the *Apology for
Aristotle's Words on the Quintessence of the Heavens*) and "Adnotatio ad librum
Domini Caesaris Cremonini de *Quinta Caeli Substantia*" (Annotation to

the book by signor Cesare Cremonini *On the Quintessence of the Heavens*).
The quotation is taken from the "Adnotatio": "la retrattatione in cose
concernenti la fede deve esser chiara, e manifesta, et non involuta, né am-
bigua." Ibid., 101.

35 Cremonini said he could alter a third treatise he planned on Aristotelian
cosmology, "De cœli efficentia," to underscore that he reasoned as a
Catholic and Christian, and that he would make sure, together with the
Paduan Inquisitor, that his book conformed to the Lateran Council (i.e.,
the decree that required authors to note discrepancies between Aristotle
and Christian faith; see above, n32). He also agreed to remain silent if
someone wanted to confute his work. See Cremonini's "Risposta del signor
Cremonino all'Inquisitor di Padova" in Poppi, "Cremonini, Galilei e gli inquisitori," 104–5. See also Del Torre, "La cosmologia di Cremonini," 378.
Cremonini responded to the Roman Inquisition with similar points. He
never published "De cœli efficentia," but the surviving manuscript shows
that he did follow through on his promise to conform to the Lateran
Council's decree. He may have avoided publishing the work so as not to
show publicly that he had surrendered in any measure to the Inquisition.
Ibid., 379–80.

36 "Non posso ne anco retrattare espositioni d'Aristotele, poiché l'intendo
così, e son pagato per dichiararlo come l'intendo, e nol facendo, sarei obligato alla restitutione della mercede; così anco non posso retrattare con-
siderationi haute circa li Interpreti e refutationi ch'habia[te] fatte delle
loro esplicationi: ci va l'honor mio, l'interesse della cathedra, e per tanto
del prencipe." See Cremonini's undated (but 1619) reply to the Inquisitor
of Padua in Poppi, "Cremonini," 105. Cremonini had previously justified
his method of teaching Aristotle by noting that the University of Padua
required teachers to explicate clearly the texts they taught. Kuhn, "Cesare
Cremonini."

37 "Responsio Caesaris Cremonini ad supradictas observationes," published
in Berti, "Di Cesare Cremonino," 287–91, and (in part, with corrections to
Berti) in Poppi, "Cremonini, Galilei e gli inquisitori," 106–9.

38 The Congregation of the Index issued decrees against the work on 15
January 1622 and 3 July 1623. Bujanda and Richter, *Index librorum prohibitorum*, 254.

39 Cremonini was denounced to the Roman Inquistion in 1626 for affirming
to a student that the soul was mortal, doubting the validity of miracles
and the worship of saints, and reporting that he only went to mass for
appearances. The student did not corroborate the charges and they were
dropped. See Berti, "Di Cesare Cremonino," 282–4.

40 According to Spini (*Ricerca dei libertini*, 156), Cremonini, "a thinker famous
for being hated by the Church," never suffered serious consequences

because he received "a protection from on high so clear and unequivocal that it stopped words ever from being uttered by those who were called to testify against him ... He was defended by the Venetian patriciate as a sort of domestic institution, who must be protected at any cost from the Church's persecution." See also Heller, *Emblems of Eloquence*, 51.

41 See Spini, *Ricerca dei libertini*, 155–9; Barbierato, *The Inquisitor*, 168–71. Spini (*Ricerca dei libertini*, 156) argues that "the naturalistic philosophy of Cremonini in essence constituted the official philosophy of the Serenissima's ruling class for a great number of years." Barbierato (*The Inquisitor*, 171) argues that Cremonini's thought also spread to other classes, which were eager to imitate the elite.

42 "[T]he Academy created a literary link through which Paduan heterodox Aristotelianism, especially in the form influenced by Cremonini, managed to take root widely within the patriciate and other social classes." Ibid., 168. In the 1640s, the friar and Incognito Antonio Rocco attracted enthusiastic crowds with his discussions of the soul's mortality and assertions of contradictions in Scripture. By 1652, more than 20 years after Cremonini's death, an anonymous denouncer worried about Cremonini's continuing influence, saying the Venetian state "was infested with the doctrine of that damned Cremonini, who in accordance with Aristotle's beliefs taught in Padua that the soul is mortal ... and other errors, which caused atheism and impiety in many." Ibid., 170.

43 "che bisogno vi è ora, e massime in Vinegia, di tal trattato, e a che proposito stamparsi tra cristiani simili materie." Copia Sulam, *Manifesto*, B1v.

44 A scholar has recently written an imaginative fictitious dialogue between Cremonini and Copia Sulam: see Centanni, "Dialogues," 302–5.

45 See Nadler, *Spinoza's Heresy*, 42–4. Nadler (ibid., 44) writes "there is no single Jewish doctrine of immortality, and ... there is nothing specific that a Jew needs to believe about the fate of the soul after death."

46 Nadler, *Spinoza's Heresy*, 63–6.

47 Fishman, *Shaking the Pillars of Exile*, 57. For an overview of Jewish beliefs on the soul's immortality, see Nadler, *Spinoza's Heresy*, 42–66; Salomon and Sassoon, "Introduction," 42–4.

48 Fishman, *Shaking the Pillars of Exile*, 57.

49 Salomon and Sassoon, "Introduction," 9. The Torah is the Written Law of 613 commandments. The Oral Law explains how the commandments should be carried out. According to orthodox Jewish dogma, both Written Law and Oral Law were products of divine revelation, given to Moses on Sinai. Ibid., 9n19. Da Costa included a revised version of this broadside in his 1624 *Exame das tradições phariseas* (discussed in chapter two, 59–60). See da Costa, *Examination*, 271–306; Salomon and Sassoon, "Introduction," 16. See also Fishman, *Shaking the Pillars of Exile*, 49–50.

On da Costa's 1616 broadside, see Petuchowski, *The Theology of Haham David Nieto*, 35–9.

50 Fishman, *Shaking the Pillars of Exile*, 50. The response has been attributed to Modena since the nineteenth century. Ibid., 199n16.

51 Salomon and Sassoon, "Introduction," 11. The transliteration is from Fishman, *Shaking the Pillars of Exile*, 50. *Magen Vi-Tzinah* circulated in manuscript and was published in 1856 by Abraham Geiger (*Leon da Modena*).

52 Salomon and Sassoon, "Introduction," 12.

53 Fishman, *Shaking the Pillars of Exile*, 50. Da Costa was also excommunicated from Hamburg, the city in which he lived, in the same year. Salomon and Sassoon, "Introduction," 12.

54 The dating is in Fishman, *Shaking the Pillars of Exile*, 50.

55 See Salomon and Sassoon, "Introduction," 24–8.

56 Da Costa's manuscript was quoted at length in the response by Semuel da Silva discussed immediately below; the quotation was accurate in its substance, as shown by da Costa's later printed work. See Ibid., 33–8. For the quotation included here, see da Silva, "Treatise on the Immortality of the Soul," 456.

57 Ibid., 430–1.

58 It was also printed by Paul van Ravesteyn; da Costa, *Examination*, 51.

59 Da Costa, *Examination*, 319.

60 Salomon and Sassoon, "Introduction," 17. At least two copies of the book survived.

61 "Book entitled *Examen das Tradições Phariseas comferidas com a ley escrita*. Entirely prohibited, in any language, with or without the name of the author, since it is Judaic and impious toward the immortality of the soul, and against the eternal rewards for the good, and suffering and punishment for the bad" (Libro intitulado, *Examen das Tradições Phariseas comferidas com a ley escrita*. Del todo se prohibe, y en qualquier lengua, con nombre de Autor, o sin el, como Iudaico, y impio contra la immortalidad del alma, y contra el premio eterno de los buenos, pena y castigo de los malos). Zapata de Mendoza, *Novus index*, 354. The book did not appear on the Roman Index. See Bujanda and Richter, *Index librorum prohibitorum*.

62 Salomon and Sassoon ("Introduction," 28–9) suggest that *Kol Sakhal* expressed some concepts that had been spread by da Costa's 1616 broadside sent to Venice. For a comparison of *Kol Sakhal* and da Costa's 1616 polemic, see Petuchowski, *The Theology of Haham David Nieto*, 35–48.

63 The *Kol Sakhal* says it was "written at Alcalá in the year of creation 5260," or in 1500, eight years after the Jewish expulsion. Salomon and Sassoon, "Introduction," 28.

64 Barzilay, "Finalizing an Issue"; Salomon and Sassoon, "Introduction," 28; Fishman, *Shaking the Pillars of Exile*, 12.

65 Rivkin, *Leone da Modena and the Kol Sakhal*; Adelman, "New Light," 109–22.

66 Fishman, *Shaking the Pillars of Exile*, 168.

67 The *Kol Sakhal* claims that the burden of proof regarding the soul's immortality rests upon those who uphold it, but it also says that immortality
of the soul is a likely possibility and that the Torah contains hidden indications of it.

68 Fishman, *Shaking the Pillars of Exile*, 90.

69 Ibid., 91.

70 Ibid., 4. On the use of the concept of heresy within Jewish communities,
see Cooperman, "Legitimizing Rhetorics."

71 On Bonifaccio (spelled as it is on the title page of his *Immortalità*), see
L. Rossi, "Baldassarre Bonifacio," 192–3; Fulco, "Sul *Paltoniere*"; Born,
"Baldassare Bonifacio," 221–37; Harrán, "A Controversy," 279n2.

72 B. Bonifaccio, *Amata. Tragedia.*

73 See L. Rossi, "Baldassarre Bonifacio," 193. In 1623, the Venetian Senate
charged the Roman ambassador with procuring Bonifaccio a bishopric,
but he declined the Candian post for health and safety concerns. Ibid.

74 Born, "Baldassare Bonifacio," 223.

75 See also chapter one, 225–6n91.

76 No written trace of the beginning of the conversation is found in sources
or archives, whereas the subsequent exchange of letters is well documented. In her letter of response, Copia Sulam recalls having seen
Bonifaccio recently.

77 Bonifaccio's comments recall those of Cremonini in his 1591 *Lecturae exordium habitum*; the modern edition is Cremonini, *Le orazioni*, 17–19.

78 "Ma se nelle cose che sono differenti di specie non si dà passaggio dall'una
nell'altra e se il corruttibile è di specie diversa dall'incorruttibile, com'esser può che un tempo fosse l'uomo immortale, s'oggidì tutti gli uomini
sono mortali?" B. Bonifaccio, *Delle amene lettere*, fascicolo 21, 11v.

79 2 Sam 14:14.

80 "Let us tend, signora, to the renewal of this temple as the itself year is
renewed, a year which I hope brings you such sunny days that – as it
does so – your mind will be cleared of clouds" (Pensiamo, signora, alla
rinovatione di questo tempio, mentre l'anno si va rinovando, il quale io
desidero che rimeni per voi così sereni i suoi giorni che siano insieme
sgombrate le nubi dall'animo vostro). B. Bonifaccio, *Delle amene lettere*,
fascicolo 21, 12r.

81 "the great learnedness of your letter was repeatedly pointed out and highly
praised by signor Paluzzi, who came here to my house to hear it read, along
with signor Corniani, which gave me the chance to discuss it with him more
than once" (l'altezza della dottrina della sua lettera è stata talmente osser-
vata e commendata dal signor Paluzzi, il quale capitò qui da me per udirla
in compagnia del signor Corniani, che mi ha dato occasione di farne seco

più che un discorso). Copia Sulam, "Al molto illustre signor Baldassare Bonifaccio," A5r; reprinted in Copia Sulam, *Jewish Poet and Intellectual*, 524–5.

82 The year was written in Venetian style as 1619 (the new year began on 1 March according to the Venetian calendar).

83 Though it is proper to question whether the ill-willed Bonifaccio provided an accurate transcript of Copia Sulam's letter, its credibility is bolstered by the fact that the priest said that he filed Copia Sulam's original letter with the notary Fabricio Beazian (he calls him Fabricio Benazzano). See B. Bonifaccio, *Risposta al Manifesto*, A4v. In the 1621 acts of this notary (indexed as Fabricio Beazian or Beaciani, together with Lucillo Beazian) there is no record of Copia Sulam's letter. Cf. ASV Beazian Records, buste 608–609; see also Boccato, "Una disputa secentesca," 600–1n24. But the letter would not likely have been included in the notary's acts. Bonifaccio invited Copia Sulam (and, implicitly, all *Risposta* readers) to go see her letter at Beazian's, as if in a public depository: "If you suspected that this copy [the one published in the *Risposta*] was in some way altered, you can see your authentic manuscript copy with signor Fabricio Beazian, public notary of this city" (Se dubitaste che la copia fosse in qualche parte alterata, potrete vederne l'autentico manuscritto vostro appresso il signor Fabricio Benazzano, publico notaio di questa città). B. Bonifaccio, *Risposta al Manifesto*, A4v. Though Bonifaccio credited Modena, not Copia Sulam, with the ideas the letter presents (see chapter three, 101–2), he said that the letter's handwriting was hers: "it is at least penned if not composed by you" (è pur, se non vostra compositione, almeno vostra scrittura). Ibid.

84 Copia Sulam ("Al molto illustre signor Baldassare Bonifaccio," A5v) wrote that to prove the corruptibility of form, not matter, she did not need to "make recourse to the sophistic doctrine of Telesio" (senza ricorrere alla sofistica dottrina di Telesio). In other words, she did not need to use Telesio's faulty logic to argue against Aristotle. In his *De rerum natura* (On the Nature of Things, 1565), Telesio replaced metaphysical Aristotelian notions of matter and form with the idea of passive matter and active force (heat and cold). Telesio's *De rerum natura* was placed *donec expurgentur* (until purged) on the Clementine Index of 1596. Ernst, *Tommaso Campanella*, 28.

85 See chapter one, 37–8, and immediately below.

86 In his published response to this letter, Bonifaccio makes clear that he considers women intellectually inferior; see chapter two, 70.

87 See chapter one, 38–9.

88 "l'anno ringiovenisce, e noi invecchiamo." B. Bonifaccio, *Delle amene lettere*, fascicolo 21, 11r.

89 It is interesting to note this Ptolemaic concept, but it would be excessive to try to deduce Copia Sulam's understanding of cosmography from this incidental remark.

90 Copia Sulam echoes Bonifaccio in discussing the new year with reference
therefore to the Gregorian calendar; by the Venetian calendar the new
year did not begin until 1 March.

91 Copia Sulam used the word "specia," or species, which in Aristotle is
tightly connected to the idea of essence. See Aristotle, *Metaphysics*, 322–5
(Z.4, 1030a11–12).

92 Ibid., 330–7 (Z.6, 1031a–1032a1–13).

93 "Don't say the essence only exists in the species and that individuals differ
by nothing more than accidents, because – even if this could be a real
opinion in some philosophies – I will say that if the essence of one man
were not different from another man's essence, then it would follow that
the death of the essence of Socrates would mean the death of the essence
of Plato, and so forth; whereby everybody would die when one individual
dies" (Né mi replichi che l'essenza sia solamente nelle specie e che gl'individui non differiscano in altro che gl'accidenti perché, se ben questa
potrebbe esser vera opinion in qualche filosofia, io dirò che se l'essenza di
un huomo non si distinguesse essentialmente dall'altra, ne seguirebbe che
mancando l'essenza di Socrate, mancasse anco quella di Platone, e così
de gl'altri, in modo che nella morte di un individuo morirebbono tutti).
Copia Sulam, "Al molto illustre signor Baldassare Bonifaccio," A5v.

94 "se di due parti componenti che vediamo nelle cose naturali, dico material
e forma, una dura eternamente e l'altra svanisce, a qual di loro sarà ragionevole di attribuire la corruttibilità?" Ibid.

95 "con pace però di Aristotile." Ibid.

96 "per qual cagione il Creatore non fece l'uomo per natura immortale, se
ebbe intenzione che tale si preservasse? O, se tale non avea stabilito che
fusse, perché costituirlo miracolosamente in essere, nel quale non avea da
durare?" Ibid., A6r.

97 Copia Sulam could be referencing the notion, seen for example in Saint
Bonaventure, that the highest good must be that which diffuses itself most
widely ("summum igitur bonum summe diffusivum est sui"). Bonaventure,
Itinerarium, 18 (chapter 6).

98 "il costituire una cosa in un esser nel quale è impossible che essa subsista
pare intollerabile negli huomini nonché in Dio." Copia Sulam, "Al molto
illustre signor Baldassare Bonifaccio," A6r.

99 2 Sam 14:14: "We all die, and like waters that return no more, we fall
down into the earth." Copia Sulam quoted the excerpt in Latin "quasi acque dilabimur"; the same verse was cited more extensively by Bonifaccio.

100 "Concedasi dunque come si cava dalla [*sic*] propositioni stesse di V[ostra]
S[ignoria] che l'huomo fu sempre di natura mortale e che perciò non habbia
fatto passaggio di una in altra specie nel cader dal primo stato, e concedasi di
conseguenza che *quasi acque dilabimur*, luogo in vero notabilissimo nella Sacra

Scrittura, poiché sì come un corrente fiume ci rappresenta avanti agli occhi acque che corrono e passano in un istante e pur sempre è quel fiume e non sempre quell'acque stessi [*sic*], così l'humana specie ci mostra ad ogn'hora individui transitorij, li quali non sono sempre li medemi benché sempre sia la specie medema." Copia Sulam, "Al molto illustre signor Baldassare Bonifaccio," A6r. The errors in the text (here and below, n102) may have come from the transcription of Copia Sulam's manuscript letter into print.

101 "altro non ne resta da desiderare nell'essere di questi nostri individui che la duratione." Ibid., A6v.

102 "Please excuse my boldness in having expressed these weak doubts out of my desire to hear in due time the explanations that your Lordship and that gentleman who is always Numen will give" (Compiacciasi ella scusar il mio ardimento nell'haver promosse queste deboli dubitatione [*sic*] per desiderio di sentire a suo tempo la dichiaratione da V.S. e da quel signor che è sempre Nume). Ibid. The use of "Nume" is likely a reference to Paluzzi's first name, Numidio.

103 Bonifaccio addresses Copia Sulam here and in his later *Risposta al Manifesto* as "Sara Copia." B. Bonifaccio, *Immortalità*, 5; B. Bonifaccio, *Risposta al Manifesto*, title page, A2r. Regarding the use of her last name, see chapter one, 229n139.

104 See Giachery, "Pinelli"; the information on Pinelli that follows is hers.

105 Ibid. See also Infelise, *I padroni dei libri*, 96 and tav. 6.

106 The office of *primicerio*, which Cornaro held from 1619 to 1632, had bishop's privileges. See [Apollonio], "The Primicerj of Saint Mark's," 167, for mention of Cornaro.

107 The brothers assumed these positions after a scuffle between the Republic and the Church. In 1629 the pope tried to appoint Federico bishop of Padua, despite Federico's own objections and the Republic's laws that prevented a doge's children from receiving posts from Rome. The crisis was resolved when, after Doge Giovanni's death in 1629 and the death of the patriarch of Venice in 1631, Federico was elected patriarch of Venice by the Senate and Marcantonio was appointed Bishop of Padua by Pope Urban VIII. See Laugier, *Storia della Repubblica di Venezia*, 11:229–30.

108 Bonifaccio dedicated his 1622 *Amata* to Molino; the tie between them would be longstanding. Fulco ("Sul *Paltoniere*," 256) calls their relationship "a central node in the biography of the humanist from Rovigo [Bonifaccio], ... a lasting liaison ... between a powerful protector of writers and a classically learned man, between a politician eager for praise and an accomplished panegyrist." In 1628, Bonifaccio published the highly celebratory *Urania ad Domenicum Molinum*, which Fulco (ibid., 257–8) calls "the highest and most compromising" of Bonifaccio's celebratory verse for Molino, which was later criticized for its exaggerated praise.

109 Cozzi, *Venezia barocca*, 327.

110 Infelise, "La Crusca a Venezia," 72.

111 "Io vado, signora, indovinando che non vi appagheranno le ragioni c'ho finora apportate." B. Bonifaccio, *Immortalità*, 24.

112 "Hor non ho io dunque disopra a sufficienza provato che l'anima non è corpo, né tratta dal corpo, e che ella è sostanza? ... Nondimeno, se volete anco dell'altre prove che l'anima possa operare senza participatione del corpo, statemi attenta." Ibid., 47.

113 "Volete ch'io vi dichiari il termine della sussistenza? ... Volete etiandio che vi provi che l'anima dell'huomo sia forma sussistente, sì che l'esser suo non habbia dependenza dal corpo ... Forse non l'ho con cento argomenti confermato?" Ibid., 54.

114 "battaglia"; "tenzone." Ibid., 6.

115 Bonifaccio contends for example (ibid., 12) that "all Platonists and all Aristotelians have always upheld and defended the immorality of the soul, except Alexander of Aphrodisias, with some other pigs from the herd of Epicurus" (tutti i platonici, e tutti gli aristotelici hanno sempre tenuta e difesa la immortalità dell'anima, eccettuato l'Afrodiseo, con alcuni altri porci della gregia d'Epicuro). For a history of the reception of Alexander's thought, see Kessler, "Alexander of Aphrodisias."

116 B. Bonifaccio, *Immortalità*, 33: "All incorporeal substances are immortal. The soul is an incorporeal substance, and therefore immortal. Here we must prove that the soul is substance, since Empedocles said that it was a harmony of contrary qualities, resulting from the symmetry of a well-organized body, just as motion results from the proper arrangement of the wheels and other mechanisms in a clock, and that motion in the clock is compared to the soul in the body ... Therefore it must be proven that the soul is simply incorporeal, since if it moved the body, it would have to touch the body, and touching it means it is a body, since there is no contact except among bodies" (Tutte le sostanze incorporee sono immortali. L'anima è sostanza incorporea. Dunque immortale. Qui bisogna provar prima che l'anima sia sostanza. Perché Empedocle disse ch'ella era un'armonia di contrarie qualità, risultante dalla simmetria del corpo ben organizzato; come dalle ruote e dagli altri instrumenti ben disposti nell'horologio risulta il moto; e quell moto nell'horologio vien an esser come l'anima nel corpo ... Dipoi bisogna provar ch'ella sia semplicemente incorporea, perché s'ella muove il corpo, convien che lo tocchi: e toccandolo, è corpo, non si facendo contatto se non tra corpi). Empedocles proposed the theory of the transmigration of souls. On the philosopher, see G. Campbell, "Empedocles."

117 See n115. On Epicurus, who "believed that, on the basis of a radical materialism which dispensed with transcendent entities such as the Platonic

Ideas or Forms, he could disprove the possibility of the soul's survival after death," see Konstan, "Epicurus."

118 B. Bonifaccio, *Immortalità*, 33. On Galen's complex and ultimately inconclusive views on the essence of the soul, see Singer, "Galen."

119 "Io mi pregio di haver trovato così dotta maestra come voi sete; né mi sdegno d'imparare da femina, perché negli intelletti non è distinzione di sesso." B. Bonifaccio, *Immortalità*, 5.

120 Diotima taught Plato the philosophy of love. Bonifaccio (ibid.) says Copia Sulam, so superior to Diotima, could well teach him, so inferior to Plato.

121 Cebà (*Lettere a Sarra Copia*, 27) made the negative valence of the term *femina* clear in a letter to Copia Sulam: "*Femine* are easy to find, most noble signora Sarra, but *donne* are not" (Delle femine si trovano assai, signora Sarra nobilissima, ma delle donne, poche). See also chapter two, 71. This statement may recall Tasso (*Discorso della virtù feminile e donnesca*, 5v–6r): "May womanly virtue and not female be considered, and may the word female [*femina*] no longer be used, but womanly [*donnesco*], which means just what *in the manner of a lady* does, so in Dante one reads, *Donnescamente, disse, viene con nui* [*sic*], that is, in the commanding manner of a lady; now considering not feminine but womanly virtue, I say that, just as among men those who exceed the human condition are considered heroes, so among women, many are born heroic in mind and virtue" (Non più la feminil virtù ma la donnesca virtù si consideri, né più si usi il nome di femina, ma quel di donnesco, il qual tanto vale, quanto signorile, onde appresso Dante si legge, *Donnescamente, disse, viene con nui* [*sic*], cioè signorilmente, & imperiosamente: hor considerando non la feminea, ma la donnesca virtù, dico che sì come fra gli huomini sono alcuni ch'eccedendo l'humana conditione sono stimati heroi, così fra le donne, molte si nascono d'animo e di virtù heroica). Marinella objects to Tasso's class-based distinction between women in the 1601 edition of her *Nobiltà* (128). She concludes her response to his treatise by saying: "About that new distinction of his between *femina* and *donna* – new, I say, since Boccaccio, Petrarch, and others have given the name of *donne* to whichever member of this sex: I have no desire to exert myself in destroying and denouncing it" (Intorno a quella sua nuova distintione di femina e di donna, nuova, dico, perciò che il Boccaccio, il Petrarca, e altri hanno dato il nome di donne a qualunque creatura di questo sesso, non mi voglio faticare a distruggerla e a vituperarla"). Ibid., 130.

122 "E quello che da Eva fu messo in forse, risolutamente affermate voi, più di lei dannosa all'humano lignaggio non solo per questo, ma perché quella donna, piegandosi alle lusinghe del serpe, fu cagione che gli huomini morissero quanto al corpo; e voi, dando orecchio alla pestifera dottrina di venenoso maestro, vi sforzate di far che gli uomini muoiano quanto all'anima." B. Bonifaccio, *Immortalità*, 5.

123 See chapter one, 233n170.

124 Harrán ("A Controversy," 284) suggests that the "poisonous teacher" is Aristotle, but it seems more likely that Bonifaccio intended Modena, since he later charged that Modena had written both the 1619 letter and the *Manifesto* that Copia Sulam signed.

125 For this issue in the Venetian context, see the introduction, 7–8.

126 See above, n83, and discussion in chapter three, 101–3. See also Bonifaccio's December 1621 letter to Uberto Manfredino: B. Bonifaccio, *Delle amene lettere*, fascicolo 20, 4v–5v. The letter is translated in part in Harrán, "A Controversy," 343–8.

127 "Because that serpent of old said to human souls: 'Not only will you not die, but you will be as gods.' On the other hand, you tell them: 'You will surely die, and you will be like beasts'" (Perché disse pur l'antico serpente alle anime humane: 'Non morirete già voi, ma sarete come iddij.' Voi dite loro all'incontro: 'Morirete al sicuro, e sarete come giumenti'). B. Bonifaccio, *Immortalità*, 59.

128 "Non dico già che uccidiate tutta voi stessa; ma quelle parti che, senza distruggere il composto, possono separarsi ... Voglio, signora, che siate crudele contra voi stessa; per poter esser maggiormente pietosa. Cuore, cuore, e non di femina: o se pur di femina, di tale c'habbia superato ogni maschio per crudeltà. Voglio che diventiate una Progne, una Medea, e, se volete alcuna delle vostre, una Maria d'Eleazaro. Svenate i vostri affetti, smembrate le vostre passioni, trucidate i vostri figliuoli, che sono i vostri peccati. Felice voi, fortunata voi, ben aventurata voi, generosa e magnanima voi, più di Delbora e di Giuditta, se strozzerete questi vostri figli. Nol credete a me; credetelo al vostro maggior profeta: *Beato chi calterisce i suoi pargoletti alla pietra*. La pietra è GIESÙ; quella pietra angolare, che fa di due uno, congiungendo il vecchio col novo Testamento. Schiacciate i vostri pargoletti con questa pietra, ma tosto, affrettatevi, perché vanno crescendo, uccideteli prima che nascano acciò che nascendo come viperini non uccidano voi." Ibid., 60. The verse is Psalms 136:9 (Vulgate/DR); 137:9 (King James).

129 Procne killed her son and fed him to her husband. Medea killed her children and others. Mary of Bethezuba, starving during the siege of Jerusalem in 70 CE, killed and ate her infant son. The story of her crime is in Josephus.

130 Judith beheaded the enemy general Holofernes, and Deborah, the prophetess and judge who incited the Israelites to rebellion against the Canaanites, foretold that a woman would be responsible for the victory. Jael in fact tricked the enemy general into lying down in a tent and resting, whereupon she drove a stake through his temple.

131 Bonifaccio's rhetoric is in sharp contrast with Cebà's, for example, which couched conversionist appeals in the language of love.

132 "voi sola tra gli hebrei dopo tante migliaia d'anni negate fede all'infallabile chirografo che scrisse Iddio di Sua mano, revocando hora in dubbio
la verità delle sacre carte." B. Bonifaccio, *Immortalità*, 5.

133 "io, che son cristiano, vorrei dichiararmi giudeo, se l'anima nostra fosse
caduca. Ma perché ella è certissimamente perpetua, voi, che sete hebrea,
vi dichiarerete cristiana. Sì, sì, vi libererete dalla servitù di cotesta abiettis-
sima Sinagoga." Ibid., 58.

134 While the terms *hebreo* and *giudeo* both mean "Jew," the latter had (and
still has) a more pejorative sense. The negative valence is documented in
the Accademia della Crusca's 1612 *Vocabolario* (389). Copia Sulam called
herself *hebrea*.

135 See chapter one, 44.

136 Ibid.

137 See chapter one, 49–50, and chapter four, 107, 113–14.

138 B. Bonifaccio, *Immortalità*, 6 (Orpheus), 24 (doves).

139 "Cotesti vostri occhi brillanti diverrano cispi, vizze diverranno le poppe, e
grinze le carni. Diverrà cadavere il corpo, e rimarrà finalmente putredine
e fango." Ibid., 11.

140 Ibid., 61.

141 "L'anima vostra, stando in fra terra nella legge natia, sarà sempre fosca
e caliginosa. Ma, separata dal continente, e circondata dal mar del
Battesimo, diverrà candida e risplendente." Ibid., 58.

142 Here Bonifaccio (ibid., 61) renews his offensive mention of dead children;
see chapter two, 71.

143 "tanto d'industria nell'eternare il vostro honorato nome con l'opere immortali del vostro divino ingegno." Ibid., 17.

144 Towards the end of his treatise, for example, Bonifaccio (ibid., 58) asked
Copia Sulam to recognize the erroneousness of the ideas that "someone or
another is planting in [her] mind" (chiunque nell'animo vostro va semi-
nando). See also chapter two, 70.

3 The Salon and the Venetian Presses (1621)

1 Bonifaccio's treatise was dated 25 June 1621 and Alberti issued the first
edition of the *Manifesto* around the middle of July.

2 "non conveniva che io interponessi dilatione di tempo né longhe dicerie
a ributtar l'offesa, per lo pericolo del danno che poteva risultarmene."
Copia Sulam, *Manifesto*, A2v.

3 The figure is from Infelise, "La Crusca a Venezia," 66. Scarsella ("Alberti,
Giovanni," 13) instead estimates his total production in Venice at about
forty-eight volumes. According to Pastorello (*Tipografi, editori, librai*, 1),
Alberti printed approximately twenty texts before the turn of the century.

See also Ascarelli and Menato, *La tipografia del '500*, 436; Borsa, *Clavis typographorum librariorumque Italiae*, 1:38. Pastorello, Ascarelli/Menato, Scarsella, and Borsa document his activity as a publisher only until 1619, though Scarsella ("Alberti, Giovanni," 13) notes that Alberti attended meetings of the booksellers' and printers' guild until 1621, the year he printed Copia Sulam's treatise. Infelise ("La Crusca a Venezia," 67) notes that Alberti issued a work by Giulio Strozzi in 1622. There is no notice of his death or indication that his enterprise passed to heirs upon his death. A printer named Giovanni Alberti, who operated in Trent from 1615–28, is sometimes assumed to be the same figure but likely is not, since the Giovanni Alberti production in Venice and in Trent is materially quite different and it would have been difficult for a printer to undertake simultaneous activity in two distant cities. Ibid., 67–8.

4 The work was printed in Venice probably because of the competitive price of paper and printing in the city. Alberti may have offered good financial terms to the Cruscanti. Considine, *Academy Dictionaries*, 23. For details of the printing, see ibid, 21–3; Scarsella, "Alberti, Giovanni," 12–13. Giacomo Sarzina reprinted the volume in 1623.

5 See Considine, *Academy Dictionaries*, 21: "Any dictionary-maker who sought to emulate the *Vocabolario* over the next two hundred years – and this meant any dictionary-maker in what would become the academy tradition – would need to take its physical presentation into account."

6 Scarsella, "Alberti, Giovanni," 12.

7 Ebreo, *Dialoghi di amore*; Terracina, *Discorso ... sopra il principio di tutti i canti d'Orlando furioso*.

8 Infelise, "La Crusca a Venezia," 67. For Pinelli's similar inclination, see chapter two, 68.

9 Sigal, *From Medievalism to Protomodernity*, 104.

10 "Avisi," 38r–38v.

11 Strozzi, *Il natal di amore* (Venice: appresso Giovanni Alberti, 1621); *L'Erotilla* (Venice: per l'Alberti, 1621). Both works were printed together as *Saggi poetici* (Venice: appresso Giovanni Alberti, 1621). Paluzzi and Berardelli had ties to Strozzi: two compositions in praise of him were published in Paluzzi's posthumous *Rime* and Berardelli would publish a poem in a 1623 collection Strozzi organized (*Il teatro delle glorie*). The librettist also published several works in 1621 with the famous publisher Giovanni Battista Ciotti, to whom salon members – and Alberti – had close ties. On salon members' ties to Ciotti, see chapter one, 31–4, 45, and chapter five, 129. Alberti and Ciotti knew each other and had collaborated on an edition of Guarini's *Lettere* in 1615. See Contò, "Ciotti, Giovanni Battista," 294. The book was issued "ad instanzia di Gio. Battista Ciotti" and "appresso Giovanni Alberti."

12 The other volumes he printed that year are Giorgio Tomasi, *Delle guerre et rivolgimenti del regno d'Ungaria e della Transilvania;* an edition of Virgil's *Bucolica, Georgica et Aeneis* (possibly a reprint of the edition of the same works he issued in 1616); and two congratulatory works (*Cinque sonetti in lode della illustriss. signora Cornelia Cornara Bragadina* and Giulio Rutati, *Cento ottave per le ... nozze del ... signor Federigo Ubaldo ... & della signora Claudia Medici*). See Griffante, *Le edizioni veneziane del Seicento,* 2:397. Some catalogs list a 1621 Alberti edition of Antonio de Torquemada's *Giardino di fiori curiosi* (*Jardín de flores curiosas*), but this seems to be a mistake that merely refers to Alberti's 1620 printing of the same work. Ciotti had published three editions of the work around the turn of the century. See Resta, "La traducción de la miscelánea española," 91.

13 Pietro Petracci, probably her associate, had worked with the printer; see chapter one, 230n148, and chapter three, 79. Additionally, Leon Modena had published *L'Ester* in 1619 with Giacomo Sarzina, who likely had business ties to Alberti. See Infelise, "La Crusca a Venezia," 68.

14 See Scarsella, "Alberti, Giovanni," 12; Infelise, "La Crusca a Venezia," 66.

15 The *editore* or *editrice* of a publication covered its cost. For the *Manifesto,* Alberti would have expected the author to cover the costs of paper, type-setting, and printing. Such was also the case for the 1612 *Vocabolario,* issued by Alberti, whose printing the Cruscanti underwrote. Considine, *Academic Dictionaries,* 23. Just as Copia Sulam occupied the role of author and *editrice* for the *Manifesto,* for the *Vocabolario* the Cruscanti were both authors and *editori.* For both volumes, Alberti played the role of the *tipografo,* or printer. With regard to this aspect of the *Vocabolario's* printing, see Infelise ("La Crusca a Venezia," 66–7); he notes that the Accademia della Crusca chose to publish with Alberti solely because of his technical expertise: he was "an experienced printer, able skillfully to finish the work." Approximately 33 per cent of authors financed their own publications in the late sixteenth and early seventeenth centuries in Venice, as can be deduced by the fact that they requested their own printing privilege. Minuzzi, "Gli autori," 11n5. I am grateful to Minuzzi for consulting with me on this matter.

16 Scarsella ("Alberti, Giovanni," 12) notes that only for one volume that Alberti printed (the 1608 *Astrologo impazzito* by Giovanni Ralli d'Arezzo) did he clearly appear as *editore.* Infelise ("La Crusca a Venezia," 66) observes that Alberti and the printer Giacomo Sarzina, who published a subsequent edition of the *Vocabolario,* were "outstanding professionals in typesetting, but showed no editorial autonomy. They were therefore talented printers, used to undertaking even challenging projects, but not entrepreneurs able to sustain their own specific and original publishing program."

17 The printing privilege would have given its requester the exclusive right to publish the work in question, prohibiting any others from reprinting it. Copia Sulam would not have sought a printing privilege for this work, since it would have been in her interest to have her work distributed as widely as possible (in other words, she aimed for self-defence and not lucre through its publication). On the function of the printing privilege in Venice, see Minuzzi, "Gli autori," 9–22.

18 Copia Sulam mentions the lasting impact she expects the text to have in her dedication to her father. See chapter three, 83.

19 See for example Salzberg, *Ephemeral City*, esp. 19–28; Carnelos, "Words on the Street."

20 See Zappella, *Le marche dei tipografi*, 1:343; 2:n.p. (figs. 1066–7).

21 Copia Sulam, *Manifesto* (G. Alberti), A2v. See immediately below.

22 Text *a*: Copia Sulam, *Manifesto* (Venice: appresso Giovanni Alberti, 1621). The copy of text *a* examined is held at the Marciana Library in Venice (Misc 2503.5). This is an octavo edition with six folios. I conclude that it is the first edition because it contains the most serious error – the inclusion of Petracci's name – which was corrected in the subsequent editions. It is also the most hastily printed, with irregularities for example in the font size and the spacing of the poetry.

23 Text *b*: Copia Sulam, *Manifesto* (Venice: appresso Ioanni Alberti, 1621). The copy of text *b* examined for this study is held at the Marciana Library in Venice (Misc 1377.3). This is a quarto edition with fourteen folios. This study considers text *b* the second edition because, while it corrected the error of including Petracci's name, it still maintained several notable typographical errors in the poetry that are corrected in text *c*.

24 Text *c*: Copia Sulam, *Manifesto* (Venice: appresso Antonio Pinelli, 1621). The copy of text *c* examined for this study is held at the British Library in London (702.d.6.[4]). Most of the prose text in *b* and *c* was paginated in the exact same manner, with the exception of the note to readers, which was set differently. However, text *c* was not a reissue of *b* (as it could have been had Alberti sold his plates to Pinelli). Instead, text *c* is a separate edition because, first, text *b* (in contrast to text *c*) includes page numbers (9–24) for the prose address to Bonifaccio and also includes on these same pages a running title: "*Manifesto*" on even (verso) pages and "*De Sarra Copia*" on odd (recto) pages. The second page of the dedication (A3v) in text *b* also has the title "*Manifesto*," while that page in text *c* does not. Second, text *c* has different ornaments and capitals for important pages (seven pages total have ornamental differences). Third, even the pages that have no ornamental differences and seem superficially identical display occasional small differences in fonts and in the spacing of the text. Although the text was reset from text *b* to text *c*, the prose text in *c* was

paginated like that in *b* perhaps because it was easier for the typesetter to work by copying the arrangement from *b* rather than reorganizing each page anew. I thank Elissa Weaver for sharing her expertise on this issue.

25 Because it is the cleanest text, I cite from text *c*, intervening only to correct errors; I also note the few important variations between the texts. For other reconstructions of the editions, see Fortis, *La "bella ebrea,"* 69n133; Harrán's note in Copia Sulam, *Jewish Poet and Intellectual*, 311n1.

26 The *Risposta* was dated 2 August 1621. See also n1 above.

27 On Pietro Petracci, see chapter one, 45. I am grateful to Sabrina Minuzzi for consulting with me about this matter.

28 Copia Sulam, *Manifesto* (G. Alberti), A2v.

29 The error may even have been corrected in the course of printing this edition: Fortis (*La "bella ebrea,"* 115–17; see also his "Nota al testo" in ibid., 100) and Harrán (Copia Sulam, *Jewish Poet and Intellectual*, 311n1, 315) do not mention the presence of Petracci's name.

30 Scarsella, "Alberti, Giovanni," 12.

31 See chapter three, 76.

32 See Pullan, *The Jews of Europe*, 145. See also chapter four, 118–20.

33 Ibid., 79. On the *Essecutori*, see also Derosas, "Moralità e giustizia."

34 See for example the account by Modena (*Autobiography*, 141) of his grandson's arrest.

35 In this instance, Modena (ibid., 147) feared for both himself and his community. See discussion of this work in chapter one, 24, and chapter three, 94.

36 Modena, *Autobiography*, 147.

37 See the introduction, 5.

38 Modena, *Autobiography*, 144–6. For a discussion of these events and their relation to Simone Luzzatto's apologetic tract, see Ravid, *Economics and Toleration*, esp. 13–18. Ravid (ibid., 18) notes that Luzzatto's tract "points out that every nation will produce a few bad individuals and that the entire group should not be judged or treated on the basis of their conduct."

39 See chapter three, 94.

40 Copia Sulam specifies the audience for her *Manifesto* as Christian; see chapter three, 87.

41 "Posso creder, benigni lettori, che sia per parervi cosa strana che il mio nome, non affatto ignoto in questa città né fuori, comparisca per la prima volta alle stampe in materia assai diversa da quella che poteva forse esser aspettata dalla mia penna. Ma l'altrui o sia stata malignità o simplicità o trascuratezza mi ha necessitata a quello a che non ero per movermi facilmente per qual si voglia occasione, ancorché io mi ritrovi qualche fatica da poter mandar alla luce, la quale, se io non fallo, potrebbe dal mondo esser più volentieri veduta e forse più gradita di questa." Copia Sulam, *Manifesto*, A2r.

42 See chapter one, 24.

43 Copia Sulam's circulation of her manuscript writing to Cebà – the letters and poems sent him – was one of the ways she included the Genoese writer in her salon.

44 Early modern women writers frequently used their fathers to justify their intellectual endeavours. See Ross, *The Birth of Feminism*, 3.

45 "Con quel poco acquisto di fama che nel mio nome forsi vedrai ... non ti sarà meno caro aver prodotto una donna per conservazione del tuo nome al mondo, di quel che ti sarebbe stato l'aver prodotto un uomo, come in questa vita mostravi estremo desiderio." Copia Sulam, *Manifesto*, A3v.

46 In Jewish communities of the period (as in Christian) great importance was attributed to male offspring, who would bear the family name. See Bonfil, *Jewish Life*, 255.

47 Ross (*Birth of Feminism*, 223) describes writer and actress Isabella Andreini's similar "unabashed statement of her aspiration to literary immortality" as her appropriation of "the syntax of masculine desire for intellectual honor."

48 See the introduction, 11, for Lucrezia Marinella's assessment of the high price women paid for fame.

49 See Cox, *Women's Writing in Italy*, 53; Robin, *Publishing Women*, 25.

50 See chapter one, 43–5, and the biographical note, 195–6.

51 On Berardelli's venal use of a dedication, see chapter five, 140.

52 See chapter two, 73.

53 Copia Sulam, *Manifesto*, A2v.

54 Ibid.

55 See Harrán's note on this image in Copia Sulam, *Jewish Poet and Intellectual*, 317n19.

56 "perfido livore." Copia Sulam, *Manifesto*, A4r.

57 "l'inchiostro ch'io spargo." Ibid., A4v.

58 See chapter two, 58.

59 "Ma quando poi leggendo più a basso trovai che il discorso era a me diretto ... non potei non prendere grandissima ammirazione e sdegno insieme della troppa audace calunnia." Copia Sulam, *Manifesto*, B1v.

60 "publicamente al mondo, per mezzo della presente scrittura, che falsissima, ingiusta e fuori di ogni ragione è l'imputazione da voi datami nel vostro discorso, che da me sia negata l'immortalità dell'anima; il che sarà solo per giustificarmi e sincerarmi appresso tutti coloro, li quali non conoscendomi potessero dar qualche credenza alla vostra accusa in quanto appartiene alla religione che io professo." Ibid., B2r.

61 "la pietà della mia legge mi fa pietosa della vostra simplicità." Ibid., B2r. Since Christianity presents itself as the religion of compassion, Copia Sulam's emphasis on the compassion of the Jewish faith can be read as

part of her broader attempt to present a Christianized version of Judaism to her Christian readers. See chapter three, 93–5.

62 J.D. Campbell (*Literary Circles*, 8) observes that such orality is common to texts that come out of debates in literary circles: "That such debates often moved from orality to textuality is clear as both male and female writers bring salon and academic discourse into their written arguments. The sense of orality shadowing the arguments employed by the writers ... underscores the immediacy of the orality/textuality relationship." Landes (*Women and the Public Sphere*, 54) observes that salons "fostered a strong relationship between speech and writing."

63 "discorriamo tra noi in questo proposito un poco più alla libera e familiarmente." Copia Sulam, *Manifesto*, B2v.

64 "ditemi dunque di grazia signor Baldassare, che cosa vi ha mosso a far quel trattato, a stamparlo, e ad imbrogliarvi il mio nome?" Ibid., B2v.

65 "non siete né filosofo né teologo ... e vi siete assicurato a stampar vostri discorsi con titolo sì sublime?" Ibid., B3v.

66 "il voler far ostentatione di se stessi in quello in che manco vagliono." Ibid., C2v. The *Galateo* is a sixteenth-century treatise on manners by Giovanni della Casa. See the recently issued translation by Rusnak: della Casa, *Galateo*.

67 "Altro non vi ha indotto a far sì longa e vana fatica se non quella vana ambizioncella che vi fa correr volentieri alle stampe credendo che la fama consista in aver di molti volumi fuori, senza aver consideratione alla stima che ne fa il mondo, il quale credo sappiate per esperienza quanto mal si sodisfaccia di cose mediocremente buone, nonché le dozinali e scioccamente composte, e però a non correr così facilmente alla stampa ci fa avvertiti la medema *Poetica* di Orazio." Copia Sulam, *Manifesto*, C3r–v.

68 This number includes the *Immortalità*. He would publish five more over the next two years, including his *Risposta al Manifesto*.

69 "vana immoderata sete di gloria." Copia Sulam, *Manifesto*, C3v.

70 "Questo non è cartello di risposta alla vostra disfida, ma un semplice manifesto per iscusarmi del mio non comparire, non essendo cagion di combattimento dove non è contrarietà di pareri né in detti né in fatti, sì che per me potete deporre affatto l'armi, che ancorché mi provocaste di nuovo con mille ingiurie, non sono più per contraporvi alcuna replica, per non consumare inutilmente il tempo, massime essendo io così nemica di sottopormi agli occhi del mondo nelle stampe come voi ve ne mostrate vago." Ibid., C4r–C4v.

71 See chapter two, 70–1.

72 "non avendo ella altro di buono che la causa che difende: nel resto è così piena di false intelligenze di termini, di storti e malintesi sentimenti di scritture, di false forme di sillogismi, di cattive connessioni, e strani

passaggi da una in altra materia, di sproposite citazioni di autori e finalmente di errori di lingua che nessuno può continuare a leggerla senza dar
qualche titolo al compositore." Copia Sulam, *Manifesto,* C2r–C2v.

73 "metter mano in pasta [to put (his) hand in the dough] circa materia sì
alta!" Ibid., B3v.

74 "mi sono disposta con la breve fatica di due giorni atterrar quanto da voi
mi è stato machinato contro con l'inutili vigilie quasi di due anni." Ibid.,
B2r.

75 "Io per me non vi parlo in questa guisa per far la maestra o la filosofessa in
insegnarvi, come voi per ischerno mi dite nel medemo tempo che venite
a farmi il pedante, poiché confesso di essere assai più ignorante di voi in
queste scienz[e]." Ibid., B4r. "Scienze" is corrected from "scienza" in texts
a, b, and *c.*

76 "da tutti coloro che vedono il vostro libro." Ibid.

77 "a che effetto sfidar una donna? E una donna che, se bene è vaga di studij,
non ha però tali scienze per sua professione?" Ibid., C3v.

78 "Di modo che, oh valoroso fidatore delle donne, il campo è tutto vostro.
Passeggiate in esso pur altiero, vibrando i colpi all'aria, oh valoroso cam-
pione, oh generoso guerriero. E senza che si oda altro strepito che della
vostra rauca tromba, gridate pur da voi stesso, 'Vittoria, Vittoria.'" Ibid.,
C4r.

79 Copia Sulam may here also have been referencing antiwoman stances
Bonifaccio took in salon debates. For her part, Copia Sulam was said to
have written "paradoxes in praise of women and against men" (see chapter
five, 275n75), which perhaps recorded her prowoman arguments in such
debates.

80 The double bias that Copia Sulam faced as a woman and a Jew – which she
here defends herself against – could be studied according to the theory
of intersectionality. "Intersectionality's most powerful argument ... is that
institutional power arrangements, rooted as they are in relations of dom-
ination and subordination, confound and constrict the life possibilities
of those who already live at the intersection of certain identity categories,
even as they elevate the possibilities of those living at more legible (and
privileged) points of intersection." Cooper, "Intersectionality," 392.

81 See chapter one, 38.

82 "massime in Vinegia." Copia Sulam, *Manifesto,* B1v. As noted in chapter
two, 56–60, the soul's eternal state was actively debated in Venice in these
years, despite Copia Sulam's characterization here.

83 "Altro ci vuole, signor mio, che il titolo di *Iuris utriusque Doctor* per trattare
dell'immortalità dell'anima." Copia Sulam, *Manifesto,* B4v. "Both Laws" are
canon and civil laws, studied together for a law degree.

84 Ibid., B4v, C1r.

85 Harrán notes that Copia Sulam (*Jewish Poet and Intellectual*, 323n59) "pleads for a literal reading of *ruah*, ignoring its anagogic connotations in the kabbalistic (and Neoplatonist) literature, with which she pretends to be unfamiliar."

86 "Perché so che voi non avete mai veduta lingua hebraica e che da altri è stato soffiato nella vostra ciarabottana, dirovvi solo che da questo fate conoscere chiaramente che anco le altre cose tutte che avete dette, vi siete assicurato a dirle senza intenderle. Almeno in questo particolare, parlando voi con una hebrea, dovevate farvi imboccare da chi meglio intendesse la proprietà della lingua." Copia Sulam, *Manifesto*, C1r.

87 She criticizes a comparison she says he made jokingly: "I believe that you made that comparison as a sort of insipid joke ..., something that is as compromising to the gravity of the subject matter that is being discussed as it is to the modesty that would befit your condition and your profession as a priest" (Io credo che quella comparatione sia stata da voi posta per occasione di scherzare insipidamente ..., cosa altretanto pregiudicante alla gravità della materia che si tratta quanto alla modestia conveniente alla vostra conditione e alla professione che fate di religioso). Ibid., C1v.

88 "Piacesse a Dio che più tosto da burla che da buon senno si morisse." B. Bonifaccio, *Immortalità*, 10.

89 "Eh, signor Bonifaccio, a che giuoco giochiamo? Credete fermamente quel che predicate o no? ... donde deriva il vostro affetto più alla presente che all'altra vita?" Copia Sulam, *Manifesto*, C2r.

90 B. Bonifaccio, *Immortalità*, 14.

91 "Avertite che questo contradirsi è cattivo segno." Copia Sulam, *Manifesto*, C2r.

92 Ibid., B4v. In Matt. 22:23–33, Jesus declares the related doctrine of resurrection to the doubting Sadducees.

93 "Vivete lieto e sperate per voi giovevole quell'immortalità che predicate, se viverete così osservatore della vostra christiana legge, come io professo di essere della mia hebrea." Copia Sulam, *Manifesto*, C4v.

94 See chapter two, 72.

95 "L'anima dell'uomo, signor Baldassare, è incorruttibile, immortale e divina, creata e infusa da DIO nel nostro corpo in quel tempo che l'organizato è reso abile nel ventre materno a poterla ricevere. E questa verità è così certa, infallabile e indubitata appresso di me come credo sia appresso ogn'ebreo e cristiano." Copia Sulam, *Manifesto*, B1r.

96 "a nessuno o hebreo o cristiano è lecito di contradire." Ibid., A2v.

97 D.M. Feldman, *Marital Relations*, 273. On Christian and Jewish views on the soul's entry into the body, see ibid., 268–75. The stakes are higher in Christianity because of the fear that the immortal soul of an embryo, if it

does not survive to baptism, could be condemned to eternal damnation.
Ibid., 270.

98 Ibid., 274.

99 Ignoring the strategic reasons Copia Sulam would have had for making this
statement, Baldassare Bonifaccio (*Delle amene lettere*, fascicolo 20, 5r) would
later write in a private letter to Uberto Manfredino: "The simple-minded
woman does not realize that this would amount to a grave heresy in her religion, since Jews believe that all souls were created at the same time, together
with the angels" (Non s'accorge la sempliciotta che questa viene ad essere
una solenne heresia nella sua religione, credendo gli hebrei che l'anime
fossero tutte create da Dio nel medesimo tempo con gli angeli). Eager to
strip Copia Sulam of responsibility for her ideas, however, Bonifaccio (ibid.)
continues on, blaming Leon Modena for her "heresies": "But of this, and
of twelve similar heresies against the dogmas of her faith, which she un-
knowingly affirms in her *Manifesto*, Jezabel was convinced by Rabbi Leon
Modena, certainly a most learned man among the Jews" (Ma di questa, e di
dodeci simili heresie contra i dogmi della sua fede, da lei nel suo *Manifesto*
inavedutamente affermate, Jezabele è stata convinta dal Rabbino Leone
Modanese, huomo tra gli hebrei certamente dottissimo). On the use of the
term "Jezabel" to refer to Copia Sulam, see chapter three, 103.

100 Adelman, "Success and Failure," 616–17.

101 "se voi havesti alcun'altra scrittura fatta dalla mano di Dio in proposito
dell'immortalità, haverei caro di vederla." Copia Sulam, *Manifesto*, C1r.

102 Adelman, "Success and Failure," 616.

103 Luzzatto also authored a philosophical dialogue on the limits of human
knowledge entitled *Socrate* (Venice: Tomasini, 1651); he dedicated this
book to the doge and Senate of Venice.

104 Cohen, "Leone da Modena's *Riti*" (1992), 445. In this tract, Modena
(*Historia de' riti hebraici* [1979], 112) emphasizes the similarity of Jewish
and Christian beliefs regarding the immortality of the soul in his discussion of the heretical Jews who did not believe in resurrection. Modena
(ibid., 123) also presents a hierarchy in the afterworld strikingly similar to
Catholic notions, with a hell, purgatory, and heaven.

105 On da Silva, see chapter two, 59. Da Silva's "Treatise on the Immortality of
the Soul," which assumed a Jewish audience, cites from the Mishnah, for
example. See ibid., 459.

106 As Bonfil (*Jewish Life*, 115) argues, it was natural for Jews, who lived in a
cultural milieu similar to that of Christians, to have a similar worldview:
"Generally speaking, I find it quite inappropriate to classify as examples
of assimilation, or of the centrifugal dynamics of Judaism, the numerous
cases involving the Jews' adoption of attitudes, aesthetic tendencies, tastes,

and cultural behaviors, to say nothing of cultural themes, ideas, and concepts, similar to those in fashion among their neighbors."

107 Bonfil (ibid., 123) notes that "the Jews *thought* like the others, shared the same kind of *mentality*, and *aspired to be like everyone else,* but since 'being *really* the same as everyone else' would have meant becoming Christians, that aspiration had to remain repressed because of their own refusal to integrate in that way, and because of the corresponding refusal of Christian society to integrate them in any other way" (my emphasis).

108 Bonfil, "Change in the Cultural Patterns," 405.

109 Copia Sulam, *Manifesto,* D1v.

110 Harrán (Copia Sulam, *Jewish Poet and Intellectual,* 330n96) reads this fount as the biblical fountain of life (the Lord). Fortis (*La "bella ebrea,"* 121–2nn6–8) reads it similarly. I believe instead that Copia Sulam – in this poem that justifies her quest for both worldly and spiritual immortality – means the term to have a double meaning: as the fountain of life and the fountain Castalia in Parnassus, from which flowed poetic inspiration. Fortis (ibid., 122n9), while calling the latter interpretation "less convincing," rightly points out that Copia Sulam echoes Horace in her phrasing here. "Né cercar dee altro **fonte**, od altro **rio**" recalls his lines on good writing that Copia Sulam cited in her *Manifesto* (B4r): "Il primo **fonte** e 'l **rio** del scrivere bene / Senza dubbio è 'l saper" (Of good writing the source and fount is wisdom). Horace, *Art of Poetry,* 477 (verse 309). Copia Sulam used Dolce's translation; see Horace, *La poetica d'Horatio,* B6r. That she echoes Horace's phrasing in her poem suggests that she was also talking about artistic creation. The interpretation of the fount as that of poetic glory is also supported with a statement by Copia Sulam reported in Cebà's *Lettere a Sarra Copia* (see below, n113). Fonseca-Wollheim ("Acque di Parnaso," 159–70, esp. 168) also makes a strong case for such a reading.

111 Christians criticized the practice of Judaism as carnal, in contrast with the spirituality of Christianity.

112 "corri, corri al lavacro, ond'hor deriva / La vita." B. Bonifaccio, *Immortalità,* 61.

113 Copia Sulam also expressed to Cebà her desire for the waters of poetic fame: Cebà (*Lettere a Sarra Copia,* †3v) reported that she "mentioned she yearned more for the waters of Parnassus than for those of baptism." On Copia Sulam's use of water images, see Fonseca-Wollheim, "Acque di Parnaso," 159–70.

114 *Mente* (mind) is a correction in text *c* of the *Mentre* (while) in texts *a* and *b,* which does not make sense in context. Harrán (Copia Sulam, *Jewish Poet and Intellectual,* 331) and Fortis (*La "bella ebrea,"* 123) also choose this reading.

115 Copia Sulam, *Manifesto*, D2r. Harrán (Copia Sulam, *Jewish Poet and Intellectual*, 332n106) sees the last two lines as a reference to Psalms 91:11 (DR 90:11).

116 "con ottimo fine, e sempre con intentione di guadagnarmi l'amore e la gratia vostra." B. Bonifaccio, *Risposta al Manifesto*, A4v.

117 "rispondere alle mie ragioni voi non potete, ed alle ingiurie vostre io non voglio." Ibid., A2r.

118 "Non havendo io ricevuto ingiuria da voi, tutto che mi chiamate aversario, non farete ch'io non vi sia vero amico. E tale mi sarete bene ancor noi [=voi], se mal non conosco la gentilezza vostra." Ibid., A2v. In his letter to Uberto Manfredino from December 1621, Bonifaccio (*Delle amene lettere*, fascicolo 20, 5v) calls Copia Sulam an enemy. See below, n135.

119 See chapter one, 38.

120 "Io sono stato da voi non dirò solamente invitato, ma spinto ancora e sforzato a scrivervi quello che scrissi." B. Bonifaccio, *Risposta al Manifesto*, A4v.

121 See the introduction, 7–8.

122 "il rabbino." B. Bonifaccio, *Risposta al Manifesto*, A2v.

123 "Col medesimo affetto amerò sempre colui che, sì come vi dettò la prima lettera ond'hebbe occasione il mio discorso dell'immortalità, così vi suggerisce questo da voi chiamato *Manifesto* ... Egli dico, e non voi, perché riconosco gli idiotismi ["idioms" and "idiocies"] del suo linguaggio e gli stessi concetti ch'egli ha sempre in bocca." Ibid.

124 Bonifaccio describes, for instance, Modena's oral speech ("those conceits that always spill out of his mouth") as distinct from Copia Sulam's. Ibid.

125 "vedo che appresso i giudei sono donne che vanno sicuramente le viscere de gli huomini perscrutando." Ibid., A3r.

126 See chapter two, 249n134.

127 Inverting roles to cast himself as lender, Bonifaccio claims he had helped Modena (perhaps financially). See Adelman, "Leon Modena, Sara Copio Sullam" 313.

128 "Hora egli, spendendo quella moneta che sola si batte nelle sue zecche, mi ricompensa con un'acerba invettiva." B. Bonifaccio, *Risposta al Manifesto*, A2v.

129 "(a)l quale par che vogliate che io christiano e voi giudea possiamo egualmente aspirare." Ibid., A4v.

130 "sì fatta contesa, essendo voi femina, mi riuscirebbe disvantaggiosa." Ibid., A2r. As in the *Immortalità*, he uses the derogatory term *femina*. See chapter two, 247n119 and 247n121.

131 "anco imparo nelle vostre scuole che il sapere è fonte del bene scrivere." B. Bonifaccio, *Risposta al Manifesto*, A3r.

132 See chapter two, 70.

133 "Non essendo io così come voi copioso di gran maestri, sotto la cui
disciplina arrivaste in un tratto a perfettion tale che vi offerite d'inseg-
narmi non pur le più recondite scienze, ma la nostra volgar favella."
B. Bonifaccio, *Risposta al Manifesto*, A3v. His use of the term *copioso* plays on
her name.

134 Bonifaccio (*Delle amene lettere*, fascicolo 20, 5r–5v) uses the term several
times in his December 1621 letter to Uberto Manfredino. On Jezabel as a
symbol for wickedness and wantonness (linked also to women teaching),
see Revelation 2:20–1 (DR): "But I have against thee a few things: because
thou sufferest the woman Jezabel, who calleth herself a prophetess, to
teach, and to seduce my servants, to commit fornication, and to eat of
things sacrificed to idols. And I gave her a time that she might do penance,
and she will not repent of her fornication." On Bonifaccio's disparagement
of Copia Sulam in this letter, see also the biographical note, 298n99.

135 Bonifaccio (*Delle amene lettere*, fascicolo 20, 5v) writes: "Jezabel, with a
cadaverous face and her limbs stripped of flesh, infamous for her unchastity, has become odious even to the Jews [*giudei*] themselves because of
the disgrace she spreads to her whole community" (Jezabele, con facia
cadaverosa, e membra spolpate, resa infame per impudicitia, vive odiosa
anco agli stessi giudei, per la ignominia che da lei si diffonde in tutta la
sua natione). Regarding the perception of Copia Sulam within the Jewish
community, Bonifaccio, who on several occasions demonstrated ill will
towards her, cannot be considered a reliable source. On the issue, see
the biographical note, 196. The wasted appearance Bonifaccio reports,
if accurate, may have been due to a recent health crisis that Copia Sulam
reported to Cebà and mentioned in her *Manifesto*. See chapter four,
262n2. In the above-cited letter to Manfredino, Bonifaccio (*Delle amene
lettere*, fascicolo 20, 5v) denies that he feels joy in Copia Sulam's pain – in
essence admitting exactly the opposite: "I am not however so little aware
of our common humanity that I relish the misery of my enemies" (Io non
son però così poco ricordevole della commune humanità ch'io mi rallegri
delle miserie degli inimici).

136 B. Bonifaccio, *Risposta al Manifesto*, A4r.

137 "il Rabbino." Ibid., A2v.

138 "sarebbe spettacolo sconciamente deforme il vedere nello steccato quinci
un prete e quindi un'hebrea giuocar di cimbottoli e stramazzoni." Ibid., A2r.

139 After having recounted a story about Apelles, Bonifaccio told Copia Sulam
that "as long as we are still alive, I will recount a half dozen of such stories,
if it is pleasing to you, in my next discourse" (di queste novelle, già che
pur ve ne compiacete, io ne conterò, s'havrem vita, nel mio seguente discorso una meza dozina). Ibid., A4v.

140 "la fama consista in aver di molti volumi fuori." Copia Sulam, *Manifesto*,
     C3v.
141 "potrebbe dal mondo esser più volentieri veduta e forse più gradita." Ibid.,
     A2r.

4 Copia Sulam Compromised (1622–1623)

 1 "una tribulazione che mi trafigge al presente"; "per qualche tempo." Cebà,
    Lettere a Sarra Copia, 126.
 2 In addition to mentions by Cebà (ibid., 119, 121–3) of her health crisis,
    Copia Sulam (*Manifesto,* A2v) wrote that an illness had recently brought
    her to the brink of death.
 3 See chapter one, 52.
 4 Cebà (*Lettere a Sarra Copia,* 126) also said a letter from her dated 31
    December 1621 had been lost.
 5 "V'accuso ben io la ricevuta della vostra Apologia, la quale insieme con
    la lettera degli otto d'agosto mi fu portata finalmente al primo di questo
    mese." Ibid., 128.
 6 "ricordatevi che non basta che crediate l'anima immortale, se non pren-
    dete anche la via che è necessaria per haverla beata." Ibid.
 7 "Lasciatemi però morire senza tribolarmi più con le vostre lettere." Ibid.,
    127.
 8 On the common trope of excessive female desire, see Ruggiero,
    Machiavelli in Love, 73–4.
 9 "Conosco io tutto quel che siete e che volete da me; e sodisfò molte volte
    con la penna al vostro desiderio." Cebà, *Lettere a Sarra Copia,* 129.
10 See LaMay, "Composing from the Throat," 380. See also Taylor, *Castration,*
    86–7.
11 "I never fool myself about the reason that impels you to seek a friendship
    with me" (non m'inganno mai nel far giudicio della cagione che vi muove
    a voler meco amicitia). Cebà, *Lettere a Sarra Copia,* 129.
12 "Gloria di mondo è quella che voi cercate, mentre per via di lettere proc-
    urate di separarvi dal volgo delle femine: ma 'l mondo, come sapete, non
    può dar cosa stabile; e quando potesse, poco monterebbe che 'l vostro
    nome fosse ricordato per molti secoli, mentre l'anima fosse tormentata
    per infiniti." Ibid.
13 For a recent discussion of the evolution of Petrarch's thoughts on glory,
    see Guastella, *Word of Mouth,* 221–50. The contrast between the rejection
    of worldly glory and embrace of eternal life is most clearly seen in the
    Trionfi (Triumphs), in which, as Guastella (ibid., 242) notes: "Time's domi-
    nance over *Fama* [glory] thus constitutes the basis for the contrast between
    the emptiness of earthly things and the truth of otherworldly existence."

14 Cebà, *Lettere a Sarra Copia*, 1. See chapter one, 30.
15 "Se non pensate di convertirvi, sospendete la vostra penna, perché, senza questa cagione, non penso d'adoperare la mia." Cebà, *Lettere a Sarra Copia*, 130.
16 "addolorato et angustiato per questo disgratiato poema." Reale Simioli, "Ansaldo Cebà," 190.
17 See chapter one, 52.
18 Reale Simioli, "Ansaldo Cebà," 167 (Marcantonio Doria letter to Alessandro d'Este, 22 July 1621).
19 Ibid., 102. Cebà included several letters to Este in his general correspondence. See for example Cebà, *Lettere a Pallavicino*, 173–9, 245, including a letter (ibid., 177) that asks Este for his opinion of *La reina Esther*. Este was named cardinal in March 1599 by Clement VIII and occupied the powerful and prestigious position of Cardinal Protector of the Crown of Spain from June 1599. He exercised considerable political power on the Italian peninsula, which he used to favour Estense family interests. Closely linked to other powerful cardinals including Roberto Bellarmino, Silvio Antoniano, Carlo Emanuele Pio di Savoia, Alessandro de' Medici, and Odoardo Farnese, Este was an influential member of the college of cardinals and played a decisive role in four conclaves. He had a lively interest in the arts and, as governor of the Tivoli estate from 1605 onward, lavishly entertained eminent literature figures such as Marino and Tassoni. See Portone, "Alessandro d'Este."
20 Reale Simioli, "Ansaldo Cebà," 103–4. Before the letters that request help for Cebà's *La reina Esther*, Doria had sent Este Cebà's books and greetings, as well as updates on the writer's health. Ibid., 104–6.
21 Reale Simioli, "Ansaldo Cebà," 165–7 (Marcantonio Doria letter to Alessandro d'Este, 16 July 1621).
22 "più nelle parole che ne' sensi." Ibid., 170. Regarding one episode in question, he wrote: "The words that I use, ... even if they are by necessity of imitation tender, are however neither filthy nor indecent such that I should be forced by this condemnation to erase them" (Le parole adunque ch'io uso ... ancorché, per la necessità dell'imitatione, sian tenere, non sono però né laide né dishoneste per modo ch'io debba essere condannato a cancellarle). Ibid.
23 "qualche piccola contrarietà che possa notarsi fra 'l testo del poema e quello della Scrittura." Ibid.
24 "molto più licentioso." Ibid., 171.
25 "L'inquisitione che sento far di questo poema a capo di sett'anni che è publicato e la somiglianza che truovo fra l'oppositioni della Congreg[atio]ne e quelle di qualch'altri mi fan sospettare che sia venuta a Roma persona ch'habbia persuaso qualche ministro di quel Tribunale ad avvertirlo ch'io

ho compilato un libro che, con le descrittioni oscenissime dell'historie
sacre e con le contrarietà scandalose delle menzogne profane, può con-
taminare gli animi di lascivie e seminar la Chiesa d'errori. Chi sia poi
questo ministro io non so ... ma dico solamente quel che mi va per l'animo." Ibid., 171. For his use of the word "inquisitione" in a letter to Copia
Sulam, see chapter one, 49–50.

26 "My suspicion of having been persecuted in this disastrous situation regarding my poem has derived, as I hinted before, from my remembering
that almost exactly the same objections had already been made to the
poem and that the person who made them even predicted that the poem
would be suspended by the Roman Congregation. He showed very clearly
that he did not have the sort of good will toward me that was merited,
given that not only did I never harm him but I never even (I think I can
say) knew him" (Et però l'haver sospettato di persecuzione nel disastro del
mio Poema è proceduto, com'accennai, dall'essermi tornato a mente che
gli furono già fatte quasi le stesse opposizioni e che la persona che le fece
predisse anche la sospension della Congregatione romana e mostrò assai
chiaramente di non havere verso di me quella volontà che richiedeva il
non essere non solamente mai stata offesa da me, ma ne anche, mi par di
poter dire, conosciuta). Ibid., 172–3 (letter dated 27 August 1621).

27 Gian Vittorio Rossi (known as Giano Nicio Eritreo or Janus Nicius
Erythraeus, 1577–1647) recounts that Cebà, in his efforts to promote *La
reina Esther*, had sent it to Cardinal Giannettino Doria (1573–1642) in
Palermo, who responded with some of his own and others' concerns about
the work. When Cebà replied curtly that the cardinal lacked an understanding of poetry, Doria responded derisively but took his true revenge
by denouncing the work to the Inquisition. Rossi, a Roman writer, philol-
ogist, and literary historian who was part of the Barberini circle, authored
several works of biblical scholarship in addition to the work for which he
is most famous: the three-volume *Pinacotheca imaginum illustrium doctrinae
vel ingenii laude virorum* (1643–8), which profiled his contemporaries. See
Hainsworth and Robey, *The Oxford Companion to Italian Literature*, 526. For
his account regarding Doria and Cebà, see Rossi, *Pinacotheca tertia*, 122–7
(entry 30, "Ansaldus Cebà"), esp. 124–7. See also Spotorno, *Storia letteraria
della Liguria*, 4:126–7. Giannettino Doria, born in Genoa to a noble family,
became a cardinal in 1604 and archbishop of Palermo in 1608. His long
tenure was marked by conflict. See Sanfilippo, "Doria, Giannettino."

28 "per lo stato miserabile in che mi truovo, conosco essere sopra le
forze mie." Reale Simioli, "Ansaldo Cebà," 173 (Ansaldo Cebà to the
Congregazione dell'Indice, undated but August/September 1621).

29 See ibid., 199–212. Though the Latin defence of *La reina Esther* is un-
signed, Reale Simioli (ibid., 144–5) thinks it is by Cebà, although it could

also have been drafted by Nicolò Riccardi, based on the detailed defence
Cebà had sent him. On Riccardi, see below, n32.

30 See Reale Simioli, "Ansaldo Cebà," 165–99.

31 See ibid., 110–11, 176–7 (Cebà to Riccardi, undated but September
1621), 181–2 (Riccardi to Cebà, 19 November 1621), 182 (Cebà to
Riccardi, undated but November 1621), 183 (Riccardi to Cebà, 10
December 1621), 191–2 (Riccardi to Cebà, 3 June 1622), 192–3 (Riccardi
to Doria, 8 July 1622).

32 See Mayer, *The Trial of Galileo*, 180–1. On Riccardi, who had an ambivalent relationship with Galileo and a prolonged conflict with Tommaso Campanella
and was known as "padre Mostro" (Father Monster [Marvel]) for his prodigious knowledge as well as his obesity, see Cavarzere, "Riccardi, Nicolò."

33 Reale Simioli, "Ansaldo Cebà," 192 (Riccardi letter to Cebà, 3 June 1622).

34 Riccardi called Barberini "the most rigorous opponent" in the voting on
the work's exoneration (il voto di più rigore). Ibid. See also ibid., 117.

35 Though, as a cardinal, Barberini had defended and protected Galileo, the scientist eventually lost Urban VIII's favour because of his defiance. In his 1632
Dialoghi, Urban said, Galileo "had dared to meddle with matters beyond his
competence ... it is an injury to religion as grievous as ever there was and of a
perverseness as bad as could be encountered." Duffy, *Saints & Sinners*, 185.

36 Doria wrote to Este on 13 May 1622 that "[Cebà's] life rests in the balance
of whether his *La reina Esther* is saved or lost" (resti bilanciata la sua vita
nella conservatione o perdita della sua Regina [*sic*] Esther). Reale Simioli,
"Ansaldo Cebà," 190. In announcing Cebà's death to Este, Doria wrote
that "the anguish that he suffered about the censure of his poem *La reina
Esther* may have taken some years from his life" (il rigore ch'ha patito nella
censura del suo poema d'Esther può haverle tolto q(u)alch'anno di vita).
Ibid., 193 (22 October 1622).

37 See ibid., 193–9. In late October, for instance, Doria implores Este to
finish the task he took on "to free the *Esther* poem" (per liberare il poema
d'Esther"). Ibid., 195 (Doria to Este, 29 October 1623).

38 Bujanda and Richter, *Index librorum prohibitorum*, 205.

39 See chapter one, 27.

40 Quondam, "Dal 'formulario' al 'formulario,'" 30.

41 See Ray, *Writing Gender*, 237n23. Cebà did include a few letters to others –
two to Giacomo Rosa and one to Copia Sulam's husband Giacob Sulam
(on the latter, see chapter one, 44–5) – but these letters primarily discussed Copia Sulam and therefore contributed to, rather than distracted
from, the volume's focus on her.

42 On the work's title, see chapter one, n30.

43 "Out of gratitude for the love this woman professed to have for me, I
wanted to ensure that some memory of her is preserved by means of these

letters" (Per gratitudine dell'amore che questa dama ha fatto profession di portarmi, ho voluto che resti di lei qualche memoria nelle presenti lettere). Cebà, *Lettere a Sarra Copia*, †2v.

44 "Il mio poema della reina Esther mosse una nobile hebrea a voler meco l'amicitia." Ibid., †2r.

45 "I did not hesitate to make love with her soul, in order to improve the condition of mine. But after four years' time, I realized that I had little aided the former and gained nothing for the latter" (Io non ricusai di far l'amore con l'anima sua, per migliorare la condizione della mia. Ma dopo lo spatio di quatt'anni mi sono avveduto d'haver avanzato poco per l'una, e guadagnato nulla per l'altra). Ibid.

46 "la Giudea, ch'io ho publicata con le mie lettere per generosa, sia riconosciuta con le vostre preghiere per christiana." Ibid., †2v.

47 "cosa alcuna contraria alla Santa Fede, né a buoni costume." Ibid., †1v.

48 Masini played an important role in Cebà's publishing life. The inquisitor's name would appear on the imprimatur for both of Cebà's posthumous letter collections, an approval his friends were careful to seek on his behalf. The works were reviewed by two of Masini's deputies. See ibid.; Cebà, *Lettere a Pallavicino*, +1v. Cebà had earlier interacted with Masini regarding his 1620 *Caratteri morali di Theofrasto* (On the Moral Characters of Theophrastus) to which the inquisitor had also objected. See Reale Simioli, "Ansaldo Cebà," 101n17. Regarding *La reina Esther*, Doria reported to Este on 16 July 1621 that Masini had not yet received an order to suspend the work, despite the Congregation of the Index's actions. He added that he would ask the inquisitor to delay the publication of such an order when received in order to allow time for Este to act. Ibid., 166–7. On Cesare Masini, who took the name Eliseo when he joined the Dominican order and was an important figure in the Inquisition, see ibid., 101n17. Black (*The Italian Inquisition*, 168) terms him "an enthusiastic book-burner." In 1621, Masini published the manual *Sacro arsenale, overo Prattica dell'officio della Santa Inquisitione* (Sacred Arsenal, or The Practice of the Office of the Holy Inquisition) with Giuseppe Pavoni, Cebà's primary publisher who printed the first edition of *La reina Esther*. See chapter one, 220n19.

49 As Ray (*Writing Gender*, 3) notes, "Self-fashioning, self-censorship, revision, masquerade – all are common to the epistolary genre." See also the further discussion in ibid., 3–4; Quondam, "Dal 'formulario' al 'formulario,'" 22–3; Najemy, *Between Friends*, 25–57; Robin, *Filelfo in Milan*, 11–55. Contemporary authors were quite conscious of such artifice. Pietro Petracci – possibly a member of Copia Sulam's salon – who edited the letters of Angelo Grillo, pointed out in his prefatory comments to Grillo's edition that "the letter pertains entirely to the

realm of literary communication – its rhetorical form is in no way 'real' but *artful*." See Quondam, "Dal 'formulario' al 'formulario,'" 144–7 (quotation on 146).

50 An example of such fabrication is the 1548 *Lettere di molte valorose donne*, a collection of more than 250 letters purportedly written by women but in fact authored by Ortensio Lando. See Ray, *Writing Gender*, 48; Pezzini, "Dissimulazione e paradosso."

51 See for example Cebà, *Lettere a Sarra Copia*, 93: Cebà told Copia Sulam that if she hadn't received his letters, "copies will be prepared to be resent to you; don't be surprised of the importance I give to our conversations, since their remarkable novelty deserves to be remembered" (saranno apparecchiate le copie da rimandarvi; né vi maravigliate del conto ch'io tengo de' nostri dialoghi, perché la novità loro è tanto notabile che merita che ne sia conservata la memoria). See also n59 below.

52 See for example Cebà, *Lettere a Sarra Copia*, 55–6, 61, 66, 85, 96, 125–6, in addition to his most forceful denunciation in the last letter: ibid., 129 (letter 53).

53 See for example ibid., 58 (letter 17 of October 1619), where he apologized for not writing sooner, but "I have no want of suffering, in body and mind" (Non mi manca da tribolare e nel corpo e nell'animo); or ibid., 88 (letter 29 of August 1620), when he wrote "I am tormented by a pain, signora Sarra, that allows me neither to live nor die; therefore do not be surprised if I speak little with you" (Io patisco un tormento, signora Sarra, che non mi lascia né vivere né morire; però non vi maravigliate se parlo poco con esso voi). In March 1621 he told her "I wrote later and less than I would have wanted, since my illness constrains me more than you believe" (Ho scritto e più tardi e più breve che non havrei voluto, perché l'infermità mi constringe più che non credete). Ibid., 111 (letter 40).

54 All of these works were issued in 1623, except the tragedy *Le gemelle capovane* (The Capuan Twins), which for reasons that are unclear remained unpublished until the eighteenth century. See Cebà, *Tragedie*, 195.

55 See chapter four, 109. Cebà and Doria discuss Cebà's health – worsened by the *La reina Esther* affair – in several other letters. On his inability to change the poem because of his health, see their correspondence published in Reale Simioli, "Ansaldo Cebà," 186, 191. On more general mentions in their letters of his poor health, see ibid., 166, 184, 188–90, 193.

56 For example, see the mention of Copia Sulam's enthusiasm for Cebà's *La reina Esther* in Modena's own work on the Old Testament queen (*L'Ester*, 3–7); the mention by Cebà (*Lettere a Sarra Copia*, 38, 68) of the correspondence between Copia Sulam and della Tolfa, which is confirmed by

Copia Sulam's autograph letter to della Tolfa (see chapter four, 122–4);
and Cebà's mention of Copia Sulam's health crisis in spring 1621, which
Copia Sulam also mentions in her *Manifesto* (see n2 above).

57 See chapter one, 37–8.

58 Ray (*Writing Gender*, 4) notes that, "under the guise of a 'private' communication between writer and addressee, the individual letters in a published *epistolario* provide readers with fragmentary sketches from which to
reconstruct an image of the writer. When considered together, these fragments form the writer's public self."

59 Cebà retained a copy of the letters he sent as standard practice; this enabled him later to publish them. See n51 above; Harrán's notes in Copia
Sulam, *Jewish Poet and Intellectual*, 128n56, 225n441. Copia Sulam may not
have done the same.

60 "Perché si tocca qualcosa in queste lettere, che non potrebbe compren-
dersi pienamente senza sapere che cagione s'havesse di dirla, si son notati
qui appresso alcuni luoghi di quelle della signora Sarra per agevolar a chi
leggerà l'intelligenza di queste." Cebà, *Lettere a Sarra Copia*, †3r. There is
no direct attribution given for this note to readers, and it is possible that
Doria could have prepared it as he readied the volume for publication.
However, since it shows detailed knowledge of Copia Sulam's letters, it is
nearly certain Cebà wrote it.

61 "si possano essere tralasciati qualch'altri luoghi necessarij per la dichiaratione sopradetta." Ibid.

62 "Havea dannata la novità della legge Christiana col seguente proverbio:
che chi 'l vecchio camin pel nova lascia spesso s'inganna e poi ne sente
ambascia"; "havea detto d'esser hebrea e non gentile & innalzata la dig-
nità della sua legge"; "havea detto di voler la tomba dov'hebbe la cuna,
cioè, che come'era nata hebrea, così volea morir hebrea"; "s'era doluta,
che fosse in lei riputato vitio l'esser nata giudea." Ibid., †3r; †3r; †3v; †4r,
respectively.

63 "Havea tocco di bramar piu l'acque di Parnaso che quelle del Battesimo";
"haveva scritto ... non haver bisogno d'acqua poiché era nata in mezzo del
mare, volendo significare che non le facea mestier di battesimo." Ibid.,
†3v; †4r, respectively. On these images, see Fonseca-Wollheim, "Acque di
Parnaso," 159–70.

64 Pullan, *The Jews of Europe*, 58.

65 "havea scritto, che Dio non si può raffigurar in questa vita ché non se lo
forma materialmente." Cebà, *Lettere a Sarra Copia*, †3r–3v.

66 In accordance with the second commandment, Exod. 20:4–5: "Thou shalt
not make to thyself a graven thing, nor the likeness of any thing that is in
heaven above, or in the earth beneath, nor of those things that are in the

waters under the earth. Thou shalt not adore them, nor serve them"; cf.
Deut. 5:8–9 (DR).

67 Pullan, *The Jews of Europe*, 14.

68 In his *Magen Vi-Tzinah* (Shield and Buckler), Leon Modena also argues
that God's incarnation is impossible. See Podet, "Christianity in the View
of Rabbi Leon Modena," 24. On Modena's *Magen Vi-Tzinah*, see chapter
two, 58–9, 241n51.

69 "havea detto non poter parlare contro la nostra fede se non da se sola
nella sua cameretta"; "havea rifiutato le preghiere per la sua conversione,
salvo se dovevano essere reciproche." Cebà, *Lettere a Sarra Copia*, †3v.

70 "haveva detto d'haver occhi lincei in materia di religione." Ibid., †3r.
The expression "avere occhi lincei" means literally "to be lynx-eyed" – in
other words, to have sharp vision or perspicuity. The acuity of the lynx's
vision was noted by Saint Albert the Great (*Man and the Beasts*, 156) in
his influential thirteenth-century treatise on animals, *De animalibus*. The
Accademia de' Lincei (Academy of the Lynx-Eyed), a scientific body
founded in Rome in 1603 that counted Galileo among its members, used
the term to advertise the group's adherence to keen-sighted scientific
observation.

71 Cebà (*Lettere a Sarra Copia*, 7) writes: "You say that you have not deigned
to read the New Testament, almost as if you would have to lower yourself
greatly to engage in similar reading" (Voi dite che non havete sdegnato di
leggere il Testamento nuovo, quasi che vi siate abbassata grandemente a
condurvi a simigliante lettione).

72 "semplice huomo." Ibid.

73 Cebà (ibid., 30) writes that her line of reasoning showed "more that you
want to demean the Christian faith than that Christianity has qualities that
allow it to be demeaned" (più voglia in voi d'abbassare la fede di Christo
che conditione in lei da poter essere abbassata).

74 Copia Sulam seems to have asked for this, probably jokingly, in response to
his suggestion that she seek baptism. Ibid., 79.

75 Pullan, *The Jews of Europe*, 58.

76 Ibid.

77 Ibid., 73.

78 Cebà, *Lettere a Sarra Copia*, 118. See also chapter one, 50.

79 On Cremonini's work, see chapter two, 56–7.

80 Pullan, *The Jews of Europe*, 71.

81 See ibid., 79; chapter three, 81.

82 See chapter three, 81–2; biographical note, 196.

83 Copia Sulam's 1620 letter to Bonifaccio on the mortality of the soul also
shows her exercising such freedom: she explicitly says that she expresses

opinions with the expectation that Bonifaccio will counter them. See chapter two, 66. She makes a similar statement in her *Manifesto*. See chapter one, 38.

84 The *Manifesto* controversy occurred more than three years into the four-year-long correspondence: 49 of the 53 letters in the *Lettere a Sarra Copia* predate it.

85 The letter is held in the Archivio di Stato di Napoli (see Bibliography – Manuscript Sources) and was published in Reale Simioli, "Tracce di letteratura ligure," 332–3.

86 "intresse che molto mi preme." Copia Sulam, "Lettera a Isabella della Tolfa."

87 The letter dated to the period of the salon debate over the immortality of the soul. See chapter one, 37–8.

88 Copia Sulam explained to della Tolfa that she had written to Doria "some days ago" (alli giorni passati) without response, but her exchanges with Cebà would have taught her that it generally took at least two weeks to receive a response from a letter sent to Genoa. Copia Sulam, "Lettera a Isabella della Tolfa."

89 Cebà (*Lettere a Sarra Copia*, 56) told her in August 1619 that in Genoa "You have friends ... who would go to greater lengths to serve you than you believe" (Voi havete amici ... che farebbono in servigio vostro più che non pensate). On her contacts in Genoa, see chapter one, 35, 39–41.

90 "se si avesse dubbio di far cosa contra la fama e volontà del sig(no)r Ansaldo ... che quella benedetta anima diede ord(in)e di tale impressione più per onorar me, sue serva, che per propria ambizione." Copia Sulam, "Lettera a Isabella della Tolfa."

5 Friends and Enemies (1621–1626)

1 The "Avisi" manuscript is held at the Correr Museum Library in Venice. Boccato ("Sara Copio Sullam," 104–218) published a transcription of the manuscript in Italian. Harrán (Copia Sulam, *Jewish Poet and Intellectual*, 349–510) translated it into English as "Notices from Parnassus." I cite from the original manuscript; all translations are mine.

2 The disease has generally been assumed to be syphilis. See for example Harrán's note in Copia Sulam, *Jewish Poet and Intellectual*, 357n43. However, early modern physicians did not distinguish between syphilis and gonorrhea, and therefore the diagnosis of "French disease" could refer to either of these conditions or another condition altogether. McGough, *Gender, Sexuality, and Syphilis*, 10.

3 The manuscript reports that Paluzzi worked behind the scenes to help Copia Sulam defend herself in that debate. It criticizes him, however,

for dragging his feet to provide comments on the draft of her *Manifesto*, stating that he eventually advised her to dramatically sharpen its tone and that he suggested some minor alterations to the work's poetry. The manuscript condemns his excessively venomous annotations of Bonifaccio's *Immortalità dell'anima*. "Avisi," 31v; 32r–32v, 50r–50v; 51v, respectively. See also chapter one, 48, 232–3n169.

4 In-text parenthetical references in this chapter are to folio numbers of the "Avisi" manuscript cited in the bibliography. The approximate dates for these and other events can be deduced from the manuscript. On the steam baths in Venice, see Boccato, "Manoscritto," 128n36. Patients at steam baths would inhale supposedly curative mercury vapour. Allen, *The Wages of Sin*, xx. On the French disease in the city, see McGough, *Gender, Sexuality, and Syphilis*, esp. 17–44.

5 The manuscript states that Paluzzi was also supported by other friends, including Giacomo Rosa, who had corresponded with Cebà and had been his agent in Venice.

6 This maid is generally called "the Moor" (la Mora) but her name is given at "Avisi," 90v. The term "moro" (feminine, "mora") could have a variety of meanings: it "could denote an Arab or Berber, but also an Ethiopian or sub-Saharan black African; it did not necessarily apply only to Muslims." Minnich, "The Catholic Church," 280. On the ethnic and racial identities of domestic workers (in this case, slaves), see Rothman, "Contested Subjecthood," esp. 428–9. See also Lowe, "Visible Lives," 415–17. On the denigration of Arnolfa in the "Avisi" based on stereotypes about Africans in Europe, see chapter 5, 166, and below, n196.

7 On Rosa, see chapter one, 26, 45–7, 49.

8 For monetary conversion, see Galilei (*Le operazioni*, 13–14), who said that 186 golden *scudi* equalled 240 ducats. For currency values, see Appendix C.

9 Copia Sulam may not have pursued charges against Paluzzi because of his compromised health, because Berardelli's crimes eclipsed Paluzzi's, or because it might have been embarrassing to pursue charges against her long-time teacher.

10 The records from the case have been lost. See Boccato, "Manoscritto," 110n15.

11 On 4 August 1626, he signed the dedication to Paluzzi's *Rime*, which he edited.

12 The title of the work, clearly intended sarcastically, recalls the Italian titles of ancient epic poems such as Virgil's *Aeneid* (in Italian *Eneide*, a celebration of Aeneas/Enea) and Statius's *Thebaid* (in Italian *Tebaide*, a celebration of Thebes/Tebe). Margherita Sarrocchi's *La*

Scanderbeide, a celebration of George Scanderbeg first published in 1606 and then in a complete version in 1623, employs the same form. In the seventeenth century, a number of parodic, satirical, or ludic works, often with vulgar content, were published with epic-like titles, including Giovanni Battista Lalli's *Moscheide ouero Domiziano il moschicida* (The Epopee of the Fly or Domitian the Fly Killer, first edition ca. 1619) and *Franceide ouero Del mal francese* (The French Feat or On the French Disease, 1629); Giambattista Marino's *Murtoleide* (Murtola's Feats, published posthumously in 1626 but composed around 1608 and widely circulated in manuscript), which mocked Marino's enemy Gaspare Murtola; and Murtola's response, *La Marineide*. On the dating of the *Murtoleide*'s composition, see Martini, "Marino, Giovan Battista," 522; on its manuscript circulation, see Corradini, *In terra di letteratura*, 25n38.

13 "scritture obbrobriossissime." "Avisi," 11v. For mentions of "Le Sareide" (or "Sarreide") by name, see ibid., 22v, 30v, 49r, 72r, 90r.

14 "si venne agli insulti, si prorupe a l'onte, fulminarvasi [*sic*] i minaci e di frapare e d'ardere." Ibid., 49r.

15 Horodowich (*Language and Statecraft*, 98) notes that it was largely this magistracy that patrolled verbal injury.

16 For Paluzzi's death, see ASV Death Records, registro 854 (1625). The document is also cited in Boccato, "Manoscritto," 105–6n4. See also the San Marcuola parochial records cited in ibid., 128n34 as well as Harrán's note in Copia Sulam, *Jewish Poet and Intellectual*, 360n62, which indicates that Paluzzi died (and presumably lived) close to the ghetto. On Paluzzi's "French disease," see n2 above.

17 See chapter one, 31.

18 Ciotti started as an apprentice in Venice around 1581 and published his first book in the city in 1583. Ascarelli and Menato, *La tipografia del '500*, 430. See also Borsa, *Clavis typographorum librariorumque Italiae*, 1:111; Rhodes, "Neglected Aspects," 229–30. As to his place of residency around the time of the *Rime*'s publication: M. Firpo ("Ciotti, Giovanni Battista," 696) states that Ciotti probably moved to Sicily shortly after his 1625 edition of the three parts of Marino's *Lira*; Rhodes ("Neglected Aspects," 225) disagrees.

19 Pastorello, *Tipografi, editori, librai*, 22.

20 Ascarelli and Menato, *La tipografia del '500*, 430.

21 M. Firpo, "Ciotti, Giovanni Battista," 693.

22 On Ciotti's association with Bruno, see Verrecchia, *Giordano Bruno*, 223–4.

23 M. Firpo, "Ciotti, Giovanni Battista," 694.

24 Cannizzaro, "Surpassing the Maestro," 375.

25 M. Firpo, "Ciotti, Giovanni Battista," 693.
26 "né dalle vostre né da altre stampe è uscito libro più scorretto e più scon-
canato di questo." Marino, *Lettere*, 29.
27 On these polemics, see the introduction, 9.
28 "è stata conosciuta, come certamente è, vero parto del suo ingegno, da
persona publica a confusione de' maligni." Marinella, *Arcadia felice* (1605),
A4v.
29 "Avisi," 35r.
30 At least until 1606 Ciotti defined himself as "Academico Veneziano." M.
Firpo, "Ciotti, Giovanni Battista," 693. On his involvement in the second
Accademia Veneziana, see also Cannizzaro ("Surpassing the Maestro,"
375–6), who observes that the academy maintained its tie to Ciotti "despite the risk of the affiliation with an individual whose unorthodoxy was
notorious."
31 At least two of the five sonnets that introduce Marinella's *La Colomba sacra*
were written by academy members – Boncio Leone (academy president)
and Teodoro Angelucci (academy assessor). See Maylender, *Storie delle accademie d'Italia*, 5:444; Lavocat, "Introduzione," xiii.
32 The modern edition and translation by Virginia Cox of Fonte's *Merito* is
entitled *The Worth of Women*. Kolsky ("Moderata Fonte," 976–7) suggests
that Marinella was a de facto member of the second Accademia Veneziana.
33 See the introduction, 10–12.
34 See Infelise, "Pallavicino, Ferrante."
35 For example, key members of the Incogniti were behind the translation of
a work that claimed women were not part of the human race and had no
souls: *Che le donne non siano della specie degli huomini*. See Infelise, "Books
and Politics," 67–9. On the academy's attitudes toward women, see the
introduction, 10–12.
36 Tarabotti's battles with certain members of the academy can be traced in
her *Lettere familiari e di complimento*. This collection is available in a modern Italian edition by Meredith K. Ray and Lynn Lara Westwater. For the
English edition and translation, also by Ray and Westwater, see Tarabotti,
Letters Familiar and Formal.
37 See Westwater, "A Rediscovered Friendship."
38 See Marinella, *Essortazioni*, 23–72; Marinella, *Exhortations*, 54–79.
39 Cannizzaro, "Guido Casoni," 547–60; Cannizzaro, "Surpassing the
Maestro," esp. 373–80.
40 Ciotti printed Strozzi's *La Venetia edificata, poema eroico* (1621) and *Le veglie
quaresimali, overo L'officio della santa settimana* (1626).
41 *Il ritorno di Damone overo La sampogna di mirtillo: Fauola siluestre* (1622). On
Cremonini's link to the Incogniti, see chapter two, 57, 239–40n40.

42 Ciotta had published Marino's works since the early 1600s and continued to do so up until his death (see the introduction, 218n73). The works of Marino printed by Ciotti include multiple editions of *La lira* from 1614 on and of *La galeria del cavalier Marino distinta in pitture & sculture* from 1619 on.

43 Accademia degli Incogniti, *Novelle amorose*, 472–83. For a fairly complete list of academy members, see Miato, *L'Accademia degli Incogniti*, 237–40; on Gabriele Zinano's possible participation, see Fonseca-Wollheim, "Faith and Fame," 133.

44 See Tasso, *Gerusalemme liberata ... con la vita di lui e con gli argomenti dell'opera del Cav. Guido Casoni*. The dedication is at ibid., A2r–A2v.

45 Infelise, "Ex ignoto notus," 218.

46 Ascarelli and Menato, *La tipografia del '500*, 430.

47 See n18 above.

48 Cannizzaro, "Studies on Guido Casoni," 309.

49 See Fonseca-Wollheim, "Faith and Fame," 136; Westwater, "Disquieting Voice," 194. Further discussion is in Boccato, "Le *Rime* postume," 112–31; Harrán, "Introduction," 67.

50 "molti errori." Paluzzi, *Rime*, A4v.

51 The name Filli is possibly a pastoral alias.

52 Ibid., 41; 30; 9; 7, respectively.

53 Ibid., 3.

54 Ibid., 1; "tolsi" in the last line of the quatrain corrected from "tosi." Cf. Petrarca, *Rerum vulgarium fragmenta*, 5 (RVF 1).

55 Paluzzi, *Rime*, 25. The lines are from the last verse of the quatrains and the first tercet. Cf. Petrarca, *Rerum vulgarium fragmenta*, 113 (RVF 134).

56 Paluzzi, *Rime*, 10, 13.

57 "Benda avvolta in testa della s[ua] d[onna]." Ibid., 24.

58 "Bella turca." Ibid., 56.

59 "In lode di bella donna hebrea." "Avisi," 21v.

60 The term "Turk" referred not only to Ottoman Turks but to all Muslims. Muslims, like Jews, were considered infidels rather than heretics because they had not relapsed from Catholicism. Ottoman Turks were forced to live segregated from the rest of the Venetian population starting in 1621. They faced similar rules to those imposed on Jews: they could not circulate from sundown to sunrise and they buried their dead (it seems) on the Lido. Ravid, "Venice and Its Minorities," 466, 468–9. See also Katz, *The Jewish Ghetto*, 53–5.

61 Coincidentally, this same cardinal may have been responsible for Cebà's troubles with the Congregation of the Index. See chapter four, 264n27.

62 Paluzzi, *Rime*, 68. See chapter one, 31.

63 Paluzzi, *Rime*, 97. On this work, see also n12 above.

64 "diede occasione ad una hebrea che gliene robbasse la maggiore e miglior parte, insieme con molte altre compositioni, in due grossi invogli,

rendendole così il guiderdone di tante opere che per lei il Paluzzi ha fatte." Ibid., A2v.

65 "ho procurato (benché con mio danno) di trarle dalle fauci dell'oblio." Ibid., A3r.

66 See chapter five, 128, 271n10.

67 "per la dolcezza, per la locutione, per la novità di concetti spiritosi, spiegati con facilità e gratia." Paluzzi, *Rime,* A2r–A2v.

68 See chapter five, 128.

69 The "Avisi" manuscript (49r, 32v) states that both the 1624 "Sareide" and the *Rime* were libelous. See also Copia Sulam, *Manifesto,* B2r.

70 "cortesi lettori." Paluzzi, *Rime,* A4r.

71 Berardelli wrote this note and the other paratextual materials, though he did not sign them. In the dedication he presents himself as the volume's editor.

72 "una feminella." Paluzzi, *Rime,* A4r.

73 See chapter two, 70, 247n121.

74 "Molte rime, dui libri di paradossi in lode delle donne contro gli huomini, e un numero grande di lettere, e un manifesto dell'imortalità dell'anima. Ella gli ha tolti in due grossi invogli la maggior e miglior parte delle rime, Della Politica, una tragedia, e li Opuscoli, i fragmenti delle quali da me adunati presto verranno fuori. E in questi si scorgerà quanto egli valesse in tutte le scienze." Paluzzi, *Rime,* A4r. On the "paradoxes," see n75 below.

75 The "paradoxes" – not mentioned by other contemporaries – were likely written in the tradition of Ortensio Lando's enormously successful *Paradossi* (1543), in which he sought to disprove prevailing wisdom – for example, poverty is better than wealth and war better than peace. Specifically, in Paradosso 25, Lando (*Paradossi,* 64) sought to prove "that women are greater than men" (che la donna è di maggior eccelentia che l'huomo). The term *paradox* in this context meant a "formal defense ... of an unexpected, unworthy or indefensible subject." Colie, *Paradoxia epidemica,* 3. In this sense, Lando's argument reinforced the validity of the "truth" of men's superiority (it posits women's superiority as absurd), but paradox could also be used to demonstrate that women were in fact superior. See Larsen, "Paradox and the Praise of Women," 767.

76 "All'anima humana." Paluzzi, *Rime,* 83.

77 One verb in the poem is altered from *esprime* (expresses) in the *Manifesto* (D2r) to *imprime* (imprints) in the *Rime* (83), but the meaning of the verse is not radically altered.

78 "Essendo stati dalla predetta hebrea rubati gli originali interi." Paluzzi, *Rime,* 72.

79 "tra le altre scritture che a l'autore sono state tolte vi è una tragedia, che mancava poco ad esser finita, della quale a pena s'è trovata questa scena." Ibid., 98.

80 "gli sono ... state rubate da quella perfida hebrea." Ibid., 120.

81 See for example, ibid., 36–9, 45, 47, 55, 74, 80, 90, 92.

82 "empia invidia"; "falsa querela." Ibid., 106. The "Avisi" manuscript (20r–20v) asserted that Berardelli (not the late Paluzzi) wrote the poem, but in Paluzzi's voice.

83 "ravvivare il nome dell'autore." Paluzzi, *Rime*, A3r.

84 "nate sotto l'istessa cattiva costellatione che'egli nacque, havendo patito parte delle istesse miserie ch'egli ha sofferto nel fine della sua vita." Ibid., A4r.

85 "di ciò ne ha havuto egli stesso la colpa." Ibid., A4r.

86 "Among these poems there are many that [Paluzzi] rejected, but they have been put here because they were his" (In queste rime ve ne son molte che egli le rifiutava, pure vi si son poste per esser sue). Ibid., A4r.

87 "presto verranno fuori." Ibid., A4r.

88 Berardelli wrote that he hoped the dedication would grant him "entry to [Soranzo's] most coveted grace" (adito alla sua desideratissima gratia). Ibid., A3v.

89 "danno." Ibid., A3r. See chapter five, 135–6. The presentation of Zinano's sonnet in praise of Berardelli (a presentation likely written by Berardelli himself; see discussion in text immediately below) also underscores the *danni* (negative consequences) Berardelli suffered for Paluzzi. Ibid., A5v.

90 See chapter one, 232–3n169.

91 See chapter five, 144.

92 On Romolo Paradiso, see the amusing account in Rossi, *Pinacotheca altera*, 166–8 (entry 54, "Romulus Paradisus"), esp. 168.

93 For these writers' verse, see Paluzzi, *Rime*, 120–30.

94 Another pair of famous friends had attracted attention in Venice a generation before. Celio Magno (1536–1602) and Orsatto Giustinian (1538–1603) published a double canzoniere in the city in 1600, *Rime di Celio Magno et di Orsatto Giustiniano*. On the friendship and the canzoniere, see McHugh, "The Gender of Desire," 72–130, esp. 109–30. McHugh notes that "the two men express their friendship for one another using the lexicon of heterosexual Petrarchan love. The two companions imagine facing heaven and hell together, they languish when apart, and meditate on portraits of one another ... [T]he overarching form of the joint canzoniere [is] presented in the text's dedicatory epistle as resulting from the authors' affective desire to link their lives and fortunes." Ibid., 110. These elements will reappear as motifs in the Barbarigo-Trevisan friendship, as discussed below. On the Giustinian-Magno dual canzoniere, see also

Erspamer, "Per un'edizione," esp. 56, 71–3; Bruscagli, "La preponderanza petrarchesca," 1611–15.

95 I follow Gaetano Cozzi's classic account of this episode, "Una vicenda della Venezia barocca" (see esp. 333–45).

96 "governare esse mie figliuole, & facoltà, come più a lui piacerà, senza obligo alcuno di dover render immaginabil conto in niun tempo, né a chi si sia, così circa le dette mie figliuole come dell'administratione delle facoltà." Cited in Strozzi, *Il Barbarigo ... seconda editione*, Bir; Cozzi, "Una vicenda," 338.

97 See ibid., 337.

98 See for example Zuccolo, *Il secolo dell'oro rinascente nella amicitia fra Nicolò Barbarigo e Marco Trivisano* (1629); Superbi, *Discorso dell'incomparabile et heroica amicitia de gl'illustrissimi signori Nicolo' Barbarigo e Marco Trivisano* (1629). Cozzi ("Una vicenda," 331–47) mentions many other works published between 1627 and 1630.

99 Zuccolo, *Dialoghi*, 174–85.

100 Zuccolo, *Nobiltà commune et heroica*, 62–79. See Cozzi, "Una vicenda," 327–31, 342.

101 Ibid., 345; Las Casas, *Istoria*.

102 "vincolo de' cori, felicità dell'anime, condimento dell'humana vita, dono incomparabile, inestimabile, incomprensibile." Ibid., +2r–v. He detailed Barbarigo and Trevisan's friendship, in particular its financial aspects. Ibid., +2r–+6v.

103 "passeggiare per le strade di Vinegia, di introdursi nelle officine delle stampe." "Avisi," 2or.

104 See also chapter three, 78.

105 *Il Barbarigo* was apparently issued first in quarto 1626 by Girolamo Piuti, with preliminary verse from several writers, including Baldassare Bonifaccio. See Bruni and Evans, *Italian Seventeenth Century Books*, 118. The copy I examined, in duodecimo, which includes a dedication to the work signed by Strozzi on 12 October 1626, lists itself as a second edition but displays neither any printing information nor the preliminary verse. A vincesimo-quarto edition, published as a second edition in 1626 and seemingly also without printing information, is also listed in catalogues. Marco Ginami reissued the work in 1628 as a second edition. Cozzi ("Una vicenda," 344) mentions only this edition. See the bibliography for the editions discussed here and in the following note.

106 A quarto edition of the first canto of *Il Barbarigo* was issued by Piuti, probably earlier that year.

107 "Vorrei poter qui registrar tutti gli honori che vengono fatti da prencipi più lontani e stranieri, e tutte le lodi, titoli e encomij che spontaneamente vengono dati, dalle penne forestiere più celebri nelle lor lettere e discorsi

e fino dalle più principali e più famose accademie d'Italia, eccitate dallo splendore e dalla suprema maraviglia di questo fatto, a questa inclita amicizia, acciò si vedesse la stima universale che vien fatta di lei." Strozzi, *Il Barbarigo ... seconda editione,* +4v–+5r.

108 Ibid., +6v; see also Cozzi, "Una vicenda," 351.

109 Berardelli later contributed poetry to a celebration of the friendship. See chapter six, 176, 286n25.

110 For a discussion of the meaning of tombs men shared and their connection to notions of male friendship and alliance, see Bray, *The Friend.* On the consequent exclusion of women, see ibid., 11.

111 Berardelli sought repayment directly, through the material benefits he would have expected for his dedication to Soranzo (see chapter five, 140) and, indirectly, through the advancement of his career he pursued by means of the volume.

112 In the end the Barbarigo women did not suffer such ill consequences, in part because Trevisan had been banished by the time of Barbarigo's death in 1644. See Cozzi, "Una vicenda," 397–8. What was at stake, however, was considerable: Venetian patrician women usually had significant power over family finances, much greater than elsewhere in Italy. See Chojnacki, *Women and Men in Renaissance Venice.*

113 Sedgwick, *Between Men,* 1–2. Sedgwick (ibid., 1) hypothesizes "the potential unbrokenness of a contiuum between homosocial and homosexual." For studies of masculinity in Italy, see for example Finucci, *The Manly Masquerade;* Milligan and Tylus, *The Poetics of Masculinity.* On male sexuality, see Ruggiero, *The Boundaries of Eros;* Ruggiero, *Machiavelli in Love.*

114 Sedgwick, *Between Men,* 2.

115 See Bray, *The Friend,* 7.

116 LaGuardia, *Intertextual Masculinity,* 4; he adds that "one of the central material practices involved in the performance of masculinity for an important class of men in the early modern period was that of reading and writing." Ibid., 6.

117 Sedgwick, *Between Men,* 25.

118 Ibid., 21–7.

119 Quaintance, *Textual Masculinity,* 10.

120 Hughes, "Distinguishing Signs," 29. Hughes (ibid., 30) asks, in fact, "If Jews were like prostitutes, were Jewish women whores?" and notes that legislation in certain parts of Italy pointed to such an association.

121 Quaintance, *Textual Masculinity,* 27. See also Bates, *Masculinity,* 93.

122 Ibid., 49.

123 See n1 above.

124 On *De' ragguagli di Parnaso,* see also the introduction, 8. The two volumes of *ragguagli,* soon supplemented with other *ragguagli,* were published

repeatedly throughout the seventeenth century, most frequently in Venice. The Guerigli press, for example, issued the volume twelve times between 1614 and 1680. See L. Firpo, "Boccalini, Traiano," 15. The work was also printed frequently elsewhere in Italy and around Europe, in Italian and in translation.

125 By 1624, for example, the Guerigli press published the fifth edition of the work.

126 The "Avisi" manuscript (3r) provides only sparse details about this betrayal: a sonnet following the dedication is addressed to Trevisan "on the incident with Strozzi that befell him" (per il caso sucessoli con lo Strozzi). Though Strozzi is not mentioned with his first name, Harrán (Copia Sulam, *Jewish Poet and Intellectual*, 355–6n27) convincingly identifies him as Giulio. A successive sonnet also addressed to Trevisan on the same incident suggests that Strozzi committed a real or figurative act of violence against him: "Non have l'empietà più fiero oggetto / de l'amico inimico; ma s'ei stringe / contro al'amico il ferro, o come è duro" (Impiety has no fiercer tool / than the unfriendly friend; and if he turns / his dagger against his friend, O how hard it is!). "Avisi," 4r. Harrán (Copia Sulam, *Jewish Poet and Intellectual*, 355–6, 351n10) suggests that Strozzi turned on Trevisan, his benefactor, whom the writer tried to stab or to challenge to a duel while the latter was visiting Strozzi's home. However, the "dagger" could also be meant metaphorically.

127 See chapter five, 144.

128 "in persona della hebrea." "Avisi," 3r. Harrán (Copia Sulam, *Jewish Poet and Intellectual*, 353n18) suggests it was authored by Solinga, possibly with Copia Sulam's collaboration. The question of authorship is addressed in chapter five, 158–63.

129 "somma pietà"; "fu larga dispensatrice." "Avisi," 7v–8r.

130 "essegranda ingratitudine." Ibid., 12v.

131 "Ogni eccesso ch'infame rende un core, / Ogni slealtà che da viltà deriva." Ibid., 13v.

132 "l'angue nel seno e ne lo snidi fuore / Pria che lo asperga di rabbia nociva." Ibid., 14r.

133 "a bello studio quello che di buono [c'era] entro a quei framenti ... di quello, dico, ne ha fatto tronchi per avalorare le sue infami mentite." Ibid., 19v.

134 "Danni e perigli per l'amico suo signor Numidio Paluzzi." Paluzzi, *Rime*, A5v.

135 "per lo eccesso dei suoi latrocini." "Avisi," 20v.

136 "Ah, infame con un tiro ha creduto di far più colpi: di parer zelante dello amico, di vendicarsi infamando falsamente la hebrea, e di ricoprire le sue infamie." Ibid., 22r.

137 "si lacerava la fama di virtuosa donna con espressissime menzogne e con essecrande maledicenze." Ibid., 15v.

138 Vittoria Colonna, a Petrarchan poet who was the most famous Italian woman writer of the sixteenth century, was praised as a model of virtue. Veronica Gambara was ruler of Correggio and another famous Petrarchan poet. On Boccalini's satire of Colonna and Gambara, see the introduction, 8. Isabella Andreini was an Italian actress, poet, and playwright born in Padua to Venetian parents. Corinna (fifth century BCE) and Sappho (seventh/sixth century BCE) were poets from ancient Greece; Sappho was regarded as one of the greatest poets of antiquity. The combination of Colonna and Gambara with Corinna and Sappho could be rooted in textual traditions that portray Colonna and Gambara as equalling, or even exceeding, the glories of their ancient forebears. See Cox, *Women's Writing in Italy*, 64, 77–8. While Andreini's inclusion is more unexpected, it may be explained by an "enduring admiration of and surprising lack of hostility towards Andreini, an actress and a writer with a decidedly pro-woman stance." Ray, *Writing Gender*, 181.

139 Aretino, who was known as the "scourge of princes" for his biting satire of figures of authority, also turned his pen against women.

140 For some of the wrongs the manuscript mentions, see "Avisi," 25r, 26r, 42v.

141 "Quel peccente guataro, quel sporco ruffiano, quel dispregiator della legge, quello incestuoso bue, quell'osceno stalone, quel pincerna de biri ... quello Araldo della infamia, quel testimonio della menzogna, quello albergo di perfidia, quel ritratto della sfacciatagine! ... quel chiromante, quel piromante che havea possibilità di commandare agli spiriti ... quello spaventoso mago, degno allievo della negra guatara." Ibid., 35r–35v. The transcription here is partially based on Boccato, "Manoscritto," 153. On the troubling characterizations of race in the manuscript, see chapter five, 166.

142 "Ardisci di appresentarti dinanzi a huomo di preclarissima integrità a cui la Giustitia appoggia il suo decoro, nel petto del quale tutte le heroiche virtudi hanno il suo nido, nel cui senno confida una tanta republica se stessa ... E di huomo tale un tuo pari vuol fasciarsi? Un qual tu se' sciagurato tanto prosume?" "Avisi," 44r.

143 Annibale Grimaldo is unidentified. See Harrán's note in Copia Sulam, *Jewish Poet and Intellectual*, 464n601.

144 The reference is to Briareus, mentioned explicitly in Grimaldo's poem at verse 2 ("Avisi," 84v), one of the three Hecatoncheires (one-hundred-handed, fifty-headed giants) who helped the Olympians defeat the Titans by throwing mountain-like rocks at them.

145 In the manuscript's Parnassian trial (ibid., 56r), Aretino concludes his tirade against the defendant by condemning him for scurrilously criticizing famous Italian writers from Petrarch and Ariosto to Marino. When the latter two writers, on a Parnassian stroll, happen by Paluzzi's trial, they are

indifferent to the fact that Paluzzi, an "ox" (*bue*) and "pedant" (*pedante*), has insulted them.

146 "O Vinegia, Vinegia, a te mi volgo, ecco ... le lor false imputationi e con qual sfaciatagine restino nelle carte signate e impresse nelle tue stampe!" Ibid., 35r.

147 "non seppe mai né la perfidia dello autore, né la detestabile iniquità del famiglio." Ibid., 59r. This interpretation recalls the anonymous letter's condemnation of Berardelli for involving his well-reputed dedicatee. See chapter five, 153.

148 Cf. Boccaccio, *Decameron*, 1:490n5 (novella 4.2).

149 "E chi è, trattone quel ladro, che affermi lui mai essersi vantato di haver composto il *Manifesto*, scrittura intessuta senza alcuno studio, solo fatta dalla hebrea per sencierarsi col mondo di quella nota onde a torto fu incaricata." "Avisi," 72v.

150 These critics include Harrán, "Introduction," 57–61; Fonseca-Wollheim, "Faith and Fame," 154–6; Boccato, "Manoscritto," 114; Cox, *Women's Writing in Italy*, 218–19; Adelman, "Educational and Literary Activities," 23; Fortis, *La "bella ebrea,"* 88.

151 For an exception to this assumption, see Harrán, "Introduction," 61.

152 See the introduction, 9; chapter three, 256n79; and chapter five, 137.

153 See for example "Avisi," 32v; Copia Sulam, *Manifesto*, C4r. This reference in the "Avisi" appears in the letter purportedly authored by Rosa; if the letter is indeed by Rosa, the similarity could indicate the *Manifesto*'s influence on, or even Copia Sulam's direct involvement in, his writing. See also chapter five, 157–8, for similar language in the two works.

154 "essendo io così nemica di sottopormi agli occhi del mondo nelle stampe come voi ve ne mostrate vago." Copia Sulam, *Manifesto*, C4v. See chapter three, 82–9.

155 Poems of Copia Sulam were published by Gabriele Zinano in 1627 but had been composed earlier. See chapter one, 46–7, and chapter six, 171–5.

156 Regarding the identity of the scribe, see n166 below.

157 "diversi originali." "Avisi," 1v.

158 The manuscript states that the extent of Paluzzi's crimes against Copia Sulam "compel us to uncover the evil deeds [of Paluzzi]" (ci sforza di dover scoprir le celeragini [*sic*] [di Paluzzi]). Ibid., 11v.

159 Regarding the *Manifesto* controversy, the "Avisi" (72v–73r) points out "how many people there are in Venice who know about this situation, with whom that virtuous woman conferred to hear their various points of view" and that "so many honorable and virtuous people ... hastened to write in defence of that worthy woman" (quanti ci siano in Vinegia a ch'è noto questo casso coi quali pur si consigliò quella virtuosa per sentire di molti il parere";

"tanti honorati virtuosi ... per quella degna s.ra allhora si mossero a scrivere). The first edition of the *Manifesto* may indicate that Pietro Petracci was
one of these writers; see chapter one, 45, and chapter three, 79–80.

160 For example, "Avisi," 10r, 21v, 31v, 52r.

161 Ibid., 31v, 32v, 50v, 51v–52r, 72v–73r.

162 DeJean, *Tender Geographies*, 95. She describes "a concept of authorship not
based on a signature with a unique, stable referent."

163 For example, Copia Sulam is called "daughter of Israel" (figliola de
Israelle) and "honored Jewess" (honorata hebrea). "Avisi," 7v, 44r.

164 Giacob Sulam is praised for generosity, for example, at ibid., 51r.

165 Flavius's work was printed in 1619 by Giovanni Alberti, the publisher of
Copia Sulam's *Manifesto*. See chapter three, 78.

166 Boccato suggests that the manuscript was copied by Modena, a hypothesis
Adelman accepts, but both Boccato and Adelman stop short of claiming
that he authored the manuscript as well. See Boccato, "Manoscritto,"
115–16; Adelman, "Educational and Literary Activities," 22–3n51. See also
Fortis, *La "bella ebrea,"* 88. On the basis of a paleographic analysis, Harrán
("Introduction," 60) rejects the hypothesis that Modena copied the manu-
script, but instead says it is possible Modena was involved in its authorship.
Harrán also, with good reason, suggests attributing a sonnet at "Avisi," 90r,
to Modena (Copia Sulam, *Jewish Poet and Intellectual*, 476–7n677); he does
the same, less convincingly, for "Avisi," 98r (Copia Sulam, *Jewish Poet and
Intellectual*, 494n781) and for "Avisi," 100v (Copia Sulam, *Jewish Poet and
Intellectual*, 498n805).

167 Basadonna is not mentioned by name but the "Avisi" (73r) say this "illustrious man" wrote in defence of Copia Sulam during the *Manifesto* crisis.
He is called "a most illustrious gentleman who loved that young woman as
a daughter and was loved by her as a cherished father and revered by her
as a most loving lord" (il.mo gentilhuomo che qual figliola amava quella
giovane dalla quale ei fu riamato come diletto padre e riverito come
amorevol sig.re). Basadonna, who was a close associate of Copia Sulam by
the time of the *Manifesto* affair, was some twenty years her senior. Harrán
(Copia Sulam, *Jewish Poet and Intellectual*, 445n505) misidentifies this
figure as Cebà, who refused to support Copia Sulam in her conflict with
Bonifaccio. See chapter one, 51–2, and chapter four, 105–7.

168 The only exception to the general use of pseudonyms is a sonnet attributed to Rosa and revised by Paluzzi that is included in Rosa's letter to
Copia Sulam. "Avisi," 40v–41v. Harrán ("Introduction," 61n395) points
out that certain poems are also attributed to Boccalini and de la Vega, but
since the poems comment on the Berardelli–Paluzzi scandal, which post-
date Boccalini's and de la Vega's deaths, the compositions are clearly part
of Parnassus fiction and were written by unnamed contemporaries.

169 Among different hypotheses Harrán ("Introduction," 61) proposes regarding "Avisi" authorship is that the names of the unknown writers were "fictitious or anagrammatic so as to provide a disguise for their Jewish identity."
I agree that the manuscript in many places communicates a Jewish perspective (as discussed immediately below), but I think it likely that pseudonyms were used to disguise both Jewish and Christian associates.

170 "fratelli hebrei." For example, "Avisi," 90r, 98r.

171 For the Jerusalem reference, see for example ibid., 90r. For further discussion of this issue, see Harrán, "Introduction," 58–61.

172 For example, "Avisi," 96v, 98v.

173 For the timeline of the *Manifesto* controversy, see chapter three, 249n1
and 253n26.

174 See "Avisi," 49r. Copia Sulam fired Paluzzi and denounced Berardelli in
July, and the "Satire" was circulated in August. See chapter five, 128.

175 "correr volentieri alle stampe"; "dozinali e scioccamente composte." Copia
Sulam, *Manifesto*, C3v.

176 "in materia assai diversa da quella che poteva forse esser aspettata dalla
mia penna." Ibid., A2r.

177 "malignità o simplicità o trascuratezza." Ibid.

178 Love, *The Culture and Commerce of Texts*, 177.

179 See chapter three, 83.

180 "mente altera / ... non spera / da vil tenzon fama illustre destare." "Avisi," 84r.

181 "da un falso suono della costui dottrina invaghita ... da quella superficie di
sapere che una gagliarda chiacchiara in lui facea apparire, adescata." Ibid.,
5r. This characterization of Paluzzi's verbal seduction of Copia Sulam
inverts the traditional stereotype of women (sirens, singers, courtesans)
attracting men to danger through their voices and writing. For an examination of this age-old trope in a seventeenth-century Venetian context, see
Heller, *Emblems of Eloquence*, 16–17, 76–7.

182 "incauta." "Avisi," 9r. The other major criticism of Copia Sulam within the
manuscript regards her handling of her judicial case against Berardelli, where
the fact that she was "most careless and impatient" (trascuratissima e impatien-
tissima), confusing her case by switching lawyers several times, led Berardelli
to get off lightly. Ibid., 61v. I discuss this criticism in chapter five, 164.

183 "con gran cuore" and "con somma pietà." "Avisi," 7r, 7v.

184 "hanno quasi posto in sterminio donna che per la lealtà de l'animo e per
lo affetto che sempre mostrò ai professori di virtù certo non meritava di
caderi in mani sì scelerate." Ibid., 2r.

185 See chapter three, 93–5.

186 Cox, *Women's Writing*, 218–19.

187 "scoprir al mondo la verità, onde ogni uno conosca qual fu il perché onde
si mosse quel ladro a lacerarne il nome della hebrea." "Avisi," 12r.

188 "Caso è questo che forse apporterà maraviglia che persona pur stimata
di giuditio in queste reti si habbia lasciata cogliere; ma se si considererà
di quai panni vada ammantata la fraude e quanto facile sia a quei lo in-
ganare che sotto la cappa di mentite dottrine, di bugiarde apparenze, di
finti costumi, di false dimostrationi e di simulato zelo, cuoprono entro
ai loro cuori infami radicato il tronco di ogni più abominevole impietà
e di onde pullular mai sempre, anzi maturi sempre si trovano i frutti
del tradimento, forsi che cesserà la maraviglia e tanto più che dei sette
concertati in questa scelerata coniura, non vi era alcuno (come si è
detto) che, per notabile, longo e continuo benefitio, non fosse obligato
della vita a honorata donna, il che rese più facile lo inganno nel quale
si perseverò da quella indegna canaglia per doi continui anni." Ibid.,
12r–12v.

189 Paluzzi came under Copia Sulam's protection on the fifteenth day of
August – the feast of the Assumption – which in Venice celebrated the
city's protection by the Virgin Mary. Ibid., 7v.

190 "terra di promisione." Ibid.

191 "honorata"; "honorata e virtuosa"; "virtuosa"; "virtuosissima"; "illustre";
"degna"; "buona"; "pregiata."

192 "nefando"; "scelerato"; "tristo."

193 "comertio ilecito che il famiglio havea con la mora, il che si facea ... per
l'empietà del costume sempre disprezzante la legge." Ibid., 17v–18r.

194 "quello spirito famigliare, care dilitie della sporca negra." Ibid., 36r.

195 "incestuoso bue." Ibid., 35r.

196 See Lowe, "The Stereotyping of Black Africans," esp. 29. For the strongly
ideological and hierarchical perceptions of skin colour, see Lowe,
"Introduction: The Black African Presence," 6, 10. Lowe (ibid., 10)
observes that "Jews and black Africans may have clashed over their place in
this pecking order."

197 "vitio nefando"; "violar d'amor le leggi, e di natura." "Avisi," 57r, 66v.
On attitudes towards sodomy in Venice, see for example Ruggiero, *The
Boundaries of Eros*, 109–45; Davidson, "Sodomy in Early Modern Venice,"
65–81.

198 Guido Guinizelli (*The Poetry of Guido Guinizelli*, 20–1) wrote the manifesto
of the school, "Al cor gentil rempaira sempre Amore" (Love returns always
to a noble heart), which Copia Sulam's phrasing ("in cor gentil / sovente
alberga") recalls.

199 "curiosa e peregrina dottrina." Copia Sulam, *Manifesto*, B1v.

200 Ibid., A4v.

201 *Telo*, from the Latin *telum*: arrow; missile; shaft; dart.

202 *Vita* implies "eternal life" (see also Fortis, La *"bella ebrea,"* 140nn3–4);
Copia Sulam thus again marries the themes of poetic glory and spiritual
immortality. See chapter three, 96.

6 The Salon's Afterlife (Post-1626)

1 Zinano published one of his most important works, *Della ragione de gli stati* (On Raison d'État) in Venice in 1625–1626. On his attendance at Copia Sulam's salon, see also chapter one, 46–7.
2 See chapter one, 231n155.
3 Zinano, *Rime diverse*, 47–8. The poem says Berardelli suffered "harm and peril" (danni e perigli) for Paluzzi, a reference to the punishment for his crimes against the Sulams.
4 See chapter five, 276n89 and 279n134.
5 "gentilhuomo venetiano che si trovò a visitar una giovane ebrea detta la sig. Sarra Copia in in [*sic*] tempo che c'era anche l'a[utore]." Zinano, *Rime diverse*, 24.
6 There is a probable printing mistake in this verse – *intendio* appears rather than *incendio*. On the word *intendio*, meaning (in Genoese) a platonic lover, male or female, see Belgrano, *Della vita privata*, 455. If the word is read *intendio*, the translation would be "whence everyone falls for the sweet lover." However, with the repeated mentions of flames and burning in the preceding verses, *incendio*, fire, is a much more likely reading.
7 Zinano, *Rime diverse*, 24–5.
8 "A un'ebrea detta la signora Sarra Copia che amava le virtù del signor Anselmo [*sic*] Cebà ancor che morto." Ibid., 46.
9 "Ma se questa Bontà chiude le porte / A quel superbo cor, ch'a lei non crede, / Dove senza il tuo Anselmo havrai tu stanza?" (But if this Goodness shuts the doors / To that haughty heart that does not believe / What place do you have without your Anselmo?) Ibid., 46.
10 Superbi, *Trionfo glorioso*, 140–1.
11 See chapter one, 229–30n140 and 230n142, and the biographical note, 301n143.
12 See the biographical note, 198.
13 Berardelli contributed an encomiastic poem to the work. Michiele, *L'arte de gli amanti*, A11v.
14 "di molto giudicio, d'intelletto nobile, & spiritoso." Superbi, *Trionfo glorioso*, 122.
15 Paluzzi, *Rime*, A6r.
16 Michiele, *Rime*, 304.
17 Michiele, *Delle poesie*, 45–6, 177–9.
18 Manso, *Poesie nomiche*, A2r–A5v.
19 Regarding Berardelli's work as a painter, Michiele (*Delle poesie*, 45–6) discusses, for instance, Berardelli's painting of Michiele's beloved in a composition entitled "Comparatione tra 'l poeta e 'l pittore" (Comparison between the Poet and the Painter).
20 Paluzzi, *Rime*, A5v (see figure 5.5); Zinano, *Rime diverse*, 47–8.

21 He requests that Berardelli paint a portrait of Pers's beloved. See Pers, "A B.A. pittore perché facesse il ritratto della sua dama" (To the painter B.A., exhorting him to make a portrait of his lady).

22 "assai noto per la industria del suo ingegno." "Avisi," 15r.

23 Strozzi, *Il teatro delle glorie*, 167–8.

24 See chapter three, 78, and chapter five, 132, 150.

25 Liceti, *L'amicitia incomparabile*, 3–12. On their heroic friendship and its relevance to the demise of Copia Sulam's salon, see chapter five, 140–50.

26 Ridolfi, *Le maraviglie*, 1:14. In his composition, Berardelli emphasizes the power of words to memorialize images. The relationship between painting and poetry is a common theme in poems that regard him.

27 Accademia degli Incogniti, *Novelle amorose*, 472–83. Berardelli's novella featured a remarried, sexually dissatisfied widow who came with her husband to Venice from Lombardy. She arranged to fulfill her sexual needs with a Venetian nobleman by tricking her husband and framing the servant who would have revealed her with having stolen food and money – crimes uncannily similar to those that Berardelli was accused of in the "Avisi" (albeit on a much smaller scale in the novella). The widow's scheme prompted the narrator to ask ironically: "Is there any limit to women's shrewdness?" (Dove non giunge la sagacità feminile). Ibid., 483. Such representation of women's excessive sexual desire is frequent in Incogniti narratives. See Cosentino, "Dee, imperatrici, cortigiane," 292.

28 "Avisi," 20r, 36v. See chapter five, 144, and chapter one, 34.

29 In discussing his publication of Manso's poetry, ostensibly against Manso's wishes, Berardelli claims that he issues the work "by means of my presses" (per mezza delle mie stampe). Manso, *Poesie nomiche*, A4r. Baba printed in Venice from at least 1626 until 1659. Bruni and Evans, *Italian Seventeenth Century Books*, 131. He issued many works by the writer Maiolino Bisaccioni, who was secretary of the Accademia degli Incogniti.

30 See Berardelli, "Albuminscriptie." The inscription probably dates from 1641. For mention of the inscription, see also Gronovius, *Johannes Fredericus Gronovius*, 177.

31 Ibid., 28, 150.

32 "le virtù e il merito ... per sempre amico e servitore." Berardelli, "Albuminscriptie."

33 Berardelli, "Sonetto."

34 See chapter five, 154–5, 166–70.

35 Ferrari, *La maga fulminata*, A11v. See also Cox, *The Prodigious Muse*, 258.

36 See chapter five, 168.

37 See Heller, *Emblems of Eloquence*, 174–5.

38 During the late 1630s, Angelico Aprosio – who had a deep network of Venetian contacts, which he would develop further in the coming decade – was actively gathering information on Copia Sulam (see chapter six, 180), yet he makes no mention of her activity in these years.

39 Their correspondence was likely a principle factor in Cebà's posthumous inclusion in the academy, which coalesced after his 1622 death. See chapter one, 31.

40 Mandosio gathered the report on Copia Sulam from Aprosio in preparation of his *Bibliotheca romana, seu romanorum scriptorum centuriae*. On Mandosio, see Ceresa, "Mandosio, Prospero."

41 "Toccò al Paluzzi di fare la parte per l'hebrea, né bisognava stasse otioso. Io che l'ho conosciuta, so non haveva tanto ingegno." Mandosio, *Bibliotheca romana*, 2:113.

42 See the biographical note, 301n145.

43 "Non però fu farina del sacco della Sarra, ma di quello del Paluzzi, che si mascherò da hebrea." Mandosio, *Bibliotheca romana*, 2:114.

44 "usare verso di quella scortesie." Ibid., 2:114.

45 "Era ... capitato in Venetia un soggetto di qualità, francese, il quale invitato dalla fama si portò anch'egli in quella casa. Era bellissimo di aspetto, ond' ella poté dire, benché accasata con Giacob Sulam, *ut vidi, ut perij*." Ibid., 2:114. Aprosio cites from Virgil's account of rapture in love in the *Eclogues*, 8.41. The translation is from Vergilius Maro, *Virgil's Eclogues*, 51.

46 "ritrovata la strada di uccellarla." Mandosio, *Bibliotheca romana*, 2:114.

47 "Non fu difficile a farle ciò credere, non lassando gli hebrei di dar opera e credito all'arte magica." Ibid., 2:114.

48 The first part of Aprosio, *La biblioteca aprosiana* (504), makes passing mention of Copia Sulam in the entry on Baldassare Bonifaccio. The second, unpublished part of the work includes a long entry on Copia Sulam that repeated the same charges of plagiarism and thievery made against her in Paluzzi's *Rime*. See MSS A.III.4 (227–30) and A.III.5 (304–6), Biblioteca Durazzo, Genoa, also cited in Harrán, "Introduction," 75–6.

49 Biga, *Una polemica antifemminista*, 15.

50 Aprosio corresponded with all of these writers and would have interacted with them in person during his Venetian sojourn. The letters are held at the Biblioteca Universitaria di Genova (BUG).

51 On Tarabotti's success suppressing the publication of Aprosio's work, see Biga, *Una polemica antifemminista*, 67–92, esp. 86–7.

52 Aprosio [Scipio Glareano pseud.], *Scudo di Rinaldo*, b8v. The original edition was issued (by Herz) in 1646. See Benedetti, "Introduction," 23–4.

53 See for example Tarabotti, *Letters Familiar and Formal*, 237.

54 "La dedica Leon Modana [*sic*] alla signora Sarra Copio Sullam [*sic*], così celebre e famosa. Il p[adre] Angelico Aprosio nella seconda parte di sua Biblioteca Aprosiana, che M.S. ho veduta, parla assai male della medesima signora Sarra Copio Sullam [*sic*], ma io fortemente dubito ch'il padre Aprosio fusse ingannato da qualche malevolo, & invidioso della detta signora, essendo di questa razza d'uomini gran dovizia anche fuori della mia patria. Certo che Leon Modana [*sic*] fu dottissimo, né ciò può mettersi in dubbio; da oltre non conosceva Sarra Copio Sullam [*sic*] per

fama ... Avendola ... praticata non poteva ingannarsi, come forse poteva
in altri succedere." Cinelli Calvoli, *Biblioteca volante*, 3:344. The 1746
edition of the work I consulted misspells Modena's name twice, though
the entry is listed as "Modena (Leone)." In the dedication to *L'Ester* (3),
Modena wrote Copia Sulam's name as it appears in this entry. Cinelli,
Biblioteca volante, 3:344.

55 "le sue rare maniere e molte virtù e scienze, avanzando gli anni e 'l sesso."
Ibid. Cf. Modena, *L'Ester*, 3.

56 On the publication of the installments of Cinelli Calvoli's work, see F.R.,
"Biblioteca volante." The later publication of the work in four alphabet-
ized volumes specifies the original *scanzia* for each entry.

57 A nineteenth-century scholar reported that "originally, [Cinelli Calvoli's]
individual volumes were restricted to a small number of copies, usually just
to be given to a few scholars and friends." Tessier, "*Biblioteca volante*," col.
170.

58 The third volume, with his report on Copia Sulam, was published in
1746. On Cinelli Calvoli and the *Biblioteca*, see Benzoni, "Cinelli Calvoli,
Giovanni."

59 Harrán ("Introduction," 77, 77n491) blames her exclusion from these
general repertories on doubts over her authorship and her eccentricity as
a woman and a Jew in the "largely Christian and androcentric orientation
of mainstream Italian literary criticism." Her limited production, the relative inaccessibility of her works (especially the "Avisi" manuscript), and
the general disdain in later centuries for seventeenth-century writing were
likely also factors.

60 "Donna a cui fuorché il lume della fede nulla mancava." Crescimbeni,
L'istoria della volgar poesia, 4:153.

61 Crescimbeni, *Commentari*, 4:136.

62 "fortissimamente." Ibid.

63 "molto vaga della nostra poesia, nella quale compose presso che bene."
Ibid.

64 "fu pur vaga della nostra poesia"; "restò di lui presa." He also said "she
was no less beautiful than learned" (era non meno vaga che scienziata).
Quadrio, *Della storia e della ragione*, 2:1:278.

65 "Giovane spiritosa e dilettante di letteratura"; "si vuole che non fosse
lavoro di essa, ma di Numidio Paluzzi romano." Mazzucchelli, "Bonifacio
(Baldassare)," 1647.

66 Busetto, "Copio (Coppio, Copia, Coppia) Sara (Sarra)"; Busetto, "La leggenda erudita."

67 Veltri, "L'anima del passato," 221–2.

68 Ibid., 222. In a more recent work, Veltri ("Jewish Philosophy in the
Ghetto," 308) instead accepts her authorship.

69 Bergalli, *Componimenti poetici*, 1:125–6.
70 "famosa e non men dotta." Pentolini, *Le donne illustri*, 1:226 (canto 3). His account was heavily indebted to Crescimbeni.
71 "delicato suo poetare"; "di tenebre e di malaugurato squallore." Fachini, *Prospetto biografico delle donne italiane*, 148, 49, respectively.
72 "donna scienziata, perita nella musica, buona rimatrice, e degna di ammirazione nello stile epistolare." Gamba, *Lettere di donne*, 251.
73 Ferri, *Biblioteca femminile italiana*, 128–9.
74 [Legrenzi], *Galleria poetica di donne veneziane*, 21–3.
75 Wolf, *Bibliotheca hebraea*, 3:1162; De Rossi, *Dizionario storico*, 1:95.
76 "femina erudita." Wolf, *Bibliotheca hebraea*, 3:1162.
77 "coltivò la poesia e le scienze e si fece ai suoi tempi un nome." De Rossi, *Dizionario storico*, 1:95.
78 On Copia Sulam's growing appeal in the context of nineteenth-century Wissenschaft des Judentums, see Harrán, "Introduction," 79; Veltri, "Body of Conversion," 332.
79 Fürst, *Bibliotheca Judaica* (1960), 1:186.
80 Graetz, *Geschichte der Juden*, 10:146–8.
81 Geiger, "Sara Copia Sullam"; Levy, "Sara Copia Sullam"; Soave, "Sara Copia Sullam"; David, "Une héroïne juive"; Kayserling, "Sara Copia Sullam."
82 Ibid.; David, "Une héroïne juive."
83 Remy [Lazarus], *Das jüdische Weib* (1896), 170–84; "moral purity" (Sittenreinheit). Ibid., 179.
84 On Kayserling and Remy Lazarus in this context, see Gerstenberger, *Truth to Tell*, 38–9.
85 An English edition was issued the same year: Rio, *The Four Martyrs* (London: Burns and Lambert, 1856); the work was in a third edition by 1862: Rio, *Les quatre martyrs* (Paris: Charles Douniol, 1862). I examined this edition, in which Rio's profile of Ansaldo Cebà, "Ansaldo Ceba ou La martyr de la Charité" (Ansaldo Cebà, or The Martyr of Charity), can be found on pages 79–134.
86 Rio was interested in the spiritual qualities of art and his *De la poésie chrétienne* was "as much a book of religious devotion as art history." Sorensen, "Rio, Alexis-François."
87 Harrán, "Introduction," 83–6; Veltri, "Body of Conversion," 332.
88 Cicogna, "Notizie intorno a Sara Copia Sulam."
89 The manuscript is one of 5,000 that Cicogna preserved and passed to the library, along with 40,000 books. On Cicogna, see Preto, "Cicogna, Emmanuele Antonio."
90 The collection is titled *Sara Copio Sullam, sonetti editi e inediti raccolti e pubblicati insieme ad alquanti cenni biografici*. On Modona, see Buttò and Petrucciani, "Modona, Leonello."

91 A 1954 article by Enzo Sarot ("Ansaldo Cebà and Sara Copio Sullam") is reminiscent of Rio's treatment.

92 For details on recent criticism regarding Copia Sulam, see the introduction, 12–13.

Biographical Note

1 On the dating of her birth, see the biographical note, 191–2, and n80 below.

2 Her sisters, Rachel and Ster (Ester), are mentioned in her father's will (see n4) and in other notarial documents.

3 On Simon Copio's activity as a merchant, see for example ASV Catti Records, busta 3357, 319v (2 September 1586) regarding his shipment of cloth that was lost in a shipwreck. On his work as an insurer, see for example ibid., 358v–359r (14 October 1586); see also Tenenti, *Naufrages*, 141, 179, 186, 189, 229, 232 (these records are from the years 1595–1598). On Simon Copio's land holdings, see the biographical note, 188, and n28 below; for his moneylending, see below, n10, and Appendix A. Regarding the terminology for Jewish lending activities, see Ravid, "Venice and Its Minorities," 474: "The full Italian name for the establishment in which the transactions took place was *banco* (plural: *banchi*) *di pegni* [bank of pawns], which was shortened to *banco* or *banchi*, with the result that their owners and managers were often referred to as *banchieri* (bankers) rather than *prestatori* or *feneratori* (moneylenders), or more accurately, pawnbrokers." For this study, I will use the terms "loanbanks" to describe the *banchi di pegni* and "moneylenders" to describe the *banchieri*, except in a few instance in which I believe that "banker" better renders the status that the title *banchiere* conveyed; I am grateful to Benjamin Ravid for his extensive consultation with me about this matter.

4 The will, hereafter ASV Will of Simon Copio, is held by the Archivio di Stato di Venezia; it is described below and is transcribed and translated in Appendix A. Many other documents that regard her father and other close family members can be found in the ASV records of notary Giovan Andrea Catti, hereafter ASV Catti Records. See Bibliography – Manuscript Sources for precise ASV references. Regarding the translation of the term "banchiere," see n3.

5 Pullan, *Rich and Poor*, 567–8.

6 See Malkiel, *A Separate Republic*, 416n4.

7 "a causa del pesante giogo loro imposto dai vari stati e príncipi." Fortis, *La "bella ebrea,"* 34.

8 See Adelman and Ravid, "Historical Notes," 224–5, note y.

9 Soave, "Sara Copia Sullam," 15 (1876–1877), 197n2.

10 "altre mercantie, ori, arzenti, zoglie, et robe de diverse sorte." ASV Will of Simon Copio. His will listed assets of 23,000 ducats, invested in his

loanbank, plus these other objects, but an instrument of division between Simon's widow and his brother Michiel shows that only 10,000 ducats were Simon's; the other 13,000 belonged to Michiel, who had been in partnership with him (though the partnership was scrupulously 50/50, Michiel received more of the loanbank assets because he was owed money from an inheritance). ASV Catti Records, busta 3383, 236r.

11 The inventory, which is held in the ASV, is transcribed and translated in Appendix B.

12 "Although its significance should not be overemphasized, it should be noted that neither the will nor the inventory of the estate of Daniel Rodgriga [d. 1603], the Portuguese-born New Christian ... reveal any trace of books or anything else of a religious or cultural nature." Ravid, "The Sephardic Jewish Merchants," 132.

13 This figure can be derived from the instrument of division between Ricca Copia and her brother-in-law Michiel Copio after Simon's death. Simon and Michiel had been equal business partners in ventures in Venice, Zante, and elsewhere. See ASV Catti Records, busta 3383, 234v–237v, esp. 236r–236v. The document shows that Michiel owes Ricca 1,694 ducats for rents from land in Zante; 250 ducats and 232 ducats for debts the partners are owed; and 77 ducats from the slightly higher valuation of Michiel's household goods with respect to Simon's, for a total of 2,253 ducats.

14 See below, n91.

15 The 1607 instrument of division between Michiel Copio and Ricca Copia shows the value of these improvements belonging equally to the two parties (ASV Catti Records, busta 3383, 236v): "They agree that the house, or rather the improvements of the house of the honorable Michieli that they have in the Ghetto Novo must remain jointly owned by the two of them for now, and what they earn from it, minus the rent that they pay to the above-mentioned honorable Michieli, must be equally divided" (Sono d'accordo che la casa, sive li miglioramenti della casa delli Clarissimi Michieli che loro possedino in ghetto novo debbi restar a loro dui indivisa per adesso così che quello che traze di essa diffalcato l'affito che si paga alli detti clarissimi Michieli debbi esser per metà). This document suggests that the Copios may have subleased part of the property. On Jews' property rights, see the biographical note, 191, and n61 below. On the significant value *miglioramenti* ("improvements") could have and their relation to property ownership, see Concina, Camerino, and Calabi, *La città degli ebrei*, 51–8.

16 For additional information on currencies and their value in the Venetian Republic, see Appendix C.

17 These brothers are mentioned in the ASV Catti Records, busta 3384, 586r–586v. The records (busta 3357, 398r–398v) also mention a Gabriel, brother of Simon.

18 Kolyvà, "The Jews of Zante," 203. Simon Copio requested and received forgiveness for custom dues for goods – including raisins and cloth – on a ship that sank.

19 The notary the family used in Venice, Giovan Andrea Catti, began practising in 1577, but Moisè appears in his records starting in 1584 and Simon in 1586, a likely indication of their arrival dates in the city. ASV Catti Records, busta 3400, index.

20 Kolyvà, "The Jews of Zante," 200. Around 200 Jews were reported on the island in a 1527 census. Ibid.

21 Ibid., 204. Romaniot Jews had lived for many centuries in the Greek-Byzantine milieu.

22 Arbel, "Introduction," 117.

23 Ibid., 118.

24 Arbel, "Colonie d'oltremare," 960.

25 Though Venetians approved the petition of upper-class Zantiot residents to segregate the Jews in a separate quarter, the project did not materialize until 1712. Kolyvà, "The Jews of Zante," 202.

26 Ibid.

27 Arbel, "Colonie d'oltremare," 980.

28 This figure assumes that Simon, Michiel, and Moisè shared equally in the earnings from the land. Simon and Michiel bought out Moisè's share of the land in 1601 (Patiel seems already to have died) and promised to pay him 500 ducats a year for the currants the lands produced as long as the crops were plentiful. See ASV Catti Records, busta 3383, 237r; busta 3357, 319v.

29 See for example ibid., busta 3383, 237r, which describes their enterprises in Zante and "Barbaria," a term used to describe regions of northern Africa and Tunisia in particular. Simon also assigned an agent in Alexandria (Egypt) to resolve problems relating to a ship that sank. Ibid., busta 3357, 319v.

30 For his activities in Ceffalonia, see for example ibid., busta 3393, 266v–267r; for ties with its residents, see ibid., busta 3381, 338v; busta 3389, 211r. For his dealings in Ferrara, see ibid., busta 3389, 498r–499r; for Verona, ibid., busta 3395, 14v–15r.

31 "I do not want [my wife], under any circumstances, to send any of my capital out of Venice, either by sea or by land, but instead want all of it to be used in this city, for the benefit and use of my daughters" (et non voglio che in nessun modo la mandi alcuno delli mei cavedali fuori di Venetia, né per mar né per terra, ma il tutto sia traficato in questa città, per beneficio et utile de mie figliole). ASV Will of Simon Copio.

32 Despite overlaps, the *ponentini* and *levantini* considered themselves distinct and were considered distinct by the Venetian government. Malkiel, *A Separate Republic*, 106–11.

33 Soave ("Sara Copia Sullam," 15 [1876–1877], 197n2) says he examined Simon's will. The version examined for the current study (see Appendix A), written shortly before Simon's death, does not contain this information, but Soave may have seen an earlier document. Other elements – including the accurate reporting of the month of Simon's death, his wife's name, and the fact he had three daughters – lend Soave's account credibility.

34 Fortis, La "bella ebrea," 34.

35 Sarsalamon, termed "Jew from Zante," left 400 Zantian ducats to the synagogue sometime before 1612, money his son Giosef later paid. ASV Catti Records, busta 3396, 216v–217r. Giosef had business ties to Moisè, Simon, and Michiel and was perhaps a cousin. See ibid., busta 3381, 270r; busta 3383, 236v.

36 Malkiel, A Separate Republic, 109. Levantine Jews "had a strong Jewish heritage," whereas Ponentine Jews "had no solid block of tradition, heritage and roots from which to draw." The Ponentine Jews kept their records in the vernacular, "which suggests that these Jews were not comfortable in Hebrew." Ibid., 108–9.

37 Ravid, "The Sephardic Jewish Merchants," 128. See also Ravid, "Venice and Its Minorities," 477–8. Such trading rights, "clear testimony to the Venetian perception of the importance of Jewish merchants," were not given to over 90 per cent of the native Christian population (those who didn't belong to the noble or citizen clases). Ravid, "The Sephardic Jewish Merchants," 128–9.

38 He signed the 1603 pan-ethnic accord (see n6) on behalf of the German community.

39 Malkiel, A Separate Republic, 379n2.

40 Ibid., 104.

41 Ibid., 111, 111n2.

42 Katz, The Jewish Ghetto, 13, 61, 74.

43 See below, n105 and n145. For the different activities that characterized the Ghetto Nuovo and the Ghetto Vecchio, see Galeazzo, "The Cosmopolitan Ghetto," 154; Cassuto, "Architectural and Urbanistic Aspects," 213.

44 Benjamin Ravid, email to author, 18 February 2019.

45 The Grassini family was one of a small number of families whose members repeatedly held positions as officials in the Large Assembly, the ghetto's pan-ethnic general assembly. Malkiel, A Separate Republic, 118.

46 "mia comissaria et sola governatrice de quanto lasso." ASV Will of Simon Copio. Ricca's maiden name is given in the ASV Catti Records, busta 3389, 451r.

47 "dona, madona et usufrutuaria de tutto il mio in vitta sua vedoando." ASV Will of Simon Copio. Adelman ("Italian Jewish Women," 151) notes that a Jewish husband could name his childless wife "donna e madonna"

of all his property in order to protect her economic interests from his
relatives. Though Ricca had children, Simon's stipulation might similarly
have been designed to protect her interests from his brothers. See below,
n53.

48 Adelman, "Italian Jewish Women," 152.

49 A contract from shortly after her husband's death between Ricca and
Samuel Spera, whom Simon had assigned to manage the loanbank,
mentions that the contract had not been concluded earlier because of
Simon's long illness. ASV Catti Records, busta 3383, 500v–504r.
An epitaph states that he had been tormented in his final years by gout
in his hands and feet. Soave, "Sara Copia Sullam," 15 (1876–1877),
197n2. Spera was later an important leader in the Jewish community, serving in 1616–1617 as communal secretary. Malkiel, *A Separate
Republic*, 26–7.

50 Adelman, "Rabbis and Reality," 34.

51 Adelman, "Italian Jewish Women," 152.

52 Adelman (ibid.) notes that husbands would use a Christian notary to
testate, "given the uncertainties of providing for a female relative under
Jewish law."

53 In appointing Ricca usufructuary of his estate, Simon wished that "no one
bother her" (che la non possi esser molestata da alcuno), a provision that
protected her from his brothers' claims. ASV Will of Simon Copio. On
similar provisions in other wills, see Adelman, "Italian Jewish Women,"
151. See above, n47.

54 See A. Luzzatto, *La comunità ebraica*, 1:227, 418.

55 See ASV Catti Records, buste 3383–3399.

56 See Adelman, "Rabbis and Reality," 35. Regarding the Venetian context, see Boccato, "Aspetti della condizione femminile," 107. In the city,
in addition to the example of Ricca Copia, there is for instance Anna,
widow of Simon dal Banco, who is listed as one of the major renters of
property within the ghetto. Concina, Camerino, and Calabi, *La città
degli ebrei*, 59.

57 See Siegmund, "La vita nei ghetti," 883.

58 Sarra's husband Giacob was also involved in this partnership. See below,
n100.

59 Ricca gave her brother-in-law and his son the 3,500-ducat dowry for
this marriage at the end of 1611. ASV Catti Records, busta 3389, 472r.
Regarding the marriage, see also ibid., busta 3399, 267v–268v. A 1607
document separating Ricca and Michiel's economic interests already
made provisions for it. This same document indicates good relations
between Ricca and Michiel, as well as between the brothers: they say the

division occurs "lovingly ... with all parties in agreement and using the same love that has always ruled the shared capital and goods of these brothers" (amorevolmente ... concordemente e con l'istesso amore che ha sempre governato li cavedali et beni di loro fratelli). Michiel travelled to Venice for the official division of their property. Ibid., busta 3383, 234v.

60 Ibid., 236v. Marco Michiel is listed as one of the original owners of the buildings where the ghetto was established. In 1519, his property was one of the first to be expanded upwards. See Concina, Camerino, and Calabi, *La città degli ebrei*, 40, 44.

61 See ibid., 51–69. The Republic's acceptance of this practice is evident in the fact that, starting in the late sixteenth century, the profits of Jews who rented out property were subject to taxation by the state. Ravid, *New Light*, 160. In general, Siegmund ("La vita nei ghetti," 850) notes that Jews in Italy were allowed to modify the real estate they rented from Christians, including dividing, remodelling, or expanding the properties.

62 ASV Catti Records, busta 3383, 236v. See above, n15.

63 Ibid., busta 3395, 27v–28r.

64 Modena reported paying 44 ducats a year in rent in 1623. Empty apartments in the ghetto were available in 1632–1633 for annual rents of 60–70 ducats, while a Levantine merchant rented a fine house for 80. Adelman, "Leon Modena: The Autobiography," 42.

65 ASV Catti Records, busta 3395, 27v–28r.

66 Baskin, "Some Parallels," 45.

67 Adelman ("Educational and Literary Activities," 13) notes that "among Jews, especially when fathers and grandfathers were preoccupied, mothers and grandmothers regularly supervised the education of the young men in their family." In the case of the Copio family, such involvement would instead have benefitted the girls.

68 "svisceratissimo genitore"; "quell'inespressibile amore, che sempre mi portasti." Sarra Copia Sullam, *Manifesto*, A3r–A3v.

69 On this dedication, see chapter three, 83.

70 "I want each of my daughters to receive a 3,000-scudo dowry, as has been promised to my first daughter, named Sara, and I want Rachel and Ster, her sisters, to have the same for their dowry" (Voglio che sia datto di dotte a ogni una de mie figliole, scudi tremille per una, sì come è stato promesso alla prima mia fiola nominata Sara, et così voglio che habino Rachel et Ster sue sorelle per dotte). ASV Will of Simon Copio.

71 ASV Catti Records, busta 3399, 267v–268v.

72 See Appendix C.

73 ASV Catti Records, busta 3395, 15v–16v.

74 Adelman, "Italian Jewish Women," 145. Ferruta ("Simone Luzzatto," 364) discusses the "enormous sums" (ingenti somme) invested in the marriages of Simone Luzzatto's children – in one case, 4,100 ducats in dowry plus wardrobe; in another, 4,600 ducats.

75 See Modena, *Autobiography*, 107–8.

76 An act from 1609 lists Giacob as the "genero" (son-in-law) of Sarra's mother Ricca. ASV Catti Records, busta 3387, 374r. The marriage contract of Sarra's cousin Diana allowed a period of three years in which the wedding could take place. Ibid., busta 3395, 15v–16v. If Sarra's marriage contract was similar and was finalized by 1606 – as Simon's will suggests – her wedding occurred by 1609 at the latest.

77 Documents show that Giacob, who was from Mantua, was involved in business in Venice with Copia Sulam's relatives by 1608. See below, n98 and n100.

78 Soave ("Sara Copia Sullam," 15 [1876–1877], 198) dates their wedding to around 1612. Kayserling ("Sara Copia Sullam," 161) dates it to the beginning of 1614. Boccato ("Lettere di Ansaldo Cebà," 173) dates it to around 1613. A. Luzzatto (*La comunità ebraica*, 1:246) dates it to around 1612–1613. And Fortis (*La "bella ebrea,"* 35n) dates it to between 1612 and 1614.

79 Adelman, "Italian Jewish Women," 143.

80 This date concurs with traditional scholarship, which dates her birth around 1590. Soave ("Sara Copia Sullam," 15 [1876–1877], 197) dates her birth to around 1590. Modona (*Sara Copio Sullam*, 11) dates it to 1588 or 1589. Sarot ("Ansaldo Cebà and Sara Copio Sullam," 140) dates it to 1590 or 1592. Boccato ("Sara Copio Sullam," 104) dates it to around 1592. Harrán ("Introduction," 15–17) instead suggests that she was born around 1600–1601. His suggestion has influenced other recent scholarship. See Cox, *The Prodigious Muse*, 219. The documents I have found confirm the earlier dating of her birth.

81 For the couple's place of residence, see n105.

82 "Et prego che la mia consorte facia che le ditte mie fiole habino li sui mariti di loro satisfatione, però nelle cose licite, et honeste, et honorate." ASV Will of Simon Copio.

83 See Tarabotti, *La semplicità ingannata* (2007); Tarabotti, *Paternal Tyranny*.

84 Adelman, "Italian Jewish Women," 145.

85 For a document on Giacob's settlement with his family, see ASV Catti Records, busta 3389, 365v–368r.

86 Ibid., 486v.

87 For example, she was able to pay her preceptor, Numidio Paluzzi. She also paid to print her *Manifesto*.

88 See Chojnacki, *Women and Men in Renaissance Venice*, cf. Adelman, "Italian Jewish Women," 146. See also Ferruta, "Simone Luzzatto," 363.

89 For an instance of an unequal division of assets between sisters and the unfortunate consequences, see ibid., 354–5.

90 "Dapoi la sua morte voglio che tutto il mio haver vada in le predette tre mie figliole equalmente. Le qual mie figliole voglio et ordino che al tempo debito le possino testar et disponer de quanto che in esse perverirà doppo la morte de ditta sua madre liberamente, come a cadauna di esse meglio parerà, et lassarla et donarla come a esse piacerà et a chi esse vorano la predetta dimissoria che in esse ha da tornare doppo ditta sua madre cossì che le siano patrone sempre absolute de ditta dimissoria, perseverando sempre nella legge nostra ebraica, et stando alla obedientia de quella." ASV Will of Simon Copio. On the term *dimissoria*, see Appendix A, 302–3n9.

91 Though the value of Simon's estate would have fluctuated over time, depending on Ricca's management of the family's assets and larger economic issues, the figure is calculated according to the value of his estate after his death and the division from his brother Michiel: 18,500 ducats (see the biographical note, 187–8). This valuation assumes that Sarra's dowry had already been subtracted out of the estate, since her marriage had been contracted when her father died and the dowry already promised. Simon's will stipulates a 3,000-scudo (3,500-ducat) dowry – like the one he had promised for Sarra – for his younger two daughters. Subtracting out those dowries, the estate in Venice would have had a value of 11,500 ducats, to be divided equally by three (3,833 ducats per daughter).

92 See n15 above.

93 That is: 3,500 ducats plus 3,833 ducats, for a total of 7,333 ducats, plus her portion of the value of real estate improvements.

94 On Salamone de Rossi's dedication, see Adelman and Ravid, "Historical Notes," 232. On Rossi more generally, see Harrán, *Salamone Rossi*. A 1611 document lists one of Giacob's four brothers as Moisè. ASV Catti Records, busta 3389, 365v–368r.

95 Giacob appears in documents in Venice beginning in 1608. See ibid., busta 3386, 469v, 506v, where he lends money to a moneylender in the ghetto. See also n98 and n100.

96 Siegmund, "La vita nei ghetti," 858.

97 An October 1611 document details the economic division between Giacob and his four brothers (Moisè, Raffael, Salamon, and Aron), who still lived in Mantua. ASV Catti Records, busta 3389, 365v–368r. Almost a decade after Giacob had come to live in Venice, he was still considered Mantuan: a document from December 1616 (1617 *stile nativitate*) lists him as "Giacob Sulam, Jew from Mantua living in this city of Venice" (Giacob Sullàn

hebreo di Mantova habitante in questa città de Venetia). Ibid., busta 3396, 2v.

98 Giacob Sulam and Moisè Copio appoint each other *commessi e procuratori* in banking matters in 1608 (ibid., busta 3386, 431r) and in 1616 Giacob appoints Moisè his *procuratore et commesso*, again in banking matters (ibid., busta 3395, 42v–43r). In 1609, Ricca named Giacob her *procuratore e commesso*; in 1611, she named him her *procuratore* to deal with a business matter in Mantova (ibid., busta 3389, 232r–232v), and in 1613, she named him her general *procuratore* (ibid., busta 3391, 109r–109v). Moisè named Giacob his *procuratore* in 1618 (ibid., busta 3397, 138v–139r). Sarra's sister Ster in 1619 named her brother-in-law her *procuratore e commesso* in matters relating to her dowry after her husband's death (ibid., busta 3398, 238r).

99 On the appointment, see ASV Inquisitorato agli ebrei Documents, 581r. See also Boccato, "Sara Copio Sullam," 104n2; Malkiel, *A Separate Republic*, 424–5. It is not clear to what extent Moisè and Giacob ran the loanbank together; Giacob is frequently listed as its sole operator, for example in March 1614. ASV Inquisitorato agli ebrei Documents, 590r. Moisè nevertheless had an important role: in 1614 and 1617, for instance, he guaranteed loans for Giacob's loanbank. ASV Catti Records, busta 3393, 12v–13v; ibid., busta 3396, 15v.

100 Moisè's documented banking activity dates to 1607, when he lent 8,000 ducats to the Di Dattoli loanbank at the high interest rate of 10.5 per cent (the Copios usually lent money at 7.5 per cent). The money had originated in Simon's loanbank and passed to Moisè through a series of transactions: Michiel, Simon's brother and former partner, received a large amount of the money that had been in the latter's loanbank when Michiel and Ricca (who was managing Simon's estate) divided their economic interests; Michiel then paid a debt to his brother Moisè. ASV, sezione notarile, atti, b. 3384, 621r-v. The money thus passed from Simon to Ricca to Michiel to Moisè. Moisè and his son Abraham were helping to run the Di Dattoli loanbank in 1610. Ibid., 3388, 422v–425v. In 1608, Ricca loaned 4,000 ducats to the same moneylenders, an indication that she was involved in the loanbank, too, or at least underwrote it. It is not clear if these transactions conformed to banking regulation. See Malkiel, *A Separate Republic*, 74. Some of the capital involved in these transactions would eventually form the basis for Giacob and Moisè's banking enterprise. In terms of other lending activity, in 1608 the partners Giacob, Ricca, and Moisè lent money to Giacob's father Angelo at a 10 per cent per annum interest rate. See ASV Catti Records, busta 3389, 486v.

101 See ibid., busta 3396, 216r–216v.

102 Ibid., busta 3393, 250r–250v.

103 See Malkiel, *A Separate Republic*, 425n1. On the power of the assessment
    committee, see ibid., 80–91; Malkiel, "The Ghetto Republic," 130–1.
104 See Malkiel, *A Separate Republic*, 425n1.
105 Her death was registered on 19 January 1615 (1614 Venetian style): "Rica
    daughter of Giacob Sulam, aged one, died in the Ghetto Nuovo after a
    month of fever" (Rica fia di Jacob Sulan heb.o d'anno uno da febre mese
    1. G.to n.o [= Ghetto Nuovo]). ASV Death Records, registro 847 (1614).
    She might have been named for Sarra's mother, even though she was
    still living, a naming practice common among non-Ashkenazi Jews; or for
    Giacob's mother, whose name was also Ricca. The epitaph on the infant's
    tombstone underscores the heartbreak her death caused: "Dawn disap-
    peared before becoming day: / Ten months old was she, her name was
    Rebecca; / Her father was Jacob Sulam, her mother Sarra: / They for her,
    and she for them, foresaw the darkness of tragedy." Translated in Harrán,
    "Introduction," 20.
106 There is no record in the ASV of Jewish deaths in this year. See ASV Death
    Records, registro 849 (1618). Cf. Boccato, "Decessi," 20.
107 Leon Modena indicates the importance ascribed to childbearing in Jewish
    women's lives by means of the blessing he gave to his infant daughter
    Esther: "May she grow up to be married and have children." Modena,
    Autobiography, 102–3. This is also underscored in the 1616 manual for
    Jewish women published in Venice by Biniamin d'Harodono: *Precetti da
    esser imparati dalle donne hebree*, 10. Modena (*Historia de' riti hebraici* [1979],
    89) says a man can divorce a woman for not having children.
108 "Women teachers and women noted for their learning in the Jewish
    community were often – but not always – widows, showing that, as in the
    Christian community, pursuing marriage and learning were not essentially
    compatible." Adelman, "Educational and Literary Activities," 15.
109 d'Harodono, *Precetti*, 95.
110 "non deve scherzare né esser famigliare con altri uomini." Ibid., 95.
111 "Guai a quelle. Quanto sarebbe meglio che fuora di casa portassero la scuf-
    fia di notte e senza adornamento, e in casa si addobbassero per sodisfare a
    lor mariti e parergli belle e non alli huomini stranieri?" Ibid., 97.
112 See the biographical note, 192.
113 "In a society governed by Jewish tradition and law, women were, from a
    legal standpoint, subject first to their fathers' and then to their husbands'
    will." Siegmund, "La vita nei ghetti," 883. On Giacob's role in the Cebà
    correspondence, see chapter one, 43–5.
114 The Sulams employed at least a washerwoman and a scullery maid. See for
    example "Avisi," 17v, 35v.
115 See the biographical note, 194, and n103 above. Malkiel ("The Ghetto
    Republic," 132) notes the Jewish community's "tendency to constantly elect

the same people" to leadership positions. He also notes that, though the community tended to elect leadership from among the elite, this elite seems not to have coveted public office. See also Malkiel, *Separate Republic*, 15–16.

116 In an obvious reference to Giacob, a poem in the "Avisi" (58r) says that Berardelli's scheme "al'hebreo fe' cangiar fortuna e stato" (altered the Jewish man's fortune and position).

117 See chapter three, n135.

118 See the introduction, 5–6 and 213n12.

119 See chapter five, 128.

120 See chapter five, 161 and 283nn170–2.

121 See Bonfil, *Jewish Life*, 117.

122 "non mi sarebbono mancate occasioni, col cangiar legge, di migliorar il mio stato: cosa nota a persone di molta autorità, che l'hanno istantemente procurato e tentato." *Manifesto*, B2v.

123 See below, n139.

124 In notary Giovan Andrea Catti's records, Moisè appears as both insurer of cargo (see for example ASV Catti Records, busta 3387, 36or) and as a merchant himself (ibid., busta 3391, 39v–40r). See also the ASV records of notary Andrea quondam Benedetto Spinelli (ASV Spinelli Records, 234v). For Moisè's activity as a broker of agricultural products, see ASV Catti Records, 3383, 20v. For his real estate dealings, see ibid., busta 3393, 33r–34v, 186v–187v, 352v–354v; busta 3396, 128v.

125 See, respectively, Malkiel, *A Separate Republic*, 379n2; ASV Catti Records, busta 3387, 337r; Malkiel, *A Separate Republic*, 256.

126 See above, n8.

127 See the biographical note, 193, and n99 above.

128 See Malkiel, *A Separate Republic*, 74–5.

129 ASV Catti Records, busta 3385, 60v–62r (1608); busta 3389, 310v (1611); busta 3391, 94v–96r (1613); busta 3396, 28r–28v, 69v–70r (1617).

130 He and Ricca were in a dispute with Isach Luzzatto in 1618. Ibid., busta 3397, 16r. Charges were levelled against Moisè and his son Abraham with the Signor di Notte al Criminal for breaking a contract. Ibid., busta 3393, 239r. On another disagreement, in 1616, see Malkiel, *A Separate Republic*, 516.

131 The exact tie between Leon Modena's wife and Moisè Copio is not clear, but it may have been the reason for the initial contact between Copia Sulam and Modena, who became close literary associates in the 1610s, as discussed in earlier chapters.

132 Modena, *Autobiography*, 104–5. On a court case brought by Abraham "together with the community," see Malkiel, *A Separate Republic*, 149–50.

133 See Adelman and Ravid, "Historical Notes," 213, note n. Modena was in contact with the family of Moisè/Francesco in 1640, long after Moisè's conversion. Ibid.

134 Moisè continued to insure cargo after 1607: a 1611 document, for instance, lists him as the insurer of a ship going from Zante to Amsterdam that was taken by pirates. ASV Catti Records, busta 3389, 282r–282v. In 1617, he was involved with others in an insurance deal. Ibid., busta 3396, 10r. On insurance rules, see Stefani, *Insurance in Venice*, 2:358 (document 30).

135 See the biographical note, 191.

136 The ASV Inquisitorato agli ebrei Documents (290r–292r [1648], 293r–295r [1650]) show his continued real estate activities in the ghetto. These documents are misfiled in a 1574 folder.

137 1654 Venetian style. See ASV Will of Abraham Copio. Moisé evidently retained relations with his son Abraham, at least for a while: in 1626 he appointed his son to be his *procuratore e commesso* to collect his debts in Zante and Ceffalonia. An Abraam Copio, possibly a younger relative, was buried in Venice in 1689. A. Luzzatto, *La comunità ebraica*, 1:522.

138 For other details of his antics, see Katz, *The Jewish Ghetto*, 64–5.

139 "Moisè Coppio hebreo, et hora Christiano d'apparenza, et chiamato Francesco Zachia." See ASV Complaint against Moisè Copio. Adinah Miller found and transcribed this document, which she generously shared with me; she also found several other documents in this file that regard irregular behaviour by Moisè alias Francesco.

140 On this pamphlet, see chapter five, 161; for the reaction in the ghetto, see the biographical note, 196.

141 "Avisi," 86r. See chapter five, 168–70.

142 Boccato ("La mortalità nel ghetto," 113) estimates that around one fifth of the Jewish population succumbed.

143 See ASV Will of Giacomo Rosa; Boccato, "La rivelazione," 123–7.

144 See chapter six, 178.

145 "Sarra wife of Giacob Sulam, approximately 40 years old, has died from a fever that lasted three months in the Ghetto Vecchio" (È morta Sarra moglie de Giacob Sulam d'anni 40 in circa da febre continua mesi 3, G.V.). ASV Death Records, registro 996 (Necrologi di ebrei, Registro morti ebrei, 1631–1656). The registration of her death mistakes her age, since there is ample evidence (described above) to date her birth to the early 1590s. It is not clear when Sarra and Giacob moved from the Ghetto Nuovo – where they were reported to reside when their infant daughter died in 1615 – to the Ghetto Vecchio.

146 See n149 below.

147 She died intestate even though her father had stipulated in his will that each of his daughters would be able to bequeath the wealth he left them. Copia Sulam – whose death notice describes a months-long illness rather than a sudden death – would have had time to draft a will but may have

considered it unnecessary since she had no direct descendants. In the absence of a will, her property would have passed directly to her husband. Giacob also left no will in Venice, perhaps a sign that he returned to Mantua at the end of his life. I give my thanks to archivist Franco Rossi at the ASV who conducted an exhaustive search of wills from the period and rules out the possibility that either Sarra's or Giacob's will exists in Venice.

148 See chapter one, 24.

149 The epitaph on her tombstone in the Jewish cemetery of San Nicolò on the Lido reads, in translation: "The tombstone of the virtuous signora Sarra Copia, / wife of the honorable signor Jacob Sullam / (may his Rock protect and preserve him!) / The oppressive angel / Shot his arrow / And a foremost lady of fine discernment / Was destroyed and killed. / Wise was she among women, / A jewel for the miserable, / And of every poor soul / A friend and companion. / If she, today, / Has been irreparably deposited / As solace for worms, / Moths, and spiders, / On the day the Redeemer comes / God will say: / Return, return, / O Sulamite. / She deceased on the eve of the sixth day, 5 Adar 5401. / May her soul dwell at ease!" Copia Sulam, *Jewish Poet and Intellectual*, 521–2.

Appendix A: Last Will and Testament of Simon Copio

1 I am grateful to Sabrina Minuzzi, Antonio Mazzucco, and Daria Perocco for their generous help in resolving the transcription and translation issues that arose in preparing Appendices A and B.

2 The *cedola* was opened at Simon's death. Copy *a* can be found at ASV, Sezione notarile, Testamenti, busta 962.387. The location of copy *b* of the will is ASV, Sezione notarile, Testamenti, busta 962, registro iiii (protocollo).

3 Regarding the translation of this term, see the biographical note, 290n3.

4 "it will please the Lord God" (piacerà al signor Dio) was written after "when" (quando) in copy *a* of the will, but was crossed out.

5 The instrument of division between Simon's widow, Ricca, and his brother Michiel shows that only 10,000 ducats were Simon's; the other 13,000 belonged to Michiel, who had been in partnership with him (cf. ASV Catti Records, busta 3383, 236r). See the biographical note, 290–1n10.

6 See Inventory, Appendix B.

7 On currency values, see Appendix C.

8 Regarding this provision, see the biographical note, 294n53.

9 The *dimissoria*, or inheritance, is not mentioned by that term above. Simon here intends the rest of his estate (beyond the promised dowries), which his widow Ricca will have in usufruct during her life and will pass to his daughters at her death. On the term *dimissoria*, see Ferro, *Dizionario del*

diritto, 1:597. *Dimissoria* can also mean a wife's property in addition to her dowry (ibid., 596–7), but this is not what Simon describes here.

10 The valuation of Simon's estate takes into account his partnership with his brother Michiel. See the biographical note, 187–8, 291n13, 291n15.

11 The transcription of the final portion of copy *a* of the will appears between double degree symbols.

12 The transcription of the final portion of copy *b* of the will appears between double asterisks.

13 On the appointment of notaries in Venice and the imperial investiture they could also receive, see Bianchi and Howard, "Life and Death in Damascus," 235.

Appendix B: Inventory of Simon Copio's House at His Death

1 This document is transcribed according to the criteria set forth in Appendix A. This document can be found at ASV, Sezione notarile, atti, b. 12526, 138r–141r.

2 ASV Catti Records, busta 3383, 235v.

3 These could also be underpants.

4 See Vitali, *La moda a Venezia*, 322.

5 On the term ruba/roba and rubon/robon (the mention of rubon is immediately below, after the three mentions of ruba) see Vitali (*La moda*, 327–31), who notes that the garment was for the upper classes, often worn at parties or ceremonies.

6 See Vitali (*La moda*, 373–4), who defines tabì as "a sort of heavy silk, watered, used to make luxury clothing." It is similar to but heavier than regular taffeta. Minuzzi, *Inventario di bottega*, 53n16. Tabì and tabby share the same etymology, from the French tabis; tabby is "a general term for silk taffeta ... applied also to silks of uniform colour waved or watered" (OED).

7 High-relief brocade.

8 See Vitali, *La moda*, 175. A kind of cloth made from linen (or hemp) and cotton. The English word "dimity" derives from dimito; the modern English word denotes a slightly different type of cloth (cf. OED).

9 Fangotti is a dialectal variation of *fagotti*. See Cortelazzo, *Dizionario veneziano*, s.v. "fagottin."

10 Ulcinj (Dulcigno in Italian) lay on the coast, across the Adriatic from Venice, and was under Venetian rule from 1405 until 1571.

Appendix C: Currency Values

1 See Appendix A and Appendix B.

2 See chapter five, 271n8.

3 ASV Catti Records, busta 3389, 472r.

4 A chart of currency values in the years 1606–1612 can be found in
Paolucci, *Le monete / The Coinage*, 80. On the money minted during this
era, see also Papadopoli Aldobrandini, *Da Leonardo Donà*, 1–42, esp. 34,
37. The comments of Nicolò Contarini (later doge) give a sense for the
era's monetary chaos: "The market for small money was creating such
angst that no one knew how much gold or silver one was spending or receiving" (Premeva il negocio delle monete ridotte in tale angustia, onde
non v'era chi sapesse né qual quantità d'oro, o d'argento spendesse, né
ricevesse). Quoted in ibid., 2. The preamble to a 1608 law blames the
instability in the exchange rate between silver and gold for rising prices:
"The prices and value of all things have increased uncontrollably, with a
harm to everyone that is most evident" (Essendo per ciò accresciuto fuor
di modo il prezio et valore di tutte le cose con danno evidentissimo universale). Quoted in Magatti, "Il mercato monetario veneziano," 316.
5 See Appendix A, 302n5.
6 See Appendix B, 204.
7 See the biographical note, 291n13.
8 See the biographical note, 297n91.
9 Plus his portion of the value of improvements on the property in the
Ghetto Nuovo. See the biographical note, 291n15.
10 Pullan, "Wage-Earners," 157.
11 Aymard, *Venise*, 121. A *staio*, or *staro*, was 83.3 litres. Ibid., 172.
12 Pullan, *Rich and Poor*, 575.
13 See Appendix B.
14 ASV Catti Records, busta 3395, 27v–28r. See also the biographical note,
191.

Bibliography

‿ܒ‿ܓ‿

Note to Reader: This bibliography is divided into primary and secondary sources. Cross-references are employed when a given item in the bibliography appears within another item. This occurs most often with introductions to critical editions and with contributions to edited collections. A secondary source may thus be cross-referenced to a primary source and vice versa; for complete bibliographical information please refer to both sections of the bibiography.

Primary Sources

Manuscript Sources

ARCHIVIO DI STATO DI VENEZIA (ASV), VENICE

Archival documents from the ASV are listed below by short titles chosen to reflect contents (e.g., Death Records); complete ASV references follow these titles. ASV documents appear in the notes by short title (for example, ASV Death Records).

Beazian Records, 1621. Sezione notarile, Atti, Fabrizio and Lucillo Beazian, busta 608–609.

Catti Records on Copio and Sulam Families, 1584–1621. Sezione notarile, Atti, Giovan Andrea Catti, buste 3355–3400.

Complaint against Moisè Copio, 9 September 1625. Provveditori sopra Monasteri, busta 267 (Processi criminali e disciplinari, maggio 1621–26).

Death Records. Provveditori alla Sanità, Necrologi.

Inquisitorato agli ebrei Documents on Copio and Sulam Families, 1613–1650. Inquisitorato agli ebrei, busta 19.

Inventory of Simon Copio's House at His Death, 1606. Sezione notarile, Atti, Gian Andrea Trevisan, busta 12526, 138r–141r.

Spinelli Records, 1607. Sezione notarile, Atti, Andrea Spinelli quondam Benedetto, busta 11928.

Will of Abraham Copio, 1655. Sezione notarile, Testamenti, Pietro Bracchi, busta 176.149.

Will of Giacomo Rosa, 1630. Sezione notarile, Testamenti, busta 1178.216.

Will of Simon Copio, 1606 (copy *a*). Sezione notarile, Testamenti, Gian Andrea Trevisan, busta 962.387 (*cedola*). [All citations are to this copy.]

Will of Simon Copio, 1606 (copy *b*). Sezione notarile, Testamenti, busta 962, registro iiii (*protocollo*).

OTHER

"Albero genealogico della famiglia Cebà," 1599. MS B.VIII.1. Biblioteca Universitaria di Genova, Genoa.

"Avisi di Parnaso," ca. 1626. Cod. Cicogna 270. Biblioteca del Museo Correr, Venice.

Barbaro, Marco. "Genealogie delle famiglie patrizie venete," 18th century. MS It. Cl. VII, 925–8 (8594–8597). Biblioteca Nazionale Marciana, Venice.

Berardelli, Alessandro. "Albuminscriptie," 1634–1646. In Johann Friedrich Gronovius, *Album amicorum*, 65r. MS 130 E 32. Koninklijke Bibliotheek, The Hague.

– "Sonetto: Nella promotione dell'emin.mo sig.r cardinal Pietro Ottobono. Felice augurio," ca. 1644. Cod. Cicogna 2357. Biblioteca del Museo Correr, Venice.

Bonifaccio, Baldassare. *Delle amene lettere di Baldassare Bonifaccio libri XXIV. Che sono una satira di scelta, e piacevole eruditione*, 1616–1655. MS Silvestriano, 226. Biblioteca dell'Accademia dei Concordi, Rovigo.

Cappellari, Girolamo Alessandro. "Campidoglio veneto," 18th century. MS It. Cl. VII, 15–18 (8304–8307). Biblioteca Nazionale Marciana, Venice.

Copia Sulam, Sarra. "Lettera a Isabella della Tolfa," 1623. Fondo Doria D'Angri, parte 2, busta 688, "Lettere senza nome di destinatario" (1609–1698), 12r. Archivio di Stato di Napoli, Naples.

Pers, Ciro [Cirio] di. "A B.A. pittore perché facesse il ritratto della sua dama," 1666. MS Ferr. 1. Biblioteca Apostolica Vaticana, Rome.

Print Sources

Accademia degli Incogniti. *Le glorie de gli Incogniti o vero gli huomini illustri dell'Accademia de' signori Incogniti di Venetia*. Venice: appresso Francesco Valvasense, 1647.

– *Novelle amorose de' signori academici Incogniti publicate da Francesco Carmeni Segretario dell'Academia*. Cremona: dal Belpieri, 1642.

Accademia della Crusca. *Vocabolario degli Accademici della Crusca, con tre indici delle voci, locuzioni, e proverbi latini e greci, posti per entro l'opera*. Venice: appresso Giovanni Alberti, 1612.

– *Vocabolario degli Accademici della Crusca, con tre indici delle voci, locuzioni, e proverbi latini e greci posti per entro l'opera.* Venice: appresso Iacopo Sarzina, 1623.

Albert the Great. *Man and the Beasts: De animalibus (Books 22–26).* Translated by James J. Scanlan. Binghamton, NY: Medieval and Renaissance Texts and Studies, 1987.

Alighieri, Dante. *The Vita Nuova or New Life of Dante Alighieri.* Translated by Frances de Meÿ. London: George Bell and Sons, 1902.

– *Vita nuova.* Milan: Garzanti, 2002.

Aprosio, Angelico [Cornelio Aspasio Antivigilmi, pseud.]. *La biblioteca aprosiana, passatempo autunnale.* Bologna: per li Manolessi, 1673.

– [Scipio Glareano, pseud.]. *Scudo di Rinaldo overo Lo specchio del disinganno.* Venice: appresso Gio. Iacomo Herz, 1654.

Aretino, Pietro. *De le lettere ... libro primo.* Venice: per Francesco Marcolini da Forlì, apresso a la chiesa de la Terneta, 1538.

Ariosto, Lodovico. *Orlando furioso.* Venice: appresso Giovanni Alberti, 1597.

Aristotle. *De anima.* Translated by R.D. Hicks. Cambridge, UK: Cambridge University Press, 1907. https://archive.org/details/aristotledeanimaoo 5947mbp/page/n141.

– *De anima.* Translated and edited by Christopher Shields. Oxford: Oxford University Press, 2016.

– *Metaphysics: Vol. 1, Books 1–9.* Translated by Hugh Tredennick. Cambridge, MA: Harvard University Press, 1933.

Battiferra degli Ammannati, Laura. *Laura Battiferra and Her Literary Circle: An Anthology.* Translated and edited by Victoria Kirkham. Chicago: University of Chicago Press, 2007.

Bellarino, Giovanni. *Doctrina catholica, ex sacro concilio tridentino et catechismo romano.* Venice: apud Ioannem de Albertis & Georgium Valentinum, 1620.

Bergalli, Luisa, ed. *Componimenti poetici delle più illustri rimatrici d'ogni secolo.* 2 vols. Venice: appresso Antonio Mora, 1726.

Boccaccio, Giovanni. *Decameron.* Edited by Vittore Branca. 3rd ed. 2 vols. Turin: Einaudi, 1992.

– *The Decameron.* Translated and edited by Wayne A. Rebhorn. New York and London: W.W. Norton & Company, 2013.

Boccalini, Traiano. *Advices from Parnassus, in Two Centuries, with the Political Touchstone, and an Appendix to It.* Edited by John Hughes. London: Printed by J.D. for Daniel Brown, 1706.

– *Delli avvisi di Parnaso, overo Compendio de' ragguagli di Trainano Boccalini centurie quattro.* Venice: appresso Francesco Prati, 1619.

– *De' ragguagli di Parnaso. Centuria prima.* Venice: appresso Pietro Farri, 1612.

– *De' ragguagli di Parnaso. Centuria seconda.* Venice: appresso Barezzo Barezzi, 1613.

Bonaventure. *Itinerarium mentis in Deum.* In Bonaventure, *Opera omnia,* edited by
    A.C. Peltier, 12:1–21. Paris: Ludovicus Vives, 1868.
Bonifaccio, Baldassare. *Amata. Tragedia.* Venice: appresso Antonio Pinelli, 1622.
– *Dell'aristocrazia, discorso.* Venice: appresso Antonio Pinelli, 1620.
– *Dell'immortalità dell'anima, discorso.* Venice: appresso Antonio Pinelli, 1621.
– *Oratione ... all'illustrissimo sig. Hieronimo Priuli, podestà e capitano di Rovigo e
    proveditor generale nel Polesino.* Venice: per Antonio Pinelli, stampator ducale,
    1620.
– *Pro inauguratione Ioannis Theupoli patriarchae venetiarum ... oratio e carmina.*
    Venice: ex tipographia Antonii Pinelli, 1619.
– *Risposta al Manifesto della signora Sarra Copia.* Venice: appresso Antonio Pinelli,
    1621.
– *Stichidion libri XVIII.* Venice: apud Pratum, 1619.
–, and Giovanni Maria Vanti. *Castore e Polluce: Rime.* Edited by Gasparo Bonifaccio.
    Venice: appresso Francesco Prati, 1618.
Bonifaccio, Gasparo. *Amor venale, favola boschereccia.* Venice: appresso Gio.
    Battista Ciotti, 1616.
– *Rosaio fiorito, a i meriti dell'illustr. sig. Vido Morosini podestà e capitano di Rovigo.*
    Venice: per Evangelista Deuchino, 1630.
– *Il vaticinio delle muse, opera scenica.* Rovigo: per Giacinto & Marino Bissuccio,
    1631.
Bujanda, Jesús Martínez de, and Marcella Richter, eds. *Index librorum prohibito-
    rum 1600–1966.* Vol. 11 of *Index des livres interdits,* edited by Jesús Martínez de
    Bujanda. Geneva: Médiaspaul-Droz, 2002.
Buoninsegni, Francesco. *Satira.* In Francesco Buoninsegni and Arcangela
    Tarabotti, *Satira e Antisatira,* edited by Elissa Weaver, 38–55. Rome: Salerno,
    1998.
Caesar, Julius. *Commentari di C. Givlio Cesare. Con le figure in rame di Andrea
    Palladio, le quali rappresentano a gl'occhi di chi legge, accampamenti, ordinanze &
    incontri di esserciti, città, fiumi, siti de paesi, & altre cose notabili contenute nell'his-
    toria. Di nuouo diligentemente corretti, e ristampati.* Venice: appresso Nicolò
    Misserini, 1619.
Campanile, Giuseppe. *Notizie di nobiltà, lettere di Giuseppe Campanile ... drizzate
    all'illustriss ... D. Bartolomeo di Capova.* Naples: per Luc'Antonio di Fusco,
    1672.
Campbell, Julie D., and Maria Galli Stampino, eds. *In Dialogue with the Other
    Voice in Sixteenth-Century Italy.* Toronto: Iter Press and the Centre for
    Reformation and Renaissance Studies, 2011.
Casoni, Guido, et al. *Giardin di rime, nel quale si leggono i fiori di nobilissimi pensieri
    di Guido Casoni, Tomaso Stigliani, Filippo Alberti, Gio. Leoni, Antonio Ongaro,
    Alessandro Gatti, Cesare Orsino.* Edited by Antonio Ongaro. Venice: presso
    Bernardo Giunti, Gio. Batt. Ciotti e compagni, 1608.

– *Ode ... seconda impressione.* Venice: presso Gio. Battista Ciotti, al segno della Minerva, 1601.

Cebà, Ansaldo. *Alcippo spartano. Tragedia di Ansaldo Cebà. A Marc'Antonio Doria.* Genoa: per Giuseppe Pavoni, 1623. [Also in Cebà, *Tragedie,* 133–92.]

– *I charatteri morali di Theofrasto interpretati per Ansaldo Cebà.* Genoa: appresso Giuseppe Pavoni, 1620.

– *Il cittadino di repubblica.* Genoa: per Giuseppe Pavoni, 1617.

– *Il cittadino nobile di repvblica.* Venice: presso Gio. Battista Combi, 1620.

– *Il Doria overo Dell'oration panegirica. Dialogo d'Ansaldo Cebà al Senato e popolo genovese.* Genoa: appresso Giuseppe Pavoni, 1621.

– *Epitafio d'Ansaldo Cebà per la memoria del Commendator Fra Gian Lanfranco suo fratello, alla valorosa militia de' Caualieri Gerosolimitani.* Genoa: per Giuseppe Pavoni, 1619.

– *Essercitii academici ... a Gian Battista Spinola di Giorgio.* Genoa: appresso Giuseppe Pavoni, 1621.

– *Furio Camillo.* Genoa: per Giuseppe Pavoni, 1623.

– *Le gemelle capovane.* In *Teatro italiano,* edited by Scipione Maffei, 2:343–424. Verona: Vallarsi, 1723. [Also in Cebà, *Tragedie,* 193–280.]

– *Il Gonzaga overo Del poema heroico. Dialogo.* Genoa: appresso Giuseppe Pavoni, 1621.

– *Lazaro il mendico.* Genoa: appresso Giuseppe Pavoni, 1614.

– *Lettere d'Ansaldo Cebà ad Agostino Pallavicino di Stefano.* Genoa: per Giuseppe Pavoni, 1623.

– *Lettere di Ansaldo Cebà scritte a Sarra Copia e dedicate a Marc'Antonio Doria.* Genoa: per Giuseppe Pavoni, 1623.

– *Oratione nell'incoronatione del Serenissimo Agostino Doria, Duce della Republica di Genoua.* Genoa: appresso Giuseppe Pavoni, 1601.

– *La principessa Silandra. Tragedia di Ansaldo Cebà.* Genoa: appresso Giuseppe Pavoni, 1621. [Also in Cebà, *Tragedie,* 3–131.]

– *Principio dell'historia romana.* Genoa: appresso Giuseppe Pavoni, 1621.

– *La reina Esther.* Genoa: appresso Giuseppe Pavoni, 1615.

– *La reina Esther.* Milan: per Gio. Battista Bidelli, 1616.

– *Rime a Leonardo Spinola Francavilla.* Rome: nella Stamperia di Bartolommeo Zannetti, 1611.

– *Rime d'Ansaldo Cebà.* Antwerp: appresso Marti Nutio, 1596.

– *Rime d'Ansaldo Cebà.* Padua: per Francesco Bolzetta, 1596.

– *Rime d'Ansaldo Cebà.* Padua: apreso Francesco Bolzetta, 1601.

– *Tragedie.* Edited by Marco Corradini. Milan: Vita e pensiero, 2001.

Che le donne non siano della specie degli huomini, discorso piacevole tradotto da Orazio Plata romano. Lyon [Venice]: Ventura [Francesco Valvasense], 1647.

Cinque sonetti in lode della illustriss. signora Cornelia Cornara Bragadina dignissima podestaressa di Treviso. Venice: appresso Giovanni Alberti, 1621.

Colbertaldo, Antonio. *Storia di Caterina Corner regina di Cipro. La prima biografia.*
Edited by Daria Perocco. Padua: Il Poligrafo, 2012.

Colonna, Vittoria. *Rime de la Divina Vettoria* [*sic*] *Colonna de Pescara inclita
Marchesana nuovamente aggiuntovi XXIIII. Sonetti spirituali, & le sue stanze, &
uno triompho de la croce di Christo non piu stampato con la sua tavola.* Venice:
Per Comin de Trino ad instantia de Nicolo d'Aristotile detto Zoppino,
1540.

Copia Sulam, Sarra. "Al molto illustre signor Baldassare Bonifaccio." In
B. Bonifaccio, *Risposta al Manifesto*, A5r–A6v.

– *Jewish Poet and Intellectual in Seventeenth-Century Venice. The Works of Sarra Copia
Sulam in Verse and Prose, Along with Writings of her Contemporaries in Her Praise,
Condemnation, or Defense.* Translated and edited by Don Harrán. Chicago:
University of Chicago Press, 2009.

– *Manifesto di Sarra Copia Sulam hebrea: Nel quale è da lei riprovata, e detestata
l'opinione negante l'immortalità dell'anima falsamente attribuitale dal sig. Baldassare
Bonifaccio.* Venice: appresso Antonio Pinelli, 1621. [Page references are to
this edition unless otherwise noted.]

– *Manifesto di Sarra Copia Sulam hebrea: Nel quale è da lei riprovata, e detestata
l'opinione negante l'immortalità dell'anima falsamente attribuitale dal sig. Baldassare
Bonifaccio.* Venice: appresso Giovanni Alberti, 1621.

– *Manifesto di Sarra Copia Sulam hebrea: Nel quale è da lei riprovata, e detestata
l'opinione negante l'immortalità dell'anima falsamente attribuitale dal sig. Baldassare
Bonifaccio.* Venice: appresso Ioanni Alberti, 1621.

– *Sara Copio Sullam, sonetti editi e inediti raccolti e pubblicati insieme ad alquanti
cenni biografici.* Edited by Leonello Modona. Bologna: Società Tipografica,
1887.

Corniani, Gianfrancesco, and Baldassare Bonifaccio. *Sinodia.* Venice: Apresso
Ambrogio Dei, 1612.

Cremonini, Cesare. *Apologia dictorum Aristotelis de quinta caeli substantia adversus
Xenarcum, Ioannem Grammaticum, et alios.* Venice: apud Roberto Meiettum,
1616.

– *Disputatio de coelo in tres partes divisa, de natura coeli, de motu coeli, de motoribus
coeli abstractis. Adiecta est apologia dictorum Aristotelis de via lactea* [et] *de facie in
orbe lunae.* Venice: apud Thomam Balionum, 1613.

– *Lecturae exordium habitum Patavii VI Kalendis Februarii 1591.* Ferrara: ex typo-
graphia Benedicti Mamarelli, 1591.

– *Le orazioni.* Edited by Antonino Poppi. Padua: Antenore, 1998.

– *Il ritorno di Damone overo La sampogna di mirtillo: Fauola siluestre.* Venice:
appresso Gio. Battista Ciotti, 1622.

da Costa, Uriel. *Examination of Pharisaic Traditions ... Supplemented with Semuel
da Silva's "Treatise on the Immortality of the Soul."* Edited by H.P. Salomon and
I.S.D. Sassoon. Leiden: E.J. Brill, 1993.

da Silva, Semuel. *Tratado da immortalidade da alma.* Amsterdam: impresso em casa de Paulo de Ravesteyn, 1623.

– "Treatise on the Immortality of the Soul." In da Costa, *Examination,* 427–554.

della Casa, Giovanni. *Galateo, or the Rules of Polite Behavior.* Translated and edited by M.F. Rusnak. Chicago: University of Chicago Press, 2013.

d'Harodono, Biniamin. *Precetti da esser imparati dalle donne hebree.* Translated by Giacob Halpron Hebreo. Venice: appresso Giacomo Sarzina, 1616.

Ebreo, Leone. *Dialoghi di amore.* Venice: appresso Giovanni Alberti, 1586.

Ferrari, Benedetto. *La maga fulminata.* Venice: presso Antonio Bariletti, [1638?].

Ferrari, Ottavio. *Prolusiones vigintisex. Epistolae. Et formulae ad capienda doctoris insignia. Item variae inscriptiones.* Padua: typis Heredum Pauli Frambotti, Bibliop., 1668.

Ficino, Marsilio. *Platonic Theology.* Translated by Michael J. B. Allen and John Warden. Edited by James Hankins with the assistance of William Bowen. 6 vols. Cambridge, MA: Harvard University Press, 2001–2006.

– *Platonica theologia de immortalitate animorum.* Florence: per Antonium Miscominum, 1482.

Fonte, Moderata. *Il merito delle donne ... oue chiaramente si scuopre quanto siano elle degne e più perfette de gli huomini.* Venice: presso Domenico Imberti, 1600.

– *The Worth of Women: Wherein Is Clearly Revealed Their Nobility and Their Superiority to Men.* Translated and edited by Virginia Cox. Chicago: University of Chicago Press, 1997.

Galilei, Galileo. *Le operazioni del compasso geometrico e militare.* Padua: per Paolo Frambotto, 1609. First published 1606.

Gamba, Bartolommeo, ed. *Lettere di donne italiane del secolo decimosesto.* Venice: Alvisopoli, 1832.

Gentile, Piergirolamo. *Della corona di Apollo, composta del piu vago de' fiori di Permesso ... parte seconda.* Venice: appresso Sebastiano Combi, 1610.

Grillo, Angelo. *Delle lettere del reverende padre abbate d. Angelo Grillo.* Edited by Pietro Petracci. 4th ed. Vol. 1. Venice: appresso Gio. Battista Ciotti, 1616.

Gronovius, Johann Friedrich. *Johannes Fredericus Gronovius, pèlerin de la République des lettres: Recherches sur le voyage savant au XVIIe siècle.* Edited by Paul Dibon and Françoise Waquet. Geneva: Librairie Droz, 1984.

Guinizelli, Guido. *The Poetry of Guido Guinizelli.* Translated and edited by Robert Edwards. New York and London: Garland Publishing, 1987.

L'heroica e incomparabile amicitia de gl'illustriss. signori Nicolò Barbarigo e Marco Trivisano ... celebrata ... da molti eccellenti ingegni del nostro secolo. Venice: Marco Ginammi, 1628.

Horace. *Art of Poetry.* In *Satires, Epistles, Art of Poetry,* 2nd ed., translated by H. Rushton Fairclough, 442–90. Cambridge, MA: Harvard University Press, 1929.

312   Bibliography

– *La poetica d'Horatio tradotta per messer Lodovico Dolce.* n.l.: n.p., 1536.

Imperiale, Gian Vincenzo. *Viaggi di Gian Vincenzo Imperiale.* Edited by Anton Giulio Barrili. *Atti della Società Ligure di Storia Patria* 29, no. 1 (1898): 7–278.

Josephus, Flavius. *Delle antichità e guerre giudaiche.* Venice: per Giovanni Alberti, 1619.

– *Delle antichità e guerre giudaiche. Nuovamente con diligenza ricorretto, & ristampato.* Venice: appresso Giovanni Alberti a Santa Foscha, 1619.

Lalli, Giovanni Battista. *Franceide overo Del mal francese. Poema giocoso.* Venice: presso Giacomo Sarzina, 1629.

– *Moscheide ouero Domiziano il moschicida, poema.* Venice: appresso Giacomo Sarzina, [1624].

Lando, Ortensio. *Paradossi, cioè sentenze fuori del commun parere.* Venice: appresso Andrea Arrivabene, 1563.

Lansperger [Lanspergio], Johann Justus. *La vita della b[eata] vergine Gertruda.* Translated by Vincenzo Buondi. Venice: appresso Giovanni Alberti, 1618.

– *La vita et le rivelationi di santa Gertruda.* Translated by Vincenzo Buondi. Venice: appresso Giovanni Alberti, 1618.

Las Casas, Bartolomé de. *Istoria o Breuissima relatione della distruttione dell'Indie occidentali.* Translated by Giacomo Castellani [Francesco Bersabita, pseud.]. Venice: presso Marco Ginammi, 1626.

Liceti, Fortunio, ed. *L'amicitia incomparabile de gl'illvstriss. signori Niccolò Barbarigo e Marco Trivisano, gentilhuomini venetiani celebrata con diuerse maniere di poesie et altre compositioni volgari et latine da molti eccellenti ingegni del nostro secolo.* Venice: appresso Marco Ginammi, 1628.

Litegato, Giacomo. *L'adige sconsolato, idilio.* Venice: appresso Gio. Batt. Ciotti, 1613.

– *La clemenza, panegirico.* Padua: per Livio Pasquato, 1632.

– *La vigilanza, panegirico.* Rovigo: appresso Giacinto & Marin Bissuccio, 1631.

Loredano, Giovan Francesco. *Bizzarrie academiche parte prima.* Venice: s.p. [Guerigli], 1648.

– *Delle bizzarrie academiche parte seconda.* Bologna: per Carlo Zenero, 1646.

Luzzatto, Simone. *Discorso circa il stato de gl'hebrei e in particolar dimoranti nell'inclita città di Venetia.* Venice: appresso Gioanne Calleoni, 1638.

– *Socrate overo Dell'humano sapere. Esercitio seriogiocoso di Simone Luzzatto hebreo venetiano. Opera nella quale si dimostra quanto sia imbecile l' humano intendimento, mentre non è diretto dalla divina rivelatione.* Venice: Tomasini, 1651.

Magno, Celio, and Orsatto Giustinian. *Rime di Celio Magno et di Orsatto Giustiniano.* Venice: presso Andrea Muschio, 1600.

Mandosio, Prospero. *Bibliotheca romana, seu romanorum scriptorum centuriae.* 2 vols. Rome: de Lazaris, 1682–1692.

Manso, Giovanni Battista. *Poesie nomiche ... divise in rime amorose, sacre e morali. Poesie di diversi a Gio. Battista Manso.* Edited by Alessandro Berardelli. Venice: appresso Francesco Baba, 1635.

Marinella, Lucrezia. *Arcadia felice.* Venice: presso Gio. Battista Ciotti, 1605.

– *Arcadia felice.* Edited by Françoise Lavocat. Florence: L.S. Olschki, 1998.

– *La Colomba sacra, poema eroico.* Venice: appresso Gio. Battista Ciotti Senese, al segno della Minerva, 1595.

– *Essortazioni alle donne e a gli altri se a loro saranno a grado ... parte prima.* Venice: per Francesco Valvasense, 1645.

– *Exhortations to Women and to Others If They Please.* Translated and edited by Laura Benedetti. Toronto: Iter Press and the Centre for Reformation and Renaissance Studies, 2012.

– *The Nobility and Excellence of Women and the Defects and Vices of Men.* Translated and edited by Anne Dunhill. Introduction by Letizia Panizza. Chicago: University of Chicago Press, 1999.

– *Le nobiltà et eccellenze delle donne et i diffetti e mancamenti de gli huomini, discorso.* Venice: appresso Giovan Battista Ciotti senese, 1600.

– *La nobiltà et l'eccellenza delle donne co' diffetti e mancamenti de gli huomini, discorso ... ricorretto & accresciutto in questa seconda impressione.* Venice: appresso Gio. Battista Ciotti sanese, all'insegna dell'Aurora, 1601.

– *La nobiltà et l'eccellenza delle donne co' diffetti e mancamenti de gli huomini, discorso ... ricorretto et accresciuto in questa terza impressione.* Venice: presso Gio. Battista Combi, 1621.

– *La nobiltà et l'eccellenza delle donne co' diffetti e mancamenti de gli huomini, discorso ... ricorretto et accresciuto in questa terza impressione.* Venice: presso Gio. Battista Combi, 1622.

– *La vita di Maria Vergine imperatrice dell'universo, descritta ... dalla ... sig. Lucrezia Marinella ... in questa seconda impressione da lei molto ampliata.* Venice: appresso Barezzo Barezzi, 1604.

Marino, Giambattista. *La galeria del cavalier Marino distinta in pitture & sculture. Seconda impression, corretta dall'autore.* Venice: dal Ciotti, 1622.

– *La galeria del cavalier Marino distinta in pitture e sculture. Terza impressione ricorretta.* Venice: dal Ciotti, 1626.

– *Della lira ... parte terza.* Venice: appresso Gio. Battista Ciotti, 1616.

– *Lettere.* Edited by Marziano Guglielminetti. Turin: Einaudi, 1966.

– *La lira ... parte prima ... parte seconda.* Venice: appresso Gio. Battista Ciotti, 1620.

– *La lira, rime ... parte prima.* Venice: appresso il Ciotti, 1625.

– *La lira, rime ... parte prima.* Venice: appresso il Ciotti, 1629.

– *La lira, rime ... parte prima ... seconda ... terza.* Venice: appresso Gio. Battista Ciotti, 1614.

– *Il Tebro festante.* Venice: appresso il Ciotti, 1624.

– *Il tempio, panegirico.* Venice: appresso il Ciotti, 1624.

–, and Gasparo Murtola. *La Murtoleide, fischiate del Cav. Marino con la Marineide, risate del Murtola.* Frankfurt: appresso Giovanni Beyer, 1626.

Masini, Elisco. *Sacro arsenale, overo Prattica dell'officio della Santa Inquisitione.* Genoa: appresso Giuseppe Pavoni, 1621.

Mauro, Pirro. *Tractatus de fideiussoribus: In quo tota fideiussionum, satisdationum & cautionum materia latissimè explicatur: omnibus tam in scholis quam in foro versantibus valde vtilis & necessarius.* Venice: apud Io. Baptistam Ciottum, 1622.

Meurs, Johannes. *Ristretto dell'Areopago.* Translated by Giovan Francesco Corniani. Venice: appresso Antonio Pinelli stampator ducale, 1626.

Michiele, Pietro. *L'arte de gli amanti.* Venice: presso Giacomo Scaglia, 1632.

– *Delle poesie postume … cioè: Le stravaganze, l'elegie, le risposte di molt' ingegni primarii e i ritratti.* Edited by Girolamo Michiele. Venice: presso Gio. Pietro Brigonci, 1671.

– *Rime … parte seconda.* Venice: appresso li Guerigli, 1642.

Modena, Leon. *The Autobiography of a Seventeenth-Century Venetian Rabbi: Leon Modena's Life of Judah.* Translated and edited by Mark R. Cohen. Princeton: Princeton University Press, 1988.

– *L'Ester. Tragedia tratta dalla Sacra Scrittura.* Venice: presso Giacomo Sarzina, 1619.

– *Galut Yehudah* (יהודה גלות). *Novo dittionario hebraico e italiano: Cioè dichiaratione di tutte le voci hebraiche più difficili delle scritture hebree nella volgar lingua italiana.* Venice: Appresso Giacomo Sarzina, 1612.

– *Historia de gli riti hebraici dove si ha breve e total relatione di tutta la vita, costumi, riti, et osservanze de gl'hebrei di questi tempi di Leon Modena Rabi hebreo di Venetia.* Edited by Jacques Gaffarel. Paris: n.p., 1637.

– *Historia de' riti hebraici. Vita e osservanze de gl'hebrei di questi tempi di Leon Modena Rabi H.o di Venetia già stampata in Parigi & hora da lui corretta e riformata.* Venice: appresso Gio. Calleoni, 1638.

– *Historia de' riti hebraici. Vita & osservanza de gl'hebrei di questi tempi … nuovamente ristampata & con diligenza ricorretta.* Venice: appresso Benedetto Miloco, 1678.

– *Historia de' riti hebraici.* Bologna: Arnaldo Forni, 1979. Facsimile of the 1678 Miloco edition.

– *Magen Vi-Tzinah.* In Abraham Geiger, *Leon da Modena, Rabbiner zu Venedig (1571–1648), und seine Stellung zur Kabbalah, zum Thalmud und zum Christenthume,* 65–105. Breslau: Kern, 1856.

Nani, Giovan Battista. *Historia della Republica Veneta.* Venice: per Combi, & La Noù, 1662.

– *Historia della Republica Veneta.* Bologna: nella Stampa di Gioseffo Longhi, 1680.

Nogarola, Isotta. *Complete Writings: Letterbook, Dialogue on Adam and Eve, Orations.* Translated and edited by Margaret L. King and Diana Robin. Chicago: University of Chicago Press, 2007.

Pallavicino, Ferrante. *La retorica delle puttane.* Edited by Laura Coci. Parma: Fondazione P. Bembo / U. Guanda, 1992.

Paluzzi, Numidio. *Rime*. Edited by Alessandro Berardelli. Venice: dal Ciotti, 1626.

Paoli, Pietro Francesco. *Rime*. Ferrara: nella Stampa Camerale, 1609.

– *Rime … amorose, pastorali, heroiche, funebri, morali*. Venice: presso Giacomo Sarzina, 1622.

– *Seconda parte delle rime*. Ferrara: nella Stamperia Camerale, 1619.

Passi, Giuseppe. *I donneschi difetti … aggiuntoui in questa quarta impressione, per compimento di essi, molte cose curiose*. Venice: appresso Vincenzo Somasco, 1618.

– *I donneschi diffetti: Nuovamente formati e posti in luce*. Venice: appresso Iacobo Antonio Somascho, 1599.

Pergamini, Giacomo. *Il memoriale della lingua italiana … in questa seconda impressione vi è il supplimento o giunta d'autori moderni*. Venice: appresso Gio. Battista Ciotti (appresso Fioravante Prati), 1617.

Petracci, Pietro. *Corona delle muse. Oda*. Venice: appresso Antonio Pinelli, stampator ducale, 1618.

– *In lode di … Giovanni Tiepolo … Oda*. Venice: appresso Antonio Pinelli, 1619.

–, ed. *Le muse sacre, scelta di rime spirituali de' più eccellenti autori d'Italia*. Venice: appresso Evangelista Deuchino e Gio. Batt. Pulciano, 1608.

Petrarca, Francesco. *Rerum vulgarium fragmenta (Rime sparse)*. In *Opere di Francesco Petrarca*, edited by Emilio Bigi, 3–264. Milan: Mursia, 1963.

Plato. *Phaedo*. Translated and edited by David Gallop. Oxford: Oxford University Press, 1993.

Poesie diverse per la partenza dell'illustrissimo signor Lorenzo Soriano podestà e capitano di Rovigo, e proveditore generale nel Polesino. Venice: per Antonio Pinelli, 1622.

Pomponazzi, Pietro. *Apologia*. [Bologna]: [Leonardi], [1518].

– *Defensorium*. [Bologna]: [Per Justinianum De Ruberia], [1519].

– *Tractatus de immortalitate animae*. Bologna: per Justinianum Leonardi Ruberiensem, 1516.

– *Tractatus de immortalitate animae*. Edited by Gianfranco Morra. Bologna: Nanni & Fiammenghi, 1954.

Pona, Francesco. *La lucerna*. Edited by Giorgio Fulco. Rome: Salerno Editrice, 1973.

Ralli d'Arezzo, Giovanni. *L'astrologo impazzito, comedia nuova e molto dilettevole*. Venice: Giovanni Alberti, 1607.

Ridolfi, Carlo. *Le maraviglie dell'arte, ouero Le vite de gl'illustri pittori veneti, e dello stato: Oue sono raccolte le opere insigni, i costumi, & i ritratti loro. Con la narratione delle historie, delle fauole, e delle moralità da quelli dipinte*. 2 vols. Venice: presso Gio. Battista Sgava, 1648.

Rocco, Antonio. *L'Alcibiade fanciullo a scola di Antonio Rocco*. Edited by Laura Coci. Rome: Salerno, 1988.

Rossi, Gian Vittorio [Janus Nicius Erythraeus, pseud.]. *Pinacotheca altera imaginum illustrium doctrinae vel ingenii laude virorum*. Cologne [Amsterdam]: apud Iodocum Kalcovium et socios [Blaeu], 1645.

– *Pinacotheca tertia imaginum virorum, aliqua ingenii et eruditionis fama illustrium.*
Cologne [Amsterdam]: apud Iodocum Kalcovium et socios [Blaeu], 1648.

Rutati, Giulio. *Cento ottave per le ... nozze del ... signor Federigo Ubaldo, principe
d'Urbino & della signora Claudia Medici, principessa di Toscana.* Venice: appresso
Giovanni Alberti, 1621.

Sannazaro, Jacopo. *Arcadia ... nuovamente ristampata & ricorretta & ornata di
alcune annotationi da Tomaso Porcacchi; con la vita dell'autore ... Rime ... novamente
ristampate et ripurgate.* Venice: appresso Giovanni Alberti, 1614.

– *Arcadia ... nuovamente ristampata & ricorretta & ornata di alcune annotationi da
Tomaso Porcacchi; con la vita dell'autore ... Rime ... novamente ristampate et ripurgate.* Venice: appresso Giovanni Alberti, 1620.

Sansovino, Francesco, and Giustiniano Martinioni. *Venetia, città nobilissima et
singolare, descritta in XIIII libri ... con aggiunta di tutte le cose notabili ... occorse
dall'anno 1580 sino al presente 1663.* Venice: appresso Stefano Curti, 1663.

Sarrocchi, Margherita. *La Scanderbeide, poema heroico.* Rome: appresso Lepido
Facij,1606.

– *La Scanderbeide, poema heroico.* Rome: Andrea Fei, 1623.

Speroni, Sperone. *Canace, tragedia: ... Sono aggiunte alcune altre sue compositioni &
una apologia, & alcune lettioni in difesa della tragedia.* Venice: presso Giovanni
Alberti, 1597.

– *Discorsi del sig. Sperone Speroni ... della precedenza de' principi, e della militia.*
Venice: appresso Giovanni Alberti, 1598.

Strozzi, Giulio. *Il Barbarigo, overo L'amico solevato ... seconda editione.* [Venice:
1626?]

– *Il Barbarigo, overo L'amico sollevato, poema eroica.* Venice: appresso Girolamo
Piuti, in Merceria, all'insegna del monte Parnaso, 1626.

– *L'Erotilla, tragedia. Saggio primo. 3a impressione.* Venice: per l'Alberti, 1621.

– *Eseqvie fatte in Venetia dalla natione fiorentina al serenissimo D. Cosimo iI quarto
gran duca di Toscana il d[ì] 25 di maggio 1621.* Venice: appresso il Ciotti, 1621.

– *Il natal di amore. Anacronismo.* Venice: appresso Giovanni Alberti, 1621.

– *Il primo canto del Barbarigo, overo Dell'amico sollevato, poema eroico di Giulio Strozzi.*
Venice: appresso Girolamo Piuti, al monte Parnaso, 1626.

– *Saggi poetici.* Venice: appresso Giovanni Alberti, 1621.

– *Le veglie quaresimali, overo L'officio della santa settimana.* Venezia: appresso il
Ciotti, 1626.

– *La Venetia edificata, poema eroico.* Venice: nella stamperia di Gio. Battista Ciotti,
1621.

–, ed. *Il teatro delle glorie della signora A. Basile, fabbricato alla virtù di lei dalle cetre
degli Anfioni di questo secolo.* Venice: per Evangelista Deuchino, 1623.

Superbi, Agostino. *Discorso dell'incomparabile et heroica amicitia de gl'illustrissimi
signori Nicolo' Barbarigo e Marco Trivisano.* Venice: n.p., 1629.

– *Trionfo glorioso d'heroi illustri et eminenti dell'inclita, & maravigliosa città di
Venetia, li quali nelle lettere fiorirono.* Venice: per Evangelista Deuchino, 1629.

[Tarabotti, Arcangela]. *Antisatira.* In *Contro 'l lusso donnesco,* Satira menippea *del Sig. Fran. Buoninsegni. Con l'*Antisatira *D.A.T. in Risposta,* 67–229. Venice: per Franc. Valvasensis, 1644.

– *Antisatira.* In Francesco Buoninsegni and Arcangela Tarabotti, *Satira e Antisatira,* edited by Elissa Weaver, 56–105. Rome: Salerno, 1998.

– [Galerana Barcitotti, pseud.]. *Che le donne siano della spetie degli huomini. Difesa delle donne, di Galerana Barcitotti, contra Horatio Plato.* Nuremberg [Venice]: Iuvann Cherchenbergher, 1651.

– *Che le donne siano della spezie degli uomini. Women are No Less Rational than Men.* Edited by Letizia Panizza. London: Institute of Romance Studies, University of London, 1994.

– *L'Inferno monacale di Arcangela Tarabotti.* Edited by Francesca Medioli. Turin: Rosenberg & Sellier, 1990.

– *Le lagrime d'Arcangela Tarabotti per la morte dell'illustrissima signora Regina Donati.* Venice: appresso li Guerigli, 1650.

– *Lettere familiari e di complimento.* Venice: appresso li Guerigli, 1650.

– *Lettere familiari e di complimento.* Edited by Meredith Ray and Lynn Westwater. Turin: Rosenberg & Sellier, 2005.

– *Letters Familiar and Formal.* Translated and edited by Meredith K. Ray and Lynn Lara Westwater. Toronto: Iter Press and the Centre for Reformation and Renaissance Studies, 2012.

– *Paradiso monacale.* Venice: presso Guglielmo Oddoni, 1663 [1643].

– *Paternal Tyranny.* Edited by Letizia Panizza. Chicago: University of Chicago Press, 2004.

– [Galerana Baratotti, pseud.]. *La semplicità ingannata.* Leiden: appresso Gio. Sambix [Elsevier], 1654.

– *La semplicità ingannata.* Edited by Simona Bortot. Padua: Il Poligrafo, 2007.

– *Women are of the Human Species.* In *"Women are not Human": An Anonymous Treatise and Responses,* edited by Theresa M. Kenney, 89–159. New York: Crossroad Publishing Company, 1998.

Tasso, Torquato. *Discorso della virtù feminile e donnesca.* Venice: appresso Bernardo Giunti e fratelli, 1582.

– *Gerusalemme liberata ... con la vita di lui e con gli argomenti dell'opera del Cav. Guido Casoni.* Venice: dal Sarzina, 1625

– *La Gierusalemme liberata ... con gli argomenti del sig. Gio. Vincenzo Imperiale, figurata da Bernardo Castello.* Genoa: per Giuseppe Pavoni, 1604.

– *La Gierusalemme liberata ... con le figure di Bernardo Castello e le annotationi di Scipio Gentili e di Giulio Guastavini.* Genoa: appresso Girolamo Bartoli, 1590.

– *Il Goffredo, ovvero Gierusalemme liberata ... con gli argomenti a ciascun canto ... et le figure a ciascun canto.* Venice: presso Gio. Battista Ciotti al segno dell'Aurora, 1599.

Terracina, Laura. *Discorso ... sopra il principio di tutti i canti d'Orlando furioso.* Venice: appresso Giovanni Alberti, 1598.

Tomasi, Giorgio. *Delle guerre et rivolgimenti del regno d'Ungaria e della Transilvania.* Venice: appresso Giovanni Alberti, 1621.

Tornabuoni de' Medici, Lucrezia. *Sacred Narratives.* Translated and edited by Jane Tylus. Chicago: Chicago University Press, 2001.

Torquemada, Antonio de. *Giardino di fiori curiosi, in forma di dialogo, diviso in sei trattati.* Translated by Celio [Orazio] Malespina. Venice: appresso Giovanni Alberti, 1620.

Uziel, Jacobo. *Dauid, poema heroico.* Venice: per Barezzo Barezzi, 1624.

Varie poesie di molti eccellenti autori in morte del m. illustre sig. cavalier Battista Guarini. Venice: appresso Gio. Battista Ciotti, 1616.

Vergilius Maro, Publius. *Bucolica, Georgica et Aeneis, una cum indice Nicolai Erythraei ... additis eiusdem Erythraei scholiis.* Venice: apud Ioannem de Albertis, 1616.

– *Bucolica, Georgica et Aeneis.* Venice: apud Ioannem de Albertis, 1621.

– *Virgil's* Eclogues: *The Latin Text with a Verse Translation and Brief Notes.* Translated and edited by Guy Lee. Liverpool: Francis Cairns, 1980.

Zapata de Mendoza, Antonio. *Novus index librorum prohibitorum et expurgatorum ... editionibus Philippi IV. R.C. & ab eius statu &c. de Consilio Supremi Senatus S. Generalis Inquisitionis.* Hispali: ex Typographeo Francisci de Lyra, 1632.

Zinano, Gabriele. *L'Eracleide.* Venice: per il Deuchino, 1623.

– *Le meraviglie d'amore pastorale.* Venice: appresso Evangelista Deuchino, 1627.

– *Della ragione de gli stati libri XII ... con due trattati, uno del Secretario, l'altro del Consigliere.* Venice: appresso Gio. Guerigli, 1625–1626.

– *Rime amorose.* Venice: appresso Evangelista Deuchino, 1627.

– *Rime diverse ... a diversi signori, & amici.* Venice: appresso Evangelista Deuchino, 1627.

– *Rime lugubri.* Venice: appresso Evangelista Deuchino, 1627.

– *Rime sacre.* Venice: appresso Evangelista Deuchino, 1627.

Zuccolo, Ludovico. *Dialoghi ... ne' quali con varietà d'eruditione si scoprono nuovi e vaghi pensieri filosofici, morali e politici.* Venice: appresso Marco Ginammi, 1625.

– *Nobiltà commune et heroica, pensier nuouo e curioso.* Venice: appresso Marco Ginammi, 1625.

– *Il secolo dell'oro rinascente nella amicitia fra Nicolò Barbarigo e Marco Trivisano.* Venice: presso Marco Ginammi, 1629.

Secondary Sources

Adelman, Howard. "The Educational and Literary Activities of Jewish Women in Italy during the Renaissance and the Catholic Restoration." In Carpi et al., *Shlomo Simonsohn Jubilee Volume,* 9–23.

– "Finding Women's Voices in Italian Jewish Literature." In *Women of the Word: Jewish Women and Jewish Writing,* edited by Judith R. Baskin, 50–69. Detroit: Wayne State University Press, 1994.

– "Italian Jewish Women." In *Jewish Women in Historical Perspective*, 2nd ed., edited by Judith R. Baskin, 150–68. Detroit: Wayne State University Press, 1998.
– "Jewish Women and Family Life, Inside and Outside the Ghetto." In Davis and Ravid, *The Jews of Early Modern Venice*, 143–65.
– "Leon Modena: The Autobiography and the Man." In Modena, *Autobiography*, 19–49.
– "Leon Modena, Sara Copio Sullam, and the Accademia degli Incogniti." In Calabi, Galeazzo, and Massaro, *Venice, the Jews and Europe*, 310–13.
– "The Literacy of Jewish Women in Early Modern Italy." In *Women's Education in Early Modern Europe, A History, 1500–1800*, edited by Barbara J. Whitehead, 133–58. New York: Garland Publishing, 1999.
– "New Light on the Life and Writings of Leon Modena." In *Approaches to Judaism in Medieval Times*, edited by David R. Blumenthal, 2:109–22. Chico, CA: Scholars Press, 1985.
– "Rabbis and Reality: Public Activities of Jewish Women in Italy during the Renaissance and the Catholic Restoration." *Jewish History* 5, no. 1 (1991): 27–40.
– "Sarra Copia Sullam." In *Jewish Women: A Comprehensive Historical Encyclopedia*, edited by Paula E. Hyman and Dalia Ofer. Jewish Women's Archive, 27 February 2009. https://jwa.org/encyclopedia/article/sullam -sara-coppia/
– "Success and Failure in the Seventeenth-Century Ghetto of Venice: The Life and Thought of Leon Modena, 1571–1648." PhD diss., Brandeis University, 1985.
–, and Benjamin Ravid. "Historical Notes." In Modena, *Autobiography*, 181–273.
Albertini, Tamara. "Marsilio Ficino (1433–1499): The Aesthetic of the One in the Soul." In *Philosophers of the Renaissance*, translated by Brian McNeil and edited by Paul Richard Blum, 82–91. Washington, DC: Catholic University of America Press, 2010.
Allen, Peter Lewis. *The Wages of Sin: Sex and Disease, Past and Present*. Chicago: University of Chicago Press, 2000.
[Apollonio, Ferdinando]. "The Primicerj of Saint Mark's." In *The Basilica of Saint Mark in Venice: Illustrated from the Points of View of Art and History by Venetian Writers*, translated by William Scott and edited by Camillo Boito, 145–70. [Venice]: F. Ongania, 1888.
Arbel, Benjamin. "Colonie d'oltremare." In *Storia di Venezia*, edited by Gino Benzoni and Antonio Menniti Ippolito, vol. 5, *Il Rinascimento: Società ed economia*, edited by Alberto Tenenti and Ugo Tucci, 947–85. Rome: Istituto della Enciclopedia Italiana, 1996.
– "Introduction." In "Minorities in Colonial Settings: The Jews in Venice's Hellenic Territories (15th–18th Centuries)." Special issue, *Mediterranean Historical Review* 27, no. 2 (2012), 117–28.

Arslan, Antonia, Adriana Chemello, and Gilberto Pizzamiglio, eds. *Le stanze ritrovate: Antologia di scrittrici venete dal Quattrocento al Novecento.* Mirano–Venice: Eidos, 1991.

Ascarelli, Fernanda, and Marco Menato. *La tipografia del '500 in Italia.* Florence: Leo S. Olschki Editore, 1989.

Aymard, Maurice. *Venise, Raguse et le commerce du blé pendant la seconde moitié du XVIᵉ siècle.* Paris: S.E.V.P.E.N., 1966.

Ballistreri, Gianni. "Bissari, Pietro Paolo." In *Dizionario biografico degli italiani,* 10:688–9. Rome: Istituto della Enciclopedia Italiana, 1968.

Barbierato, Federico. *The Inquisitor in the Hat Shop: Inquisition, Forbidden Books and Unbelief in Early Modern Venice.* Farnham, UK: Ashgate, 2012.

Barzilay, Isaac E. "Finalizing an Issue: Modena's Authorship of the 'Qol Sakhal.'" In *Salo Wittmayer Baron Jubilee Volume on the Occasion of his Eightieth Birthday,* edited by Saul Lieberman and Arthur Hyman, 1:135–66. Jerusalem and New York: American Academy for Jewish Research, 1974.

Baskin, Judith R. "Some Parallels in the Education of Medieval Jewish and Christian Women." *Jewish History* 5, no. 1 (1991): 41–51.

Bates, Catherine. *Masculinity, Gender and Identity in the English Renaissance Lyric.* Cambridge, UK: Cambridge University Press, 2007.

Belgrano, L.T. *Della vita privata dei genovesi.* 2nd ed. Genoa: R. Istituto Sordo-Muti, 1875.

Benedetti, Laura. "Introduction." In Marinella, *Exhortations,* 1–38.

Benzoni, Gino. "Le accademie." In *Storia della cultura veneta,* vol. 4, *Dalla Controriforma alla fine della repubblica. Il Seicento,* edited by Girolamo Arnaldi and Manlio Pastore Stocchi, 1:131–62. Vicenza: Neri Pozza Editore, 1983.

– *Gli affanni della cultura: Intellettuali e potere nell'Italia della Controriforma e barocca.* Milan: Feltrinelli, 1978.

– "Cinelli Calvoli, Giovanni." In *Dizionario biografico degli italiani,* 25:583–9. Rome: Istituto della Enciclopedia Italiana, 1981.

–, and Gaetano Cozzi, eds. *La Venezia barocca.* Vol. 7 of *Storia di Venezia,* edited by Gino Benzoni and Antonio Menniti Ippolito. Roma: Istituto della Enciclopedia Italiana, 1997.

Berliner, Abraham, ed. *200 Inschriften aus Venedig, 16 u. 17 Jahrhundert.* Vol. 1 of *Hebräische Grabschriften in Italien.* Frankfurt: Kauffmann, 1881.

Berti, Domenico. "Di Cesare Cremonino e della sua controversia con l'Inquisizione di Padova e di Roma." *Atti della R. Accademia dei Lincei, memorie della classe di scienze morali, storiche e filologiche,* 3ʳᵈ ser., 2 (1877–1878): 273–99.

Bettella, Patrizia. "Women and the Academies in Seventeenth-Century Italy: Elena Lucrezia Cornaro Piscopia's Role in Literary Academies." *Italian Culture* 36, no. 2 (2018): 100–19.

Bianchi, Francesco, and Deborah Howard. "Life and Death in Damascus: The Material Culture of Venetians in the Syrian Capital in the Mid-Fifteenth Century." *Studi veneziani*, n.s., 46 (2003): 233–301.

Biavati, Giuliana. "Castello, Bernardo." In *Dizionario biografico degli italiani*, 21:781–6. Rome: Istituto della Enciclopedia Italiana, 1978.

Biga, Emilia. *Una polemica antifemminista del '600:* La maschera scoperta *di Angelico Aprosio.* Ventimiglia: Civica Biblioteca Aprosiana, 1989.

Black, Christopher F. *The Italian Inquisition.* New Haven: Yale University Press, 2009.

Bloch, R. Howard. *Medieval Misogyny and the Invention of Western Romantic Love.* Chicago: University of Chicago Press, 1991.

Boccato, Carla. "Un altro documento inedito su Sara Copio Sullam: il Codice di Giulia Soliga." *Rassegna mensile di Israel* 40, no. 7/8 (1974): 303–16.

– "Aspetti della condizione femminile nel ghetto di Venezia (secolo XVII): I testamenti." *Italia* 10 (1993): 105–35.

– "Decessi di ebrei veneziani nelle registrazioni dei Provveditori alla Sanità." *Rassegna mensile di Israel* 50, nos. 1–4 (1984): 11–22.

– "Una disputa secentesca sull'immortalità dell'anima. Contributi d'archivio." *Rassegna mensile di Israel* 54, no. 3 (1988): 593–606.

– "Un episodio della vita di Sara Copio Sullam: Il Manifesto *sull'immortalità dell'anima.*" *Rassegna mensile di Israel* 39, no. 11 (1973): 633–46.

– "Lettere di Ansaldo Cebà, genovese, a Sara Copio Sullam, poetessa del Ghetto di Venezia." *Rassegna Mensile di Israel* 40, no. 4 (1974): 169–91.

– "La mortalità nel ghetto di Venezia durante la peste del 1630." *Archivio veneto*, 5th ser., 175 (1993): 111–46.

– "Nuove testimonianze su Sara Copio Sullam." *Rassegna mensile di Israel* 46, no. 9/10 (1980): 272–87.

– "Il presunto ritratto di Sara Copio Sullam." *Rassegna mensile di Israel* 52, no. 1 (1986): 191–204.

– "Le *Rime* postume di Numidio Paluzzi: Un contributo alla lirica barocca a Venezia nel primo Seicento." *Lettere italiane* 57, no. 1 (2005): 112–31.

– "La rivelazione delle cedole testamentarie: Procedura ed esempi in documenti veneziani del secolo XVII." *Archivio veneto*, 5th ser., 137 (1991): 119–30.

– "Sara Copio Sullam, la poetessa del ghetto di Venezia: episodi della sua vita in un manoscritto del secolo XVII." *Italia* 6, no. 1–2 (1987): 104–218.

Bonfil, Robert. "Change in the Cultural Patterns of a Jewish Society in Crisis: Italian Jewry at the Close of the Sixteenth Century." In *Essential Papers on Jewish Culture in Renaissance and Baroque Italy*, edited by David B. Ruderman, 401–25. New York: New York University Press, 1992.

– "The Devil and the Jews in the Christian Consciousness of the Middle Ages." In *Antisemitism through the Ages*, translated by Nathan H. Reisner and edited by Shmuel Almog, 91–8. Oxford: Pergamon Press, 1988.

– *Jewish Life in Renaissance Italy*. Translated by Anthony Oldcorn. Berkeley: University of California Press, 1994.
– *Rabbis and Jewish Communities in Renaissance Italy*. Translated by Jonathan Chipman. Oxford: Oxford University Press, 1990.
Born, Lester K. "Baldassare Bonifacio and His Essay 'De Archivis.'" *American Archivist* 4, no. 4 (October 1941): 221–37.
Borsa, Gedeon. *Clavis typographorum librariorumque Italiae 1465–1600*. 2 vols. Aureliae Aquensis [Baden-Baden]: Valentini Koerner, 1980.
Bray, Alan. *The Friend*. Chicago: University of Chicago Press, 2003.
Bruni, Roberto L., and D. Wyn Evans. *Italian 17th-Century Books in Cambridge Libraries*. Florence: L.S. Olschki, 1997.
– *Italian Seventeenth Century Books: Indexes of Authors, Titles, Dates, Printers and Publishers Alphabetically and by Place, Based on the Libreria Vinciana's Autori italiani del '600*. Exeter: Exeter University Library, 1984.
Bruscagli, Riccardo. "La preponderanza petrarchesca." In *Storia letteraria d'Italia – Il Cinquecento*, edited by Giovanni Da Pozzo, part 3, *La letteratura tra l'eroico e il quotidiano: La nuova religione dell'utopia e della scienza (1573–1600)*, 1559–1615. Padua: Piccin Nuova Libraria, 2007.
Buccini, Stefania. "Note sulle edizioni de 'La lucerna' di Francesco Pona." *Italica* 82, no. 3/4 (2005): 510–24.
Burns, Norman T. *Christian Mortalism from Tyndale to Milton*. Cambridge, MA: Harvard University Press, 1972.
Busetto, Giorgio. "Copio (Coppio, Copia, Coppia) Sara (Sarra)." In *Dizionario biografico degli italiani*, 28:582–4. Rome: Istituto della Enciclopedia Italiana, 1983.
– "La leggenda erudita di Sara Copio Sullam, letterata del ghetto di Venezia." In *Il gran secolo di Angelico Aprosio*, edited by Serena Leone Vatta and Alberto Naso, 45–66. Ventimiglia: Civica Biblioteca Aprosiana, 1981.
– "Sara Copio Sullam." In *Le stanze ritrovate: Antologia di scrittrici venete dal Quattrocento al Novecento*, edited by Antonia Arslan, Adriana Chemello, and Gilberto Pizzamiglio, 109–16. Mirano: Eidos, 1991.
Buttò, Simonetta, and Alberto Petrucciani. "Modona, Leonello." In *Dizionario bio-bibliografico dei bibliotecari italiani del XX secolo*, edited by Simonetta Buttò and Alberto Petrucciani. Associazione Italiana Biblioteche, 2013. https:// www.aib.it/aib/editoria/dbbi20/modona.htm
Calabi, Donatella. "Il ghetto e la città." In *La città degli ebrei*, 201–301.
–, Ludovica Galeazzo, and Martina Massaro, eds. *Venice, the Jews and Europe: 1516–2016*. Venice: Marsilio, 2016.
Calimani, Riccardo. *Storia del ghetto di Venezia*. Milan: Mondadori, 1995.
Campbell, Gordon. "Empedocles (c. 492–432 BCE)." In *Internet Encyclopedia of Philosophy*, edited by James Fieser and Bradley Dowden. https://www.iep.utm.edu/empedocl/

Campbell, Julie D. *Literary Circles and Gender in Early Modern Europe: A Cross-Cultural Approach.* Hampshire, UK: Ashgate, 2006.

– "The *Querelle des femmes.*" In *The Ashgate Research Companion to Women and Gender in Early Modern Europe,* edited by Allyson M. Poska, Jane Couchman, and Katherine A. McIver, 363–79. Burlington, VT: Ashgate, 2013.

–, and Anne R. Larsen, eds. *Early Modern Women and Transnational Communities of Letters.* Farnham, UK: Ashgate, 2009.

Cannizzaro, Nina. "Guido Casoni, padre degli Incogniti." In *I luoghi dell'immaginario barocco: Atti del convegno di Siena, 21–23 ottobre 1999,* edited by Lucia Strappini, 547–60. Naples: Liguori, 2001.

– "The Nile, Nothingness & Knowledge: The Incogniti Impresa." In *Coming About ... A Festschrift for John Shearman,* edited by Lars R. Jones and Louisa Chevalier Matthew, 325–32. Cambridge, MA: Harvard University Art Museums, 2001.

– "Studies on Guido Casoni (1561–1642) and Venetian Academies." PhD diss., Harvard University, 2001.

– "Surpassing the Maestro: Loredano, Colluraffi, Casoni and the Origins of the Accademia degli Incogniti." *Annali di storia moderna e contemporanea* 9 (2003): 369–97.

Carinci, Eleonora. "Una lettera autografa inedita di Moderata Fonte (al granduca di Toscana Francesco I)." *Critica del testo* 5, no. 3 (2002): 671–81.

Carminati, Clizia. "La prima edizione della *Messalina* di Francesco Pona (1633)." *Studi secenteschi* 47 (2006): 337–47.

Carnelos, Laura. "Words on the Street: Selling Small Printed 'Things' in Sixteenth- and Seventeenth-Century Venice." In *News Networks in Early Modern Europe,* edited by Joad Raymond and Noah Moxham, 739–55. Leiden: Brill, 2016.

Carpi, Daniel. "Le 'convenzioni' degli anni 1624 e 1645 tra le tre 'nazioni' della communità di Venezia." In Carpi et al., *Shlomo Simonsohn Jubilee Volume,* 25–70.

–, et al., eds. *Shlomo Simonsohn Jubilee Volume: Studies on the History of the Jews in the Middle Ages and Renaissance Periods.* Tel Aviv: Tel Aviv University, Faculty of Humanities, Chaim Rosenberg School of Jewish Studies, 1993.

Cassuto, David. "Architectural and Urbanistic Aspects of the Venice Ghetto." In Calabi, Galeazzo, and Massaro, *Venice, the Jews and Europe,* 212–15.

Cavanna Ciappina, Mariastella. "Doria, Marcantonio." In *Dizionario biografico degli italiani,* 41:408–9. Rome: Istituto della Enciclopedia Italiana, 1992.

Cavarocchi Arbib, Marina. "Rivisitando la biblica Ester: Implicazioni sottese all'immagine femminile ebraica nell'Italia del Seicento." In Honess and Jones, *Le donne delle minoranze,* 143–57.

Cavarzere, Marco. "Riccardi, Nicolò." In *Dizionario biografico degli italiani,* 87:166–71. Rome: Istituto della Enciclopedia Italiana, 2016.

Centanni, Monica. "Dialogues." In Calabi, Galeazzo, and Massaro, *Venice, the Jews and Europe*, 298–305.

Ceresa, Massimo. "Mandosio, Prospero." In *Dizionario biografico degli italiani*, 68:585–7. Rome: Istituto della Enciclopedia Italiana, 2007.

Chemello, Adriana. "La donna, il modello, l'immaginario: Moderata Fonte e Lucrezia Marinella." In *Nel cerchio della luna: Figure di donna in alcuni testi del XVI secolo*, edited by Marina Zancan, 95–170. Venice: Marsilio, 1983.

– "The Rhetoric of Euology in Marinella's *La nobiltá et l'eccellenza delle donne*." In *Women in Italian Renaissance Culture and Society*, edited by Letizia Panizza, 463–77. Oxford: Legenda European Humanities Research Centre, University of Oxford, 2000.

Cherchi, Paolo. *Polimatia di riuso: Mezzo secolo di plagio (1539–89)*. Rome: Bulzoni, 1998.

Chojnacki, Stanley. *Women and Men in Renaissance Venice: Twelve Essays on Patrician Society*. Baltimore: Johns Hopkins University Press, 2000.

Cicogna, Emmanuele Antonio. *Delle iscrizioni veneziane*. 6 vols. Venice: presso Giuseppe Molinari Stampatore, 1824–1853.

– "Notizie intorno a Sara Copia Sulam, coltissima ebrea veneziana del secolo XVII." *Memorie del Regio Istituto Veneto di Scienze, Lettere ed Arti* 12 (1864): 227–46.

Cinelli Calvoli, Giovanni. *Biblioteca volante ... continuata dal dottor Dionigi Andrea Sancassani*. 2nd ed. 4 vols. Venice: presso Giambattista Albrizzi q. Girolamo, 1734–1747.

Coci, Laura. "Introduzione." In Pallavicino, *La retorica delle puttane*, ix–c.

– "Nota introduttiva." In Rocco, *L'Alcibiade*, 7–34.

Cohen, Mark R. "Leone da Modena's *Riti*: A Seventeenth-Century Plea for Social Toleration of Jews." *Jewish Social Studies* 34, no. 4 (1972): 287–321.

– "Leone da Modena's *Riti*: A Seventeenth-Century Plea for Social Toleration of Jews." In *Essential Papers on Jewish Culture in Rennaissance and Baroque Italy*, edited by David B. Ruderman, 429–73. New York: New York University Press, 1992.

Colie, Rosalie L. *Paradoxia epidemica: The Renaissance Tradition of Paradox*. Princeton: Princeton University Press, 1966.

Compagni, Vittoria Perrone. "Pomponazzi, Pietro." In *Dizionario biografico degli italiani*, 84:704–11. Rome: Istituto della Enciclopedia Italiana, 2015.

Concina, Ennio, Ugo Camerino, and Donatella Calabi. *La città degli ebrei: Il ghetto di Venezia, architettura e urbanistica*. Venice: Albrizzi Editore, 1991.

Considine, John. *Academy Dictionaries 1600–1800*. Cambridge, UK: Cambridge University Press, 2014.

Constant, Eric A. "A Reinterpretation of the Fifth Lateran Council Decree *Apostolici regiminis* (1513)." *Sixteenth Century Journal* 33, no. 2 (2002): 353–79.

Contò, Agostino. "Ciotti, Giovanni Battista." In *Dizionario dei tipografi e degli editori italiani. Il Cinquecento*, vol. 1, *A–F*, edited by Marco Menato, Ennio Sandal, and Giuseppina Zappella, 293–5. Milan: Editrice Bibliografica, 1997.

Cooper, Brittney. "Intersectionality." In *The Oxford Handbook of Feminist Theory*, edited by Lisa Disch and Mary Hawkesworth, 385–97. New York: Oxford University Press, 2016.

Cooperman, Bernard Dov. "Legitimizing Rhetorics: Jewish 'Heresy' in Early Modern Italy." *Etudes épistémè* 31 (2017). https://journals.openedition.org/episteme/1764.

Corradini, Marco. "Etica e politica nella 'Reina Ester' di Ansaldo Cebà." In *Genova e il barocco. Studi su Angelo Grillo, Ansaldo Cebà, Anton Giulio Brignole Sale*, edited by Marco Corradini, 125–246. Milan: Vita e Pensiero, 1994.

– *In terra di letteratura. Poesia e poetica di Giovan Battista Marino*. Lecce: Argo, 2012.

– "Introduzione." In Cebà, *Tragedie*, ix–lviii.

Cortelazzo, Manlio. *Dizionario veneziano della lingua e della cultura popolare nel XVI secolo*. Limena [Padua]: La linea, 2007.

Cosentino, Paola. "Dee, imperatrici, cortigiane: La natura della donna nei romanzi degli Incogniti (Venezia)." In Everson, Reidy, and Sampson, *The Italian Academies*, 292–305.

Costa-Zalessow, Natalia. "La condanna all'Indice della *Semplicità ingannata* di Arcangela Tarabotti alla luce di manoscritti inediti." *Nouvelles de la république des lettres*, no. 1 (2002): 97–113.

– "Sara Copio Sullam." In *Scrittrici italiane dal XIII al XX secolo. Testi e critica*, edited by Natalia Costa-Zalessow, 123–7. Ravenna: Longo Editore, 1982.

– "Tarabotti's *La semplicità ingannata* and its Twentieth-Century Interpreters, with Unpublished Documents Regarding its Condemnation to the Index." *Italica* 78, no. 3 (2001): 314–25.

Cox, Virginia. "Members, Muses, Mascots: Women and Italian Academies." In Everson, Reidy, and Sampson, *The Italian Academies*, 132–69.

– "Moderata Fonte and *The Worth of Women*." In Fonte, *The Worth of Women*, 1–23.

– *The Prodigious Muse: Women's Writing in Counter-Reformation Italy*. Baltimore: Johns Hopkins University Press, 2011.

– "The Single Self: Feminist Thought and the Marriage Market in Early Modern Venice." *Renaissance Quarterly* 48, no. 3 (1995): 513–81.

– *Women's Writing in Italy 1400–1650*. Baltimore: Johns Hopkins University Press, 2008.

Cozzi, Gaetano. *Giustizia 'contaminata': Vicende giudiziarie di nobili ed ebrei nella Venezia del Seicento*. Venice: Marsilio, 1996.

– *Venezia barocca. Conflitti di uomini e idee nella crisi del Seicento veneziano*. Venice: Il Cardo, 1995.

– "Una vicenda della Venezia barocca: Marco Trevisan e la sua 'eroica amicizia.'"
Bollettino dell'Istituto di Storia della Società e dello Stato Veneziano 2 (1960): 61–154.
[Page references are to the reprint in Cozzi, *Venezia barocca*, 327–409.]

–, ed. *Gli ebrei e Venezia, secoli XIV–XVIII. Atti del convegno internazionale ... 5–10 giugno 1983.* Milan: Edizioni Comunità, 1987.

Crescimbeni, Giovanni Mario. *Commentari intorno alla sua istoria della volgar poesia.* 5 vols. Venice: Lorenzo Basegio, 1730.

– *L'istoria della volgar poesia.* 6 vols. Rome: Crachas, 1698.

David, Ernest. "Une héroine juive au XVIIe siècle: Sara Copia Sullam." *Les archives israélites* 37 (1876): 377–81, 407–11, 440–3, 471–4, 502–5, 536–40, 567–71, 599–603, 663–6, 694–7, 759–62; 38 (1877): 54–8.

Davidson, N.S. "Sodomy in Early Modern Venice." In *Sodomy in Early Modern Europe*, edited by Tom Betteridge, 65–81. Manchester: Manchester University Press, 2002.

Davis, Robert C., and Benjamin Ravid, eds. *The Jews of Early Modern Venice.* Baltimore: Johns Hopkins University Press, 2001.

De Bellis, Ennio. *Nicoletto Vernia: Studi sull'aristotelismo del XV secolo.* Florence: Olschki, 2012.

DeJean, Joan. *Tender Geographies: Women and the Origins of the Novel in France.* New York: Columbia University Press, 1991.

Del Torre, Maria Assunta. "Gli aspetti complessivi dell'opera di Cesare Cremonini." In *Cesare Cremonini (1550–1631): Il suo pensiero e il suo tempo, convegno di studi, Cento, 7 aprile 1984,* 17–28. Cento, Italy: Centro Studi Girolamo Baruffaldi, 1990.

– "La cosmologia di Cremonini e l'inedito 'De coeli efficentia.'" *Rivista critica di storia della filosofia* 21, no. 4 (1966): 373–97.

Derosas, Renzo. "Moralità e giustizia a Venezia nel '500–'600: Gli Esecutori contro la Bestemmia." In *Stato, società e giustizia nella Repubblica Veneta (sec. XV–XVIII)*, edited by Gaetano Cozzi, 1:431–528. Rome: Jouvence, 1980.

De Rossi, Giovanni Bernardo. *Dizionario storico degli autori ebrei e delle loro opere.* 2 vols. Parma: Dalla Reale Stamperia, 1802.

Dersofi, Nancy. "Copio Sullam, Sara." In *The Feminist Encyclopedia of Italian Literature*, edited by Rinaldina Russell, 53–4. Westport, CT: Greenwood Press, 1997.

Diemling, Maria, and Giuseppe Veltri, eds. *The Jewish Body: Corporeality, Society, and Identity in the Renaissance and Early Modern Period.* Leiden: Brill, 2009.

Di Filippo Bareggi, Claudia. *Il mestiere di scrivere: Lavoro intellettuale e mercato librario a Venezia nel Cinquecento.* Roma: Bulzoni, 1988.

Dimont, Max I. *Jews, God and History.* New York: Simon and Schuster, 1962.

Duffy, Eamon. *Saints & Sinners: A History of the Popes.* New Haven: Yale University Press, 1997.

Duggan, Anne E. *Salonnières, Furies, and Fairies: The Politics of Gender and Cultural Change in Absolutist France.* Newark: University of Delaware Press, 2005.

Earle, T.F., and K.J.P. Lowe, eds. *Black Africans in Renaissance Europe.* Cambridge, UK: Cambridge University Press, 2005.

Eisenstein, Elizabeth L. *The Printing Press as an Agent of Change: Communications and Cultural Transformations in Early Modern Europe.* 2 vols. Cambridge, UK: Cambridge University Press, 1979.

Ernst, Germana. *Tommaso Campanella: The Book and the Body of Nature.* Translated by David Marshall. Dordrecht: Springer, 2010.

Erspamer, Franscesco. "Per un'edizione delle rime di Celio Magno." *Studi di filologia italiana* 41 (1983): 45–73.

Everson, Jane E., Denis V. Reidy, and Lisa Sampson, eds. *The Italian Academies 1525–1700: Networks of Culture, Innovation and Dissent.* Oxford: Legenda, 2016.

F.R. "Biblioteca volante di Giovanni Cinelli Calvoli." *Giornale degli eruditi e curiosi* 1 (1882–83): col. 307–8.

Fachini, Ginevra Canonici. *Prospetto biografico delle donne italiane rinomate in letteratura, dal secolo decimoquarto fino a' giorni nostri.* Venice: Alvisopoli, 1824.

Fahy, Conor. "Women and Italian Cinquecento Literary Academies." In *Women in Italian Renaissance Culture and Society,* edited by Letizia Panizza, 438–52. Oxford: Legenda, 2000.

Febvre, Lucien, and Henri-Jean Martin. *The Coming of the Book: The Impact of Printing 1450–1800.* Translated by David Gerard. Edited by Geoffrey Nowell-Smith and David Wootton. London: N.L.B., 1976.

Feldman, David M. *Birth Control in Jewish Law; Marital Relations, Contraception, and Abortion as Set Forth in the Classic Texts of Jewish Law.* New York: New York University Press, 1968.

– *Marital Relations, Birth Control and Abortion in Jewish Law ... with Comparative Reference to Christian Tradition.* New York: Schocken, 1974.

Feldman, Martha. *City Culture and the Madrigal at Venice.* Berkeley: University of California Press, 1995.

Ferraro, Joanne Marie. *Marriage Wars in Late Renaissance Venice.* Oxford: Oxford University Press, 2001.

Ferri, Pietro Leopoldo. *Biblioteca femminile italiana, raccolta, posseduta e descritta.* Padua: Crescini, 1842.

Ferro, Marco. *Dizionario del diritto comune e veneto.* 2nd ed. 2 vols. Venice: Andrea Santini e Figlio, 1845.

Ferruta, Paola. "Simone Luzzatto e la sua cerchia familiare: Questioni di affari, parentela e vita privata." In *Filosofo e rabbino nella Venezia del Seicento: Studi su Simone Luzzatto con documenti inediti dall'Archivio di Stato di Venezia,* edited by Giuseppi Veltri, 341–71. Rome: Aracne, 2015.

Findlen, Paula. "Academies." In *Encyclopedia of the Renaissance,* edited by Paul F. Grendler, 1:4–6. New York: Charles Scribner's Sons, 1999.

Finucci, Valeria. *The Manly Masquerade: Masculinity, Paternity, and Castration in the Italian Renaissance.* Durham, NC: Duke University Press, 2003.

Firpo, Luigi. "Boccalini, Traiano." In *Dizionario biografico degli italiani*, 11:10–19. Rome: Istituto della Enciclopedia Italiana, 1969.

Firpo, Massimo. "Ciotti, Giovanni Battista." In *Dizionario biografico degli italiani*, 25:692–6. Rome: Istituto della Enciclopedia Italiana, 1981.

Fishman, Talya. *Shaking the Pillars of Exile: 'Voice of the Fool,' an Early Modern Jewish Critique of Rabbinic Culture.* Stanford, CA: Stanford University Press, 1997.

Foa, Anna. *Ebrei in Europa: Dalla peste nera all'emancipazione XIV–XVIII secolo.* Rome: Laterza, 1992.

Fonseca-Wollheim, Corinna da. "Acque di Parnaso, acque di battesimo: Fede e fama nell'opera di Sara Copio Sullam." In Honess and Jones, *Le donne delle minoranze*, 159–70.

– "Faith and Fame in the Life and Works of the Venetian Jewish Poet Sara Copio Sullam (1592?–1641)." PhD diss., Cambridge University, 2000.

Fontana, Giovanni L., and Ennio Sandal, eds. *Cartai e stampatori in Veneto.* Brescia: Grafo, 2001.

Forlivesi, Marco. "Cesare Cremonini." In *Enciclopedia italiana di scienze, lettere ed arti*, edited by Giovanni Gentile et al., appendix 8, *Il contributo italiano alla storia del pensiero: Filosofia*, edited by M. Ciliberto, 250–7. Rome: Istituto della Enciclopedia Italiana, 2012.

Fortis, Umberto. *La "bella ebrea": Sara Copio Sullam, poetessa nel ghetto di Venezia del '600.* Turin: Silvio Zamorani editore, 2003.

– "Il dialogo negato: Per una lettura della poesia di Sara Copio Sullam." In *Miscellanea di studi: Liceo Ginnasio Statale Raimondo Franchetti Venezia Mestre 3*, 109–51. Venice: Storti, 1998.

Fulco, Giorgio. "Introduction." In Pona, *La lucerna*, ix–lvi.

– "Sul *Paltoniere* di Baldassare Bonifacio." *Strumenti critici* 36–7 (February 1978): 253–74.

Fumagalli, Giuseppe. *Giunte e correzioni al* Lexicon typographicum Italie *di G.F.* Florence: L.S. Olschki, 1938.

Fürst, Julius. *Bibliotheca Judaica: Bibliographisches Handbuch der gesamten jüdischen Literatur.* 3 vols. Leipzig: Wilhelm Engelmann, 1849–1863. Reprint, Hildesheim: Georg Olms Verlagsbuchhandlung, 1960.

Galeazzo, Ludovica. "The Cosmopolitan Ghetto." In Calabi, Galeazzo, and Massaro, *Venice, the Jews and Europe*, 152–9.

Geiger, Abraham. "Sara Copia Sullam." *Jüdische Zeitschrift für Wissenschaft und Leben* 7 (1868): 178–83.

Gerstenberger, Katharina. *Truth to Tell: German Women's Autobiographies and Turn-of-the-Century Culture. Social History, Popular Culture, and Politics in Germany.* Ann Arbor: University of Michigan Press, 2000.

Giachery, Alessia. "Pinelli." In *Dizionario biografico degli italiani*, 83:711–16. Rome: Istituto della Enciclopedia Italiana, 2015.

Gilson, Ètienne. "L'affaire de l'immortalité de l'âme à Venise au début du XVIe siècle." In *Umanesimo europeo e umanesimo veneziano*, edited by Vittore Branca, 31–61. Florence: Sansoni, 1963.

– "Autour de Pomponazzi. Problématique de l'immortalité de l'âme en Italie au début du XVIe siècle." *Archives d'histoire doctrinale et littéraire du Moyen Âge* 28 (1961): 163–279.

Glixon, Beth L., and Jonathan E. Glixon. *Inventing the Business of Opera: The Impresario and His World in Seventeenth-Century Venice*. Oxford: Oxford University Press, 2006.

Goldsmith, Elizabeth C., and Dena Goodman, eds. *Going Public: Women and Publishing in Early Modern France*. Ithaca: Cornell University Press, 1995.

Goodman, Dena. *The Republic of Letters: A Cultural History of the French Enlightenment*. Ithaca: Cornell University Press, 1994.

Graetz, Heinrich. *Geschichte der Juden von den ältesten Zeiten bis auf die Gegenwart*. 11 vols. Leipzig: O. Leiner, 1853–1876.

Grafton, Anthony, Glenn W. Most, and Salvatore Settis, eds. *The Classical Tradition*. Cambridge, MA: The Belknap Press of Harvard University Press, 2010.

Grendler, Paul F. "The Leaders of the Venetian State, 1540–1609: A Prosopographical Analysis." In Paul F. Grendler, *Renaissance Education between Religion and Politics*, section 11, 35–85. Aldershot, UK: Ashgate, 2006.

– *The Roman Inquisition and the Venetian Press, 1540–1605*. Princeton: Princeton University Press, 1977.

– *Schooling in Renaissance Italy: Literacy and Learning, 1300–1600*. Baltimore: Johns Hopkins University Press, 1989.

– *The Universities of the Italian Renaissance*. Baltimore: Johns Hopkins University Press, 2002.

Griffante, Caterina, ed., with Alessia Giachery and Sabrina Minuzzi. *Le edizioni veneziane del Seicento. Censimento*. 2 vols. Milan: Editrice Bibliografica, 2003–2006.

Griffin, Clive. *Journeymen-Printers, Heresy, and the Inquisition in Sixteenth-Century Spain*. Oxford: Oxford University Press, 2005.

[Grimaldo, Giuseppe]. *Numismatica veneta o Serie di monete e medaglie dei Dogi di Venezia*. Venice: Giuseppe Grimaldo Editore, 1854.

Guastella, Gianni. *Word of Mouth: Fama and Its Personifications in Art and Literature from Ancient Rome to the Middle Ages*. Oxford: Oxford University Press, 2017.

Gullino, Giuseppe. *I Pisani dal Banco e Moretta: Storia di due famiglie veneziane in età moderna e delle loro vicende patrimoniali tra 1705 e 1836*. Roma: Istituto Storico Italiano per l'Età Moderna e Contemporanea, 1984.

Hainsworth, Peter, and David Robey, eds. *The Oxford Companion to Italian Literature.* Oxford: Oxford University Press, 2002.

Haliczer, Stephen, ed. and trans. *Inquisition and Society in Early Modern Europe.* Totowa, NJ: Barnes & Noble, 1987.

Harrán, Don. "A Controversy on the Immortality of the Soul." In Copia Sulam, *Jewish Poet and Intellectual,* 269–348.

– "Doubly Tainted, Doubly Talented: The Jewish Poet Sara Copio (d. 1641) as a Heroic Singer." In *Musica Franka: Essays in Honor of Frank A. D'Accone,* edited by Irene Alm, Alyson McLamore, and Colleen Reardon, 367–422. Stuyvesant, NY: Pendragon Press, 1996.

– "Introduction." In Copia Sulam, *Jewish Poet and Intellectual,* 1–90.

– "Madama Europa, Jewish Singer in Late Renaissance Manuta." In *Festa Musicologica: Essays in Honor of George J. Buelow,* edited by Thomas J. Mathiesen and Benito V. Rivera, 197–231. Stuyvesant, NY: Pendragon Press, 1995.

– *Salamone Rossi: Jewish Musician in Late Renaissance Mantua.* Oxford: Oxford University Press, 1999.

Haskins, Susan. "Vexatious Litigant, or the Case of Lucrezia Marinella? New Documents Concerning Her Life." *Nouvelles de la république des lettres,* no. 1 (2006): 81–128.

– "Vexatious Litigant, or the Case of Lucrezia Marinella? New Documents Concerning Her Life (Part II)." *Nouvelles de la république des lettres,* nos. 1–2 (2007): 203–30.

Haym, Nicola Francesco. *Biblioteca italiana, ossia Notizia de' libri rari italiani divisa in quattro parti cioè istoria, poesia, prose, arti e scienze.* 4 vols. Milan: G. Silvestri, 1803.

Heller, Wendy. *Emblems of Eloquence: Opera and Women's Voices in Seventeenth-Century Venice.* Berkeley: University of California Press, 2003.

Hester, Nathalie. *Literature and Identity in Baroque Travel Writing.* Aldershot, UK; Burlington, VT: Ashgate, 2008.

Honess, Claire E., and Verina R. Jones, eds. *Le donne delle minoranze: Le ebree e le protestanti d'Italia.* Turin: Claudiana, 1999.

Horodowich, Elizabeth. *Language and Statecraft in Early Modern Venice.* Cambridge, UK: Cambridge University Press, 2008.

Hughes, Diane Owen. "Distinguishing Signs: Ear-Rings, Jews and Franciscan Rhetoric in the Italian Renaissance City." *Past and Present* 112 (1986): 3–59.

– "Sumptuary Law and Social Relations in Renaissance Italy." In *Disputes and Settlements: Law and Human Relations in the West,* edited by John Bossy, 69–99. Cambridge, UK: Cambridge University Press, 1983.

Infelise, Mario. "Books and Politics in Arcangela Tarabotti's Venice." In Weaver, *Arcangela Tarabotti,* 57–72.

– "La Crusca a Venezia. Solo tipografia?" In *Il vocabolario degli Accademici della Crusca (1612) e la storia della lessicografia italiana,* edited by Lorenzo Tomasin, 65–72. Florence: Franco Cesati Editore, 2013.

– "Ex ignoto notus? Note sul tipografo Sarzina e l'Accademia degli Incogniti." In *Libri, tipografi, biblioteche. Ricerche storiche dedicate a Luigi Balsamo*, edited by Istituto di Biblioteconomia e Paleografia, Università degli Studi, Parma, 1:207–23. Florence: Leo S. Olschki, 1997.

– "Libri e politica nella Venezia di Arcangela Tarabotti." *Annali di Storia Moderna e Contemporanea* 8 (2002): 31–45.

– *I libri proibiti. Da Gutenberg all'Encyclopédie*. Roma: Editori Laterza, 2013.

– *I padroni dei libri. Il controllo sulla stampa nella prima età moderna*. Roma: Editori Laterza, 2014.

– "Pallavicino, Ferrante." In *Dizionario biografico degli italiani*, 80:506–11. Rome: Istituto della Enciclopedia Italiana, 2014.

– *Prima dei giornali: Alle origini della pubblica informazione (secoli XVI e XVII)*. Roma: Laterza, 2002.

Jones, Ann Rosalind. *The Currency of Eros: Women's Love Lyric in Europe, 1540–1620*. Bloomington: Indiana University Press, 1990.

Katz, Dana E. *The Jewish Ghetto and the Visual Imagination of Early Modern Venice*. Cambridge, UK: Cambridge University Press, 2017.

Kayserling, Meyer. "Sara Copia Sullam." In *Die jüdischen Frauen in der Geschichte, Literatur und Kunst*, 159–70. Leipzig: F.A. Brockhaus, 1879.

Kelso, Ruth. *Doctrine for the Lady of the Renaissance*. Urbana: University of Illinois Press, 1956.

Kennedy, Leonard A. "Cesare Cremonini and the Immortality of the Human Soul." *Vivarium* 18, no. 2 (1980): 143–58.

Kessler, Eckhard. "Alexander of Aphrodisias and His Doctrine of the Soul: 1400 Years of Lasting Significance." *Early Science and Medicine* 16, no. 1 (2011): 1–93.

King, Margaret L. *Humanism, Venice, and Women: Essays on the Italian Renaissance*. Aldershot, UK: Ashgate, 2005.

–, and Diana Robin. "Volume Editors' Introduction." In Nogarola, *Complete Writings*, 1–19.

Kirkham, Victoria. "Volume Editor's Introduction." In Battiferra degli Ammannati, *Laura Battiferra*, 1–54.

Kirshner, Julius. "Raymond de Roover on Scholastic Economic Thought." In *Business, Banking and Economic Thought in Late Medieval and Early Modern Europe: Selected Studies of Raymond de Roover*, edited by Julius Kirshner, 15–36. Chicago: University of Chicago Press, 1974.

Klein, Luce A. *Portrait de la Juive dans la littérature française*. Paris: Nizet, 1970.

Knox, Dilwyn. "Immortality of the Soul." In Grafton, Most, and Settis, *The Classical Tradition*, 475–81.

Kolsky, Stephen. "Moderata Fonte, Lucrezia Marinella, Giuseppe Passi: An Early Seventeenth-Century Feminist Controversy." *Modern Language Review* 96, no. 4 (2001): 973–89.

Kolyvà, Marianna. "The Jews of Zante between the Serenissima and the Sublime Porte: The Local Community and the Jewish Consuls (Sixteenth to Seventeenth Centuries)." In "Minorities in Colonial Settings: The Jews in Venice's Hellenic Territories (15th–18th Centuries)." Special issue, *Mediterranean Historical Review* 27, no. 2 (2012): 199–213.

Konstan, David. "Epicurus." In *The Stanford Encyclopedia of Philosophy*, summer 2018 edition, edited by Edward N. Zalta. https://plato.stanford.edu/archives/sum2018/entries/epicurus/

Kraye, Jill. "Pietro Pomponazzi (1462–1525): Secular Aristotelianism in the Renaissance." In *Philosophers of the Renaissance*, translated by Brian McNeil and edited by Paul Richard Blum, 92–115. Washington, DC: Catholic University of America Press, 2010.

Kristeller, Paul Oskar. *Eight Philosophers of the Italian Renaissance*. Palo Alto, CA: Stanford University Press, 1964.

– "The Theory of Immortality in Marsilio Ficino." *Journal of the History of Ideas* 1, no. 3 (1940): 299–319.

Kuhn, Heinrich C. "Cesare Cremonini: Volti e maschere di un filosofo scomodo per tre secoli e mezzo." In *Cesare Cremonini: Aspetti del pensiero e scritti*, edited by Ezio Riondato and Antonino Poppi, 1:153–68. Padua: La Garangola, 2000.

Labalme, Patricia H. "Venetian Women on Women: Three Early Modern Feminists." *Archivio veneto*, 5th ser., 117 (1981): 81–108.

LaGuardia, David P. *Intertextual Masculinity in French Renaissance Literature: Rabelais, Brantôme, and the* Cent nouvelles nouvelles. Aldershot, UK: Ashgate, 2008.

LaMay, Thomasin. "Composing from the Throat: Madalena Casulana's *Primo Libro de madrigali*, 1568." In *Musical Voices of Early Modern Women: Many-Headed Melodies*, edited by Thomasin LaMay, 365–97. Burlington, VT: Ashgate, 2005.

Landes, Joan B. *Women and the Public Sphere in the Age of the French Revolution*. Ithaca and London: Cornell University Press, 1988.

Larsen, Ann. "Paradox and the Praise of Women: From Ortensio Lando and Charles Estienne to Marie de Romieu." *The Sixteenth Century Journal* 28, no. 3 (1997): 759–74.

Laugier, Marc Antoine. *Storia della Repubblica di Venezia dalla sua fondazione fino al presente*. 12 vols. Venice: presso Carlo Palese e Gasparo Storti, 1769.

Lavocat, Françoise. "Introduzione." In Marinella, *Arcadia felice* (1998), vii–lx.

[Legrenzi, Domenico], ed. *Galleria poetica di donne veneziane, strennetta per l'anno nuovo, compilata da D.L.* Mestre: Antonio Sacchetto, [1852].

Levy, Moritz Abraham. "Sara Copia Sullam: Lebensbild einer jüdischen italienischen Dichterin aus dem siebzehnten Jahrhundert." *Jahrbuch für die Geschichte der Juden und des Judenthums* 3 (1863): 65–93.

Lorenz, Hendrik. "Ancient Theories of Soul." In *The Stanford Encyclopedia of Philosophy*, summer 2009 edition, edited by Edward N. Zalta. http://plato .stanford.edu/archives/sum2009/entries/ancient-soul.

Love, Harold. *The Culture and Commerce of Texts: Scribal Publication in Seventeenth-Century England.* Amherst: University of Massachusetts Press, 1998.

Lowe, Kate. "Introduction: The Black African Presence in Renaissance Europe." In Earle and Lowe, *Black Africans in Renaissance Europe*, 1–14.

– "The Stereotyping of Black Africans in Renaissance Europe." In Earle and Lowe, *Black Africans in Renaissance Europe*, 17–47.

– "Visible Lives: Black Gondoliers and Other Black Africans in Renaissance Venice." *Renaissance Quarterly* 66, no. 2 (2013): 412–52.

Lubello, Sergio. "Pergamini, Giacomo." *Dizionario biografico degli italiani*, 82:362–5. Rome: Istituto della Enciclopedia Italiana, 2015.

Luzzatto, Aldo, ed. *La comunità ebraica di Venezia e il suo antico cimitero.* 2 vols. Milan: Il Polifolo, 2000.

Magatti, Enrico. "Il mercato monetario veneziano alla fine del secolo XVI." *Nuovo Archivio veneto*, n.s., 27 (1914): 245–323.

Maggi, Armando. "The Discourse of Sodom in a Seventeenth-Century Venetian Text." *Journal of Homosexuality* 33, nos. 3–4 (1997): 25–43.

– *In the Company of Demons: Unnatural Beings, Love, and Identity in the Italian Renaissance.* Chicago: University of Chicago Press, 2006.

Magnanini, Suzanne. *Fairy-Tale Science: Monstrous Generation in the Tales of Straparola and Basile.* Toronto: University of Toronto Press, 2008.

–, ed. "Giuseppe Passi's Attacks on Women in *The Defects of Women*." Translated by Suzanne Magnanini (Italian) and David Lamari (Latin). In J.D. Campbell and Stampino, *In Dialogue with the Other Voice*, 143–94.

Malkiel, David. "The Ghetto Republic." In Davis and Ravid, *The Jews of Early Modern Venice*, 117–42.

– *A Separate Republic: The Mechanism and Dynamics of Venetian Jewish Self-Government.* Jerusalem: Magnes Press, Hebrew University, 1991.

Mancini, Albert N. "La narrativa libertina degli Incogniti. Tipologia e forme." *Forum italicum* 16, no. 3 (1982): 203–29.

Mannucci, Francesco Luigi. *La vita e le opere di Agostino Mascardi con appendici di lettere e altri scritti inediti e un saggio bibliografico.* Vol. 42 of *Atti della Società Ligure di Storia Patria.* Genoa: Tipografia della Gioventù, 1908.

Martin, Craig. *Subverting Aristotle: Religion, History, and Philosophy in Early Modern Science.* Baltimore: Johns Hopkins University Press, 2014.

Martini, Alessandro. "Marino, Giovan Battista." In *Dizionario biografico degli italiani*, 70:517–31. Rome: Istituto della Enciclopedia Italiana, 2008.

Mayer, Thomas F., ed. *The Trial of Galileo, 1612–1633.* Toronto: University of Toronto Press, 2012.

Maylender, Michele. *Storie delle accademie d'Italia*. 5 vols. Bologna: Licinio Cappelli, 1926–1930.

Mazzucchelli, Giammaria. "Bonifacio (Baldassare)." In *Gli scrittori d'Italia, cioè Notizie storiche e critiche intorno alle vite e agli scritti dei letterati italiani*, 2:3: 1644–1650 Brescia: Giambattista Bossini, 1762.

McClure, George. *Parlour Games and the Public Life of Women in Renaissance Italy*. Toronto: University of Toronto Press, 2013.

McGough, Laura J. *Gender, Sexuality, and Syphilis in Early Modern Venice: The Disease That Came to Stay*. New York: Palgrave Macmillan, 2011.

McHugh, Shannon. "The Gender of Desire: Feminine and Masculine Voices in Early Modern Italian Lyric Poetry." PhD diss., New York University, 2015.

McInerny, Ralph, and John O'Callaghan. "Saint Thomas Aquinas." *The Stanford Encyclopedia of Philosophy*, spring 2015 edition, edited by Edward N. Zalta. http://plato.stanford.edu/archives/spr2015/entries/aquinas.

Medioli, Francesca. "Alcune lettere autografe di Arcangela Tarabotti: Autocensura e immagine di sé." *Rivista di storia e letteratura religiosa* 32, no. 1 (1996): 133–41.

Melzi, Gaetano, Gaetano Zardetti, and Giovanni Antonio Melzi. *Dizionario di opere anonime e pseudonime di scrittori italiani, o come che sia aventi relazione all'Italia*. 3 vols. Milan: Luigi di Giacomo Pirola, 1848–1859.

Menegatti, Tiziana. *"Ex ignoto notus": Bibliografia delle opere a stampa del Principe degli Incogniti: Giovan Francesco Loredano*. Padua: Il Poligrafo, 2000.

Miato, Monica. *L'Accademia degli Incogniti di Giovan Francesco Loredano: Venezia, 1630–1661*. Florence: Leo S. Olschki Editore, 1998.

Miller, Fred D., Jr. "Aristotle's Philosophy of Soul." *The Review of Metaphysics* 53, no. 2 (1999): 309–37.

Milligan, Gerry. "Unlikely Heroines in Lucrezia Tornabuoni's 'Judith' and 'Esther.'" *Italica* 88, no. 4 (Winter 2011): 538–64.

–, and Jane Tylus, eds. *The Poetics of Masculinity in Early Modern Italy and Spain*. Toronto: Iter Press and the Centre for Reformation and Renaissance Studies, 2010.

Minnich, Nelson H. "The Catholic Church and the Pastoral Care of Black Africans in Renaissance Italy." In Earle and Lowe, *Black Africans in Renaissance Europe*, 280–300.

Minuzzi, Sabrina. "Gli autori ovvero gli 'inventori di qualche cosa novella.'" In *L'invenzione dell'autore: Privilegi di stampa nella Venezia del Rinascimento*, edited by Sabrina Minuzzi, 9–22. Venice: Marsilio, 2016.

– *Inventario di bottega di Antonio Bosio veneziano (1646–1694)*. Venice: Edizioni Ca' Foscari, 2013.

– *Il secolo di carta. Antonio Bosio artigiano di testi e immagini nella Venezia del Seicento*. Milan: FrancoAngeli, 2009.

Modestino, Carmine. *Della dimora di Torquato Tasso in Napoli negli anni 1588, 1592, 1594. Discorsi tre. Discorso secondo.* Naples: Stabilimento Tipografico di Giuseppe Cataneo, 1863.

Muir, Edward. *Civic Ritual in Renaissance Venice.* Princeton: Princeton University Press, 1981.

– *The Culture Wars of the Late Renaissance: Skeptics, Libertines, and Opera.* Cambridge, MA: Harvard University Press, 2007.

Mutini, Claudio. "Cebà, Ansaldo." In *Dizionario biografico degli italiani,* 23:184–6. Rome: Istituto della Enciclopedia Italiana, 1979.

Nadler, Steven M. *Spinoza's Heresy: Immortality and the Jewish Mind.* Oxford: Clarendon, 2004.

Najemy, John M. *Between Friends: Discourses of Power and Desire in the Machiavelli-Vettori Letters of 1513–1515.* Princeton: Princeton University Press, 1993.

Neri, Achille. "Il vero autore dell'*Alcibiade fanciullo a scola.*" *Giornale storico della letteratura italiana* 12 (1888): 219–27.

Nuovo, Angela. *Il commercio librario nell'Italia del Rinascimento.* Milano: F. Angeli, 1998.

–, and Ennio Sandal, eds. *Il libro nell'Italia del Rinascimento.* Brescia: Grafo, 1998.

Nussbaum, Martha C., and Hillary Putnam. "Changing Aristotle's Mind." In Nussbaum and Rorty, *Essays on Aristotle's* De anima, 27–56.

Nussbaum, Martha C., and Amélie Oksenberg Rorty, eds. *Essays on Aristotle's* De anima. Oxford: Clarendon Press, 1992.

Ottolenghi, Adolfo. "Origine e vicende dell'*Historia de riti hebraici* di Leon da Modena." *Rassegna mensile di Israel* 7, nos. 7–8 (1932): 287–92.

Pal, Carol. *Republic of Women: Rethinking the Republic of Letters in the Seventeenth Century.* Cambridge, UK: Cambridge University Press, 2012.

Panizza, Letizia. "Introduction to the Translation." In Marinella, *Nobility,* 1–34.

–, and Sharon Wood, eds. *A History of Women's Writing in Italy.* Cambridge, UK: Cambridge University Press, 2000.

Paolucci, Raffaele. *Le monete dei dogi di Venezia / The Coinage of the Doges of Venice.* Padua: Raffaele Paolucci Editore, 1990.

Papadopoli Aldobrandini, Nicolò. *Da Leonardo Donà a Lodovico Manin, 1606–1797.* Vol. 3.1 of *Le monete di Venezia.* Venice: Tipografia Libreria Emiliana, 1919.

Pastorello, Ester. *Tipografi, editori, librai a Venezia nel secolo XVI.* Florence: L.S. Olschki, 1924.

Penslar, Derek J. *Shylock's Children: Economics and Jewish Identity in Modern Europe.* Berkeley: University of California Press, 2001.

Pentolini, Francesco Clodoveo Maria. *Le donne illustri canti dieci.* 2 vols. Livorno: Gio Vincenzo Falorni, 1776–1777.

Perocco, Daria. "Prose Production in Venice in the Early Seicento." In Weaver, *Arcangela Tarabotti,* 73–87.

Petuchowski, Jakob J. *The Theology of Haham David Nieto: An Eighteenth-Century Defense of the Jewish Tradition.* New York: KTAV Publishing House, 1970.

Pezzini, Serena. "Dissimulazione e paradosso nelle *Lettere di molte valorose donne* (1548) a cura di Ortensio Lando," *Italianistica* 31, no. 1 (2002): 67–83.

Piattelli, Abramo A. "*L'Ester.* L'unico dramma di Leon da Modena giunto fino a noi." *Rassegna mensile di Israel* 34, no. 3 (1968): 163–72.

Plebani, Tiziana. *Il 'genere' dei libri: Storie e rappresentazioni della lettura al femminile e al maschile tra medioevo e età moderna.* Milan: FrancoAngeli, 2001.

Podet, Allen H. "Christianity in the View of Rabbi Leon Modena." *European Judaism: A Journal for the New Europe* 20, no. 2 (1986): 22–4.

Poliakov, Léon. *The History of Anti-Semitism.* 3 vols. Translated by Richard Howard. New York: Vanguard Press, 1965.

Poppi, Antonino. "Cremonini, Galilei e gli inquisitori del Santo a Padova." *Il Santo: Rivista antoniana di storia dottrina arte,* 2nd ser., 33, nos. 1–2 (1993): 5–112.

–, ed. *Cremonini e Galilei inquisiti a Padova nel 1604: Nuovi documenti d'archivio.* Padua: Antenore, 1992.

Portone, Paolo. "Alessandro d'Este." In *Dizionario biografico degli italiani,* 43:310–12. Rome: Istituto della Enciclopedia Italiana, 1993.

Preto, Paolo. "Cicogna, Emmanuele Antonio." In *Dizionario biografico degli italiani,* 25:394–7. Rome: Istituto della Enciclopedia Italiana, 1981.

Price, Paola Malpezzi, and Christine Ristaino. *Lucrezia Marinella and the "Querelle des Femmes" in Seventeenth-Century Italy.* Madison, NJ: Fairleigh Dickinson University Press, 2008.

Pullan, Brian. *The Jews of Europe and the Inquisition of Venice, 1550–1670.* Oxford: Basil Blackwell, 1983.

– *Rich and Poor in Renaissance Venice: The Social Institutions of a Catholic State, to 1620.* Oxford: Basil Blackwell, 1971.

– "Wage-Earners and the Venetian Economy, 1550–1630." In *Crisis and Change in the Venetian Economy in the Sixteenth and Seventeenth Centuries,* edited by Brian Pullan, 146–74. London: Methuen, 1968.

Quadrio, Francesco Saverio. *Della storia e della ragione d'ogni poesia.* 4 vols. Bologna: Pisarri, 1741.

Quaintance, Courtney. *Textual Masculinity and the Exchange of Women in Renaissance Venice.* Toronto: University of Toronto Press, 2015.

Quondam, Amedeo. "Dal 'formulario' al 'formulario': Cento anni di 'libri di lettere.'" In *Le "carte messaggiere." Retorica e modelli di comunicazione epistolare: Per un indice dei libri di lettere del Cinquecento,* edited by Amedeo Quondam, 13–156. Rome: Bulzoni, 1981.

Ravid, Benjamin. "Curfew Time in the Ghetto of Venice." In *Medieval and Renaissance Venice,* edited by Ellen E. Kittell and Thomas F. Madden, 237–75. Urbana: University of Illinois Press, 1999.

– *Economics and Toleration in Seventeenth-Century Venice: The Background and Context of the* Discorso *of Simone Luzzatto.* Jerusalem: American Academy for Jewish Research, 1978.

– "The First Charter of the Jewish Merchants of Venice, 1589." *AJS Review* 1 (1976): 187–222.

– "From Yellow to Red: On the Distinguishing Head-Covering of the Jews of Venice." *Jewish History* 6, nos. 1–2, The Frank Talmage Memorial Volume (1992): 179–210.

– "Ghetto: Etymology, Original Definition, Reality, and Diffusion." In *The Ghetto in Global History, 1500 to the Present,* edited by Wendy Z. Goldman and Joe William Trotter, Jr., 23–39. Abingdon and New York: Routledge, 2018.

– "'Kosher Bread' in Baroque Venice." *Italia* 6, nos. 1–2 (1987): 20–9.

– "New Light on the *Ghetti* of Venice." In Carpi et al., *Shlomo Simonsohn Jubilee Volume,* 149–76.

– "The Religious, Economic and Social Background and Context of the Establishment of the Ghetti of Venice." In Cozzi, *Gli ebrei e Venezia,* 211–59.

– "The Sephardic Jewish Merchants of Venice, Port Jews, and the Road to Modernity." In *From Catalonia to the Caribbean: The Sephardic Orbit from Medieval to Modern Times. Essays in Honor of Jane S. Gerber,* edited by Federica Francesconi, Stanley Mirvis, and Brian M. Smollet, 117–35. Leiden and Boston: Brill, 2018.

– *Studies on the Jews of Venice, 1382–1797.* Alershot, UK: Ashgate, 2003.

– "Venice and Its Minorities." In *A Companion to Venetian History, 1400–1797,* edited by Eric R. Dursteler, 449–85. Leiden and Boston: Brill, 2013.

– "The Venetian Government and the Jews." In Davis and Ravid, *The Jews of Early Modern Venice,* 3–30.

Ray, Meredith K. *Daughters of Alchemy: Women and Scientific Culture in Early Modern Italy.* Cambridge, MA: Harvard University Press, 2015.

– *Margherita Sarrocchi's Letters to Galileo: Astronomy, Astrology, and Poetics in Seventeenth-Century Italy.* New York: Palgrave Macmillan, 2016.

– *Writing Gender in Women's Letter Collections of the Italian Renaissance.* Toronto: University of Toronto Press, 2009.

Reale Simioli, Carmela. "Ansaldo Cebà e la Congregazione dell'Indice." *Campania sacra. Studi e documenti* 11–12 (1980–1): 96–212.

– "Tracce di letteratura ligure (1617–1650) nelle carte napoletane dell'Archivio Doria d'Angri." *Accademie e biblioteche d'Italia* 49 (1981): 321–39.

Remy [Lazarus], Nahida [Ruth]. *Das jüdische Weib.* 3rd ed. Berlin: Siegfried Cronbach, 1896. First published Leipzig: Malende, 1891.

Renan, Ernest. *Averroès et l'averroïsme: Essai historique.* Paris: A. Durand, 1852.

Resta, Ilaria. "La traducción de la miscelánea española en la Italia del XVI: El *Jardín de flores curiosas* en la versión de Malespini." *Artifara* 17 (2017): 83–98.

Rhodes, Dennis E. "Some Neglected Aspects of the Career of Giovanni Battista Ciotti." *The Library*, 6th ser., 9, no. 3 (1987): 225–39.

Rio, Alexis François. *The Four Martyrs*. London: Burns and Lambert, 1856.

– *Les quatre martyrs*. Paris: Bray, 1856.

– *Les quatre martyrs*. 3rd ed. Paris: Charles Douniol, 1862.

Rivkin, Ellis. *Leone da Modena and the Kol Sakhal*. Cincinnati: Hebrew Union College Press, 1952.

Robin, Diana. "Editor's Introduction." In Cassandra Fedele, *Letters and Orations*, translated and edited by Diana Robin, 3–15. Chicago: University of Chicago Press, 2000.

– *Filelfo in Milan: Writings, 1451–1477*. Princeton: Princeton University Press, 1991.

– "Gender." In *The Oxford Handbook of Neo-Latin*, edited by Sarah Knight and Stefan Tilg, 363–77. Oxford: Oxford University Press, 2015.

– *Publishing Women: Salons, the Presses, and the Counter-Reformation in Sixteenth-Century Italy*. Chicago: University of Chicago Press, 2007.

Rosand, Ellen. "Barbara Strozzi, virtuosissima cantatrice: The Composer's Voice." *Journal of the American Musicological Society* 31, no. 2 (1978): 241–81.

– *Opera in Seventeenth-Century Venice: The Creation of a Genre*. Berkeley: University of California Press, 1991.

Rosenthal, Margaret F. *The Honest Courtesan: Veronica Franco, Citizen and Writer in Sixteenth-Century Venice*. Chicago: University of Chicago Press, 1992.

Ross, Sarah Gwyneth. *The Birth of Feminism: Woman as Intellect in Renaissance Italy and England*. Cambridge, MA: Harvard University Press, 2009.

Rossi, Lovanio. "Baldassarre Bonifacio." In *Dizionario biografico degli italiani*, 12:192–3. Rome: Istituto della Enciclopedia Italiana, 1970.

Rothman, E. Natalie. "Contested Subjecthood: Runaway Slaves in Early Modern Venice." *Quaderni storici*, n.s., 47, no. 140.2 (2012): 425–41.

Ruderman, David B. *Early Modern Jewry: A New Cultural History*. Princeton: Princeton University Press, 2010.

– "The Italian Renaissance and Jewish Thought." In *Renaissance Humanism: Foundations, Forms, and Legacy*, vol. 1, *Humanism in Italy*, edited by Albert Rabil, Jr., 382–433. Philadelphia: University of Pennsylvania Press, 1988.

– *Jewish Thought and Scientific Discovery in Early Modern Europe*. New Haven: Yale University Press, 1995.

–, ed. *Preachers of the Italian Ghetto*. Berkeley: University of California Press, 1992.

–, and Giuseppe Veltri, eds. *Cultural Intermediaries: Jewish Intellectuals in Early Modern Italy*. Philadelphia: University of Pennsylvania Press, 2004.

Ruffini, Graziano. "Note su Giuseppe Pavoni stampatore a Genova dal 1598 al 1641." *La Bibliofilia* 91 (1989): 267–85.

Ruggiero, Guido. *The Boundaries of Eros: Sex Crime and Sexuality in Renaissance Venice*. New York: Oxford University Press, 1985.

– *Machiavelli in Love: Sex, Self, and Society in the Italian Renaissance.* Baltimore: Johns Hopkins University Press, 2006.

Salomon, H.P., and I.S.D. Sassoon. "Introduction." In da Costa, *Examination*, 1–50.

Salzberg, Rosa. *Ephemeral City: Cheap Print and Urban Culture in Renaissance Venice.* Manchester: Manchester University Press, 2014.

Sanfilippo, Matteo. "Doria, Giannettino." In *Dizionario biografico degli italiani*, 41:345–8. Rome: Istituto della Enciclopedia Italiana, 1991.

Sarot, Enzo. "Ansaldo Cebà and Sara Copio Sullam." *Italica* 31, no. 3 (1954): 138–50.

Sartori, Claudio. *Dizionario degli editori musicali italiani: Tipografi, incisori, librai-editori.* Florence: L.S. Olschki, 1958.

Scarsella, Alessandro. "Alberti, Giovanni." In *Dizionario dei tipografi e degli editori italiani. Il Cinquecento*, vol. 1, A–F, edited by Marco Menato, Ennio Sandal, and Giuseppina Zappella, 11–13. Milan: Editrice Bibliografica, 1997.

Schiesari, Julia. "In Praise of Virtuous Women? For a Genealogy of Gender Morals in Renaissance Italy." *Annali d'italianistica* 7 (1989): 66–87.

Schmitt, Charles B. "Cremonini, Cesare." In *Dizionario biografico degli italiani*, 30:618–22. Rome: Istituto della Enciclopedia Italiana, 1984.

Schutte, Anne Jacobson. *Aspiring Saints: Pretense of Holiness, Inquisition, and Gender in the Republic of Venice, 1618–1750.* Baltimore: Johns Hopkins University Press, 2001.

– *By Force and Fear: Taking and Breaking Monastic Vows in Early Modern Europe.* Ithaca: Cornell University Press, 2011.

Sedgwick, Eve Kosofsky. *Between Men: English Literature and Male Homosocial Desire.* New York: Columbia University Press, 1985.

Shemek, Deanna. *Ladies Errant: Wayward Women and Social Order in Early Modern Italy.* Durham, NC: Duke University Press, 1998.

Shepherd, Naomi. *A Price Below Rubies: Jewish Women as Rebels and Radicals.* Cambridge, MA: Harvard University Press, 1993.

Sherberg, Michael. *The Governance of Friendship: Law and Gender in the Decameron.* Columbus: Ohio State University Press, 2011.

Siegmund, Stephanie. "La vita nei ghetti." In Vivanti, *Storia d'Italia*, 11:1:845–92.

Sigal, Phillip. *From Medievalism to Protomodernity in the Sixteenth and Seventeenth Centuries.* Vol. 3 of *The Emergence of Contemporary Judaism.* Eugene, Oregon: Pickwick Publications, 1986.

Simonsohn, Shlomo. "Discussione." In Cozzi, *Gli ebrei e Venezia*, 537–62.

Singer, P.N. "Galen." In *The Stanford Encyclopedia of Philosophy*, winter 2016 edition, edited by Edward N. Zalta. https://plato.stanford.edu/archives /win2016/entries/galen/

Soave, Moisè. "Sara Copia Sullam." *Corriere Israelitico* (September 1863): 157–60; (October 1863): 88–96; 2 (1863–1864): 157–96; 15 (1876–1877): 196–8, 220–3, 245–8, 272–5; 16 (1877–1878): 5–7, 28–31.

– *Sara Copia Sullam (Dalla biografia di Leon da Modena che si sta pubblicando nel* Corriere Israelitico *di Trieste).* Trieste: C. Coen, 1864.

Soranzo, Girolamo. *Bibliografia veneziana, in aggiunta e continuazione del saggio di Emmanuele Antonio Cicogna.* Venice: Pietro Naratovich, 1885.

Sorensen, Lee R. "Rio, Alexis-François." In *Dictionary of Art Historians*, edited by Lee R. Sorensen. http://arthistorians.info/rioa.

Spini, Giorgio. *Ricerca dei libertini: La teoria dell'impostura delle religioni nel Seicento italiano.* Florence: La Nuova Italia, 1983 [1950].

Spotorno, Giovanni Battista. *Storia letteraria della Liguria.* 5 vols. Genoa: Ponthenier, 1824–1858.

Stefani, Giuseppe. *Insurance in Venice from the Origins to the End of the Serenissima.* 2 vols. Trieste: Assicurazioni generali di Trieste e Venezia, 1958.

Storchi, Maria Luisa. "Formazione e organizzazione di un archivio gentilizio: L'archivio Doria d'Angri tra XV e XX secolo." In *Per la storia del Mezzogiorno medievale e moderno: Studi in memoria di Jole Mazzoleni*, 2:547–87. Rome: Ministero per i Beni Culturali e Ambientali. Ufficio Centrale per i Beni Archivistici, 1998.

Tanner, Norman P., ed. *Decrees of the Ecumenical Councils.* 2 vols. London: Sheed & Ward, 1990.

Taylor, Gary. *Castration: An Abbreviated History of Western Manhood.* New York: Routledge, 2002.

Tenenti, Alberto. *Naufrages, corsaires et assurances maritimes à Venise 1592–1609.* Paris: S.E.V.P.E.N., 1959.

Tessier, Andrea. "*Biblioteca volante* di Giovanni Cinelli Calvoli." *Giornale degli eruditi e curiosi* 1 (1882–1883): col. 168–71.

Testa, Simone. *Italian Academies and Their Networks 1525–1700: From Local to Global.* New York: Palgrave Macmillan, 2015.

Tiraboschi, Girolamo. *Storia della letteratura italiana.* 10 vols. Modena: presso la Società Tipografica, 1772–1782.

– "Zinani Gabriello Reggiano." In *Biblioteca modenese, o, Notizie della vita e delle opere degli scrittori natii degli stati del serenissimo signor duca di Modena*, 5:415–33. Modena: presso la Società Tipografica, 1784.

Tirosh-Rothschild, Hava. "Jewish Culture in Renaissance Italy – A Methodological Survey." *Italia* 7, nos. 1–2 (1989): 63–96.

Todeschini, Giacomo. "Franciscan Economics and Jews in the Middle Ages: From a Theological to an Economic Lexicon." In *The Medieval Franciscans*, edited by Steven J. McMichael, vol. 2, *Friars and Jews in the Middle Ages and Renaissance*, edited by Steven J. McMichael and Susan E. Myers, 99–117. Leiden: Brill, 2004.

Trachtenberg, Joshua. *The Devil and the Jews: The Medieval Conception of the Jew and Its Relation to Modern Antisemitism.* New York: Harper & Row, 1966.

Tylus, Jane. *Writing and Vulnerability in the Late Renaissance.* Stanford: Stanford University Press, 1993.

Ultsch, Lori J. "Sara Copio Sullam: A Jewish Woman of Letters in 17th-Century Venice." *Italian Culture* 18 (2000): 73–86.

Ulvioni, P. "Stampa e censura a Venezia nel Seicento." *Archivio veneto,* 5th ser., 106 (1975): 45–93.

– "Stampatori e librai a Venezia nel Seicento." *Archivio veneto,* 5th ser., 109 (1977): 93–124.

Valverde, José Manuel García. "Averroistic Themes in Girolamo Cardano's *De Immortalitate Animorum.*" In *Renaissance Averroism and its Aftermath: Arabic Philosophy in Early Modern Europe,* edited by Anna Akasoy and Guido Giglioni, 145–71. Dordrecht: Springer, 2013.

Vazzoler, Franco. "Le *Rime* di Ansaldo Cebà fra esperienza autobiografica e miti eroici e civili." *Studi di filologia e letteratura* 6 (1984): 121–49.

– "La soluzione tragica del pessimismo politico nell'ultimo Cebà." In *Dibattito politico e problemi di governo a Genova nella prima metà del Seicento,* 75–114. Florence: La Nuova Italia, 1976.

Veltri, Giuseppe. "L'anima del passato: Studi e testi recenti (Azaria de' Rossi, Moshe da Rieti e Sara Copio Sullam)." *Henoch* 26, no. 2 (2004): 210–23.

– "Body of Conversion and the Immortality of the Soul: The 'Beautiful Jewess' Sara Copio Sullam." In Diemling and Veltri, *The Jewish Body,* 331–52.

– "Jewish Philosophy in the Ghetto: Simone Luzzatto and Sara Copio Sullam." In Calabi, Galeazzo, and Massaro, *Venice, the Jews and Europe,* 306–9.

Verrecchia, Anacleto. *Giordano Bruno: La falena dello spirito (Giordano Bruno: Nachtfalter des Geistes).* Rome: Donzelli, 2002.

Vitali, Achille. *La moda a Venezia attraverso i secoli. Lessico ragionato.* Venice: Filippi Editori, 1992.

Vivanti, Corrado, ed. *Storia d'Italia.* Annali 11, *Gli ebrei in Italia.* Vol. 1, *Dall'alto medioevo all'età dei ghetti.* Turin: Einaudi, 1996.

Walfish, Barry Dov. *Esther in Medieval Garb: Jewish Interpretations of the* Book of Esther *in the Middle Ages.* Albany: State University of New York Press, 1993.

Weaver, Elissa B., ed. *Arcangela Tarabotti: A Literary Nun in Baroque Venice.* Ravenna: Longo, 2006.

– *Convent Theatre in Early Modern Italy: Spiritual Fun and Learning for Women.* Cambridge, UK: Cambridge University Press, 2002.

Westwater, Lynn Lara. "A Cloistered Nun Abroad: Arcangela Tarabotti's International Literary Career." In *Women Writing Back / Writing Women Back: Transnational Perspectives from the Late Middle Ages to the Dawn of the Modern Era,* edited by Anke Gilleir, Alicia C. Montoya, and Suzan van Dijk, 283–308. Leiden: Brill, 2010.

- "Copio Sullam, Sara." In *Encyclopedia of Women in the Renaissance: Italy, France, and England*, edited by Diana Maury Robin, Anne R. Larsen, and Carole Levin, 96–8. Santa Barbara, CA: ABC–CLIO, 2007.
- "The Disquieting Voice: Women's Writing and Anti-Feminism in Seventeenth-Century Venice." PhD diss., University of Chicago, 2003.
- "'Le false obiezioni de' nostri calunniatori': Lucrezia Marinella Responds to the Misogynist Tradition." *Bruniana & Campanelliana* 12, no. 1 (2006): 95–109.
- "A Rediscovered Friendship in the Republic of Letters: The Unpublished Correspondence of Arcangela Tarabotti and Ismaël Boulliau." *Renaissance Quarterly* 65, no. 1 (2012): 67–134.

Wolf, Johann Christoph. *Bibliotheca hebraea*. 4 vols. Hamburg and Leipzig: Christian Liebezeit (vol. 1); Hamburg: Theodor Christoph Felginer (vol. 2); Hamburg: Widow of Theodor Christoph Felginer (vols. 3–4), 1715–1733.

Zafran, Eric, ed. *Renaissance to Rococo: Masterpieces from the Wadsworth Atheneum Museum of Art*. New Haven and London: Wadsworth Atheneum Museum of Art, in association with Yale University Press, 2004.

Zanette, Emilio. "Su Ansaldo Cebà." *Convivium* 4, no. 1 (1932): 94–123.
- *Suor Arcangela, Monaca del Seicento veneziano*. Rome and Venice: Istituto per la Collaborazione Culturale, 1960.

Zappella, Giuseppina. *Le marche dei tipografi e degli editori italiani del Cinquecento. Repertorio di figure, simboli e soggetti e dei relativi motti*. 2 vols. Milan: Editrice Bibliografica, 1986.

Zorattini, Pier Cesare Ioly. "Gli ebrei nel Veneto dal secondo Cinquecento a tutto il Seicento." In *Storia della cultura veneta*, vol. 4, *Dalla Controriforma alla fine della repubblica. Il Seicento*, edited by Girolamo Arnaldi and Manlio Pastore Stocchi, 2:281–312. Vicenza: Neri Pozza, 1984.

Index

Page references to figures appear in italics.

Love, Harold, 162
Luther, Martin, 56
Luzzatto, Rabbi Simone, 6, 16, 94,
    253n38, 296n74

Manifesto: dedication, 78, 84, 87, 98–9;
    defense of Judaism, 120–1; editions,
    79–81; on fame, 16, 83–4, 88, 96,
    103–4, 168; paratext, 78, 84, 87;
    and print culture, 82–7; publication,
    76–8, 121; responses (see Bonifaccio,
    Baldassare: Risposta al Manifesto);
    sonnets, 79, 84–6, 87, 95–9. See
    also Dell'immortalità dell'anima; Copia
    Sulam, Sarra: works
Manso, Giovanni Battista, 176–7
Marinella, Lucrezia, xvii, xix, xxii,
    8–13, 129–32, 175, 180, 223n60,
    247n121
Marino, Giambattista, 31, 34, 45,
    129, 132–3, 263n19, 271n12,
    280n145
marriage, 11, 20, 44, 187; dowries,
    11, 192, 210; individual choice, 9,
    192, 197; in Jewish communities,
    27, 190–4, 199. See also Copia
    Sulam, Sarra: marriage
Mascardi, Agostino, 51
Masini, Eliseo, 111
Mazzucchelli, Giovanni Maria, 182
Medici, Giovanni de', 135
men: authorship, 64; literary
    constructs of masculinity, 91;
    marriage, 27, 43–5; reading
    practices, 147; role in Judaism,
    27, 43–5, 81–2; sexuality, 146–8;
    social roles, 11–12, 228n128. See
    also friendship; gender; misogyny;
    women
Michiele, Pietro, 132, 140, 176, 180
Misserini, Nicolò, 31, 32–3. See also
    Caesar, Julius

misogyny, 10–12, 72, 131, 217n71.
    See also academies; feminism;
    gender; querelle des femmes
Modena, Rabbi Leon: attacks against,
    70, 93–4; autobiography, 81–2;
    L'Ester, xviii, xxii, 24; Historia de' riti
    hebraici, 16, 23, 24, 78, 81–2, 94;
    relationship with Copia/o family,
    187, 191, 197–8; relationship with
    Copia Sulam, xxii, 5–6, 22, 24,
    198; role in Copia Sulam's salon,
    34–5, 59–60; on soul debate, xviii,
    58–60 (see also soul)
Modona, Leonello, 185
Molino, Domenico, 68

Neoplatonism, 26, 55, 257n85
Nogarola, Isotta, 7

oral culture, 87, 101, 217n71. See also
    print culture
Orpheus, 72
orthodoxy, 15, 17, 47–8, 51–2,
    68–9, 93, 101, 108, 111–13;
    Christian, 15, 47, 53, 66; Counter-
    Reformation, 98; Jewish, 15, 38,
    53, 66, 105, 125, 240n49. See also
    heresy; heterodoxy; Inquisition
Ottoman Empire, 36, 135, 188–9

Pagnoni, Giovanni, 45
Pallavicino, Ferrante, 11
Paluzzi, Numidio: accusations against
    Copia Sulam, 48, 135–9, 162 (see
    also "Le Sareide"; Rime [Paluzzi]);
    arrival in Venice, xviii, 31, 34;
    death, xx, 17–18, 158; defrauding
    of Copia Sulam, xviii, xix–xx, xxii,
    17–18, 126–9, 151, 162–3 (see
    also "Avisi di Parnaso"); friendship
    with Berardelli, xviii–xxi, 17–18,
    34, 126–8, 140–8, 151, 175–6

women in, 9, 11–13 (*see also*
women; women writers)
Vernia, Nicoletto, 54–5

Wolf, Johann Christoph, 184
women: accusations of promiscuity,
10–12, 14–15, 17, 43–4, 48–50,
103, 179; education of, xxii, 6–7,
187, 191, 195; sexuality, 3, 10–12,
165–6; virtue, 8, 44, 150, 163, 165–6;
writers (*see* women writers). *See
also* academies; feminism; gender;
marriage; misogyny; salons; Venice

women writers: accusations against,
7–8, 12, 75, 92, 131, 180;
authorship, 19, 101, 159, 182–3;
in early modern Venice, 7–12,
75, 131; modesty tropes, 66, 90;
publishing, 4; scholarship on,
12–13, 19, 171, 180–5
Wotton, Henry, 24

Zacchia, Francesco. *See* Copio, Moisè
Zinano, Gabriele, xx, xxiii, 18, 22,
46–7, 132, 140, 171–6
Zuccolo, Ludovico, 142